Writing for Pleasure

This book explores what writing for pleasure means, and how it can be realised as a much-needed pedagogy whose aim is to develop children, young people, and their teachers as extraordinary and life-long writers. The approach described is grounded in what global research has long been telling us are the most effective ways of teaching writing and contains a description of the authors' own research project into what exceptional teachers of writing do that makes the difference.

The authors describe ways of building communities of committed and successful writers who write with purpose, power, and pleasure, and they underline the importance of the affective aspects of writing teaching, including promoting in apprentice writers a sense of self-efficacy, agency, self-regulation, volition, motivation, and writer-identity. They define and discuss 14 research-informed principles which constitute a *Writing for Pleasure* pedagogy and show how they are applied by teachers in classroom practice. Case studies of outstanding teachers across the globe further illustrate what world-class writing teaching is.

This ground-breaking text is essential reading for anyone who is concerned about the current status and nature of writing teaching in schools. The rich *Writing for Pleasure* pedagogy presented here is a radical new conception of what it means to teach young writers effectively today.

Ross Young is the founder of The Writing For Pleasure Centre. He holds an MA in applied linguistics in education. As a passionate writer-teacher, he now works around the UK and abroad helping teachers and schools develop extraordinary young writers. He was a primary school teacher for ten years and holds an MA in applied linguistics in education. He now works around the UK and abroad helping teachers and schools develop young writers. He is also a visiting lecturer at a number of UK universities and is a passionate writer-teacher. Ross was the lead researcher on *What is it Writing For Pleasure teachers do that makes the difference?* His work continues to focus on the learning and teaching of young writers and is informed by his ongoing work with classroom teachers and early years educators.

Felicity Ferguson was a primary school teacher for 40 years, working as an EAL specialist, SENCO, deputy, and head teacher. A writer herself, she has MA degrees in applied linguistics and children's literature and has been involved in a number of literacy-based projects, including children's reading development. She was a primary school teacher for 40 years, working as an EAL specialist, SENCO, deputy and head teacher. She has MA degrees in applied linguistics and children's literature and has been involved in a number of literacy-based projects, including children's reading development. An avid writer herself, Felicity, along with Ross, was the series creator of the Power English: Writing approach written for Pearson Education. Her current interest is in how classroom talk affects the development of children as writers.

Writing for Pleasure
Theory, Research and Practice

Ross Young and Felicity Ferguson

LONDON AND NEW YORK

First published 2021
by Routledge
2 Park Square, Milton Park, Abingdon, Oxon OX14 4RN

and by Routledge
52 Vanderbilt Avenue, New York, NY 10017

Routledge is an imprint of the Taylor & Francis Group, an informa business

© 2021 Ross Young & Felicity Ferguson

The right of Ross Young & Felicity Ferguson to be identified as authors of this work has been asserted by them in accordance with sections 77 and 78 of the Copyright, Designs and Patents Act 1988.

All rights reserved. No part of this book may be reprinted or reproduced or utilised in any form or by any electronic, mechanical, or other means, now known or hereafter invented, including photocopying and recording, or in any information storage or retrieval system, without permission in writing from the publishers.

Trademark notice: Product or corporate names may be trademarks or registered trademarks, and are used only for identification and explanation without intent to infringe.

British Library Cataloguing-in-Publication Data
A catalogue record for this book is available from the British Library

Library of Congress Cataloging-in-Publication Data
Title: Writing for pleasure : theory, research, and practice / Ross Young & Felicity Ferguson.
Description: Abingdon, Oxon ; New York, NY : Routledge, 2021. |
Includes bibliographical references and index. | Identifiers: LCCN 2020038760 |
ISBN 9780367219505 (hardback) | ISBN 9780367219529 (paperback) |
ISBN 9780429268984 (ebook)
Subjects: LCSH: English language--Composition and exercises--Study and teaching (Elementary) | Creative writing (Elementary education)
Classification: LCC LB1576 .Y62 2021 | DDC 372.6--dc23
LC record available at https://lccn.loc.gov/2020038760

ISBN: 978-0-367-21950-5 (hbk)
ISBN: 978-0-367-21952-9 (pbk)
ISBN: 978-0-429-26898-4 (ebk)

Typeset in Bembo
by Deanta Global Publishing Services, Chennai, India

Contents

Preface   vii
Acknowledgements   ix
The Writing For Pleasure Centre   x

1   Teachers' orientations towards teaching writing and young writers   1

2   Defining writing for pleasure   20

3   The affective domains of *Writing for Pleasure*   26

4   Self-efficacy   29

5   Self-regulation   35

6   Agency   42

7   Motivation   49

8   Volition   58

9   Writer-identity   64

10   The enduring principles of effective writing teaching   75

11   Create a community of writers   86

12	Treat every child as a writer	94
13	Read, share, think, and talk about writing	101
14	Pursue authentic and purposeful writing projects	112
15	Teach the writing processes	124
16	Set writing goals	144
17	Be reassuringly consistent	159
18	Personal writing projects	166
19	Balance composition and transcription	177
20	Teach mini-lessons	187
21	Be a writer-teacher	199
22	Pupil conference: Meet children where they are	211
23	Literacy for pleasure: Connect reading and writing	220
24	Conclusion: An action plan for world-class writing teaching	240

Index   255

Preface

What we learn with pleasure we never forget – Alfred Mercier

This book has been written by two passionate writer-teacher researchers. Writer-teachers are writers who teach and teachers who write. Years ago, we started teaching writing in what we felt to be a new way. We began reading research to support our work. Subsequently, we started conducting and disseminating our own research and observing what outstanding teachers were doing. While academic colleagues have been encouraging during the writing of the book, it has always been important for us to keep in mind that, ultimately, all the roads we follow must lead us back to teachers and children writing and writing together successfully and with pleasure.

The idea that children can be taught exceptionally well *and* enjoy the craft of writing should be at the heart of every writing curriculum. It is entirely reasonable to suppose that children who are taught to write successfully and see themselves as writers enjoy their writing, and that when children enjoy being writers, they learn more effectively. However, surveys and reports of English children's attitudes to and attainments in writing consistently tell us that such a happy state of affairs is by no means widespread. Something needs to change, and so we were moved to write this book.

The book describes, to the best of our current knowledge, what constitutes world-class writing teaching, with the fervent hope that as many children as possible will receive such teaching and so have the opportunity to become extraordinary writers. The evidence suggests that this is best achieved through a *Writing For Pleasure* pedagogy, which is the subject of the book. The pedagogy is based on what we currently know about the most effective teaching practices as documented in educational research and in what action research and case studies have learnt from exceptional classroom teachers of writing. One of the questions we try to answer is, what is it they do that makes the difference?

Writing For Pleasure is a robust and rigorous pedagogy. It does not advocate for a 'creative writing' approach, though it encourages children to write creatively. It does not call for a return to a 'growth', 'naturalistic', or 'romantic' conception of writing, though it does want children to grow as writers. It wants children to learn about linguistic and literary features, grammar, and punctuation, but in such a way as to help them craft meaningful and successful texts. It wants children to write in an environment of collective responsibility but also to be able to develop their own individual voice. Finally, it wants children to learn the behaviours, dispositions, knowledge, skills, and techniques of writers, to write with purpose, power, precision, and pleasure, and to *write for life*. And running beneath it like an underground stream is the conviction that we as teachers should be helping children to see writing not as being directed solely towards a set of efficient outcomes, but as an enterprise in which they can and should express their values, ideals, and aspirations.

We do not assume that our job as writer-teacher researchers is done. What we have discovered today will undoubtedly be built on in the future, and, through our work at The Writing For Pleasure Centre, we will continue to question, investigate, and share how best to develop children as writers and consider how we deliver world-class writing teaching. We hope that what we have proposed is demanding, stimulating, and thought-provoking. And a first step on the road to bringing about much-needed change.

Acknowledgements

I dedicate this book to my nan who never learnt to write. RY

I dedicate this book to my daughter, a writer in her own write. FF

The Writing For Pleasure Centre

The Writing For Pleasure Centre
- Promoting research informed writing teaching

The mission of The Writing For Pleasure Centre is to help all young people become passionate and successful writers. We look to accomplish this goal by investigating what world-class writing teaching might be. We do this through:

- Our school residencies and teacher training workshops.
- Curriculum development and creating resources.
- Conducting, disseminating, and publishing research.
- Working with children, teachers, school leaders, teacher-educators, and charities.

We have developed a research-rich website which shares the most effective writing teaching practices. It's our hope that teachers regard The Writing For Pleasure Centre as a place where they can access a specialist network and continued professional development, and where they can read action research and examples of practice written by other teachers.

The centre enables us to provide research-informed CPD through our school residencies, specialist teacher institutes, and our single or multi-day school-based teacher workshops. We also provide teacher and pupil writing retreats as well as creative school-based writing days.

School residencies

Our school residencies last for at least a year and involve visiting for several days to work with senior leadership, teachers, and children. Over the course of our week's visit, we provide after-school teacher workshops, observe and mentor teachers in their classrooms, and provide each teacher with their own summary report. Once the residency is over, schools are encouraged to engage in action research and to work on their own examples of practice. We maintain contact with our school affiliates over the long term and continue to make ourselves available to staff who need us for the rest of the academic year. We see this as embedded professional development based on what research tells us is the most effective type of teacher development.

Institutes

We have created our out-of-term-time institutes so that teachers can come together and enjoy a 'working holiday' learning about different aspects of teaching writing and can network and enjoy the company of like-minded colleagues. We have found that these working holidays can be particularly attractive to schools that are committed to improving children's writing experiences and outcomes but may have limited budgets.

Writing retreats

We run affordable retreats, throughout the year, for writer-teachers who want to develop their own writing craft and enjoy some time talking, writing, and networking with sympathetic fellow writers and teachers. Our retreats take place in sites of natural beauty where everyone can throw themselves into days of expressive and immersive writing.

Our retreats for schools provide an opportunity for children to enjoy the great outdoors. Children explore a huge range of poetic forms whilst learning to think poetically and mould feelings into words. Generally, a few schools join together, with each one sending a small number of children and a teacher. We begin the project as strangers, but by the end we are friends, united through our shared experience as writers.

For more information, please contact us at **www.writing4pleasure.com/contact** or follow us on Twitter **@WritingRocks_17**

CHAPTER 1

Teachers' orientations towards teaching writing and young writers

How one was taught to write at school, for better or for worse, will have a profound influence on one's present and future perceptions of writing and, importantly, of oneself as a writer (Graham et al. 2001; Street 2003; Cremin 2006, 2019; Leigh 2014; Gardner 2014). A teacher's perspective on writing teaching is shaped and guided by their own past school experiences, how they were trained, how they themselves undertake writing as an adult, their choice of reading on the subject, and of course by school and government policies (Parker 1988; Frank 2003; Hall and Grisham-Brown 2011; McCarthey and Mkhize 2013; Dobson 2016).

We begin this chapter by considering some of the views of writing held by educators, drawing on how they have been articulated by academic theorists and researchers such as Dixon (1967), Hillocks (1986), Bereiter and Scardamalia (1987), Street (1995), Maybin (2001), Hyland (2002), Ivanič (2004) Locke (2015) and Gardner (2018). It is not our intention to give a historical overview of favoured approaches to the teaching of writing at various times (these can be found in Kinneavy 1980; Graham and Kelly 2009; Gibbons 2017; Durrant et al. 2019), but simply to describe a range of different ideologies and beliefs which may be held at the present time and which may sometimes appear to be in conflict with each other. All these orientations have the power to govern classroom pedagogy.

We anticipate that readers of this chapter will recognise aspects of their own beliefs and practices in many of the descriptions of different orientations, but will understand that we have written them in a somewhat caricatured way.

The presentational orientation

The presentational orientation is also referred to as the exercise approach, the tutelage approach, the 'assigned tasks' approach, retrieve-and-write, the immediate training for immediate performance approach (Kellogg 2008), the autonomous approach (Street 1995), the compliant scribe approach (Gardner 2018), drill and skill, one-shot perfect-product approach, the algorithm approach, writing as object and rules, the mechanistic approach, authoritarian, high-stakes, evaluative, codification writing, mechanics, regurgitating, recite for writing, artificial, the memorization approach, the transactional approach, the banking concept (Freire 1996), and, rather bluntly, according to Wray and Beard (1988), as the 'dead-dead-end' approach. This orientation sees writing essentially as a set of complex cognitive skills. Children are required to master these skills and then to present their competence by producing an accurate writing product or outcome to their teacher's specifications, ready for evaluation. Without learning these skills, any attempt to craft text and share meaning is likely to fail. Therefore, the teacher sees their role as primarily to teach children how to write passable texts, but not necessarily how to be writers.

The conception of writing and the writer

A presentational-orientated teacher largely views writing as rules and processes to be followed, an outcome, a piece of evidence that shows how or whether students are fulfilling the objective, which is to apply and showcase skills learnt with a high degree of accuracy. Whether the writing was meaningful in its intent and successful according to its readership is seen as less important than correctness. The teacher gains satisfaction from their pupils building on these skills incrementally over time.

The relationship between teacher and pupil

This approach is teacher centred, with the teacher as the gatekeeper and controller of knowledge, cognition, and skills. Teaching is focused on the individual student, with little sense of the social or collaborative aspects of composition and meaning making. Students are seen as empty vessels to be filled, coming into school with nothing that would be useful to them in learning how to write (Smith 1988a).

The content of the writing curriculum

The teacher's priority is typically the teaching of correct spelling, handwriting, punctuation, vocabulary, correct grammar usage, sentence combination, cohesive devices, and the conventions of Standard English.

Teaching strategies

Writing tasks and assignments are chosen by the teacher. These are largely set for evaluation purposes and may take several forms. For example, the teacher transmits content knowledge and students are then required to show their application and understanding of it through drill exercises or error-recognition tasks. Artificial writing tasks might be set which have a pseudo-authentic purpose and a pseudo-audience. In either case, all pieces of work are marked and corrected, and the student may or may not be asked to attend to the errors and corrections. A major teaching strategy is to provide a model for the student to internalise and imitate. Children are required to arrange sentences and paragraphs into prescribed patterns and to follow pro-forma instructions which over time become more syntactically complex.

Limitations

- It is essential that children internalise the key basic skills, processes, and strategies involved in crafting texts (MacArthur and Graham 2017). However, the main limitation of a presentational approach is not so much its focus on the teaching of these skills but rather the vast amount it ignores when developing children as writers (Locke 2015; Eyres 2017). It appears that presentational-orientated teachers excel at teaching children to produce what Zoellner (1969) called 'Skinner box' writing, where, like mice, children can perform certain actions in response to specific stimuli. However, these teachers do not see the necessity of teaching children to be independent writers.
- Children's personal growth, motivation, and enjoyment as writers are largely seen as unimportant factors in ensuring academic success. Instead, the teacher's focus is solely on the written product and not on the young writer who produced it.
- Children's writing is deemed successful largely because it is transcriptionally accurate or syntactically complex. This can result in children writing 'impeccable nonsense'. There is often a lack of attention given to text-level and genre-based teaching and little focus on purpose and audience.
- The favouring of skill exercises and contrived writing tasks coupled with a lack of emphasis on children's agency does not help children understand how they can write for their own purposes and audiences at school, at home, and in the future. Instead, they become the passive recipients of their teacher's writing voice, ideas, models, and desires.
- Since children are producing the same piece as one another, their texts tell teachers very little about how individuals are developing as writers (Graham et al. 2013).
- Because, in this conception, learning tasks are so often limited in terms of the application of new learning, the process of 'equilibration and cognitive restructuring – necessary for deep learning – will likely fail to occur' (Allal 2019, p. 3). Children are offered little opportunity to develop higher-order skills or 'the mental operations necessary for writing expertise' (Chuy et al. 2011, p. 181). In this conception, children are routinely taught to mentally store 'single-use' procedures for constructing writing and are not required or taught to develop a long-term and general understanding of the strategies and acts of cognition needed to be able to write independently for their own purposes and in response to their own urges. Essentially, teachers in this orientation end up assuming the cognitive responsibility for the children's writing (Chuy et al. 2011).
- The emphasis on product devalues the importance of the writing processes, with the exception of those which are to be assessed. The processes of writing are therefore seen as largely unimportant, and the practices of writers out in the world are largely ignored.
- The approach assumes that children will be interested in the content knowledge being taught to support the writing task, and that they will retain enough information in their working memory to recreate it in their writing. Both these

factors, if not realised by the child, can adversely affect the teacher's judgement as to whether or not they have been academically successful.

- Children are only ever taught; they never get to teach others. They are not invited to comment or advise on the learning process; they are simply subjected to it.

- Children are not seen as capable of choosing their own subjects or ideas for writing; the teacher may also actively oppose their writing desires (Rosen 2017). Subjects and ideas for writing are generated for them and imposed on them and children are therefore only ever spectators and not creators of writing. In many ways, it is the teacher and the stimulus doing the 'writing', but children are given the illusion that they are the ones crafting their text. In this conception, children spend a lot of time writing without ever composing. They become, to use a computing analogy, automators of *writing* and not authentic *writers*.

- At its worst, the presentational orientation towards writing turns it into an utterly unnatural set of mechanical and nonsensical procedures which are far from how writers craft and work. Not only does such an approach decontextualise writing; it also decontextualises the writer (Street 1995).

The self-expression or naturalistic orientation

Terms which are associated with this conception of writing include composition centric, language experience, language awareness, child centred, humanised, libertarian, creative writing, free writing, romantic, teacher as psychoanalyst, the free-to-be-me approach, self-discovery, personal growth or, as Bernstein (1996 cited in Rose 2008) called it, the invisible approach. This approach believes that the young writer is sovereign and that a high degree of teacher intervention only ever results in the stifling of their processes and compositions. The teacher does not provide a purpose or context for the writing since projects are to be determined by the children.

The conception of writing and the writer

Hyland (2008) sees this approach as one which stresses the essentially creative nature of writing, where writers discover and express themselves in a natural way through engagement in personally significant projects. The apprentice writer is of paramount importance and is accorded much time and personal freedom.

The relationship between teacher and pupil

As the less dominant partner in this relationship, the teacher's role is largely as a facilitator, fostering positive dispositions in young writers which, it is hoped, will encourage them to continue writing into adulthood as a life-long pursuit. Focus is thus centred on the individual pupil, who is left to take personal responsibility for their own writing processes, practices, and products. The pupil is thus liberated from the limitations of the teacher's vision and from linguistic oppression. It is worth noting at this point Ivanič's (2004) view that this orientation, at its best, can challenge elitist ideas of what counts as relevant or valid writing, and has the potential to promote and legitimise the voices of minority or marginalised young writers.

The content of the writing curriculum

The objectives of instruction tend to be generalised and include, for example, how to revise drafts, how to give 'sentimental' feedback to peers, and how to improve fluency in drafting.

Teaching strategies

Teachers who subscribe to this view do not set particular writing tasks, criteria, purposes, or audiences. Hyland (2008) asserts that teachers may typically ask students to read stories, discuss them, and then use the ideas, themes, or events in them as a stimulus for writing about their own experiences. These stories are not necessarily recommended as literary models. Teachers also set up opportunities for exploratory talk between pupils to support them in generating and refining their own ideas for writing, and allow daily time for 'free writing' (Murray 1978; Elbow 1998). The rationale for free writing is that writers do not always know at the outset what they intend to write; the form, purpose, and audience for the piece may only emerge during or even after the free writing. Peer-sharing is an important part of the approach, as is the (albeit rather 'loose') conferencing of individual pupils by the teacher while writing is going on.

Limitations

- This conception of writing is limiting for pupils since the lack of genre-focused teaching and attention to, for example, transcriptional skills does not give them mastery of the functional writing of the 'real world of work' (Fishman and McCarthy 1992; Kress 1994).
- It can all too easily separate writing from the rest of the curriculum.
- The pursuit of self-expression can also be limiting in the sense that children will not be directed towards engaging in a rich range of writing across many genres and with a variety of purposes and audiences (McCarthy 1994).
- The finished writing pieces are not necessarily required to fulfil the standards needed for final publication. In fact, the 'product', which may never be formally published, is seen as unimportant when compared to the creative effort which went into the writing of it.
- Because of the individualistic nature of this ideology, the social consequences of writing and being a writer can be neglected (Smagorinsky 1987). For example, in this largely asocial approach, it is unlikely that the teacher and therefore the pupils will consider the importance of a critical literacy stance when writing (Lensmire 1998).
- This kind of approach might be considered unrealistic given the demands of modern curricula, or could be viewed as a potential violation of children's

privacy or as a cultural intrusion (Sudol and Sudol 1991; McCarthy 1994; Dutro and Kazemi 2006; Zacarian et al. 2017). For example, some consider the approach to hold an outdated romantic or elitist view of writing, creating purely hedonistic writers (Lensmire 1998), that it may only suit 'the brightest middle class children', and that a refusal by teachers to teach only reinforces the success of ruling-class children in education, with other children 'supportively encouraged to fail' (Martin cited in Cremin and Myhill 2012, p. 20).

- Research has clearly shown that implicit teaching is not enough if we want to create successful and thoughtful writers. Children need direct and explicit instruction in the skills and processes involved in crafting texts (Hillocks 1986; Graham and Perin 2007; Hmelo-Silver et al. 2007).

The structuralist or genre orientation

Terms which are associated with this position include: the forms of writing approach, rhetoric, semiotic, writing as design, academic socialisation, textual competence, the textual analysis approach, the conformity approach, the recipe approach, painting by numbers (Rosen 2017), the standardised approach, the textual police approach (Watkins 1999) and what Dixon (1987) calls the 'strait-jacket' approach. The genre orientation insists on children's mastery of different forms of writing in order to be successful in the world. Genre knowledge is seen as powerful, giving children access to important cultural capital. In contrast to the self-expressionist orientation, it maintains that writing products have just as much importance as the processes experienced in their creation. One particular focus is on learning the expository genres since these will be of future use to children both academically and economically (Kress 1994). Genre teaching is seen by some as a social justice issue, giving all children equal access to the highly valued social practices and purposes of writing (Bazerman et al. 2017).

The conception of writing and the writer

'We learn genres as we learn the language, and communication would be impossible without them' (Maybin 2001, p. 66). Literacy is seen essentially as a social and functional practice as well as an individual one. The writer writes with the understanding that their writing will be socially situated, and that therefore there is a need to consider its purpose and audience (Coffin 2006; Martin and Rose 2008; Halliday 2013). The teacher gains satisfaction from seeing children apply genre conventions and write in a variety of different forms.

The relationship between teacher and pupil

The teacher's role is dominant. There is some similarity with the presentational approach here, with the teacher setting the writing task, specifying that certain linguistic or organisational features related to the genre be used, and constructing what is most often a pseudo-authentic purpose and audience for the writing. Pupils have a subordinate role; their performance is judged by the extent to which they have fulfilled the teacher's generated criteria for success.

The content of the writing curriculum

The focus of a genre-based curriculum is on the transmission from teacher to pupil of knowledge about the structural and linguistic features necessary for effective communication in certain (often privileged or outdated) genres. The view is that genres follow rules which can and should be taught to children. Grammar is taught largely in a functional way, related to the purposes and audiences for writing. Attention is paid to the various register features of field, tenor, mode, and to how writers can make readers feel 'at home' in their texts (Halliday 2013).

Teaching strategies

The central strategy in this approach is for the teacher to present good examples of written genres. Pupils are asked to discuss and study such texts from the point of view of a reader, and to identify what makes them successful illustrations. They then create their own versions, adhering to the parameters set by the teacher.

Limitations

- This view takes little account of the fact that genres change over time and according to circumstances, and are often manipulated and hybridised by writers. The idea of 'genre play' through experimentation and exploration is not made available to children in this restricted and conventional conception (Freedman 1994; Rosen 2017). Children are simply asked to reproduce the genre, not to reimagine it.
- The prescriptive stance means that children are given no opportunity to create their own genres and are unlikely to be exposed to new and emerging ones such as digital literacies. They only learn to reproduce the given text structures decided upon by the teacher (Richardson 1998).
- There is often a failure to see that expository texts can be enhanced when hybridised with expressive genres (Maybin 2001).
- The genres children are interested in or use outside of the school environment are seen as secondary or irrelevant to the genres the teacher deems as important or socially significant.
- Writing may be judged as 'successful' mainly in terms of the application of 'genre features', and not in its own right in terms of attention to purpose and audience. Nor is the quality of content, style, originality, and interest of the writing considered. Indeed, the children's writing rarely achieves a true social purpose but is instead a fake artefact produced solely for the teacher's evaluation (Watkins 1999; Rosen 2017).
- It is utterly possible that children know about and can already write successfully and creatively in the dominant genres of society. Lengthy and explicit teaching of linguistic 'rules' may therefore contribute little to their development (Schneider 2003). Children may be taught a very large number of genres but not necessarily in depth, with textual features overshadowing purpose. As a result, teachers 'obscure the forest by planting so many trees' (Chuy et al. 2011, p. 178).

- There can often be little concern for children's personal growth as writers and for their personal writing projects.

The literature-based orientation

The pedagogy derived from a literature-based orientation is typically associated with terms such as book planning, novel study, basalisation, literature as a unit of study, the manufactured approach (Mason and Giovanelli 2017), the formalist approach, the analysis-paralysis approach (Grainger et al. 2005), or what Rohman calls 'the echo approach' (1965 cited in Hyland 2002). It places considerable value on the literary cultural heritage and believes literary texts to be more important than non-literary ones (Bishop 1999; Locke 2015). Teachers who share this viewpoint approach the task of writing teaching more from the position of a lover of reading rather than a lover of writing, and are, in reality, more aligned to the teaching of reading than to teaching writing composition and the craft knowledge involved in writing and being a writer (Cremin et al. 2014, 2019; Shanahan 2016). They believe that the study of literary texts is the most effective way to help children produce high-quality writing.

The conception of writing and the writer

Apprentice writers are regarded as being in need of the major support of a literary text as both a stimulus and a model for writing. Writing is interpreted as the study of a text, followed by the setting of a number of arbitrary writing tasks related to it, which are to be completed to the teacher's specification and for the teacher's evaluation. The teacher gains satisfaction from seeing children engaging with reading through the writing tasks.

The relationship between teacher and pupil

There are many similarities here with the presentational orientation. The teacher is the gatekeeper of what is best in terms of a suitable literary text and the pupil is the receiver of the teacher's choice, interpretation, and subsequent associated writing ideas.

The content of the writing curriculum

Selected high-quality literary texts are presented and studied as models in terms of theme, character, plot, structure, and language.

Teaching strategies

Practitioners focus on teaching 'the content' – the comprehension of the text and how it can act as a stimulus for writing in various genres. The writing tasks which follow or accompany the reading of the text are devised by the teacher and take the form of preformatted activities and pseudo-authentic assignments carrying ill-defined writing goals. These goals are often set for assessment purposes, to evaluate not only children's writing competency but also their comprehension of the text as the teacher sees it.

Limitations

- Part of the model is that teachers choose and set a text on behalf of their students. This is a dangerous limitation since it assumes that culture is to be defined and communicated by the teacher (or the purchased scheme), and implies that children's cultures outside the school gates are not a useful resource for teaching them to be writers. As part of this process, children have to shed their culture and take on one that is liked or reflected by the teacher (Rosen 2017). Here we see parallels with the presentational and genre orientations.
- A rich network of attitudes, experiences, 'funds of knowledge', and personal reflections that children bring into the classroom every day are largely ignored. As a result, children do not learn how they can transmit their culture out into the world through the act of writing, nor that they have the right to do so.
- Dixon (1967) and Subero et al. (2016) argue that in this approach pupils only ever become readers, recipients, and duplicators of someone else's writing ideas and voice instead of constructing their own. At its worst, and thus not in keeping with the spirit of intertextuality, the writing has not actually been achieved by the children but rather by the combination of the chosen text and the teacher's view of it. It is as if what could be a rich wildflower meadow of interpretation and response is instead turned into a field of artificially cultivated and identical crops.
- 'Teaching the book' is often done at the expense of teaching the generalities, acts of cognition, the craft of writing, and how writers genuinely read and use texts to support their own writing (Graham and Harris 2019). The book itself becomes the central focus. 'Great' books are treated as topics that can in some way be 'done' and on which often arbitrary writing tasks can be hung. Writing thus becomes merely a subordinate component of a teacher's or school's reading programme (Shanahan 2016).
- Teachers may be inadvertently teaching literary criticism or English literature instead of composition, and neglecting to show children how they can use texts to craft their very own fiction, non-fiction, and 'faction' texts. Differences between reading and writing can become blurred, with explicit writing instruction sidelined in favour of reading instruction (Cremin et al. 2014, 2019; Shanahan 2016). The teaching of composition becomes more difficult because the teacher, whilst able to admire and point out aspects of quality composition, is unable to describe the decisions, strategies, and techniques the author, who is not present, will have employed to create the text.
- There is an assumption that a particular text will engage and feel relevant to all the children in the class. However, if children do not have a positive response to the text, or are not motivated by the subsequent tasks, adverse judgements of

their writing competency may be formed. It is also erroneously assumed that children are able to use what they have learnt from the study of a particular book in future writing projects (Shanahan 2016).

- Children's writing competency may also be judged on how well they have shown themselves to comprehend the text as their *teacher* sees it, and not by the quality of their writing. It has been said that such an approach, rather than giving children access to literature, actually snatches literature out of children's hands (Harwayne 1992; McGuinn 2005).
- The approach denies children exposure to those very vital compositional processes which are used throughout life: generating and publishing original thoughts, ideas, and concepts; reacting on lived experiences; reactions to one's own reading material; wanting to share something we know a lot about; and giving an opinion and wanting to make changes to the world. In other words, strategies which could show children how writing can and will relate to their own life are largely sidelined or even refused.
- Finally, children grow up with a warped understanding of what it means to be a writer. For example, they may believe that you can only be an author if you are formally and commercially published (Young 2019).

The critical literacy orientation

The concept of critical literacy has many terminological associations. These include: a 'Writing Realities' approach (Young et al. in press), a critical writing pedagogy (Kamler 2001), culturally relevant (Ladson-Billings 1995; Morrison et al. 2008), culturally responsive (Zacarian and Soto 2020), cultural competence, sociopolitical, pluralistic pedagogy, engagement literacy, inclusion and social justice literacy, a multimodal approach, 21st-century literacies, new literacy studies, multiliteracies, third space writing, emancipatory literacy, the critical sociocultural perspective, the critical democratic approach, culturally sustaining, critical framing, critical consciousness, critical-cultural approach, funds of identity, and 'action for change' literacy.

Inspired by the work of Paulo Freire (1996), this orientation is based on the premise that no text is neutral. Language comes attached to social relations, cultural models, power and politics, oppression of minority or marginalised groups, perspectives on experience, values and attitudes, and things and places in the world (The Talk Workshop Group 1982; Smagorinsky and Smith 1992; Street 1995; Maybin 2001; Perry 2012; Subero et al. 2016; Laman et al. 2018). Therefore, writers must be critical of what they write and have a profound sense of responsibility towards others (Gutiérrez 2008). Critical literacy proposes that writing be undertaken as a collective, and for the purposes of transformative social action and the challenging of injustice (Searle 1973). In common with the community/environmental orientation discussed below, traditional genres can be used in fresh ways towards the production of a literacy which develops new understandings of oneself and one's place in a 21st-century world (Flint and Laman 2012).

The conception of writing and the writer

As in the genre-based conception of writing, texts are considered to be socially constructed, carrying underlying values and assumptions. Critical literacy interrogates the images of race, gender, class, and disability offered in texts, considers who is privileged and whose voices are included and excluded, and examines the power structures reflected in writing (Fairclough 1989). Children are taught to empower themselves and see their existing knowledge and home cultures as an asset they can utilise, therefore ensuring that a multiplicity of voices is heard and that no one is marginalised (Lensmire 1998; Lankshear and Knobel 2009; Kinloch 2017). The writer is seen as proactive, with the power to use literacy to make societal changes and for affirmation of their own identity and culture (Searle 1973). The teacher gains satisfaction from seeing the development of children's ability to work and write with a collective voice, celebrate and validate who they are, share and appreciate multiple individual voices, funds of identities, funds of knowledge and experiences, and, through student-led activism, fight for and critically reflect on issues of social justice, educational justice, linguistic oppression, inequality, and prejudice.

The relationship between teacher and pupil

The teacher's role is to support pupils by raising their awareness, developing in them a critical stance, and ensuring they understand their ethical responsibilities as writers to safeguard against oppression by others. Pupils may be encouraged towards the establishment and nurturing of both an individual and collective identity through their writing and the building of a writing community within the classroom (Gutiérrez 2008; Lankshear and Knobel 2009). Critical dialogue between students and teachers and the creation of a loving learning environment is therefore seen as essential (Lensmire 1998; Kinloch 2017).

The writing curriculum and teaching strategies

It is believed that writers are at their best when they are able to work in a social and co-operative classroom environment. They will often write collaboratively and on collective projects. Their home cultures, the local community, and their identities are a resource that can be championed and used in their writing at school (Lankshear and Knobel 2009; Rowsell and Pahl 2011; Kinloch 2018). Analysing the language, patterns, and structures of texts is vital to the understanding of how they work to act for or against the reader and writer. Pupils may study articles and exemplar texts to gain an insight into bias or 'fake news'; they may also be encouraged to appropriate them for their own purposes (Lensmire 1998). They are invited to write nonconformist or subversive texts which represent people who are often seen as marginal, to transgress conventions, to challenge the status quo, and so bring about new thinking to their own community of writers and beyond. Teachers recognise that technology, multiliteracies, and new emerging literacies have a profound part to play in the development of these young writers who not only write texts but also 'make' and perform them (Cazden et al. 1992; Merchant 2009).

Limitations

- Can critical literacy alienate children or make them fearful to compose texts?
- What happens if and when the texts produced create conflict or cause offence?
- How much political understanding is required by children to take part in such an approach? When and how is this taught?
- Should teachers be engaging in politics? Should schooling and politics be kept separate? Is this even possible?
- What happens if children do not have access to the required technology?
- If texts carry different meanings for different people and are written in a largely co-operative way, how do teachers begin the task of assessing individual progress (Locke 2015)?

The community or environmental orientation

There are a number of terms associated with this orientation: meaning making/meaning sharing, connected learning, the 'writing event' approach, the communicative approach, the environmental approach, inquiry, situation of expression approach (Nystrand 1987), function and aims (Beard 2000), social connection, social interaction, social participation, social construction (Bishop 1999), the socioliterate approach (Johns 1997), the writing for a reader approach (Nystrand 1989), the post-process writing workshop (Taylor 2000), problem-posing, funds of knowledge, funds of identity, literacy as a social practice, literacy-in-action, the community ideology, knowledge building (Scardamalia and Bereiter 2003), everyday life literacy, meaningful literacy, relevant literacy, literacy of the person (Gardner 2018), or the 'living the literate life' approach (Kaufman 2009). Through this orientation, the classroom is seen as a community which has the collective mission of fulfilling different purposes, communicating with different audiences, creating successful texts, achieving social goals, and contributing to a variety of social groups and contexts (Lensmire 1998; Schultz and Fecho 2000; Bazerman 2016). There is a sense of collective effort towards creating a variety of meaningful texts which can then be distributed for others' learning, reflection, or entertainment. It recognises that genre and writing cannot be separated. However, it also sees that genre teaching can too often be far removed from the way writers craft texts. In this conception, teachers are less prescriptive and less anxiously devoted to the inclusion of any arbitrary genre features. Instead, they place more emphasis on children writing successful and meaningful texts for authentic and purposeful reasons which match the needs of their audiences.

The conception of writing and the writer

The community orientation has some similarities with the genre-based approach in that it regards writing as inherently social and writers as the producers of texts written accurately and appropriately to serve a social purpose and audience (Watkins 1999). It extends this conception of writers to include the more humanistic viewpoint that all children have something vital, worthwhile, and personal to share out into different communities. James Britton (1972) argued that a child's writing should be doing work, be in 'operation', and that artificial stimuli are unnecessary since the world is always ready and waiting for the child to write about it and for it. Writers are seen as active, discerning, experimenting, and engaging in the world through writing (Hymes 1974; Subero et al. 2016; Rosen 2017). Essentially, writing and being a writer is seen as a shared, reader-orientated and social enterprise. The teacher gains satisfaction from seeing children develop their own writer's process and the ability to write successful and meaningful texts which fulfil their own intentions and reach genuine audiences.

The relationship between teachers and pupils

Cremin and Myhill (2012) use the word 'reciprocal' to describe a relationship of equality between teacher and pupil. The term characterises this approach, where the teacher's role is to create a community of writers, or a 'literacy club' (Smith 1988b) of which all children feel they have membership. Teachers are active participants in the community, working, learning, teaching, and writing alongside and amongst their pupils. Children cease being consumers of writing and instead become proactive producers in an environment where differing voices, experiences, and texts are published for others to enjoy, respond to, and learn from (Subero et al. 2016). In this way, the community of the classroom shares a variety of knowledge through writing, as opposed to simply producing multiple examples of a single and possibly decontextualised piece of writing.

The content of the writing curriculum

Children are invited to participate in the choosing of their own writing ideas for class writing projects. They are given instruction in genre (where discussion is focused on the purpose and future audience for the writing), the writing craft, and writing procedures. Community-orientated teachers ensure that children learn about and are engaged in all the writing processes in order to produce high-quality final written products which are successful and meaningful in their own right. In these ways, the community curriculum approach is significantly different from the laissez-faire stance taken by teachers who subscribe to a self-expressionist orientation.

Teaching strategies

Writing problems are tackled in a spirit of inquiry and problem-solving within a contemporary writing workshop environment (Young and Ferguson 2020). For example, teachers draw pupils' attention to the purposes, meaningfulness, and features of 'information texts' and then provide an opportunity in which they can apply this knowledge using their own chosen ideas. These pieces will then be revised, edited, and published for authentic reasons. Therefore, time is spent defining and then understanding the future readership. Children are taught strategies, techniques, and procedures which they can apply in the current writing project but which are also generalised and useful enough to be applied in future projects.

Limitations

- It is possible that some children might remove themselves from classroom interactions (such as sharing and publishing) because they feel they have 'no friends' there and that their writing voice is not seen as legitimate in the community of the classroom (Lensmire 2000).
- Children may choose subjects for writing which have the potential to cause tensions or feelings of offence (Collier 2010).
- Children may value some class writing projects more than others.
- There may be tensions between children expressing themselves and the teacher being required to evaluate the outcome.
- Some teachers might find it problematic to join the community of writers whilst at the same time providing more formal instruction.
- When compared to a naturalistic approach, there is less time devoted to the individual writer's personal writing projects.

Conclusion

It is interesting to note that Hillocks' (1986) report on the meta-analysis of 73 studies stated that the *community* or *environmental* orientation towards writing teaching was two to three times more effective than the *self-expression* or *naturalistic* approach and over four times more effective than the *presentational* approach. The presentational orientation was observed to be the least effective. It seems that the community approach is able to bring the presentational and the naturalistic together since it encourages teachers to present skills, genres, models and criteria, and then to facilitate their use in class writing projects which are led by the young writers (Young and Ferguson 2020). As this chapter has shown, adopting a multi-dimensional approach to the teaching of writing is necessary if we are to take the greatest strengths from each orientation. At a point in time where we are clearly seeing profound underachievement in writing (Ofsted 2012; DfE 2012, 2017) and an increase in young people's indifference to or dislike of it (Clark 2016; Clark and Teravainen 2017), we propose an approach which combines rigorous instruction in the processes and craft of writing with principles which contribute significantly to children's enjoyment and satisfaction. An approach which is neither teacher centred nor child centred but rather one centred around creating successful writers. We term such a model *Writing For Pleasure*, which brings together the very best aspects of all the orientations described in this chapter to form a rigorous, fresh, holistic, and inclusive philosophy and pedagogy for writing.

In the next chapter we will define exactly what we mean by writing for pleasure.

QUESTIONS WORTH ASKING YOURSELF

- Did you enjoy learning to write? Why? Why not?
- How many teachers can you attribute this to?

- Do you think you're a good writer now? Why? Why not?
- How does your experience with writing affect your view of how writing should be taught?
- Which teacher orientation would you have wanted to have been taught by most?
- Which orientation(s) do you feel best represent(s) your personal theory of writing teaching?

References

Allal, L. (2019). Assessment and the co-regulation of learning in the classroom, *Assessment in Education: Principles, Policy & Practice*. 27:4, 332-349 DOI: 10.1080/0969594X.2019.1609411.

Bazerman, C. (2016). What do sociocultural studies of writing tell us about learning to write. In *Handbook of Writing Research*, MacArthur, C., Graham, S., and Fitzgerald, J. (Eds.) (2nd Ed.) (pp. 11–23). New York: The Guilford Press.

Bazerman, C., Applebee, A., Berninger, V., Brandt, D., Graham, S., Matsuda, P., Murphy, S., Rowe, D., and Schleppegrell, M. (2017). Taking the long view on writing development. *Research in the Teaching of English*, 51, 351–360.

Beard, R. (2000). *Developing Writing 3–13*. Oxon: Hodder & Stoughton.

Bereiter, C., and M. Scardamalia. (1987). an attainable version of high literacy: Approaches to teaching higher-order skills in reading and writing. *Curriculum Inquiry*, 17(1), 19–30.

Bishop, W. (1999). Place to stand: The reflective writer-teacher-writer in composition. *College Composition and Communication*, 51(1), 9–31.

Britton, J. (1972). Writing to learn and learning to write. In *Prospect and Retrospect: Selected Essays of James Britton*, Pradl, G. (Ed.) (pp. 94–112). London: Heinemann.

Cazden, C., Cope, B., Fairclough, N., and Gee, J. (1992). A pedagogy of multiliteracies: Designing social futures. *Harvard Educational Review*, 66(1), 60–92.

Chuy, M., Scardamalia, M., and Bereiter, C. (2011). Development of ideational writing through knowledge building: Theoretical and empirical bases. In *Handbook of Writing: A Mosaic of New Perspectives*, Grigorenko, E., Mambrino, E., and Preiss, D. (Eds.) (pp. 175–190). New York: Psychology Press.

Clark, C. (2016). *Children's and Young People's Writing in 2015*. London: National Literacy Trust.

Clark, C., and Teravainen, A. (2017). *Writing for Enjoyment and Its Link to Wider Writing*. London: National Literacy Trust.

Coffin, C. (2006). Mapping subject-specific literacies. *NALDIC Quarterly*, 3(3), 13–26.

Collier, D. (2010). Journey to becoming a writer: Review of research about children's identities as writers. *Language and Literacy*, 12(10), 147–164.

Cremin, T. (2006). Creativity, uncertainty and discomfort: Teachers as writers. *Cambridge Journal of Education*, 36(3), 415–433.

Cremin, T. and Myhill, D. (2012). *Writing Voices: Creating Communities of Writers*. London: Routledge.

Cremin, T., Myhill, D., Eyres, I., Nash, T., Wilson, A., and Oliver, L. (2019). Teachers as writers: Learning together with others. *Literacy*. 54(2) pp.49-59 doi.org/10.1111/lit.12201

Cremin, T., Mottram, M., Collins, F., Powell, S., and Safford, K. (2014). *Building Communities of Engaged Readers: Reading for Pleasure*. London: Routledge.

DfE (2012). *What is the Research Evidence on Writing?* Education Standards Research Team, London: Department for Education.

DfE (2017). *National Curriculum Assessments at Key Stage 2 in England, 2017 (revised)*. London: Department for Education

Dixon, J. (1967). *Growth in English*. London: Oxford University Press.

Dixon, J. (1987). The question of genres. In *The Place of Genre in Learning: Current Debates*, Reid, I. (Ed.) (pp. 22–34). Deakin: Deakin University Press.

Dobson, T. (2016). Just because I'm not a published author does not mean that I'm not a writer": Primary trainee teachers' identities as creative writers. *Writing in Practice: The Journal of Creative Writing Research*, 2.

Durrant, C., Sawyer, W., Scherff, L., and Goodwyn, A. (2019). *The Future of English Teaching Worldwide* London: Routledge.

Dutro, E., and Kazemi, E. (2006). Making sense of 'the boy who died': Tales of a struggling successful writer. *Reading and Writing Quarterly*, 22, 325–356.

Elbow, P. (1998). *Writing Without Teachers*. New York: Oxford University Press.

Eyres, I. (2017). Conceptualising writing and identity. In *Writer Identity and the Teaching and Learning of Writing*, Cremin, T., and Locke, T. (Eds.) (pp. 3–18). London: Routledge.

Fairclough, N. (1989). *Language and Power*. London: Longman.

Fishman, S., and McCarthy, L. (1992). Is expressivism dead? Reconsidering its romantic roots and its relation to social constructionism. *College English*, 54(6), 647–661.

Flint, A. S., and Laman, T. (2012). Where poems hide: Finding reflective, critical spaces inside writing workshop. *Theory Into Practice*, 51(1), 12–19.

Frank, C. (2003). Mapping our stories: Teachers' reflections on themselves as writers. *Language Arts*, 80(3), 185–195.

Freedman, A. (1994). Anyone for tennis? In *Genre and the New Rhetoric*, Freedman, A., and Medway, P. (Eds.) (pp. 43–66). London: Taylor & Francis.

Freire, P. (1996). *Pedagogy of the Oppressed* (2nd Ed.). London: Penguin Press.

Gardner, P. (2014). Becoming a teacher of writing: Primary student teachers reviewing their relationship with writing. *English in Education*, 48(2), 128–148.

Gardner, P. (2018). Writing and writer identity: the poor relation and the search for voice in 'personal literacy'. *Literacy*, 52(1), 11–19.

Gibbons, S. (2017). *English and Its Teachers*. London: Routledge.

Graham, J., and Kelly, A. (2009). *Writing Under Control*. London: Routledge.

Graham, S., and Harris, K. (2019). Evidence-based practices in writing. In *Best Practices in Writing Instruction*, Graham, S., MacArthur, C., and Hebert, M. (Eds.) (3rd Ed.) (pp. 3–31). New York: The Guilford Press.

Graham, S., & Perin, D. (2007). Writing next: Effective strategies to improve writing of adolescents in middle and high schools – A report to Carnegie Corporation of New York. Washington, DC: Alliance for Excellent Education.

Graham, S., Harris, K.R., Fink, B., and MacArthur, C.A. (2001). Teacher efficacy in writing: A construct validation with primary grade teachers. *Scientific Studies of Reading*, 56, 177–202.

Graham, S., Harris, K.R., and Mckeown, D. (2013). The writing of students with LD and a meta-analysis of SRSD writing intervention studies: Redux. In *Handbook of Learning Disabilities*, Swanson, L., Harris, K., and Graham, S. (Eds.) (2nd Ed.) (pp. 405–438). New York: Guilford Press.

Grainger, T., Goouch, K., and Lambirth, A. (2005). *Creativity and Writing: Developing Voice and Verve in the Classroom*. London: Routledge.

Gutiérrez, K. (2008) 'Developing a sociocritical literacy in the Third Space'. *Reading Research Quarterly*, 43(2), 148–164.

Hall, A., and Grisham-Brown, J. (2011). Writing development over time: Examining preservice teachers' attitudes and beliefs about writing. *Journal of Early Childhood Teacher Education*, 32, 148–158.

Halliday, M. (2013). *Introduction to Functional Grammar* (4th Ed.). London: Routledge.

Harwayne, S. (1992). *Lasting Impressions Weaving Literature into the Writing Workshop*. Portsmouth, NH: Heinemann.

Hillocks, G. (1986). *Research on Written Composition: New Directions for Teaching*. Urbana, IL: National Council of Teachers of English.

Hmelo-Silver, C., Duncan, R., and Chinn, C. (2007). Scaffolding and achievement in problem-based and inquiry learning: A response to Kirschner, Sweller, and Clark (2006). *Educational Psychologist*, 42(2), 99–107.

Hyland, K. (2002). *Teaching and Researching Writing*. Oxford: Pearson Education.

Hyland, K. (2008). Writing theories and writing pedagogies. *Indonesian Journal of English Language Teaching*, 4(2), 91–110.

Hymes, D. (1974). *Foundations in Sociolinguistics*. Philadelphia, PA: University of Pennsylvania Press.

Ivanič, R. (2004). Discourses of writing and learning to write. *Language and Education*, 18(3), 220–245.

Johns, A. (1997). *Text, Role and Context: Developing Academic Literacies*. Cambridge: Cambridge University Press.

Kamler, B. (2001). *Relocating the Personal: A Critical Writing Pedagogy*. Albany: State University Press of New York.

Kaufman, D. (2009). A teacher educator writes and shares: Student perceptions of a publicly literate life. *Journal of Teacher Education*, 60, 228.

Kellogg, R. T. (2008). Training writing skills: A cognitive developmental perspective. *Journal of Writing Research* 1(1), 1–26.

Kinloch, V. (2017). 'You ain't making me write': Culturally sustaining pedagogies and black youths' performance of resistance. In *Culturally Sustaining Pedagogies*, Paris, D., and Alim, S. (Eds.)(pp.25–42). New York: Teachers' College Press.

Kinloch, V. (2018). Necessary disruptions: Examining justice, engagement, and humanizing approaches to teaching and teacher education. In *Teaching Works*. Pittsburgh, PA: University of Pittsburgh.

Kinneavy, J. (1980). *A Theory of Discourse*. New York: W.W Norton.

Kress, G. (1994). *Learning to Write* (2nd Ed.). London: Routledge.

Ladson-Billings, G. (1995). Toward a theory of culturally relevant pedagogy. *American Educational Research Journal*, 32(3), 465–491.

Laman, T., Davis, T., and Henderson, J. (2018). My hair has a lot of stories!": Unpacking culturally sustaining writing pedagogies in an elementary mediated field experience for teacher candidates. *Action in Teacher Education*, 40(4), 374–390.

Lankshear, C., and Knobel, M. (2009). More than words: Chris Searle's approach to critical literacy as cultural action. *Race & Class*, 51(2), 59–78.

Leigh, S.R. (2014). *Wounded Writers: Am I Doing it Write?* Netherlands: Sense.

Lensmire, T. (1998). Rewriting student voice. *Journal of Curriculum Studies*, 30(3), 261–291.

Lensmire, T. (2000). *Powerful Writing Responsible Teaching*. New York: Teachers' College Press

Locke, T. (2015). *Developing Writing Teachers*. London: Routledge.

MacArthur, C., and Graham, S. (2017). Writing research from a cognitive perspective. In *Handbook of Writing Research*, MacArthur, C., Graham, S., and Fitzgerald, J. (Eds.) (2nd Ed.) (pp. 24–40). London: Guildford Press.

Martin, J., and Rose, D. (2008). *Genre Relations: mapping Culture*. Sheffield: Equinox.

Mason, J., & Giovanelli, M. (2017). 'What do you think?' Let me tell you: Discourse about texts and the literature classroom. *Changing English*, 24(3), 318–329.

Maybin, J. (2001). Language, struggle and voice: The bakhtin/volosinov writings. In *Discourse Theory and Practice: A Reader*, Wetherell, M., Taylor, S., and Yates, S. (Eds.) (pp. 64–71). London: Sage.

McCarthey, S. (1994). Opportunities and risks of writing from personal experience. *Children's And Adolescent Literature: Writing, Illustrating, Publishing, Reading, Responding, Teaching*, 71(3), 182–191.

McCarthey, S., and Mkhize, D. (2013). Teachers' Orientations towards writing. *Journal of Writing Research*, 5(1), 1–33.

McGuinn, N. (2005). A place for the personal voice? Gunther Kress and the English curriculum. *Changing English*, 12(2), 205–217.

Merchant, G. (2009). Web 2.0, new literacies, and the idea of learning through participation. *English Teaching: Practice and Critique*, 8(3), 107–122.

Morrison, K., Robbins, H., and Gregory Rose, H. (2008). Operationalizing culturally relevant pedagogy: A synthesis of classroom-based research. *Equity & Excellence in Education*, 41(4), 433–452.

Murray, D. (1978). Write before writing. *College Composition and Communication*, 29(4), 375–381.

Nystrand, M. (1987). The role of context in written communication. In *Comprehending Oral and Written Language*, Horowitz, R., and Samuels, S.J. (Eds.) (pp. 197–214). Cambridge, MA: Academic Press.

Nystrand, M. (1989). A social interactive model of writing. *Written Communication*, 6, 66–85.

Ofsted (2012). *Moving English Forward*. London: Ofsted

Parker, R. (1988). Theories of writing instruction: having them, use them, change them. *English Education*, 20(1), 18–40.

Perry, K. (2012). What is literacy? A critical overview of sociocultural perspectives. *Journal of Language and Literacy Education*, 8(1), 50–71.

Richardson, P. (1998). Literacy, learning and teaching. *Educational Review*, 50(2), 115–134.

Rose, D. (2008). Writing as linguistic mastery: The development of genre-based literacy pedagogy. In *Handbook of Writing Development*, Myhill, D., Beard, R., Nystrand, M., and Riley, J. (Eds.). London: Sage.

Rosen, H. (2017). The politics of writing. In *Harold Rosen Writings on Life, Language and Learning 1958–2008*, Richmond, J. (Ed.) (pp. 347–361). London: UCL IOE Press.

Rowsell, J., and Pahl, K. (2011). The material and the situated. In *Handbook of Research on Teaching the English Language Arts*, Lapp, D., and Fisher, D. (Eds.) (pp. 175–181). London: Routledge.

Scardamalia, M., and Bereiter, C. (2003). Knowledge building. In *Encyclopedia of Education* (2nd Ed.) (pp. 1370–1373). New York: Macmillan Reference.

Schneider, J. (2003). Contexts, genres, and imagination: An examination of the idiosyncratic writing performances of three elementary children within multiple contexts of writing instruction. *Research in the Teaching of English*, 37: 329–379.

Schultz, K., and Fecho, B. (2000). Society's child: Social context and writing development. *Educational Psychologist*, 35(1), 51–62.

Searle, C. (1973). *This New Season: Our Class, Our Schools, Our World*. London: Calder & Boyars.

Shanahan, T. (2016). Relationships between reading and writing development. In *Handbook of Writing Research*, MacArthur, C., Graham, S., and Fitzgerald, J. (Eds.) (2nd Ed.) (pp. 194–207). New York: The Guilford Press.

Smagorinsky, P. (1987). Graves revisited: A look at the methods and conclusions of the New Hampshire study. *Written Communication*, 4(4), 331–342.

Smagorinsky, P., and Smith, M. (1992). The nature of knowledge in composition and literary understanding: The question of specificity. *Review of Educational Research*, 62(3), 279–305.

Smith, F. (1988a). *Insult to Intelligence*. Portsmouth, NH: Heinemann.

Smith, F. (1988b). *Joining the Literacy Club*. Portsmouth, NH: Heinemann.

Street, B. (1995). *Social Literacies: Critical Approaches to Literacy in Development, Ethnography and Education*. London: Routledge.

Street, C. (2003). Pre-service teachers' attitudes about writing and learning to teach writing: Implications for teacher educators. *Teacher Education Quarterly* Summer, 30, 33–50.

Subero, D., Vujasinović E., and Esteban-Guitart, M. (2016). Mobilising funds of identity in and out of school. *Cambridge Journal of Education*, 47(2), 247–263.

Sudol, D., and Sudol, P. (1991). Another story: Putting Graves, Calkins, and Atwell into practice and perspective. *Language Arts*, 68(4), 292–300.

Taylor, M. (2000). Nancie Atwell's 'In the Middle' and the ongoing transformation of the writing workshop. *The English Journal*, 90(1), 46–52.

The Talk Workshop Group. (1982). *Becoming Our Own Experts*. London: Redwood Burn.

Watkins, M. (1999). Policing the text: Structuralism's stranglehold on Australian language and literacy pedagogy. *Language and Education*, 13(2), 118–132.

Wray, D., and Beard, R. (1988) *Teacher Handbooks: Developing Children's Writing*. Oxford: Scholastic.

Young, R., (2019) *What is it 'Writing For Pleasure' teachers do that makes the difference?* The University Of Sussex: The Goldsmiths' Company

Young, R., and Ferguson F. (2020). *Real-World Writers: A Handbook for Teaching Writing with 7–11 Year Olds*. London: Routledge.

Young, R., Govender, N., Kaufman, D. (in press) *Writing Realities*. Leicester: UKLA

Zacarian, D., and Soto, I. (2020). *Responsive Schooling for Culturally and Linguistically Diverse Students*. New York: Norton.

Zacarian, D., Alvarez-Ortiz, L., and Haynes, J. (2017) *Teaching to Strengths: Supporting Students Living with Trauma, Violence, and Chronic Stress*. Alexandria, VA: ASCD.

Zoellner, R. (1969). Talk-write: A behavioral pedagogy for composition. *College English*, 30(4), 267–320.

CHAPTER

2

Defining writing for pleasure

Why should children be writing for pleasure?

'The first object of any act of learning, over and beyond the pleasure it may give, is that it should serve us in the future' (Bruner 1963, p. 17). Recent surveys conducted by the National Literacy Trust (Clark 2016; Clark and Teravainen 2017) make it clear that for many years there has been a decline or stagnation in children's enjoyment, volition, and motivation to write both in and out of school, with around half showing indifference to or an active dislike of writing. Graham and Johnson (2012, p. 110) confirm this finding when they note, in a review of perceptions of writing in their classroom, that: 'while 75% of the children demonstrated a positive attitude towards their reading experiences, only 10% of the same children described positive or happy associations in their writing memories. The majority of children ... associated the writing experience with incompetence or anxiety; even those children who were perceived by me to be able writers did not consider the experience to be emotionally rewarding ... children who were competent in their literacy skills, who met their targets, who could write successfully in a variety of genres, failed to express any sense of joy in their written achievements'.

Evidence shows that, for a number of years, too many students in England have been underachieving, with one in five primary school pupils not attaining the expected standard in English and with far more pupils failing to achieve the standard in writing (Ofsted 2009, 2012). Ofsted (2012, p. 9) states that 'only 69% of boys achieved national expectations in writing' with, as Ofsted (2009, p. 4) elsewhere notes, 'white British boys eligible for free school meals ... amongst the lowest performers in the country'. This is repeated in 2018, where according to the Department for Education (DfE 2018) we see the largest attainment gap between boys and girls, with only 72% of boys reaching the expected standard. Further, 'standards are not yet high enough for all pupils and there has been too little improvement in primary schools' (Ofsted 2012, p. 4). We see this again in 2017, where 'attainment at the expected standard, as measured by teacher assessment ... is lowest in writing. This is similar to the pattern in 2016' (DfE 2017). In 2019, only one in five children in England were achieving above the basic level in writing (DfE

2019). Finally, the DfE (2012, p. 3) remarks that 'writing is the subject with the worst performance compared with reading, maths and science at Key Stages 1 and 2'.

We can conclude that it is likely that children are underachieving as a result of their dislike of writing. Clark and Teravainen (2017, p. 14) state that 'eight times as many children and young people who do not enjoy writing write below the expected level compared with those who enjoy writing', and this is further supported by Ofsted's (2019) latest research, which states that pupils' motivation and positive attitudes towards learning are important predictors for attainment. Finally, the National Literacy Trust points out in their 2017 annual survey that their findings 'highlight the importance of writing enjoyment for children's outcomes and warrant a call for more attention on writing enjoyment in schools, research and policy' (Clark and Teravainen 2017, p. 15). Our own research conducted in 2019 aimed to answer that very call (Young 2019).

Educational research consistently tells us that there are significant academic benefits to be gained through engagement with the personal and affective (Zins et al. 2007; Clark and Teravainen 2017). It will therefore come as no surprise to learn that children's enjoyment of writing in school contributes significantly to their greater academic success and achievement (Bruning and Horn 2000; Purcell-Gates et al. 2007; Dignath et al. 2008; Bruning et al. 2013; Zumbrunn et al. 2017; DeSmedt et al. 2018). According to some studies, the most important pointers to high attainment in writing are motivation and volition (Hillocks 1986; Beard 2000; Alexander 2009; Clark 2016) with the best single motivator being agency (Lave and Wenger 1991; Ketter and Pool 2001; Dyson and Freedman 2003; Watanabe 2007; Au and Gourd 2013).

Agency, volition, and motivation have very clear links to the experience of pleasure in writing. In his review of 100 years of literacy research, Hillocks (2011, p. 189) sums up the issue forcefully: 'we know from a very wide variety of studies in English and out of it, that students who are authentically engaged with the tasks of their learning are likely to learn much more than those who are not'.

Defining *Writing For Pleasure*

As literate adults, most of us would have little difficulty in defining what we mean by *reading* for pleasure, and indeed its promotion is now a statutory part of the English National Curriculum (DfE 2013). Cremin et al. (2014, p. 5) state 'at the core of reading for pleasure is the reader's volition, their agency and desire to read, their anticipation of the satisfaction gained through the experience and/or afterwards in interaction with others'. However, little consideration has been given to what *writing* for pleasure might mean, particularly in the context of the classroom.

It is known that children who enjoy writing and are motivated to write are seven times more likely to achieve well academically (Clark and Teravainen 2017). Therefore, writing for pleasure is a vital consideration when teaching young writers. If we examine what professional writers have said on the subject (Cremin and Oliver 2017), alongside the definition of reading for pleasure given by Cremin et al. (2014), we can define writing for pleasure as a volitional act of writing undertaken for enjoyment and satisfaction. The specific sources of enjoyment and satisfaction in writing are many and varied and will be different for individual writers in different contexts. In their book *Real-World Writers,* Young and Ferguson (2020, pp. 4–7) consider some of the reasons why young writers are *moved* to write, including to:

- **Teach** others by sharing their experience and knowledge or teach themselves by writing to learn.
- **Persuade or influence** others by sharing their thoughts and opinions.
- **Entertain** themselves or others by sharing stories – both real and imagined.
- **Paint with words** to show their artistry and their ability to see things differently, or to simply play around and have fun.
- **Reflect** in order to better understand themselves, their place in the world or their response to a new subject.
- **Make a record** of something to look back on in the future.

Writing can of course involve a variety of these simultaneously. In our own research (Young 2019), we also argue that there are two types of pleasure in writing: writing *as* pleasure (enjoyment) and writing *for* pleasure (satisfaction).

Writing as pleasure

We describe this kind of pleasure as:

- Feeling a need to write and experiencing enjoyment in practising the craft of writing.
- Feeling confident and content when engaging in the different processes of writing.
- Enjoying being part of a writing community, discussing your own writing and how it feels to be a writer.

Writing *as* pleasure is pleasure gained from practising the craft of writing, from engaging in the process or in particular parts of the process, whether it be generating ideas; dabbling; getting the words down on paper or screen for the first time; revising a section till you get it just so; editing to perfection; or publishing the final product with care. Joyce Carol Oates and Ernest Hemingway both recorded that, for them, the pleasure was all in the revising. Ellen Goodman likens editing to cleaning up a house. And for some, the pleasure ends with the completion of the act of writing; the prospect of others reading their text can fill them with dread.

Writing for pleasure

Gene Fowler is said to have remarked that writing is easy: 'all you do is sit staring at a blank sheet of paper until the drops of blood form on your forehead'. T.S. Eliot stated that writing is an intolerable wrestle with words and their meanings. So, the act of writing isn't always pleasurable. Why then do we put ourselves through it? Maybe for the kind of pleasure we describe below:

- Having the sense of a purpose fulfilled.
- The expectation of a response.

- Sharing something to be proud of and feeling you have achieved something significant.
- The discovery of your own writing voice.

This type of pleasure is the satisfaction that comes *after* the act of writing: it comes from knowing that you will receive a response from your audience and that your writing will be put to work – sharing your memories, knowledge, ideas, thoughts, artistry, or opinions with others. There can also be pleasure in hearing the meanings other people take from your text. It can come from hearing your own writing voice as you read back, from knowing you said what you meant to say, or from achieving what you wanted your reader to feel or understand. Writing *for* pleasure presents children with a feeling of empowerment and that their writing has enriched their lives and the lives of others.

It is our contention that there is not only value and satisfaction to be gained from a finished text, but that something significant occurs during the crafting of it. You will have noticed that the elements of writing *as* and *for* pleasure are strongly present in some of the orientations described in Chapter 1, notably: the achieving of a purpose, the expectation of a response, a feeling of empowerment, sharing something significant, being part of a community, pleasure in the craft of writing, and in producing something to be proud of. In summary, it could be said that *Writing For Pleasure* is the difference between being 'schooled' in writing and being truly educated in the craft of being a writer.

A working definition of a *Writing For Pleasure* pedagogy

> Writing for pleasure is a volitional act of writing undertaken for enjoyment and satisfaction. Therefore, a Writing For Pleasure pedagogy is any research-informed pedagogy which seeks to create the conditions in which writing and being a writer is a pleasurable, purposeful and satisfying experience. It has as its goal the use of effective writing practices with young apprentice writers and the promotion of the affective aspects of writing and of being a writer.
>
> (Young 2019, p. 13)

An introduction to our research

In 2019, we carried out a research project entitled *What is it 'Writing For Pleasure' teachers do that makes the difference?* The principal purpose of the classroom-based research was to investigate and describe the kind of writing teaching which constitutes a *Writing For Pleasure* pedagogy. It was a requirement that the practices of the teachers participating in the research were based on what studies tell us is the most effective writing teaching associated with high levels of pupil motivation, self-efficacy, agency, self-regulation, volition, writer-identity, and pleasure in writing. Teachers were also required to provide evidence of exceptional or above expected academic progress among their pupils. The research observed and identified the practices employed by the most *effective* teachers of writing and connected them to the *affective domains* of *Writing For Pleasure*. The aim was to begin sharing ways in which the profession can address children's lack of enjoyment and therefore underachievement in writing, and to bring to light what effective *Writing For Pleasure* teachers do that makes the difference, both in terms of pupils' exceptional academic progress and their attitudes towards writing and being writers.

Our next chapter will draw on this research and on the research of others to discuss exactly what the affective domains of writing for pleasure are, and how they can be attended to in classroom practice.

References

Alexander, R. (2009). *Cambridge Primary Review*. London: Routledge.
Au, W., and Gourd, K. (2013). Asinine assessment: Why high-stakes testing is bad for everyone, including English teachers. *The English Journal*, 103(1), 14–19.
Beard, R. (2000). *Developing Writing 3–13*. Oxon: Hodder & Stoughton.
Bruner, J. (1963). *The Process of Education*. Cambridge, MA: Harvard University Press.
Bruning, R., and Horn, C. (2000). Developing motivation to write. *Educational Psychologist*, 35(1), 25–37.
Bruning, R., Dempsey, M., Kauffman, D., McKim, C., and Zumbrunn, S. (2013). Examining dimensions of self-efficacy for writing. *Journal of Educational Psychology*, 105(1), 25–38.
Clark, C. (2016). *Children's and Young People's Writing in 2015*. London: National Literacy Trust.
Clark, C., and Teravainen, A. (2017). *Writing for Enjoyment and Its Link to Wider Writing*. London: National Literacy Trust.
Cremin, T., Mottram, M., Collins, F., Powell, S., and Safford, K. (2014). *Building Communities of Engaged Readers: Reading For Pleasure*, London: Routledge.
Cremin, T., and Oliver, L. (2017). Teachers as writers: A systematic review. In *Research Papers in Education*, 32(3), 269–295.
DeSmedt, F., Merchie, E., Barendse, M., Rosseel, Y., De Naeghel, J., and Van Keer, H. (2018). Cognitive and motivational challenges in writing: Studying the relationship with writing performance across students' gender and achievement level. *Reading Research Quarterly*, 53(2), 249–272.
DfE. (2012). *What is the Research Evidence on Writing? Education Standards Research Team*. London: Department for Education.
DfE. (2013) *National curriculum in England: Primary Curriculum*. London: Department For Education.
DfE. (2017). *National Curriculum Assessments at Key Stage 2 in England, 2017 (revised)*. London: Department for Education.
DfE. (2018). *National Curriculum Assessments at Key Stage 2 in England, 2018 (provisional)*. London: Department for Education.
DfE. (2019) *National curriculum assessments at key stage 2 in England, 2019 (revised)* London: Department for Education.
Dignath, C., Buettner, G., and Langfeldt, H. (2008). how can primary school students learn self-regulated learning strategies most effectively? A meta-analysis on self-regulation training programmes. *Educational Research Review*, 3, 101–129.
Dyson, A.H., and Freedman, S.W. (2003). Writing. In *Handbook of Research on Teaching the English Language Arts*, Flood, J., Jensen, J., Lapp, D., and Squire, R. J. (Eds.) (pp. 967–992). Mahwah, NJ: Erlbaum.
Graham, L., and Johnson, A. (2012). *Children's Writing Journals*. Royston: United Kingdom Literacy Association.
Hillocks, G. (1986). *Research on Written Composition: New Directions for Teaching*. Urbana, IL: National Council of Teachers of English.

Hillocks, G. (2011). Commentary on "Research in secondary English, 1912–2011: Historical continuities and discontinuities in the NCTE imprint." *Research in the Teaching of English*, 46(2), 187–192.

Ketter, J., and Pool, J. (2001). Exploring the impact of a high-stakes direct writing assessment in two high school classrooms. In *Research in the Teaching of English*, 35(3), 344–393.

Lave, J., and Wenger, E. (1991). *Situated Learning: Legitimate Peripheral Participation*. London: Cambridge University Press.

Ofsted. (2009). *English at the Crossroads*. London: Ofsted.

Ofsted. (2012). *Moving English Forward*. London: Ofsted.

Ofsted. (2019). *Education Inspection Framework: Overview of Research*. London: Ofsted.

Purcell-Gates, V., Duke, N., and Martineau, J. (2007). Learning to read and write genre-specific text: Roles of authentic experience and explicit teaching. *Reading Research Quarterly*, 42(1), 8–45.

Watanabe, M. (2007). Displaced teacher and state priorities in a high-stakes accountability context. *Educational Policy*, 21(2), 311–368.

Young, R. (2019). *What is it 'Writing for Pleasure' teachers do that makes the difference?* The University Of Sussex: The Goldsmiths' Company [Online] Available: www.writing4pleasure.com.

Young, R., and Ferguson, F. (2020). *Real-World Writers: A Handbook for Teaching Writing with 7–11 Year Olds*. London: Routledge.

Zins, J., Bloodworth, M., Weissberg, R., and Walberg, H. (2007). The scientific base linking social and emotional learning to school success. *Journal of Educational and Psychological Consultation*, 17(2–3), 191–210.

Zumbrunn, S., Ekholm, E., Stringer J.K., McKnight, K., and DeBusk-Lane, M. (2017). Student experiences with writing: Taking the temperature of the classroom. *The Reading Teacher*, 70(6), 667–677.

CHAPTER

3

The affective domains of *Writing for Pleasure*

Neuroscientists Immordino-Yang and Damasio (2007, p. 9) state simply that when we feel, we learn, warning that 'when we educators fail to appreciate the importance of students' emotions, we fail to appreciate a critical force in students' learning. One could argue, in fact, that we fail to appreciate the very reason that students learn at all'. This warning should make us look at the way we teach writing in school.

Writing is something that is both personal and intensely social, both analytical and emotive. The concept of writing for pleasure sees it as an enjoyable activity bringing about a sense of satisfaction; *Writing For Pleasure* as a pedagogy is therefore based on the affective domains – the feelings, emotions, and attitudes involved in learning. It appears that 'students' views toward writing have received little attention from researchers' (Piazza and Sibert 2008, p. 275), and so our own research wanted to begin the process of filling this gap (Young 2019). In the context of writing teaching, our readings led us to define the affective domains as: self-efficacy, agency, self-regulation, motivation, volition, and writer-identity. These domains are associated with the experiences of feeling, emotion, disposition, drive, anxiety, desire, instinct, value, worth, mood and attitude, as described by affective and motivational science (Brand 1991; McLeod 1991). Affective and motivational science, cognitive and social cognitive psychology and sociocultural theory will continue to be interesting territories for educational researchers and for teachers of writing (Brand 1987; Bishop 1993; Lensmire 1998, 2000; Pintrich 2003; Piazza and Sibert 2008) (see Figure 3.1).

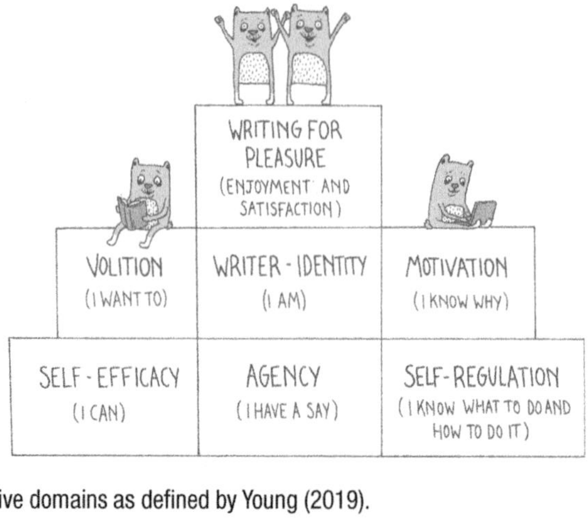

FIGURE 3.1 The affective domains as defined by Young (2019).

Hall and Axelrod (2014 p. 35) tell us that 'by listening to children and studying their experiences, the importance of social influences on writing development and achievement can be illustrated'. Listening can inspire us to re-examine what have been considered effective curriculum and teaching practices. For example, we explain throughout this book how attention to the affective domains strongly influences the promotion and teaching of cognitive factors such as ability, craft knowledge, knowledge of processes, procedures, strategies and techniques, and social factors such as community of practice, positive learning environments, and purposeful and meaningful writing projects (Zins 2007; Piazza and Sibert 2008). Indeed, Colognesi and Niwese (2020) have shown that when children are taught using the research-based effective practices described throughout this book, they not only achieve better than peers who do not receive such teaching, but they write with more desire, pleasure, and enthusiasm. These findings are repeated in Young's (2019) research where he was able to observe teachers connecting the affective domains of young writers with 14 principles of effective writing teaching and bringing them together as a cohesive whole. How these principles were identified is the subject of Chapter 10 and we recommend that you read that chapter first before continuing here.

Welcome back. The focus of the following chapters is to show the relationship between the affective domains and what research says are the most effective writing practices. According to Piazza and Sibert (2008), the affective domains account 'for more variance in school learning than a combination of factors related to peer groups, direct instruction, and school culture', and so it can be said that nurturing the affective domains is in itself the most effective practice teachers can employ. We hope that the next chapters will develop an understanding of how *Writing For Pleasure* can be realised as a highly effective, affective, and *affecting* pedagogy.

References

Bishop, W. (1993). Writing is/and therapy? Raising questions about writing classrooms and writing program administration. *Journal of Advanced Composition*, 13(2), 503–516.

Brand, A. (1987). The why of cognition: Emotion and the writing process. *College Composition and Communication*, 38(4), 436–443.

Brand, A. (1991). Social cognition emotions, and the psychology of writing. *Journal of Advanced Composition*, 11(2), 395–407.

Colognesi, S., and Niwese, M. (2020). Do effective practices for teaching writing change students' relationship to writing? Exploratory study with students aged 10–12 years. *L1-Educational Studies in Language and Literature*, 20, 1–25.

Hall, A., and Axelrod, Y. (2014). 'I am kind of a good writer and kind of not': Examining students' writing attitudes. *Journal of Research in Education*, 24(2), 34–50.

Immordino-Yang, M., and Damasio, A. (2007). We feel, therefore we learn: The relevance of affective and social neuroscience to education. *Mind, Brain & Education*, 1(1), 3–10.

Lensmire, T. (1998). Rewriting student voice. *Journal of Curriculum Studies*, 30(3), 261–291.

Lensmire, T. (2000). *Powerful Writing Responsible Teaching*. New York: Teachers' College Press.

McLeod, S. (1991). The affective domain and the writing process: Working definitions. *Journal of Advanced Composition*, 11(1), 95–105.

Piazza, C., and Siebert, C. (2008). Development and validation of a writing dispositions scale for elementary and middle school students. *The Journal of Educational Research*, 101(5), 275–285.

Pintrich, P. (2003). A motivational science perspective on the role of student motivation in learning and teaching contexts. *Journal of Educational Psychology*, 95(4), 667–686.

Young, R. (2019). *What is it 'Writing For Pleasure' teachers do that makes the difference?* The University of Sussex: The Goldsmiths' Company [Online] Available: www.writing4pleasure.com.

Zins, J., Bloodworth, M., Weissberg, R., and Walberg, H. (2007). The scientific base linking social and emotional learning to school success. *Journal of Educational and Psychological Consultation*, 17(2), 191–210.

CHAPTER 4

Self-efficacy

Introduction and context

> *At the start of my writing I feel like 'I can do this' and then I look at it and think I did it!*
>
> (Young 2019)

Self-efficacy, also described as self-belief, self-esteem, self-worth, self-affirmation, self-integrity, and associated with having a positive self-image, is recognised as one of the affective domains of *Writing For Pleasure,* and is a vital force not only in the achievement of academic success but also in the promotion of personal well-being (Pajares 2003; Pajares et al. 2007). A feeling of competence is obviously a necessary part of becoming a confident and effective writer; children with a high degree of self-efficacy believe they can generate meaningful and successful writing ideas, manage the processes involved in producing a good writing product, and write accurately (Bruning et al. 2013). Knowing that you are being successful as you achieve your writing goals, that you have been successful in the past, and that your writing will continue to be successful creates positive feelings and also has a powerful influence on academic achievement in writing (Andrade and Brooke 2010; Bruning et al. 2013; Collie et al. 2016). Self-efficacy is also linked to other affective domains such as motivation, self-regulation, agency, and volition (Pajares 2003; Garcia-Sanchez and Caso-Fuertes 2005; Graham et al. 2007; Bayraktar 2013; Bruning et al. 2013; Lensmire 1998, 2000; Lazowski and Hulleman 2016; Limpo and Alves 2017).

Bruning et al. (2013) have pointed to the large body of research evidence detailing the ways in which a feeling of self-efficacy enables children to excel in writing. According to such research, confident apprentice writers are more willing to participate, make a greater effort, show perseverance, and seek and find solutions to their own writing problems. They also try out higher-level strategies and writerly techniques, set themselves more ambitious writing goals, show greater commitment to class writing projects, are prepared to take risks, have strong volition to write, are better able to teach themselves and others, and are more aware of their own potential as writers (Pajares and Valiante 1997; Garcia-Sanchez and Caso-Fuertes 2005;

Schunk 2003; Schunk and Zimmerman 2007; Raphael et al. 2008; Bayraktar 2013). Finally, when young writers feel that they can be successful in writing, they are more likely to value it as a life-long pursuit (Pajares and Valiante 1997). Limpo and Alves (2017) observe that self-efficacy, knowing you are proficient in the cognitive skills of writing, is closely aligned to the motivational will to write. Therefore, teachers must focus on the skills *and* on the will of their young apprentice writers.

Low self-efficacy affects young writers in profound ways. Children with low self-confidence as writers generally dislike writing (Boscolo et al. 2012). They believe they cannot improve and therefore do not seek writing advice. They write the minimum required, have low aspirations, feel a sense of learned helplessness, and show little commitment to writing projects. They express negative views of themselves and may even be depressed (Pajares and Valiante 1997; Bayraktar 2013). Interestingly, both very young children (Shell et al. 1995) and children with special educational needs (Garcia-Sanchez and Caso-Fuertes 2005) often overestimate their ability to write; teachers need to be aware of this and find ways of sensitively helping them towards achievement.

Finally, and most importantly, our own and others' research (Fletcher 2016; Young 2019) shows that self-efficacy *alone* is not guaranteed to raise the quality of children's writing nor to increase the likelihood of writing for pleasure. Instead, teaching needs to be directed towards giving children a rich combination of self-efficacy, agency, and self-regulation.

Self-efficacy and the principles of effective practice

Build a community of writers

The writing classroom must be a safe and democratic place in which children can talk, read, and share their writing readily, and where they have plenty of time to complete their projects. Children enjoy feeling part of the social writing group as modelled by their teacher, and benefit from the opportunity to observe and emulate the behaviours and strategies of their successful peers and their writer-teacher (Schunk and Zimmerman 2007; Kaufman 2009).

Treat every child as a writer

Teachers can increase children's self-efficacy by abandoning a high-stakes performance-orientated stance and communicating the idea of writing as improvement through repeated practice. When children hold a similarly incremental view of learning to write and of being a writer, they believe that they can and will improve over time (Schunk and Zimmerman 2007).

Read, share, think, and talk about writing

Reflecting, critiquing, receiving and acting on advice can both support and increase levels of self-efficacy (Garcia-Sanchez and Caso-Fuertes 2005). Therefore, children should regularly be given time to examine and discuss their own writing and that of other apprentice writers.

Pursue purposeful and authentic writing projects

All children are able to experience a great feeling of positivity and optimism through undertaking purposeful and authentic writing projects (Miller and Meece 1999). If they feel confident that a project is leading towards a positive final goal, such as publication or performance, they are more likely to engage in and value it (Schunk and Zimmerman 2007; Raphael et al. 2008; Limpo and Alves 2017). As far as possible, all children should hear about the impact their writing has had on their readership once it is published.

Teach the writing processes

Explicitly teaching the writing processes is a principle of effective practice which greatly supports children's self-efficacy (McKeod 1987). Teachers should encourage and allow children to use the processes in a way which best suits them. Finally, children should not be expected to focus on composition and transcriptional accuracy simultaneously but should be allowed to give full cognitive attention to each one separately, thereby ensuring a better chance of success (McKeod 1987).

Set writing goals

Setting writing goals is a further principle of effective practice that can have a significant impact on children's feelings of self-efficacy (Andrade and Brooke 2010; McTigue and Liew 2011). A distant goal is set by the whole writing community at the start of a class writing project; children then learn how to set product goals effectively in collaboration with their peers and their teacher. They can also be asked to have a process goal in mind before they begin writing. Not surprisingly, children gain confidence and enjoyment from achieving each separate goal (Corden 2003; Andrade and Brooke 2010).

Be reassuringly consistent

Research suggests that having a consistent daily routine of mini-lesson, writing time, and class sharing can increase children's confidence, self-esteem, and sense of a writer-identity (Hachem et al. 2008). For example, concluding each writing session with Author's Chair or class sharing enables children to discuss with the community what they feel they have done well during that session's writing time and to have it approved and confirmed (Limpo and Alves 2017).

Teach daily mini-lessons

In daily mini-lessons, children learn about writing strategies and processes and how to use them successfully in their own writing. Teachers must also be quick to deliver responsive teaching through mini-lessons if they notice a lack of confidence in any aspect of writing composition, process, or transcription. During these lessons, writer-teachers often discuss mentor texts (Alber-Morgan et al. 2007) and their own strategies, techniques, and writing models. This kind of sharing is known to increase the self-efficacy of other writers (Pajares 2003; Gadd et al. 2019), especially if they have the explicit assurance that it will help them produce a better piece for their readership to enjoy (Schunk and Zimmerman 2007). It is also worth noting the suggestion that young writers modelling their own writing strategies and techniques for others to learn from is a procedure which may build self-belief even more effectively than when it's done by the teacher. (McTigue and Liew 2011).

Children's feelings of self-efficacy will not be enhanced if they cannot apply the instruction they receive in their own independent writing (MacArthur and Graham 2017). Therefore, instruction must be relevant and children should be encouraged to apply it in that day's writing time. And of course, when a strategy can be meaningfully applied, children are more likely to remember it and use it confidently in future writing projects.

According to Hmelo-Silver et al. (2007), instructionally guiding rather than directing apprentice writers promotes pleasure in writing through securing greater engagement and feelings of self-efficacy (Schunk and Zimmerman 2007; Graham et al. 2011, ; Limpo and Alves 2013).

Pupil conference: meet children where they are

Pupil conferences can play a vital role in increasing children's confidence, desire to write, and desire to share (Bayraktar 2013). During conferences, teachers should draw attention to writing strengths and praise the use of any new or challenging writing techniques or strategies. It will come as no surprise that children who receive encouraging feedback from their teachers, peers, and readership are more likely to feel efficacious and work harder to ensure their writing is successful (Schunk and Zimmerman 2007; Limpo and Alves 2017).

A word of wisdom

Teachers would be wise to collect from their students questionnaire and interview data about the affective aspects of learning to write and being a young writer. Research has shown that the teacher's response to and use of such data could have as much impact on children's future writing progress as the use of conventional assessment data (Pajares and Valiante 1997; Phillips 2019; Walker 2019).

The Writing For Pleasure teachers

- 'If I say yes I can do this, it means I have a plan, I know what to do – and I feel like that most of the time'.
- 'At the start of my writing I feel like "I can do this" and then I look at it and think I did it!'

- 'If I know what I'm doing and I feel confident with it – I feel like yeah I can do this!'

In our own research (Young 2019), the case study teachers who promoted self-efficacy to the highest level of proficiency did so by relating current writing projects to previous learning. This meant children saw writing as a mastery process through repeated practice as opposed to simply a performance-related task set by the teacher for evaluative purposes. Children understood that in the project they were currently undertaking they could and should employ skills, strategies, and techniques used in previous writing projects. Teachers reminded their children of such strategies and referred them to the posters on display in the classroom. There was a strong individual and collective focus on achieving goals and building on them incrementally; distant, process, and product goals were evident in rich combination. For example, the children knew the ultimate aim of the writing and what its purpose and future audience was to be, and they had an emotional and social investment in it. They set themselves writing deadlines to achieve throughout the project and were praised when they reached their goals. Both the teachers and the children understood the product goals that would determine the success of their compositions, and the teachers explicitly praised children for attending to them. Self-belief was very apparent in the children's responses during their interview. In essence, they were made to feel good about themselves, that they were developing as writers, and that their writing was achieving something significant.

References

Alber-Morgan, S., Hessler, T., and Konrad, M. (2007). Teaching writing for keeps. *Education and Treatment of Children*, 30, 107–128.

Andrade, H., and Brooke, G. (2010). Self-assessment and learning to write. In *Writing: Processes, Tools and Techniques*, Mertens, N. (Ed.) (pp.74–89). Nova Science Publishers.

Bayraktar, A. (2013). Nature of interactions during teacher-student writing conferences, revisiting the potential effects of self-efficacy beliefs. *Eurasian Journal of Educational Research*, 50, 63–85.

Boscolo, P., Gelati, C., and Galvan, N. (2012). Teaching elementary school students to play with meanings and genre. *Reading & Writing Quarterly*, 28(1), 29–50.

Bruning, R., Dempsey, M., Kauffman, D., McKim, C., and Zumbrunn, S. (2013). Examining dimensions of self-efficacy for writing. *Journal of Educational Psychology*, 105(1), 25–38.

Collie, R., Martin, A., and Curwood, J. (2016). Multidimensional motivation and engagement for writing: Construct validation with a sample of boys. *Educational Psychology*, 36(4), 771–791.

Corden, R. (2003). Writing is more than 'exciting': Equipping primary children to become reflective writers. *Reading Literacy and Language*, 37, 18–26.

Fletcher, A. (2016). Exceeding expectations: Scaffolding agentic engagement through assessment as learning. *Educational Research*, 58(4), 400–419.

Gadd, M., Parr, J., Robertson, J., Carran, L., Ali, Z., Gendall, L., and Watson K. (2019). Portrait of the student as a young writer: Some student survey findings about attitudes to writing and self-efficacy as writers. *Literacy*, 53(4), 226–235.

Garcia-Sanchez and Caso-Fuertes. (2005). Comparison of the effects on writing attitudes and writing self-efficacy of three different training programs in students with learning disabilities. *International Journal of Educational Research*, 43(4–5), 272–289.

Graham, S., Berninger, V., and Fan, W. (2007). The structural relationship between writing attitude and writing achievement in first and third grade students. *Contemporary Educational Psychology*, 32, 516–535.

Graham, S., Harris, K., and Mason, L. (2011). Self-regulated strategy development for students with writing difficulties. *Theory Into Practice*. 50(1), 20–27.

Hachem, A., Nabhani, M., and Bahous, R. (2008). 'We can write!' The writing workshop for young learners. *Education 3–13*, 36(4), 325–337.

Hmelo-Silver, C.E., Duncan, R.G., and Chinn, C.A. (2007). Scaffolding and achievement in problem-based and inquiry learning: a response to Kirschner, Sweller, and. *Educational Psychologist*, 42(2), 99–107.

Kaufman, D. (2009). A teacher educator writes and shares: student perceptions of a publicly literate life. *Journal of Teacher Education*, 60, 228.

Lazowski, R., and Hulleman, C. (2016). Motivation interventions in Education: A meta-analytic review. *Review of Educational Research*, 86(2), 602–640.

Limpo, T., and Alves, R. (2013). Teaching planning or sentence-combining strategies: Effective SRSD interventions at different levels of written composition. *Contemporary Educational Psychology* 38, 328–341.

Lensmire, T. (1998). Rewriting student voice. *Journal of Curriculum Studies*, 30(3), 261–291.

Lensmire, T. (2000). *Powerful Writing Responsible Teaching*. Teachers' College Press.

Limpo, T., and Alves, R. (2017). Relating beliefs in writing skill malleability to writing performance: The mediating role of achievement goals and self-efficacy. *Journal of Writing Research*, 9(2), 97–125.

MacArthur, C., and Graham, S. (2017). Writing research from a cognitive perspective. In *Handbook of Writing Research*, C. MacArthur., S. Graham., and J. Fitgerald (Eds.) (2nd Ed.) (pp. 24–40). Guilford Press.

McKeod, S. (1987). Some thoughts about feelings: The affective domains and the writing process. *College Composition and Communication*, 38(4), 426–435.

McTigue, E., and Liew, J. (2011). Principles and practices for building academic self-efficacy in middle grades language arts classrooms. *The Clearing House*, 84(3), 114–118.

Miller, S., and Meece, J. (1999). Third graders' motivational preferences for reading and writing tasks. *The Elementary Journal*, 100(1), 19–35.

Pajares, F. (2003). Self-efficacy beliefs, motivation, and achievement in writing: A review of the literature. *Reading and Writing Quarterly*, 19(2), 139–158.

Pajares, F., and Valiante, G. (1997). Influence of self-efficacy on elementary students' writing. *The Journal of Educational Research*, 90(6), 353–360.

Pajares, F., Johnson, M., and Usher, E. (2007). Sources of writing self-efficacy beliefs of elementary, middle, and high school students. *Research in the Teaching of English*, 42(1), 104–120.

Phillips, S. (2019). *Writing Rivers*. Available: https://writing4pleasure.com/writing-rivers/.

Raphael, L., Pressley, M., and Mohan, L. (2008). Engaging instruction in middle school classrooms: Observational study of nine teachers. *The Elementary School Journal*, 109(1), 61–81.

Schunk, D.H. (2003). Self-efficacy for reading and writing: Influence of modeling, goal setting, and self-evaluation. *Reading and Writing Quarterly*, 19, 159–172.

Schunk, D.H., and Zimmerman, B.J. (2007). Influencing children's self-efficacy and self-regulation of reading and writing through modeling. *Reading and Writing Quarterly*, 23, 7–25.

Shell, D.F., Colvin, C., and Bruning, R.H. (1995). Self-efficacy, attribution, and outcome expectancy mechanisms in reading and writing achievement: Grade-level and achievement-level differences. *Journal of Educational Psychology*, 87, 386–398.

Walker, J. (2019). *Sharing Our Perceptions of Writing* Available: https://writing4pleasure.com/sharing-our-perceptions-of-writing.

Young, R. (2019). *What is it 'Writing For Pleasure' teachers do that makes the difference?* The University of Sussex: The Goldsmiths' Company [Online] Available: www.writing4pleasure.com.

CHAPTER 5

Self-regulation

Introduction and context

Self-regulation, also described as autonomy-supporting, self-reliance, self-initiation, self-activation, self-generating, self-organising, self-directed, self-discipline, self-monitoring, self-evaluation, responsible decision-making, co-regulation, relationship management, time planning, self-management, socially shared regulation, and meta-cognition, is the feeling of independence from external intervention and is closely associated with the concept of *Writing For Pleasure* (Zimmerman and Risemberg 1997). According to Robson et al. (2020), building a child's sense of self-regulation increases their social skills, academic performance, and wellbeing in adulthood. In terms of children's development as writers, being self-regulating is knowing what to do and how to do it for yourself. Studies show that self-regulation can increase children's pleasure in writing (Englert et al. 1991; Sexton et al. 1998; Harris et al. 2006; Graham et al. 2011). Knowing what to do and how to do it gives them a sense of self-efficacy, control and ownership over their own writing craft and products, and relatedness – the pleasant feeling of belonging to a social group (Paris and Winograd 2003). This domain is clearly linked to the other domains of writing for pleasure, notably agency, volition, and motivation (Pintrich 2003; Dignath et al. 2008).

Research into self-regulation is extensive. According to Dignath et al. (2008), the large amount of empirical evidence now available has led to a consensus about the positive link between self-regulated metacognitive learning and academic achievement. Graham's (2006) meta-analysis of 39 studies indicated that self-regulation significantly improves the writing of high-achieving, typical, and struggling writers, as well as students with learning disabilities (Lane et al. 2010; Johnson et al. 2012; Zumbrunn and Bruning 2013). Further, research consistently demonstrates the effectiveness of teaching self-regulatory strategies within a contemporary writing workshop approach (Danoff et al. 1993; Alber-Morgan, Hessler and Konrad 2007; McQuitty 2014). For example, the average effect size for strategy instruction within this approach was 1.15 (0.32 and above is typically seen as significantly effective). This meant that a loosely interpreted version of a writing workshop taught in an unsystematic, naturalistic, or laissez-faire way was shown overall to be far less effective than a more robust approach (Chapter 1; Graham and Perin, 2007; Graham and Sandmel, 2011).

Teaching self-regulation strategies opens up the opportunity to improve children's general 'craft knowledge'. Young writers learn more about the 'generalities' of writing and acquire many procedures and writerly or literary techniques to help them manage the writing processes and produce successful and meaningful texts in a variety of forms (Englert et al. 1991; Graham 2006; Graham et al. 2011; Schunk & Zimmerman 2007). These strategies include knowing how to:

- Set their own writing goals and deadlines.
- Look after and use their writing environment positively.
- Seek assistance from peers or their teacher.
- Use mentor texts as aids to their own compositions.
- Gather information and make notes.
- Plan.
- Produce rich literary descriptions.
- Check their developing composition against set writing goals.
- Review their developing composition.
- Revise.
- Proof-read.

(MacArthur and Graham 2017)

Finally, the importance of learning self-regulation cannot be underestimated, as is clear from the following readily recognisable profiles emerging from some research studies:

- Children with high levels of self-regulation are better able to transfer learning from one writing project to another and can, of their own volition, initiate actions to drive their own academic performance (Paris and Winograd 2003; Alber-Morgan et al. 2007; Perry et al. 2008; Graham et al. 2011). Further, they value their personal progress and view errors as an opportunity to learn (Perry and VandeKamp 2000).
- Children with low levels of self-regulation often lack the strategies and techniques to sustain a piece of writing successfully. They will use avoidance tactics such as procrastination and hiding their work and will spend as little time as possible engaged in the writing processes. They will focus mainly on their handwriting, spelling, and punctuation, have difficulty in generating ideas, lack the ability to plan, omit or fail to attend to writing goals, struggle to revise their compositions, and fail to proof-read their final drafts (Perry and VandeKamp 2000; Graham et al. 2011).

Self-regulation and the principles of effective practice

Build a community of writers

The best writing classrooms are ones which promote both individual responsibility and communal sharing and learning (Perry and Drummond 2002). Research has found that social and co-regulating writing environments, such as *Writing For Pleasure* classrooms, are linked to positive academic performance and intellectual outcomes (Zins et al. 2007).

Developing writerly or 'craft' knowledge is critical to children's growth as writers (Perry and VandeKamp 2000; Graham et al. 2011), and part of the building of a writing community involves sharing this knowledge among its members. Children need to know *what* writing strategies there are, *how* they can be used, and decide for themselves *when* is the best time to employ them. They also need to know how to use the writing environment successfully and about the writing process, forms of writing, the textual features of typical genres, literary techniques, and potential audiences and purposes. And of course, as Perry and Drummond (2002) point out, when children are in tune with the identity of the writing community they are better able to learn and use the craft knowledge, skills, procedures, strategies and techniques of its members.

Teachers in *Writing For Pleasure* communities do all they can to foster children's independence. They are well-organised, communicate very clear behavioural expectations, and ensure children understand their responsibilities (Atwell 2014; Young and Ferguson 2020). They meticulously provide resources, prompts, charts, posters, rubrics, checklists, and other visual displays, often in collaboration with the children and always subject to adjustment. Any problems are quickly identified and attended to in mini-lessons. The writing environment is one where children feel they can trial newly learnt writing strategies and discuss and practise them collaboratively, with time made for feedback (Paris and Winograd 2003; Marrs et al. 2016).

Read, share, think, and talk about writing

According to Zimmerman and Risemberg (1997, p. 95): 'the critical aspect of effective writers is their proactive efforts to seek out others who can be helpful'. In this context, Hadwin and Oshige (2011) usefully expand the concept of self-regulation to include the ideas of co-regulation and socially shared regulation. Co-regulation is when children employ the self-regulatory strategy of seeking help or advice from their teacher or a peer. Socially shared regulation involves the community of writers coming together as a collective and sharing and reflecting on their progress. Cazden (cited in Lensmire 1998) claims that a writing workshop approach is one of the best environments for co-regulation and co-operative learning to take place in schools.

Teach the writing processes

We would agree with Collier's (2010) view that giving children access to writing strategies and techniques that help them think and write for themselves is vital. According to Schneider (2003), a great deal of research shows that children's success in becoming writers is inevitably impacted by their ability to regulate their *own* writing process. Therefore, coming to use personalised writing processes is a valuable contribution towards learning self-regulation (Perry and VandeKamp 2000). As an example, using planning grids, graphic organisers, rubrics, drawing as planning, and free writing can all be strategies at a young writer's disposal, employed as they suit the individual best (Young and Ferguson 2019).

Set writing goals

Once a strategy or technique has been introduced to a class, teachers will often invite children to try it out during that day's writing time by setting it as a writing goal (Butler and Winne 1995). Having a set of product goals for a class writing project, established through discussion and dialogue in the community of writers, helps children feel a sense of independence through knowing what to do and how to do it to achieve success (Andrade and Brooke 2010; Allal 2019). They can also be self-regulating through monitoring their own developing drafts against the set class writing goals. In addition, Zimmerman's (2000) work suggests that children's self-regulation can be promoted by having them routinely set themselves a process goal (writing deadline) to achieve during that day's writing time. A useful suggestion is that children can also be given a calendar or time chart on which to record what they plan to do in each writing session towards final publication or performance (Zimmerman and Risemberg 1997).

Be reassuringly consistent

According to Alber-Morgan et al. (2007), children are more likely to become self-regulating if they are taught through a reassuringly consistent routine of mini-lesson, writing time, and class sharing. This type of routine allows children to internalise through repeated practice the strategies, procedures, processes, and techniques which are part of being a writer. Sustained and regular writing time for class and personal projects provides children with the opportunity they need to practise and internalise self-regulated learning strategies which will impact on self-efficacy, motivation, and volition to write (Perry and VandeKamp 2000; Perry and Drummond 2002).

Teach daily mini-lessons

Through the teaching of daily mini-lessons, teachers can help their pupils towards self-regulation by teaching them strategies, techniques, processes, procedures, and how to use resources (Alber-Morgan et al. 2007; Graham et al. 2014). Teachers first give a rationale for the strategy they are teaching; they then discuss their own use of the strategy or model it live before inviting children to use it for themselves in that day's writing time. Teachers can then provide further support and feedback through pupil conferencing.

Be a writer-teacher

According to Paris and Winograd (2003), teachers themselves must engage in writing and being a writer and must understand the writing strategies and processes they themselves employ. They are then able to present their personal self-regulating strategies and discuss the benefits from a position of knowledge and experience

Perry et al. 2008; Graham et al. 2011; Marrs et al. 2016). In addition, children are likely to adopt behaviours that their teacher shows to be important (Graham et al. 2013; White 2017).

A particular kind of reflective writing practice takes place when teachers illustrate and model self-regulation while constructing their own texts alongside their learners. As writer-teachers, they provide exemplar texts and samples written by themselves to showcase how they have used or are using a strategy or technique successfully and also how they deal with typical writing difficulties (Marrs et al. 2016). For example, teachers can show how they themselves use mentor texts and other authors to help them craft their own (White 2017). Graham et al. (2011) assert that teachers' modelling of the strategies they use is critical in establishing self-regulation amongst their pupils. They can do this by describing the strategy, asking for pupils' comments, and then demonstrating how to use it in relation to the whole writing process (Regan and Berkeley 2012). For example, a teacher might explain: 'once I've drafted my short story, I often read through it and look for the moment where I introduce my characters for the first time. I can now revise it by adding into my piece some description to develop my characters more for my reader'.

Pupil conference: meet children where they are

Ongoing formative feedback is strongly recommended as a way of supporting self-regulation (Butler and Winne 1995). When conferencing, writer-teachers are well placed to understand, teach, and recommend effective writerly strategies that children can employ to help them solve their writing problems (Englert et al. 1991; Butler and Winne 1995). Writer-teachers who point out and celebrate the strategies and techniques children are using to good effect also increase children's self-efficacy, motivation, and self-regulation in writing (Marrs et al. 2016).

The writing for pleasure teachers

Our own research (Young 2019) shows that children with high levels of self-regulation also feel a desire to write and have a stronger writer identity. The case study teachers regularly taught children strategies and techniques and provided resources which always aimed to support self-regulation (Hayden 2020). For example, in one class, the children were asked to think about what type of writing process they preferred to use: 'adventurer', 'planner', 'vomiter', 'paragraph piler', or 'sentence stacker' (Young and Ferguson 2020). They were taught techniques for revising their compositions and were also given checklists to help with proof-reading. Children were shown how to support each other during writing time and would share their 'tips, tricks and opinions' with one another. A rich combination of knowing what to do and how to do it, feeling confident of success, and being given some agency over their writing processes and writing topic seemed to make a real difference to the children's pleasure and subsequent academic success.

References

Alber-Morgan, S., Hessler, T., and Konrad, M. (2007). Teaching writing for keeps. *Education and Treatment of Children*, 30, 107–128.

Allal, L. (2019). Assessment and the co-regulation of learning in the classroom. *Assessment in Education: Principles, Policy & Practice*. 27, 332–349. DOI: 10.1080/0969594X.2019.1609411.

Andrade, H., and Brooke, G. (2010). Self-assessment and learning to write. In *Writing: Processes, Tools and Techniques*, Mertens, N. (Ed.) (pp.74–89). New York: Nova Science Publishers.

Atwell, N. (2014). *In the Middle* (3rd Ed.). Heinemann.

Butler, D.L., and Winne, P.H. (1995). Feedback and self-regulated learning: A theoretical synthesis. *Review of Educational Research*, 65(3), 245–274.

Collier, D.R. (2010). Journey to becoming a writer: Review of research about children's identities as writers, *Language and Literacy*, 12(1), 147–164.

Danoff, B., Harris, K.R., and Graham, S. (1993). Incorporating strategy instruction within the writing process in the regular classroom: Effects on the writing of students with and without learning disabilities. *Journal of Reading Behavior*, 25(3), 295–322.

Dignath, C., Buettner, G., and Langfeldt, H. (2008). How can primary school students learn self-regulated learning strategies most effectively? A meta-analysis on self-regulation training programmes. *Educational Research Review*, 3, 101–129.

Englert, C.S., Raphael, T.E., Anderson, L.M., Anthony, H.M., and Stevens, D.D. (1991). Making strategies and self-talk visible: Writing instruction in regular and special education classrooms. *American Educational Research Journal*, 28(2), 337–372.

Graham, S. (2006). Strategy instruction and the teaching of writing: A meta-analysis. In *Handbook of Writing Research*, McArthur, C., Graham, S., and Fitzgerald, J. (Ed.) (pp.187–207). New York: Guilford Press.

Graham, S., Harris, K., and Mason, L. (2011). Self-regulated strategy development for students with writing difficulties. *Theory Into Practice*, 50(1), 20–27.

Graham, S., Harris, K., and Mckeown, D. (2013). The writing of students with LD and a meta-analysis of SRSD writing intervention studies: Redux. In *Handbook of Learning Disabilities Guilford Press,* Swanson, L., Harris, K., and Graham, S. (Eds) (2nd Ed.) (pp.405–438). New York: Guilford Press.

Graham, S., Harris, K., and Mason, L. (2014). Improving the writing performance, knowledge, and self-efficacy of struggling young writers: The effects of self-regulated strategy development. *Contemporary Educational Psychology*, 30(2), 207–241.

Hadwin, A., and Oshige, M. (2011). Self-regulation, coregulation, and socially shared regulation: Exploring perspectives of social in self-regulated learning theory. Teachers College Record, 113, 240–264.

Harris, K., Graham, S., & Mason, L. (2006). Improving the writing, knowledge, and motivation of struggling young writers: Effects of self- regulated strategy development with and without peer support. *American Educational Research Journal*, 43(2), 295–340.

Hayden, T. (2020). *No more draft-dodging*. Available: https://writing4pleasure.com/no-more-draft-dodging.

Johnson, E., Hancock, C., Carter, D, and Pool, J. (2012). Self-regulated strategy development as a tier 2 writing intervention. *Intervention in School and Clinic*, 48(4), 218–222.

Lane, K., Graham, S., Harris, K., Little, M., Sandmel, K., and Brindle, M. (2010). The effects of self-regulated strategy development for second-grade students with writing and behavioral difficulties. *The Journal of Special Education*, 44(2), 107–128.

Lensmire, T. (1998). Rewriting student voice. *Journal of Curriculum Studies*, 30(3), 261–291.

MacArthur, C., and Graham, S. (2017). Writing research from a cognitive perspective. In *Handbook of Writing Research*, MacArthur, C., Graham, S., and Fitzgerald, J. (Ed.) (2nd Ed.) (pp. 24–40). London: Guildford Press.

Marrs, S., Zumbrunn, S., McBride, C., and Stringer, J.K. (2016). Exploring elementary student perceptions of writing feedback. *Journal on Educational Psychology*, 10, 16–28.

McQuitty, V. (2014). Process-oriented writing instruction in elementary classrooms: Evidence of effective practices from the research literature. *Writing & Pedagogy*, 6(3), 467–495.

Paris, S.G., & Winograd, P. (2003). *The role of self-regulated learning in contextual teaching: Principles and practices for teacher preparation* (CIERA Report) Retrieved from https://files.eric.ed.gov/fulltext/ED479905.pdf.

Perry, N.E., and Drummond, L. (2002). Helping young students become self-regulated researchers and writers. *The Reading Teacher*, 56, 298–310.

Perry, N.E., and VandeKamp, K.J.O. (2000). Creating classroom contexts that support young children's development of self-regulated learning. *International Journal of Educational Research*, 33(7), 821–843.

Perry, N.E., Hutchinson, L., and Thauberger, C. (2008). Talking about teaching self-regulated learning: Scaffolding student teachers' development and use of practices that promote self-regulated learning. *International Journal of Educational Research*, 47(2), 97–108.

Pintrich, P. (2003). A motivational science perspective on the role of student motivation in learning and teaching contexts. *Journal of Educational Psychology*, 95(4), 667–686.

Regan, K., and Berkeley, S. (2012). Effective reading and writing instruction: A focus on modelling. *Intervention in School and Clinic*, 47(5), 276–282.

Robson, D., Allen, M., and Howard, S. (2020). Self-regulation in childhood as a predictor of future outcomes: A meta-analytic review. *Psychological Bulletin*, 146(4), 324–354.

Schneider, J. (2003). Contexts, genres, and imagination: An examination of the idiosyncratic writing performances of three elementary children within multiple contexts of writing instruction. *Research in the Teaching of English*, 37, 329–379.

Schunk, D.H., and Zimmerman, B.J. (2007). Influencing children's self-efficacy and self-regulation of reading and writing through modelling. *Reading and Writing Quarterly*, 23(1), 7–25.

Sexton, M., Harris, K.R., and Graham, S. (1998). Self-regulated strategy development and the writing process: Effects on essay writing and attributions. *Exceptional Children*, 64(3), 295–311.

White, M. (2017). Cognitive modeling and self-regulation of learning instructional settings. Teachers College Record, 119(13), 1–26.

Young, R. (2019). *What is it 'Writing For Pleasure' teachers do that makes the difference?* The University Of Sussex: The Goldsmiths' Company [Online] Available: www.writing4pleasure.com.

Young, R., and Ferguson, F. (2019). *Power English Writing: Teacher's Guide Year 6*. Oxford: Pearson.

Young, R., and Ferguson, F. (2020). *Real-World Writers: A Handbook for Teaching Writing with 7–11 Year Olds*. London: Routledge.

Zimmerman, B. (2000). Self-efficacy: An essential motive to learn. *Contemporary Educational Psychology*, 25(1), 82–91.

Zimmerman B., and Risemberg, R. (1997). Becoming a self-regulated writer: A social cognitive perspective. *Contemporary Educational Psychology*, 22, 73–101.

Zins, J., Bloodworth, M., Weissberg, R., and Walberg, H. (2007). The scientific base linking social and emotional learning to school success. *Journal of Educational and Psychological Consultation*, 17(2–3), 191–210.

Zumbrunn, S, and Bruning, R. (2013). Improving the writing and knowledge of emergent writers: The effects of self-regulated strategy development reading and writing. *An Interdisciplinary Journal*, 26(1), 91–110.

CHAPTER 6

Agency

Introduction and context

> *He isn't forcing us to do something we don't want to do; we actually want to go and do it.*
>
> (Young 2019)

Agency, also known as personal control, epistemic agency (Scardamalia 2002), personal or collective responsibility, or agentic learning (Fletcher 2016), is in this context about having choice, freedom, autonomy, and ownership of writing ideas, writing processes, and even how you are taught (Collier 2010). Agency is included in the affective domains of writing for pleasure because it is a vital force in increasing writers' engagement and their writing performance (Rief 2006; Niemiec and Ryan 2009; Zumbrunn and Krause 2012; Behizadeh 2014; Fletcher 2016). Put simply, 'students who believe they have more personal control of their own learning and behaviour are more likely to do well and achieve at a higher level' than those who do not (Pintrich 2003, p. 673). The sense of agency is clearly linked to other components of writing for pleasure, notably self-regulation, self-efficacy, motivation, and writer-identity (Grainger, Goouch, and Lambirth 2005; Flint and Fisher 2014; Fletcher 2016).

According to Purcell-Gates et al. (2007), a critical number of scholars from a range of theoretical and pedagogical orientations agree that agency is essential to children's ability to produce successful and meaningful texts. According to their research, having a level of agency has impressive results, with young writers exceeding expectations, improving their academic achievement, feeling increased engagement and motivation in writing and becoming a writer, connecting better with new genres or topics, showing more persistence and effort, and feeling a greater sense of satisfaction in their compositions (Turner and Paris 1995; Behizadeh 2014, 2018; Fletcher 2016). Research also shows that having a sense of agency improves the writing performance of low-achieving or poorly motivated children in particular (Fletcher 2016). A contrasting picture is given by Grainger, Goouch, and Lambirth (2005), who report that, in underperforming schools, children are given little agency as writers, are not in control of their writing processes, and are not involved in discussions about purpose and audience for class writing projects. Bruning and Horn (2000) add that children who have no say over writing topics are often assigned tasks whose content they know or care little about.

Interestingly and ironically, apprentice writers who are given control over the content of their writing and their writing process show more willingness to steer their writing towards the goals of the curriculum objectives (Fletcher 2016). For example, Bruning and Horn (2000) found that children who were given the freedom to choose subjects which they were knowledgeable about and interested in wrote pieces which were more logical, better organised, and more accomplished overall.

Agency and the principles of effective practice

Build a community of writers

Ultimately, the promotion of agency is about teaching children how to have control over their writing lives. Dyson (1997) describes how, by giving agency, teachers can develop a writing community based on what she calls a 'pedagogy of responsibility', where children feel themselves to be experts and operate with increased levels of self-regulation and self-efficacy. Teachers thus have more time to observe and work with individuals and groups in what becomes a 'literacy club' (Smith 1988).

In a classroom where agentic learning takes place, children can be active participants, requesting the instruction they feel they require most to be successful. They can share their intellectual, social, and cultural capital with others, thus creating a democratic space where they know they can learn from one another (James 2020). In this way, agency is influential in forming a mutually supportive community of writers. In terms of the critical literacy orientation of writing teaching (see Chapter 1), pupils in this kind of classroom are more likely to feel safe enough to approach 'gritty', difficult, and culturally sustaining topics in their writing (Dyson 1997; Laman et al. 2018; Young et al. in press).

Pursue purposeful and authentic class writing projects

Since early childhood, apprentice writers have been capable of generating their own ideas for writing (Rowe and Neitzel 2010). However, it is a sad fact that once they reach the age of seven or eight and even before, that opportunity is often removed, and the teacher assumes responsibility for the choice of topic. This happens for no good reason and has largely negative consequences (Graves 1982; Harmey 2020).

It is important that all children, of whatever age, be given the opportunity to choose their own topics for class writing projects (Graves 1982; Gadd et al. 2019). When this happens, they are able to make connections with their own identities, thoughts, feelings, opinions, cultures, and funds of knowledge. They become much more what Fletcher (2016) calls 'critical connectors' between what the task requires and the necessary learning process. They are also able to reflect on and monitor their own progress in a meaningful way. And as Behizadeh (2014) states, children's perception of class writing projects as personally relevant and worthwhile also contributes significantly to academic success.

Some points to consider

- Children who have a long experience of teacher-chosen writing topics are likely to need specific instruction in making authentic writing choices (Seban and Tavsanli 2015), and so idea generation techniques must become a teaching priority (Young and Ferguson 2019, 2020).
- Teachers may need to consider whether or not certain topics chosen by children are their best, and then to discuss with children whether alternatives should be found (Young and Ferguson 2020).
- As Flint and Fisher (2014) say, agency over purpose and audience has a natural part to play in learning to write in a particular genre. However, if genres are taught as decontextualised and school-only 'units', children's writing development is impeded (Purcell-Gates et al. 2007; Flint and Fisher 2014).
- Finally, as Bazerman et al. (2017) warn, if every child is writing in the same way on the same assigned topic, there is little scope for comparison or measurement across all the pieces. Each text has little to tell us about how children are developing as writers, and potentially rich insights are lost.

Teach the writing processes

Children who feel they have control over the way they employ the writing processes, are more likely to achieve and achieve well (Fletcher 2016). They should therefore understand that, when confident, they can choose their own strategies and write at their own pace.

Set writing goals

When children are invited to be co-developers in class writing projects, they can achieve above academic expectations (Fletcher 2016). Children write effectively when they are afforded high levels of autonomy over topic choice and when they are participants in the setting of product goals (Purcell-Gates et al. 2007). Teachers can present mentor texts for discussion – written by peers, themselves, or published authors – and use them as a basis for the collaborative generation of possible writing goals (Flint and Fisher 2014). Finally, giving children personal responsibility for achieving certain writing deadlines on their journey towards final publication or performance is seen as crucial (Turner and Paris 1995).

Pursue personal writing projects

In personal writing projects children have to take responsibility for themselves as writers. Their writing is of course informed by knowledge and experience but is also driven by the desire to communicate with selves and with others. It is writing for real.

According to Grainger, Goouch, and Lambirth (2005), children need time to decide on the topic, genre, purpose, and audience for their writing and to set their own process deadlines and goals. They also state that personal writing projects improve children's capacity for self-regulation and increase the volition to write, and suggest that teachers can support personal projects by offering lists of writing purposes and genres and idea generating techniques. Teachers, they say, 'will notice that ideas and themes begin to travel around the class and groups of writers begin to form around common interests, prompting collaborative writing and much conversation' (Grainger, Goouch, and Lambirth 2005, p. 60). Owning a writer's notebook in which to write and keep records of possible future writing ideas is invaluable for agentic learning (Young and Ferguson 2020).

Pupil conference: meet children where they are

Fletcher's (2016) research shows that, when children are pursuing a writing project they have chosen and feel a personal commitment to, they are more likely to seek and accept advice from a teacher during pupil conferencing.

The Writing For Pleasure teachers

- 'If we weren't asked what we wanted to write about, it could be a bit boring'.
- 'When you haven't been learning much and you don't know what to write … when you haven't really learnt about the thing you're writing, like in topic and science, it's hard'.
- 'If we are writing about something I don't know about – if we are writing and I have no idea what it is – I just don't know what to do'.
- 'I don't like writing when it's things I don't like or it's something I'm not interested in – I'm like, do I really have to write about that?'

Our own research (Young 2019) showed there to be a fundamental and highly significant relationship between self-efficacy, self-regulation, and agency. The children's interview and questionnaire data showed that agency is really important to them. Those who felt that they had a degree of ownership and control over their writing were more likely to want to write, saw their writing as purposeful, felt more motivation, and had high levels of self-regulation.

In interview, children repeatedly stated that they felt more confidence when they were able to generate and use their own ideas in a class writing project. For example, 'we don't have to write what the teacher says. It's actually better if you choose what you're going to write because you know about the thing you're going to write about'. This view was expressed by other children who felt some of their self-efficacy and motivation was lost when their teacher chose the ideas for a class project.

The children stated that they felt a greater sense of satisfaction when seeing their own writing idea through to publication. They explained that they were able to share thoughts, knowledge, identity, and imagination when they had agency over their topics. Finally, it is important to note that although *Writing For Pleasure* advocates for pupil choice, this does not make it a child-centred pedagogy as understood in the *naturalistic* tradition (see Chapter 1). Rather, it is learner-centred or, even better, writer-centred. Children learn and are rightly given instruction from their peers and from their more experienced writer-teacher, but they must see that their teacher is also there to learn from them.

One of the most significant outcomes of our research was the conviction that giving children high levels of agency over their ideas and their writing process would not by itself ensure they write for pleasure. Niemiec and Ryan (2009) suggest that, without direct instruction in how to use their agency, children's ability to write for pleasure may even be negatively impacted. The need for instruction was felt by children and was strongly implied in the following interview statement: 'when I know what to do, and when I can write about what I feel inside kind of – I know I can write and I want to write'. It appears to be critical that agency sits alongside and is supported by a solid foundation of self-efficacy and self-regulation (see Figure 6.1). Beyond agency, children want to feel that they can write and that they know how to write successfully. The teachers in the research project ensured children understood the writing processes and how to set themselves process goals, and that they knew what their own favoured processes and strategies were.

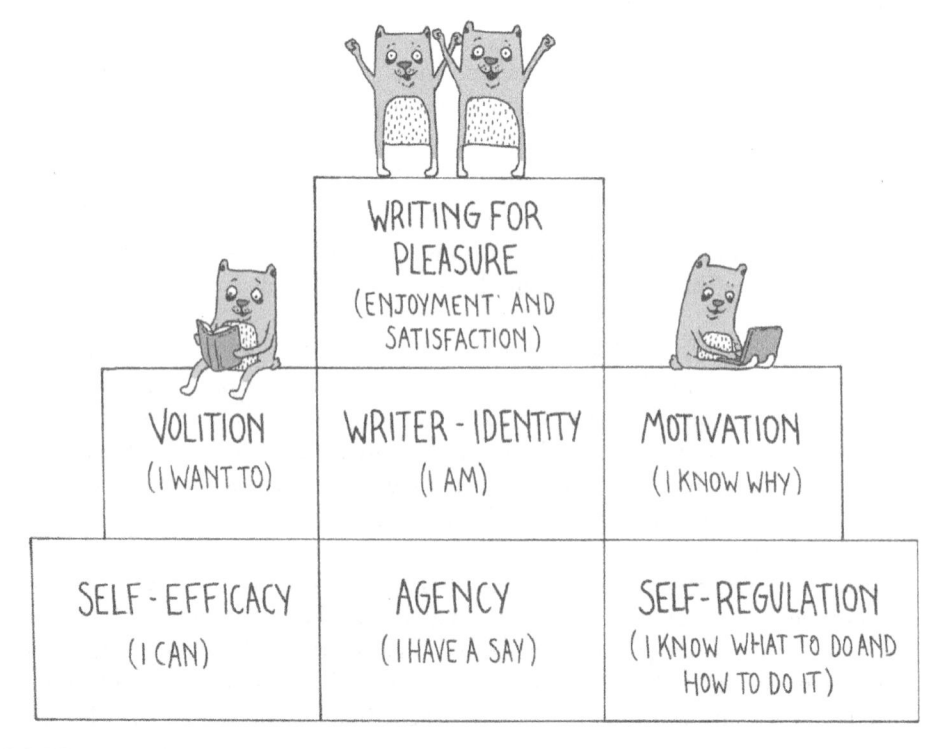

FIGURE 6.1 The affective domains as defined by Young (2019).

Children were given explicit instruction by their teachers in techniques and strategies to help them generate ideas for both class and personal writing projects (Young and Ferguson 2019, 2020). Specific time was set aside near the beginning of a project for generating possible ideas alone, in groups, or as a whole class; the children then individually decided what they were going to write about. One of the teachers introduced class writing projects in what was called a 'genre week'. The week comprised a series of lessons which included discussion of what the class writing project was going to be in terms of genre, what genuine purpose published pieces were going to serve, and instruction and discussion about what the children would need to do to write something successful and meaningful (Young and Ferguson 2020). Children were then given agency over their writing topic and audience. This was a very effective and efficient way of ensuring children had a sense of self-efficacy, self-regulation, and agency in rich combination.

References

Bazerman, C., Applebee, A., Berninger, V., Brandt, D., Graham, S., Matsuda, P., Murphy, S., Rowe, D., and Schleppegrell, M. (2017). Taking the long view on writing development. *Research in the Teaching of English*, 51, 351–360.

Behizadeh, N. (2014). Xavier's take on authentic writing: Structuring choices for expression and impact. *Journal of Adolescent & Adult Literacy*, 58(4), 289–298.

Behizadeh, N. (2018). Aiming for authenticity: Successes and struggles of an attempt to increase authenticity in writing. *Journal of Adolescent & Adult Literacy*, 62(4), 411–419.

Bruning, R., and Horn, C. (2000). Developing motivation to write. *Educational Psychologist*, 35(1), 25–37.

Collier, D.R. (2010). Journey to becoming a writer: Review of research about children's identities as writers. *Language and Literacy*, 12(1), 147–164.

Dyson, A.H. (1997). *Writing Superheroes: Contemporary Childhood, Popular Culture and Classroom Literacy*. New York: Teachers College Press.

Fletcher, A. (2016). Exceeding expectations: Scaffolding agentic engagement through assessment as learning. *Educational Research*, 58(4), 400–419.

Flint, A.S., and Fisher, T. (2014). Writing their worlds: Young english language learners navigate writing workshop. In *Writing & Pedagogy*, 6(3), 1756–5839.

Gadd, M., Parr, J., Robertson, J., Carran, L., Ali, Z., Gendall, L., and Watson K. (2019). Portrait of the student as a young writer: Some student survey findings about attitudes to writing and self-efficacy as writers. *Literacy*, 53(4), 226–235.

Grainger, T., Goouch, K., and Lambirth, A. (2005). *Creativity and Writing: Developing Voice and Verve in the Classroom*. London: Routledge.

Graves, D. (1982). Break the welfare cycle: Let writers choose their topics. The English Composition Board, 3(2), 75–78.

Harmey, S. (2020). Co-constructing writing: handing over the reins to young authors. *Education 3-13*, 3–11.

James, S. (2020). *Let's make a 'Guess Who?' book! Writing character descriptions in Year Two* Available: https://writing4pleasure.com/lets-make-a-guess-who-book-writing-character-descriptions-in-year-two.

Laman, T., Davis, T., and Henderson, J. (2018). 'My hair has a lot of stories!': Unpacking culturally sustaining writing pedagogies in an elementary mediated field experience for teacher candidates. *Action in Teacher Education*, 40(4), 374–390.

Niemiec, C., and Ryan, R. (2009). Autonomy, competence and relatedness in the classroom: Applying self-determination theory to educational practice. *Theory & Research in Education*, 7(2), 133–144.

Pintrich, P. (2003). A motivational science perspective on the role of student motivation in learning and teaching contexts. *Journal of Educational Psychology*, 95(4), 667–686.

Purcell-Gates, V., Duke, N., and Martineau, J. (2007). Learning to read and write genre-specific text: Roles of authentic experience and explicit teaching. *Reading Research Quarterly*, 42(1), 8–45

Rief, L. (2006). What's right about writing? *Voices from the Middle*, 13(4), 32–39.

Rowe, D., and Neitzel, C. (2010). Interest and agency in 2- and 3-year-olds' participation in emergent writing. *Reading Research Quarterly*, 45(2), 169–195.

Scardamalia, M. (2002). Collective cognitive responsibility for the advancement of knowledge. In *Liberal Education in a Knowledge Society*, Smith, B. (Ed.) (ppl. 67–98). Chicago, IL: Open Court.

Seban, D., and Tavsanli, Ö. (2015). Children's sense of being a writer: Identity construction in second grade writers workshop. *International Electronic Journal of Elementary Education*, 7(2), 217–234.

Smith, F. (1988). *Joining the Literacy Club*. Oxford: Heinemann.

Turner, J., and Paris, S. (1995). How literacy tasks influence children's motivation for literacy. *The Reading Teacher*, 48(8), 662–673.

Young, R. (2019). *What is it 'Writing For Pleasure' teachers do that makes the difference?* The University Of Sussex: The Goldsmiths' Company [Online] Available: www.writing4pleasure.com.

Young, R., and Ferguson, F. (2019). *Power English Writing: Teacher's Guide Year 6*. Oxford: Pearson Education.

Young, R., and Ferguson, F. (2020). *Real-World Writers: A Handbook for Teaching Writing with 7–11 Year Olds*. London: Routledge.

Young, R., Govender, N., and Kaufman, D. (in press) *Writing Realities*. Leicester: UKLA

Zumbrunn, S., and Krause, K. (2012). Conversations with leaders: Principles of effective writing instruction. *The Reading Teacher*, 65(5), 346–353.

CHAPTER 7

Motivation

Introduction and context

Motivation, also related to ideas about goal theory, self-determination, engaging instruction, writer attitude and interest, and value theory, is closely associated with the concept of writing for pleasure (Eccles and Wigfield 2002; Hidi and Renninger 2006; Boscolo 2009; Lazowski and Hulleman 2016) and has strong links to self-regulation, self-efficacy, volition, and writer-identity (Turner and Paris 1995; Bruning and Horn 2000; Eccles and Wigfield 2002; Pajares 2003; Troia et al. 2013; DeSmedt et al. 2018a, b). Teachers should give special attention to practices which foster a positive disposition; children need to feel the relevance and importance of writing because, as Bruning and Horn (2000) rightly say, motivation is often what gets them through this cognitively demanding act successfully.

The body of research looking specifically into children's motivation to write is strong and growing (Bruning and Horn, 2000; Boscolo 2009; Garrett and Moltzen 2011). According to DeSmedt et al. (2018b), a lack of motivation is at the heart of writing underperformance, and attending to it is just as important for academic attainment as focusing on cognitive learning. Other empirical findings consistently show how motivational factors are positively and directly related to students' writing performance and achievement (Miller and Meece 1999; DeSmedt et al. 2018a; Graham et al. 2007), substantiated by examples such as the one given by Harmey (2020), who observes that children make less academic progress and are less successful when forced to pursue topics they are not motivated to write about. With this observation in mind, the findings of DeSmedt et al. (2018a) that boys are typically less motivated to write than girls should therefore give practitioners food for thought.

Hall and Axelrod (2014, p. 46) remind us how important it is 'that teachers understand the relationship between writing motivation and writing achievement', and indeed effective teachers of writing consider their pupils' motivation to be a high priority. They stimulate children's curiosity, encourage pride in persistence, and promote the idea that good writing can often require sustained effort over many writing sessions (Pressley et al. 1997). In their observations of highly motivating writing-teachers, Turner and Paris (1995) observed that these practitioners focused on what the authors call the six 'Cs':

- Children having **choice** over their writing ideas.
- The undertaking of **challenging** and **constructive** writing projects which were authentic and meaningful.
- **Control** over their writing processes and writing deadlines.
- A classroom environment which encouraged **collaboration.**
- The **consequences** of such teaching decisions resulting in competence and confidence.

Children who are motivated writers will persist with their writing and show commitment to it by giving it high levels of attention and focus. They also have a greater understanding of why they are writing and who they are writing for (Eccles and Wigfield 2002; Troia et al. 2013; DeSmedt et al. 2018a). Low motivation can result from the teacher transmitting an excessive concern with evaluation, which may exacerbate anxiety and the fear of engaging and risk-taking (Bruning and Horn 2000). Poorly motivated children also tend to find writing more difficult and harder to concentrate on (Oldfather 2002; DeSmedt et al. 2018a).

Intrinsic, extrinsic, and situational motivation

Research has also looked at the nature of different kinds of motivation in writing. Being **intrinsically motivated** means being engaged because you are interested in the writing project you are undertaking; you are finding personal value in it; you are experiencing pleasure in the craft of writing and you anticipate inherent satisfaction when you are finished. Empirical findings also show that intrinsic motivation can be related to a drive to challenge yourself, to learn through interest or curiosity, to improve your skills, and to achieve well academically (Turner and Paris 1995; Eccles and Wigfield 2002; Brophy 2008). Studies confirm the positive benefits of being intrinsically motivated. These include having a higher level of self-determination, persistence and well-being, together with writing better texts and feeling more positive about being at school (DeSmedt et al. 2018a). According to DeSmedt et al. (2018b), intrinsic motivation has a positive impact on the writing performance of all children.

As its name suggests, **extrinsic motivation** is externally generated. Children may write in response to feelings of pressure, the threat of punishment, or through feelings of guilt (Brophy 2008; DeSmedt et al. 2018a). They may also write with the expectation of receiving an immediate reward (Eccles and Wigfield 2002), such as the teacher's praise or the chance to win a writing competition. However, if relied upon too heavily, extrinsic motivation can lead to the fear of making errors and an excessive focus on producing 'correct' writing. As a result, children may neglect or avoid those higher-order writing techniques and skills which ordinarily result in higher academic achievement (DeSmedt et al. 2018b). This view is supported by Eccles and Wigfield (2002), who claim that extrinsic motivation can actually undermine children's ability to produce successful writing. Teachers should therefore try to avoid an overtly performance-oriented stance (Brophy 2008; Troia et al. 2013).

However, promotion of both extrinsic and intrinsic motivation is rightly seen as important.

Finally, Boscolo (2009) suggests that motivation, whether positive or negative, is often shared and can spread across a whole classroom environment. **Situational motivation** is the motivation that can be felt as a result of being in an environment which is passionate, energetic, and welcoming. The electricity and productiveness within a community of writers can rub off onto other children in profound ways (Boscolo and Hidi 2006).

Agency, self-efficacy, and self-regulation

In keeping with our own research (Young 2019), other studies show that motivation to write is positively affected by a sense of ownership and agency, along with direct instruction in strategies, techniques, and processes to ensure confidence (self-efficacy) and a sound knowledge of what to do and how to do it (self-regulation) (Turner and Paris 1995; Brophy 2008; DeSmedt et al. 2018a).

Motivation and the principles of effective practice

Build a community of writers

Teachers have an enormous power over the conditions in which children are asked to write. Creating an environment where children feel they are part of a community, can write alongside their peers in a social workspace, and are discovering their literacy as a cohesive group, helps build situational motivation over the long term (Oldfather 2002; Miller 2003; Boscolo and Hidi 2006; Raphael et al. 2008; Lazowski and Hulleman 2016; De Smedt 2018a).

According to Bruning and Horn (2000), a class needs a motivated and committed writer-teacher with a sound conception of what it actually means to live a life in which writing and being a writer are valuable and important. Children are susceptible to the attitudes of their teachers; therefore, if a teacher's past and present experiences of writing are narrow, socially isolated, evaluatively oriented, and anxiety provoking, they are very unlikely to create positive and motivational conditions for their students to write in (Miller and Meece 1999; Zumbrunn and Krause 2012).

In their study of 'engaging teachers', Raphael et al. (2008) reported that they care deeply about their students, create positive atmospheres, treat their classes as communities, and encourage prosocial behaviours. Finally, Boscolo (2009) and Lamb and Wedell (2015) suggest that teachers need to find ways of instilling the long-term intrinsic motivation which can best lead children to engage in writing as a life-long activity.

The modern conception of the writing workshop approach (Atwell 2014; Calkins et al. 2015 (USA); Young and Ferguson 2020 (UK)) with, as outlined in Chapter 1, its elements of both a self-expression and a community orientation towards writing, allows confident, volitional, self-determined, and highly motivated writers to develop (Bruning and Horn 2000; Nolen 2007; Magnifico 2010). Such an approach engages children to be intrinsically motivated. When they are writing about what interests them most, engagement, concentration, and 'flow' become fundamental characteristics of the writing classroom, where participants are absorbed and self-determined in the crafting of their writing (Abbott 2000). Finally, the findings of Vanknin-Nusbaum et al. (2020) show that, by nurturing confident and motivated young *readers,* teachers can also produce confident and motivated writers.

Read, share, think, and talk about writing

Co-operative learning, working with and around others instead of alone, increases children's motivation and often produces significant academic benefits (Pressley et al. 2003; Alber-Morgan et al. 2007). Getting a response from a peer acting as the future reader for your piece of writing most often has positive effects on motivation. When children know that their text is to be read, seen, or heard by a 'reader' who is interested in the content, they become more involved in its creation and, according to Miller (2003) and Hoogeveen (2012), experience pleasure as a result. Children also enjoy adjusting their texts to meet the needs of their audience.

Pursue purposeful and authentic class writing projects

In purposeful and authentic class writing projects, the explicit goals of a curriculum can meet the implicit reasons children are moved to write. According to Miller and Meece (1999), children dislike assigned writing tasks because they require minimal thought, are often boring, and lack personal meaning; children will not feel it necessary to produce a good writing product and so will write to a lower standard (Boscolo and Gelati 2019). Teachers who understand the importance of motivation give children a rationale for why they are taking part in a class writing project. They will ensure the project engages with their pupils' outside worlds and interests, inviting them to make a personal connection with it (Raphael et al. 2008; Zumbrunn and Krause 2012; Gadd et al. 2019). According to Maloch (2005) literacy projects that do not allow children to take advantage of their strengths and preoccupations are not motivating, and children will not participate in them in any meaningful way. We would heartily agree with Oldfather (2002) when he states that teachers should also take time to actively teach idea generation techniques and help children find a significant and self-relevant topic for class writing projects. These projects should also have a real-world purpose and should be written for and with true communicative and expressive intentions (Boscolo et al. 2012).

According to Magnifico (2010), motivation comes from doing this kind of purposeful and authentic writing; it is vital for writers to feel that a project has personal value and social relevance, creating in them a sense of self-worth and identity. In essence, class writing projects simply must be significant for both the writer and the reader. Bruning and Horn (2000), Miller (2003), and Timperley and Parr (2009) all point out that such projects benefit writers of all abilities, with Miller noting that 'lowest achievers' gain most in terms of motivation and also of academic outcomes. Finally, children are motivated when they know their writing is going to be valued, used by others, and published or performed (Hickey 2003; Alber-Morgan et al. 2007). We would stress that these are entirely logical, natural, and admirable aspirations for an authentic project.

Finally, when children feel they are writing for their own real purposes and audiences and see themselves as active in their own learning, they are more likely to be motivated to apply techniques and features to their writing that are high-level and challenging (Miller and Meece 1999; Eccles and Wigfield 2002). They are also motivated by being introduced to a variety of discourses, styles, and genres for writing and will want to learn how to utilise them in their own way (Bruning and Horn 2000; Troia et al. 2013). As Miller (2003) observes, motivation may increase when children see they can use strategies and techniques from previous writing projects. Links with self-efficacy and self-regulation are obvious here.

Teach the writing processes

Cognitive science has for a long time understood that children develop best as writers in a supportive social environment and when instruction in the processes of writing is linked to motivational and other affective needs. For example, in his model of the writing process, Hayes (2012) shows that, before anything else, writers must be motivated to write. They must have a *why*, a reason they are moved to write in the first place (Figure 7.1).

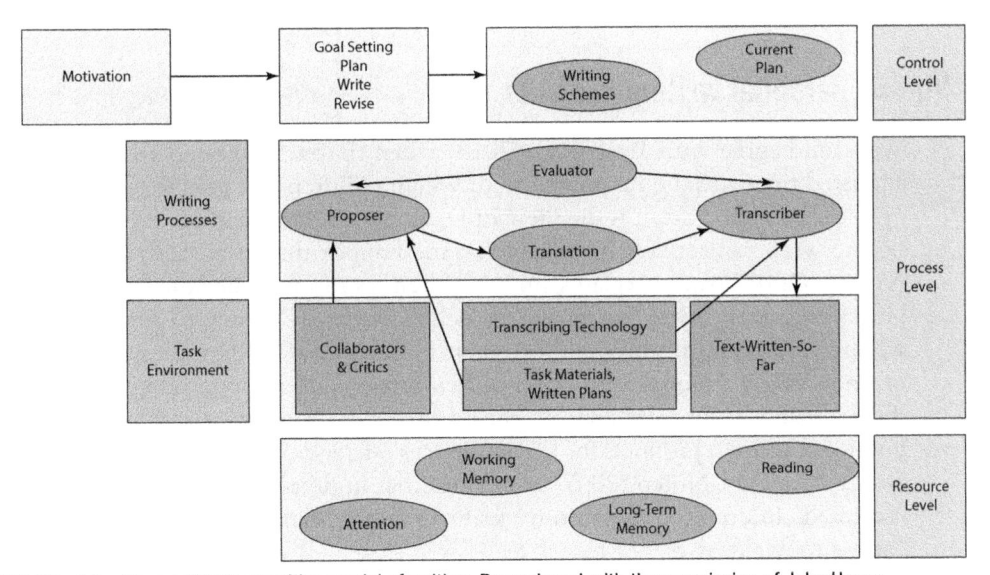

FIGURE 7.1 John Hayes' (2012) cognitive model of writing. Reproduced with the permission of John Hayes.

In the model, we can see that children having and maintaining control over how they use the writing processes is critical. Providing them with the rationale for certain planning, drafting, revising, and editing techniques, examining exemplar texts, and offering ample time and opportunity for writing are all ways in which a teacher can sustain and increase motivation (DeSmedt 2018a). It is through such means that children see how this craft knowledge can help them better fulfil their writing desire and intentions.

Set writing goals

Achievement goal theory is an aspect of *Writing For Pleasure* where children are encouraged to see writing as mastery over processes, strategies, and techniques and not just about producing a final product for evaluation by an external other (Lazowski and Hulleman 2016). It is about the journey *and* the destination. Therefore, children should know what the distant goal for a writing project is and keep it 'in sight' throughout the project (Eccles and Wigfield 2002). If a class writing project is shaped through the setting of both process and product goals (Troia et al. 2003), children will see their intended outcome gradually materialising as they near the final goal of publication or performance. This is highly motivating (Lazowski and Hulleman 2016).

Teach daily mini-lessons

Engaging teachers explain to children the importance and relevance of the instruction they are about to give in the mini-lesson (Miller and Meece 1999; Brophy 2008; Raphael et al. 2008). Children are motivated further if they are allowed an input into what they are to be taught during mini-lessons and are able to request instruction in things they think will better help them achieve their writing goals.

Pursue personal writing projects

We would agree with Troia et al. (2013) when they recommend an increase in the allocated time and the frequency with which children can pursue personal writing projects. Furthermore, it is the view of DeSmedt (2018a) that the desire and motivation to write can actually be damaged if such opportunities are restricted or denied. Nolen's (2007) study explains how children were given personal writing project books and were invited to write in them daily, with a view to maintaining their writing 'momentum' and therefore their motivation. Children drew on their funds of knowledge, interests, out-of-school cultures, opinions, and imaginative ideas in their writing. They were encouraged to turn any promising personal projects into published written products for real audiences – friends, parents, caregivers, and other family members. Nolen (2007) concludes that undertaking these personal projects increased children's motivation to write, turning them from 'we *have* to' writers to 'we *get* to' writers.

Pupil conference: meet children where they are

Children's desire to write and continue writing is directly influenced by their teacher's expressions of genuine warmth and interest. In classrooms where trust, care, and mutual concern are a high priority, students are situationally motivated to engage (Bruning and Horn 2000). Conferencing with pupils is one medium through which such an ambience can be created and motivation sustained. For example, when a teacher feels a child has a real personal investment in the writing they are crafting, it has an effect on them too. They begin to care deeply for the child's piece and really want it to be as successful and as meaningful as possible (Young and Ferguson 2020).

The Writing For Pleasure teachers

In our own research (Young 2019), we observed a significant and somewhat surprising difference among the participating teachers in how they were attending to children's motivation. Data derived from the pupil questionnaire revealed that some children did not always know *why* they were writing and did not always feel that their writing was serving real purposes. They also felt that their writing was not seen by a variety of audiences throughout the year.

However, the teachers who scored well in this domain could certainly be designated 'autonomous motivating teachers' (de Smedt et al. 2018a). These teachers did make the effort for their children's writing to leave the classroom and be published elsewhere. They always ensured children knew who they were writing for. For example, in one class, children's writing contributed to a National Literacy Trust poetry anthology and to a literature festival, and their collectively written story chapter was published in a children's book. Their writing was also shared closer to home in the local community and church halls. The children also felt that their writing had personal value and was for their own fulfilment as well as for others to read and enjoy. Essentially, they were motivated for their writing to be the best it could be because they believed in and cared about it on several different levels.

The teachers all created a nurturing community of writers in their classrooms. They allowed children to read, talk, write together, and share their developing pieces with others in the class. Children had agency over the topics for their class writing project and plenty of time and opportunity to pursue personal projects. Direct instruction was given about different approaches to the writing processes and children were taught self-regulation writing strategies to help them feel more independent. We observed that, because children felt they knew why they were writing and how to do it, they also experienced a high level of motivation to write.

References

Abbott, J. (2000). 'Blinking out' and 'Having the touch' two fifth-grade boys talk about flow experiences in writing. *Written Communication*, 17(1), 53–92.

Alber-Morgan, S., Hessler, T., and Konrad, M. (2007). Teaching writing for keeps. *Education and Treatment of Children*, 30, 107–128.

Atwell, N. (2014). *In the Middle* (3rd Ed.). Portsmouth, NH: Heinemann.

Boscolo, P. (2009). Engaging and motivating children to write. In *The SAGE Handbook of Writing Development*, Beard, R., Myhill, D., Riley, J., and Nystrand, M. London: Routledge.

Boscolo, P., and Gelati, C. (2019). Motivating writers. In *Best Practices in Writing Instruction*, Graham, S., MacArthur, C., and Hebert, M. (Eds.) (3rd Ed) (pp. 51–78). New York: The Guilford Press.

Boscolo, P., and Hidi, S. (2006). *Writing & Motivation*. Holland: Elsevier Science.

Boscolo, P., Gelati, C., and Galvan, N. (2012). Teaching elementary school students to play with meanings and genre. *Reading & Writing Quarterly*, 28(1), 29–50.

Brophy, J. (2008). Developing students' appreciation for what is taught. School, Educational Psychologist, 43(3), 132–141.
Bruning, R., and Horn, C. (2000). Developing motivation to write. *Educational Psychologist*, 35(1), 25–37.
Calkins, L., Hohne, K., and Robb, A. (2015). *Writing Pathways*. Portsmouth, NH: Heinemann.
De Smedt, F., Graham, S., and Van Keer, H. (2018a). The bright and dark side of writing motivation: Effects of explicit instruction and peer assistance. *The Journal of Educational Research*, 112(2), 152–167.
De Smedt, F., Merchie, E., Barendse, M., Rosseel, Y., De Naeghel, J., and Van Keer, H. (2018b). Cognitive and motivational challenges in writing: Studying the relationship with writing performance across students' gender and achievement level. *Reading Research Quarterly*, 53(2), 249–272.
Eccles, J., and Wigfield, A. (2002). Motivational beliefs, values and goals. *Annual Review of Psychology*, 53, 109–132.
Gadd, M., Parr, J., Robertson, J., Carran, L., Ali, Z., Gendall, L., and Watson K. (2019). Portrait of the student as a young writer: some student survey findings about attitudes to writing and self-efficacy as writers. *Literacy* 53(4), 226–235.
Garrett, L., and Moltzen, R. (2011). Writing because I want to, not because I have to: Young gifted writers' perspectives on the factors that "matter" in developing expertise. *English Teaching: Practice and Critique*, 10(1), 165–180.
Graham, S., Berninger, V., and Fan, W. (2007). The structural relationship between writing attitude and writing achievement in first and third grade students. *Contemporary Educational Psychology*, 32(3), 516–536.
Hall, A., and Axelrod, Y. (2014). 'I am kind of a good writer and kind of not': Examining students' writing attitudes. *Journal of Research in Education*, 24(2), 34–50.
Harmey, S. (2020). Co-constructing writing: Handing over the reins to young authors. *Education 3-13*, 3–11.
Hayes, J.R. (2012). Modeling and remodeling writing. *Written Communication*, 29(3), 369–388.
Hickey, D.T. (2003). Engaged participation versus marginal nonparticipation: A stridently sociocultural approach to achievement motivation. *The Elementary School Journal*, 103(4), 401–429.
Hidi, S., and Renninger, A. (2006). The four-phase model of interest development. *Educational Psychologist*, 41(2), 111–127.
Hoogeveen, M. (2012). *Writing with Peer Response Using Genre Knowledge* (Thesis). University of Twente. Available: https://ris.utwente.nl/ws/portalfiles/portal/6062163/thesis_M_Hoogeveen.pdf.
Lamb, M., and Wedell, M. (2015). Cultural contrasts and commonalities in inspiring language teaching. *Language Teaching Research*, 19(2), 207–224.
Lazowski, R., and Hulleman, C. (2016). Motivation interventions in Education: A meta-analytic review, *Review of Educational Research*, 86(2), 602–640.
Magnifico, A. (2010). Writing for whom? cognition, motivation, and a writer's audience. *Educational Psychologist*, 45(3), 167–184.
Maloch, B. (2005). Moments by which change is made: A cross-case exploration of teacher mediation and student participation in literacy events. *Journal of Literacy Research*, 37(1), 95–142.
Miller, S. (2003). How high- and low-challenge tasks affect motivation and learning: Implications for struggling learners. *Reading & Writing Quarterly*, 19(1), 39–57.
Miller, S., and Meece, J. (1999). Third graders' motivational preferences for reading and writing tasks. *The Elementary Journal*, 100(1), 19–35.
Nolen, S. (2007). Young children's motivation to read and write: Development in social contexts. *Cognition and Instruction*, 25(2–3), 219–270.
Oldfather, P. (2002). Students' experiences when not initially motivated for literacy learning. *Reading & Writing Quarterly*, 18(3), 231–256.

Pajares, F. (2003). Self-efficacy beliefs, motivation, and achievement in writing: A review of the literature. *Reading & Writing Quarterly*, 19(2), 139–158.

Pressley, M., Yokoi, L., Rankin, J., Wharton-McDonald, R., and Mistretta, J. (1997). A survey of the instructional practices of grade 5 teachers nominated as effective in promoting literacy, *Scientific Studies of Reading*, 1(2), 145–160.

Pressley, M., Dolezal, S., Raphael, L., Mohan, L., and Roehrig, A. (2003). Increasing academic motivation in primary grades. *Catholic Education: A Journal of Inquiry and Practice*, 6(3), 372–392.

Raphael, L., Pressley, M., and Mohan, L. (2008). Engaging instruction in middle school classrooms: Observational study of nine teachers. *The Elementary School Journal*, 109(1), 61–81.

Timperley, H. and Parr, J. (2009). What is this lesson about? Instructional processes and student understandings in writing classrooms. *The Curriculum Journal*, 20(1), 43–60.

Troia, G., Harbaugh, A., Shankland, R., Wolbers, K., and Lawrence, A. (2013). Relationships between writing motivation, writing activity, and writing performance: Effects of grade, sex, and ability. *Reading and Writing*, 26(1), 17–44.

Turner, J., and Paris, S. (1995). How literacy tasks influence children's motivation for literacy. *The Reading Teacher*, 48(8), 662–673.

Vaknin-Nusbaum, V., Nevo, E., Brande, S., and Gambrell, L. (2020). Reading and writing motivation of third to sixth graders. *Reading Psychology*, 41(1), 44–70.

Young, R. (2019). *What is it 'Writing For Pleasure' teachers do that makes the difference?* The University Of Sussex: The Goldsmiths' Company [Online]. Available: www.writing4pleasure.com.

Young, R., and Ferguson, F. (2020). *Real-world writers*: A Handbook for Teaching Writing to 7–11 Year Olds. London: Routledge.

Zumbrunn, S., and Krause, K. (2012). Conversations with leaders: Principles of effective writing instruction. *The Reading Teacher*, 65(5), 346–353.

CHAPTER 8

Volition

Introduction and context

Donald Graves, the much-respected and influential writer, educator, and master of the deceptively simple but deeply significant statement, tells us: 'children want to write. They want to write the first day they attend school' (1983, p. 1). We define volition as the need, desire, urge, or the internal compulsion to write, sometimes described as purposive striving or, mystifyingly, personal endorsement. It is a component of the concept of writing *as* pleasure (Garrett and Moltzen 2011) since the urge to write can be fed by the knowledge that the craft of writing can bring pleasurable and desirable sensations. Volition can also be engaged through realising the possibility of saying something strongly through writing. This is writing *for* the pleasure of getting a subject, topic, or idea 'off your chest' – quite literally releasing it through publishing or performance (Nauman 2007).

Research specifically studying children's volition in writing is scarce (Garrett and Moltzen 2011; Nauman 2007), but the drive to write has been related to other aspects of writing for pleasure, such as self-efficacy, motivation, self-regulation, and writer-identity (Abbott 2000; Bruning and Horn 2000; Eccles and Wigfield 2002; Brophy 2008; DeSmedt et al. 2018; Troia et al. 2013). Engagement of volition, for example, stimulates the child's desire to harness the knowledge and skills necessary for the creation of an excellent written piece (Colognesi and Niwese 2020).

Bruning and Horn's (2000) study makes the claim that teachers have a responsibility to help children learn not only how to write but also how to *want* to write. The challenge is to help students see that the benefits of writing outweigh the considerable effort and time involved, and that being a writer brings great intellectual, social, and personal rewards. Interestingly, their study also claims that *all* writing is volitional except when it is being carried out mechanically or under duress. In other words, volition is an innate psychological force which, in the context of writing, may be at risk of being weakened by some authoritarian teacher interventions, such as those we draw attention to in Chapter 1. Niemiec and Ryan (2009) echo this view and claim that, all too often, teachers place external demands on children's writing which can diminish their volition to write. According to Nauman (2007), teaching practices which are likely to have this effect include: overuse of writing prompts and teacher-assigned topics, setting up inauthentic writing activities, and focusing almost exclusively on transcriptional errors in a high-stakes performance-oriented classroom culture.

According to both Elbow (1998) and DeSmedt (2018b), the more children write volitionally, the better they write, with Olthouse (2012, p. 117) agreeing that children's desire to write 'is such an important factor in the development of writing talent'. Nauman (2007) suggests that those children whose internal desire to write has always been understood and nurtured find writing easier, which in turn enables them to develop the skills needed to write successfully. Garrett and Moltzen (2011) conducted an interesting study of young gifted female writers in which they showed that those who testified to having strong volition had felt the desire to write from a very early age and wrote because they had an emotional need to do so, often in response to their life experiences or the imaginative dreams they had had. Eccles and Wigfield (2002) found that children with a high level of volition are also likely to be able to cope with any anxiety experienced over writing and remain motivated even if others around them are not. They make their own environment conducive to writing, for example by resisting distractions, having resources to hand, and making use of peer support productively.

In her very engaging study of two young boy writers, Abbott (2000) notes that, when children are given ownership and control over their writing and enjoy what they are doing, they can become utterly absorbed in crafting their writing. She notes that they write with deep concentration and clear intention, that they set themselves high standards, seem to have no fear of failure, and are unaware of the passing of time. The boys in the study vividly described their experience of what they called 'flow'.

Finally, Colognesi and Niwese (2020, p. 20) found that when children are taught using the evidence-based writing practices described in this book, not only does their writing improve but their desire to write increases significantly, and they write 'with enthusiasm and pleasure'.

Volition and the principles of effective practice

Create a community of writers

Garrett and Moltzen (2011) state that, unsurprisingly, volitional writers feel supported by their teacher's creation of an environment in which they can write with confidence and ease alongside like-minded peers. The young volitional writers interviewed by Olthouse (2012) stated that they liked the feeling of connection with their fellow writers, and that they sometimes wrote as a class to create a sense of belonging.

Pursue purposeful and authentic class writing projects

According to Nauman (2007), the best way a teacher can respond to children's desire, need, urge, and compulsion to write is to allow them to write about their natural enthusiasms. Studies by Nauman (2007) and Garrett and Moltzen (2011) agree that teachers would do well to rethink tasks which are set solely for evaluative purposes and afford children little personal involvement. Garrett and Moltzen observe how children will often choose voluntarily to write about topics of local, national, or global significance. Here we can see a link between volition and the critical literacy orientation for writing described in Chapter 1; the determination to share strong opinions and feelings about the world can often feed children's drive to write. This is illustrated in our own reworking of Kinneavy's (1980) framework for English. In the figure below, you can see that all writing comes either from a desire to impose or enact *on* the world or else to reflect or react *to* the world. These texts are then sometimes shared with others. Words and the world are inextricably linked (Figure 8.1).

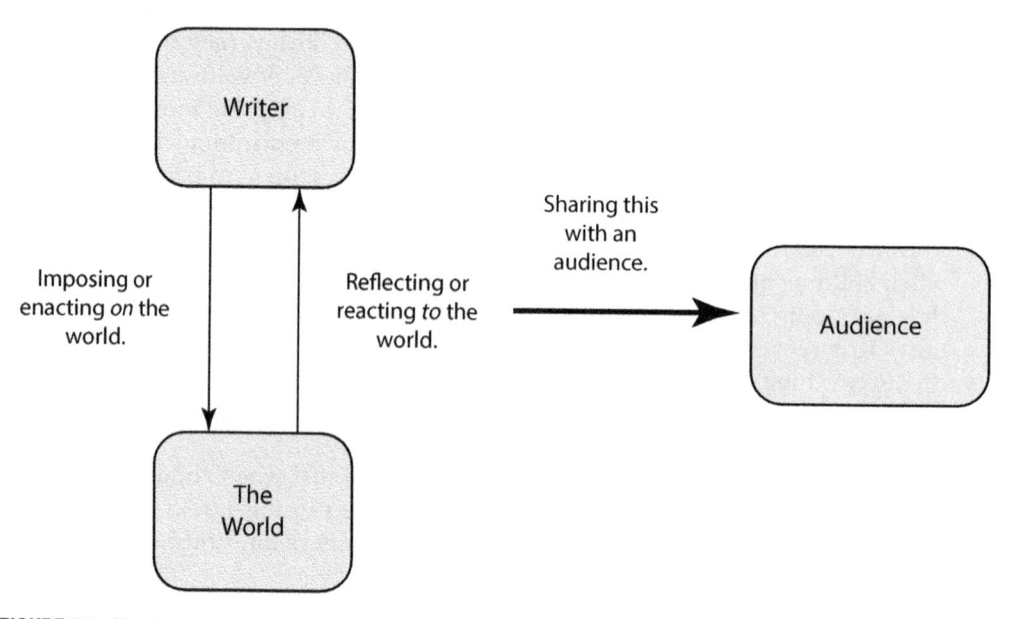

FIGURE 8.1 Showing our desire to create text as a result of wanting to express ourselves in the world, make sense of the world, or impose ourselves upon it.

Balance composition and transcription

Knowing that their teacher will balance compositional and transcriptional teaching supports children's volition. By focusing on the content and voice in a child's piece during the drafting phases, the teacher connects with the writer, who in turn enjoys the teacher's interest in how the composition is going. Attention is paid to children's transcription later on in the process (Nauman 2007).

Pursue personal writing projects

A number of studies show that volition is maintained and better learning outcomes achieved when learners engage autonomously in a self-chosen activity rather than when a task is imposed and regulated by others (Brophy 2008). Therefore, children need the freedom and space in which to develop personal projects (Garrett and Moltzen 2011).

Several studies have focused on children's volitional writing out of school. Nauman (2007) suggests that children should be encouraged to write regularly in a personal writing journal and to regard writing as a genuine recreational activity, a hobby, or even a 'job' that they can do outside of school. Parents and caregivers should support personal writing projects and, if possible, provide a space and some materials to enable children to write freely at home. However, Garrett and Moltzen (2011) point to evidence that the drive to write sometimes comes from the need to metaphorically 'escape' from unsupportive or stressful family circumstances. Bruning and Horn (2000) remind us too that school may be the best, the safest, and the only space where children ever get the opportunity to write for themselves. Therefore, schools must take this responsibility incredibly seriously and provide children with space and time in which to write solely for their own purposes (Chamberlain 2015; Young and Ferguson 2020a) (Figure 8.2).

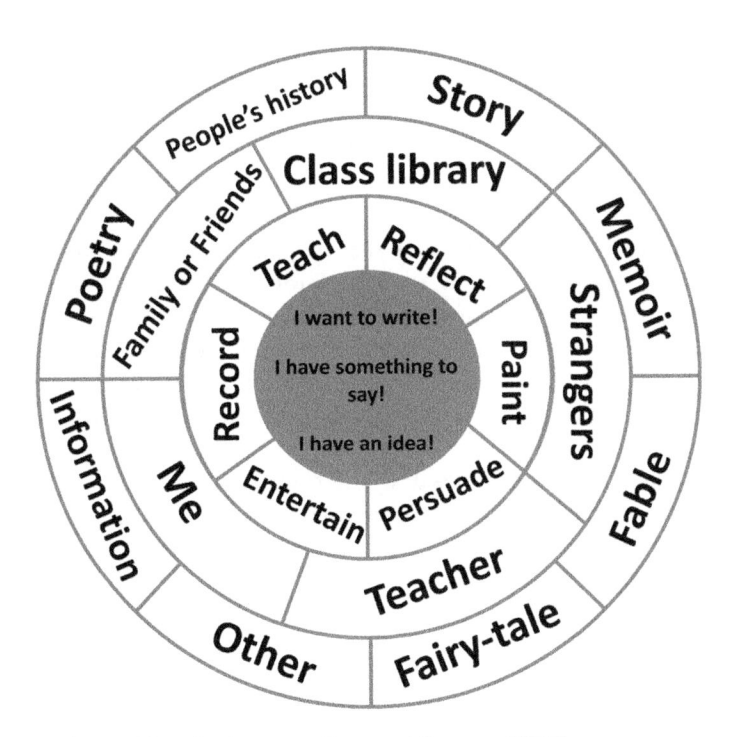

FIGURE 8.2 A year three writing wheel resource (Young and Ferguson 2020b).

In the resource above, we can see that children begin by being *moved* to write. They sit down knowing at the very least that they want to write and on many occasions knowing *why* they want to write: usually to entertain, paint with words, reflect on something personal, or share their opinion on some matter. They may also have an audience in mind. This knowledge then leads them consciously or not to choose an appropriate genre to help them fulfil their needs. Clearly, desire is closely linked to motivation. A desire to write is fuelled by knowing why you want to do it, and motivation is enhanced when you have a desire and a reason to get something done.

Be a writer-teacher

'A strong writing teacher creates the itch to write' (Zumbrunn and Krause 2012). Through modelling, producing mentor texts, and explaining their own processes and reasons for writing, writer-teachers can increase children's knowledge of the whole business of composition and stimulate their desire to write (Nauman 2007). Writing alongside or with the children in their class is therefore vital.

Literacy for pleasure: connect reading and writing

Garrett and Moltzen's (2011) study appears to show that children with high levels of volition had a desire to imaginatively reinvent the texts they were reading. Teachers' practice of modelling positive reading behaviours and creating a community of readers alongside a community of writers is seen as hugely significant in children's writerly development (Nauman 2007; Young 2019).

The *Writing For Pleasure* teachers

Our own research (Young 2019) confirmed that children who want to write do so because they feel a strong sense of self-efficacy, anticipated pleasure, and satisfaction, and have a clear perception of themselves as writers.

The teachers in our study knew that they had a responsibility to engage children's volition and develop in them a belief in the relevance and importance of writing. They gave sound instruction in the writing processes and the craft of writing, became writer-teachers, talked writer to writer, let their children have agency over their writing topics, and allowed ample time for them to pursue personal writing projects which the teachers held in high regard and for which they maintained high expectations.

They also shared and talked about their own reading, established good class libraries, read aloud to their classes regularly, and encouraged much informal book-talk. Finally, the data gathered through our questionnaire showed that the majority of children who expressed a strong volition to write also had strong reader-identities (Nauman 2007).

References

Abbott, J. (2000). 'Blinking out' and 'having the touch' two fifth-grade boys talk about flow experiences in writing. *Written Communication*, 17(1), 53–92.

Brophy, J. (2008). Developing students' appreciation for what is taught. School, Educational Psychologist, 43(3), 132–141.

Bruning, R., and Horn, C. (2000). Developing motivation to write. *Educational Psychologist*, 35(1), 25–37.

Chamberlain, L. (2015). *Exploring the out-of-school writing practices of three children aged 9–10 years old and how these practices travel across and within the domains of home and school* (PhD thesis). The Open University.

Colognesi, S., and Niwese, M. (2020). Do effective practices for teaching writing change students' relationship to writing? Exploratory study with students aged 10–12 years. *L1-Educational Studies in Language and Literature*, 20, 1–25.

De Smedt, F., Merchie, E., Barendse, M., Rosseel, Y., De Naeghel, J., and Van Keer, H. (2018). Cognitive and motivational challenges in writing: Studying the relationship with writing performance across students' gender and achievement level. *Reading Research Quarterly*, 53(2), 249–272.

Eccles, J., and Wigfield, A. (2002). Motivational beliefs, values and goals. *Annual Review of Psychology*, 53, 109–132.

Elbow, P. (1998). *Writing Without Teachers*. New York: Oxford University Press.

Garrett, L., and Moltzen, R. (2011). Writing because I want to, not because I have to: Young gifted writers' perspectives on the factors that 'matter' in developing expertise. *English Teaching: Practice and Critique*, 10(1), 165–180.

Graves, D. (1983). *Writing: Teachers and Children at Work*. Portsmouth, NH: Heinemann.

Kinneavy, J. (1980). *A Theory of Discourse*. New York: W.W Norton.

Nauman, A. (2007). Writing in the primary grades: Tapping young children's enthusiasm to help them become good writers. Illinois Reading Council, 35(4), 16–28.

Niemiec, C., and Ryan, R. (2009). Autonomy, competence and relatedness in the classroom: Applying self-determination theory to educational practice. *Theory & Research in Education*, 7(2), 133–144.

Olthouse, J. (2012). Why I write: What talented creative writers need their teachers to know. *Gifted Child Today*, 35(2), 117–121.

Troia, G., Harbaugh, A., Shankland, R., Wolbers, K., and Lawrence, A. (2013). Relationships between writing motivation, writing activity, and writing performance: Effects of grade, sex, and ability. *Reading and Writing*, 26(1), 17–44.

Young, R. (2019). *What is it 'writing for pleasure' teachers do that makes the difference?* The University of Sussex: The Goldsmiths' Company [Online] Available: www.writing4pleasure.com.

Young, R., and Ferguson, F. (2020a). *Real-World Writers: A Handbook for Teaching Writing with 7–11 Year Olds*. London: Routledge.

Young, R., and Ferguson, F. (2020b). *Year Three Writing Wheel* [Online] Available: www.writing4pleasure.com/class-writing-projects.

Zumbrunn, S., and Krause, K. (2012). Conversations with leaders: Principles of effective writing instruction. *The Reading Teacher*, 65(5), 346–353.

CHAPTER

9

Writer-identity

Introduction and context

Writer-identity is one of the most complex aspects of the theory of writing for pleasure. Also known as self-perception, self-concept, social belonging, possible selves (Lazowski and Hulleman 2016), writer-belief or having ownership of your writer's voice, writer-identity is your understanding of what writing means and your belief that you are a writer (McKeod 1987; Boscolo and Hidi 2006; Collier 2010; Seban and Tavsanli 2015; Gardner 2018). Writer-identity is about doing, being, valuing, feeling, and believing (Johnston et al. 2001; Eyres 2017). For Lensmire (1998) it is in a continuous state of 'becoming'.

Moje et al. (2009) present what they call five metaphors of identity. First, there is what makes us broadly different from one another, such as our national, ethnic, and cultural identity. Next, is the sense of self we pursue in our own writing – the 'I' which makes us uniquely who we are. There is then writer-identity constructed through consciousness, how writing can be used as a tool for gathering our thoughts and articulating and sharing our knowledge. Next, is the idea that we share our identities through the experiences we have and the stories we tell. These can quite literally be the personal stories of everyday life told as vignettes, anecdotes, personal narrative, people's history, and personal, family, and community biographies, part of which will be the fictional narratives and the artefacts, media, and reading we use to create them (See Chapter 23 for more detail). Finally, our identities are revealed through the positions we adopt or even resist in our writing.

Children's writer-identities

Students' beliefs about themselves as writers and how they undertake writing are important (Frank 2001; Zumbrunn et al. 2017; Gutiérrez 2008). Specifically, how they perceive their own intellectual abilities has either a positive or a negative effect on their sense of writer-identity (Seban and Tavsanli 2015) and on how they carry out their writing. Children with strong writer-identities are more disposed to redraft and revise, write of their own accord, and consider their own writing processes and purposes

(Grainger, Goouch, and Lambirth 2003; Hicks 2008; Seban and Tavsanli 2015) while, unsurprisingly, those whose writer-identity is weak often lack the volition to write (Brown et al. 2011). Beach and Ward (2013) add the caution that children's writer-identities may not always be stable and can be subject to pressure and influence.

Implications for teaching

How children perceive themselves as writers has an effect on their academic performance (Beach and Ward 2013; Zumbrunn et al. 2017). The message for practitioners is plain: a writer's identity must be part of their assessment profile. We should not measure a child's writing development simply by their command of written conventions but should also take into account the affective dimensions of self-belief, self-esteem, and motivation. It will be clear, then, that writer-identity is dependent on and closely related to the other aspects of *Writing For Pleasure* (Grainger et al. 2003; Boscolo and Hidi 2006; Young 2019).

Children's writer identities are constructed for the most part through engagement in the kinds of writing events, behaviours and projects which take place in the classroom. Therefore, and as Beach and Ward (2013) and Seban and Tavsanli (2015) point out, the teacher's influence is critical. Leung and Hicks (2014) citing Ray (2001) state that children should be provided with the type of instruction and writing environment that enables them to practise all the things a writer really does: research, explore, collect, interview, talk, read, stare off into space, co-author, pre-write, draft, revise, edit, and publish. This is best achieved in the classroom through the reassuringly consistent writing workshop approach (Chelsea and Snyders 2014; Leung and Hicks 2014; Seban and Tavsanli 2015; Young and Ferguson 2020). The more children write in this sympathetic environment, the more likely they are to join 'the literacy club', to write outside of school, and to show greater investment and involvement in their written work (Hicks 2008; Leung and Hicks 2014). However, too often, the way writing is taught in schools actually prevents children from constructing their identities as authors (Brown et al. 2011; Laman et al. 2018; Young et al in press). Grainger et al. (2003) make the particular claim that the teacher's imposing of writing tasks negatively impacts on children's writer-identities, while Au and Gourd (2013) and Chelsea and Snyders (2014) make the point that the requirement to write for inauthentic purposes and audiences results in the suppression of children's own writing voices. Writing-teaching loses the quality of 'write as a writer writes' when the focus shifts to a narrow conception of genre over content, assessment over quality, and product over process (Au and Gourd 2013; Barrs 1983 see also Chapter 1).

According to Hicks (2008, p. 4) 'writing identity should be a crucial goal for any type of writing pedagogy because it helps students to see writing as something they can do outside of the classroom'. Beach and Ward (2013) and Chamberlain (2015) take up this theme when they encourage teachers to consider and take seriously children's writer-identities outside of school.

'Funds of knowledge' and 'funds of identity'

Collier (2010, p. 147) says 'through the making of texts, writers are able to remake themselves and their relations with the world'. The point she and others make is that a person's writing cannot be separated from their identity; they are deeply intertwined (Johnston et al. 2001; Dutro and Kazemi 2006; Compton-Lilly 2006; Rowsell and Pahl 2007; Seban and Tavsanli 2015). This valuable observation has clear implications for classroom practice. Writer-identities will be influenced by so many different factors: school pedagogy, how you perceive yourself as a reader, home literacy, race, gender, culture, socioeconomic circumstances, multilingualism, and second language learning (Bourne 2002). Teachers who promote 'funds of knowledge' (Gonzalez et al. 2005) and 'funds of identity' (Subero et al. 2016) in the writing classroom allow children to bring in their outside-school learning experiences, cultural capital, interests, passions, hobbies, objects, artefacts, activities, talents, popular cultures and knowledge, and connect them with what they are learning about writing and being a writer in school. Significantly, and contrary to received wisdom, children having this kind of writing experience achieve school-based objectives more effectively and efficiently because they are simply more engaged and keen to express their interests, curiosities, and outside pleasures in their writing (Subero et al. 2016).

Writer-identity and the principles of effective practice

Build a community of writers

Jacky, one of the authors of a study by Leung and Hicks (2014, p. 584), movingly describes how the writing community to which she belonged was instrumental in helping her construct her own sense of a writer-identity: 'most of my classmates came from low-income families, and many grew up in broken homes, lived with relatives or in foster care. We defined ourselves as a class of writers. I relished our classroom culture and told anyone who would listen'. According to Rowsell and Pahl (2007), the kinds of writing practices and attitudes that are created, promoted, and valued in a classroom will surface in the texts children produce. Thus, as Jacky testified, and as Gee (1999) reiterates, the writing community created by teachers will have a profound and lasting effect on children's identities as writers. Johnston, Woodside-Jiron, and Day (2001), citing Vygotsky (1978), broaden the community idea to include the whole enveloping language environment where children acquire a set of cultural practices, values, and beliefs from which they can construct their identity. For example, a community might collaboratively create a piece of writing which expresses their collective identity and send it out into the world. Such a project was described by Tarrés et al. (2012). Over the course of a year, a unique story was developed with the participation of all the students in a school, helped by their teachers, two authors, and three illustrators. Drawing on their funds of social and family knowledge, each class wrote their own story, deciding together on characters, setting, and action; transitions were then devised between the story created by one age group and the next. The final piece was achieved in the spirit of democratic decision-making and respect for the linguistic and cultural diversity of the student writers and was thus an artefact of a shared community writer-identity.

Treat every child as a writer

Graves (1983) challenges us all to teach first the writer, then the writing. According to Brown, Morrell, and Rowlands (2011), if we fail to do this, we will have little impact on children's writing development. However, teachers sometimes find it difficult to see all children as writers. Those who are not, for whatever reasons, identified as such may be given very different experiences in the writing classroom and fewer opportunities than their classmates to participate in authentic and purposeful writing projects. Instead, teachers may allocate them worksheets and writing exercises, thereby in effect removing them from the writing community and impairing their chances of developing a positive writer-identity (Bourne 2002; Collier 2010). Hicks (2008), however, offers the reassurance that struggling students have a far greater chance of emerging as writers if taught through a contemporary writing workshop approach.

Read, share, think, and talk about writing

We would agree with Leung and Hicks (2014) when they state that creating a classroom where students define *each other* as writers is just as important as individuals defining themselves that way. Children should be regularly publishing their own writing for others to read, responding to their peers' on-going work, and sharing with one another their techniques, strategies, and ways of managing the writing process. Zumbrunn et al. (2017) suggest that teachers should continually be monitoring how students are relating to the content and style of their teaching. Continually 'checking the temperature' by observing students during writing time, by conversing, and by engaging in pupil conferences is invaluable (Piazza and Siebert 2008; Zumbrunn et al 2017). It is our view that no teacher should ever make the blanket assertion that 'all my class loved that writing project!' without finding out whether this was actually true.

Boscolo and Gelati (2007) regard such conversations as an essential element in helping children to appreciate and enjoy writing as both process *and* product. In dialogic classrooms, teachers value reciprocal talk and understand that it mediates learning. Both Kaufman (2006) and Zumbrunn et al. (2017) suggest that children can be asked to *draw* what they feel about the writing experiences they have at school. They can also be invited to draw a picture which reflects their writer-identity – a valuable resource for a teacher moving forward.

Pursue purposeful and authentic writing projects

Lensmire (1998) sees writer-identity as a project in itself. It can be worked on, built upon, and developed over time. In his view, class writing projects which explore many different genres offer a variety of spaces for young writers to expand into. For example, as Seban and Tavsanli (2015) remind us, students may have a natural preference for a particular type of writing, and so it is important to provide a multi-genre writing curriculum, giving all students the chance of success, a belief in themselves as writers, and the opportunity to push their writing forward into unknown and exciting territories.

Through writing and being a writer, children say, 'hey world, here I am. This is me. This is what I think, feel, know, imagine and want to share with you'. As we have discussed, giving children ownership over their topic choice within a class writing project is instrumental in increasing their enjoyment of writing since, as Calkins (1994) states, it stimulates their very natural desire to express themselves. Chelsea and Snyders (2014) take this idea further when they observe that children are more likely to develop a writer-identity if teachers set up authentic and genuinely purposeful writing projects.

It is crucially important that teachers take account of children's existing cultural capital (Seban and Tavsanli 2015). Dyson (2003), along with Rosen (1972), Edelsky (2006), Fisher (2006), and Cummins (2011), warns against making the dangerous assumption that some children (particularly those new to English, or children who are economically disadvantaged) have nothing – no identity – that they can profitably bring to class. She proves that even the youngest of children, regardless of background, can bring their home identities to school writing in the form of symbolic objects, games, books, drawings, toys, artefacts, and images, which they can use as rich sources of inspiration within class writing projects. She adds that they also have access to talk, singing, and experiences with friends and family, as well as radio, music, TV, film, online material, and other aspects of popular culture to draw on. All these resources can feed into class writing projects and help form writer-identities. As Boscolo (2009) points out, when children write from a position of knowledge and expertise, the sense of writer-identity is strengthened. We would also agree with Au and Gourd (2013) that the curriculum is more engaging when it pays attention to the lives, cultures, communities, and identities of the students.

We know that, despite the research of Dyson and others referred to above, many teachers hold the belief that topics chosen by the children will not be worthwhile and will jar with the culture or style of school writing. However, in a culturally sustaining writing classroom with its acceptance of and respect for the variety of children's identities and their different lives, it is easy for teachers to validate children's authorial decision-making (Young et al in press). The topics chosen may not be of the usual kind. For example, they may not sit well with neoliberal or white middle-class sensibilities, might be topics which are traditionally less sanctioned, or be taken from children's popular or local cultures (Hoewisch 2001; Dyson 2020). However, McCarthy and Mkhize (2013) and Laman et al. (2018) make the depressing observation that teachers working in schools with high levels of poverty often implement the exact opposite – a narrow writing curriculum with limited opportunities for students to write for authentic reasons.

Teach the writing processes

Teaching children how to use the writing processes (generate ideas, plan, draft, revise, edit, publish) and the many tools available when undertaking them creates a real depth of understanding that could be compared to a mastery based approach (Leung and Hicks 2014). Contemporary writing workshop (Atwell 2014; Calkins et al. 2015 (USA); Young and Ferguson 2020 (UK)), as a process approach, supports young writers' identities in that it highlights the social aspect of writing. It puts young writers at the centre of writing projects and gives them time to develop their pieces and an opportunity to respond to their own and others' writing in many different ways. Through exploring the processes involved in writing many times over, students develop an understanding of themselves as writers who use writing projects in their own way depending on their personal and social purposes (Chelsea and Snyders 2014).

Teach daily mini-lessons

The sense of a writer-identity allows children to better explain what they feel they need from their teacher to develop further as writers (Grainger et al. 2003). Through daily writing mini-lessons, children feel that they are exploring, thinking, and having rich discussions about the writers' craft and are gaining valuable writerly knowledge (Chelsea and Snyders 2014).

Pursue personal writing projects

The conviction that 'I'm an author!' is what motivates students to pursue writing on their own and in their own time (Leung and Hicks 2014). It is therefore important that, as teachers, we allow children time to write for their own purposes and in their own ways. An obvious way of doing this, of course, is to provide regular and ample time for children to write in personal writing journals, as Grainger, Goouch, and Lambirth (2003) reported. Graves (1983) notes that when children begin to see themselves as genuine writers, they begin to live what could be called the 'writer's life'. His study noted the amount of 'off-stage' thinking and writing that was done by children when they felt they were writers; they would continue to compose and consider their writing both in and out of school. Children who have access to personal writing project books will think and write in their free time, evenings, and weekends and can be invited to continue such writing in school on a Monday morning (Young and Ferguson 2020).

Be reassuringly consistent

Students need daily, sustained classroom time devoted to writing instruction and writing practice to become confident, engaged, and successful writers. This requirement is at the centre of the contemporary writing workshop and influences students' identity as writers (Hicks 2008; Atwell 2014; Young and Ferguson 2020). Teachers provide students with a consistent routine of mini-lesson, writing time, and class sharing. Jacky, (Hicks 2008), whom we mentioned earlier, explained how her teacher's use of this consistent writing workshop structure specifically helped her build her identity as a writer. She described how, during mini-lessons, her teacher would share new writing strategies using books, newspaper clippings, and examples from her own writing. The daily ritual of presenting writing to peers helped students focus on the goal of writing for an audience. It also helped the classroom develop into a literacy community where students interacted with one another as fellow authors.

The workshop routine creates what Leung and Hicks (2014) call a 'metacognitive' environment which allows students to assemble, as Chamberlain (2018) says, an internal toolbox of writing strategies to be opened over and over again. With practice, students internalise their own most frequently used strategies and employ them without much cognitive energy being expended. This gives them space to turn their attention to learning new strategies (Atwell 2014; Calkins et al. 2015; Young and Ferguson 2019). Through such a routine, teachers create an ever-evolving chain of writing growth that leads to children's stronger writer-identity as they work and behave as professional and recreational writers do.

Be a writer-teacher

Teachers should write with their students. Writing for and with students has numerous benefits, according to Zumbrunn et al. (2017), but perhaps the most important is that it allows students to see that their teacher also has a writer-identity (Cremin and Locke 2017).

According to Laman, Davis, and Henderson (2018) and Johnston, Woodside-Jiron, and Day (2001), teachers need to know that their perceptions of what a writer is and how a writer works will have a direct impact on children's own developing writer-identities. They need to be aware of personal biases and prejudices and that what they see as legitimate or illegitimate in terms of writing behaviour, writer dialect, subject choice, and writing process can have potentially serious negative consequences for children's writer-identities (Young et al in press). Children do not just learn about *writing* from their teacher, they also learn about what it means to be a *writer*.

Pupil conference: meet children where they are

Not surprisingly, all children find harsh criticism damaging to their sense of themselves as writers (Seban and Tavsanli 2015). However, practices such as pupil conferencing and class sharing are directed towards providing children with a daily opportunity to celebrate who they are as writers (Chelsea and Snyders 2014). Because children's identities cannot be separated from their writing, it is important for teachers to create time for individual conversations with children about being a writer, their likes and dislikes, what they enjoy most, what they struggle with most, and the content of their writing. Children with fragile writer-identities often need these sorts of conversations the most (Dutro and Kazemi 2006).

Literacy for pleasure: connect reading and writing

A literature-rich classroom is vital for children's sense of a writer-identity. Surrounding apprentice writers with the works of other authors gives children role models to learn from and be inspired to emulate. According to Leung and Hicks (2014), if children are to learn to read like writers, they first have to see themselves as writers. And as Graham et al. (2017) point out, once students start thinking of themselves in such a way, they connect more deeply with what they read. Indeed, children with strong reader-identities usually carry strong writer-identities too (Harwayne 1992; Young 2019).

The *Writing For Pleasure* teachers

In our own research (Young 2019), writer-identity was, along with motivation, one of the weaker domains encountered across the study. Importantly, those children who did identify strongly as writers also scored highly across all the other affective domains. They saw writing as a pleasurable activity; they felt a sense of self-efficacy; they had a strong desire to write; they were motivated by their writing projects; they felt they knew what to do and how to do it; they wrote *for* pleasure and felt a sense of satisfaction and pride in their texts. They felt that they were legitimate authors right now and several stated that writing was one of their 'hobbies'. They said they felt most like authors when they were writing stories or poems; one reason for this is perhaps that these types of class writing projects afford children the agency they believe other writers have. Indeed, they stated that they felt like writers when they were given the agency to generate their own ideas for a writing project. Not surprisingly, children who identified as writers were also more likely to identify as readers. They enjoyed reading, read volitionally, and used intertextuality regularly in their writing (see Chapter 23).

However, it appeared that some children did not have a good understanding of what a writer is or can be. Many of them certainly did not seem to know that a hobbyist or a recreational writer can also identify themselves as a writer. Instead, they felt that writers were only those who were good at it, could write a great quantity, wrote books like the ones in their class libraries, wrote for a living, were formally published, or were in some way famous. Additionally, they did not feel like writers because they were not convinced their writing was always serving a legitimate purpose or was always read by 'real' audiences beyond the classroom. The teachers whose classes did show strong writer-identities made a conscious effort for their children's writing to leave the classroom and for it to be published or performed elsewhere. These teachers also tried to be role-models by identifying as writers themselves, discussing, and promoting their writerly life with their classes.

Some of the teachers played an unintentional but powerful role in signalling that only some children were 'writers'. They did this through their manner, praise, and interactions with certain members of their class. Some teachers also seemed to hold commercially published authors in disproportionately high regard. This too could have negatively impacted on what children thought about themselves as writers. Finally, some children were unwilling to identify as writers because of a feeling that their teacher did not see them as 'good' at it or perhaps that their subjects for writing or style differed from what their teachers 'liked to read'.

References

Atwell, N. (2014). *In the Middle* (3rd Ed). Portsmouth, NH: Heinemann.

Au, W., and Gourd, K. (2013). Asinine assessment: Why high-stakes testing is bad for everyone, including english teachers. *The English Journal*, 103(1), 14–19.

Barrs, M. (1983). The new orthodoxy about writing: Confusing process and pedagogy. *Language Arts*, 60(7), 829–840.

Beach, S., and Ward, A. (2013). Insights into engaged literacy learning: Stories of literate identity. *Journal of Research in Childhood Education*, 27(2), 239–255.

Boscolo, P. (2009). Engaging and motivating children to write. In *The SAGE Handbook of Writing Development*, Beard, R., Myhill, D., Riley, J., and Nystrand, M. (Eds.). London: Routledge.

Boscolo, P., and Gelati, C. (2007). Best practices in promoting motivation for writing. In *Best Practices in Writing Instruction*, Graham, S., MacArthur, C., and Fitzgerald, J. (Eds.) (pp. 202–221). New York: Guildford.

Boscolo, P., and Hidi, S. (2006). *Writing & Motivation*. Holland: Elsevier Science.

Bourne, J. (2002). Oh, what will Miss say!: Constructing texts and identities in the discursive processes of classroom writing. *Language and Education*, 16(4), 241–259.

Brown, M., Morrell, J., and Rowlands, K. (2011). Never more crucial: Transforming young writers' attitudes toward writing and becoming writers. *California English*, 17(2), 15–17.

Calkins, L. (1994). *The Art of Teaching Writing*. Portsmouth, NH: Heinemann.

Calkins, L., Hohne, K., and Robb, A. (2015). *Writing Pathways*. Portsmouth, NH: Heinemann.

Chamberlain, L. (2015). *Exploring the out-of-school writing practices of three children aged 9–10 years old and how these practices travel across and within the domains of home and school* (PhD thesis). The Open University.

Chamberlain, L. (2018). *Inspiring Writing in Primary School* (2nd Ed.). London: Sage.

Chelsea, S., and Snyders, B. (2014). 'I wish we could make books all day!' An observational study of kindergarten children during writing workshop. *Early Childhood Educational Journal*, 42, 405–414.

Collier, D.R. (2010). Journey to becoming a writer: Review of research about children's identities as writers. *Language and Literacy*, 12(1), 147–164.

Compton-Lilly, C. (2006). Identity, childhood culture, and literacy learning: A case study. *Journal of Early Childhood Studies*, 6(1), 57–76.

Cremin, T., and Locke, T. (2017). *Writer-identity and the teaching and learning of writing*. London: Routledge.

Cummins, J. (2011). Identity matters: From evidence-free to evidence-based policies for promoting achievement among students from marginalized social groups. *Writing & Pedagogy*, 3(2), 189–216.

Dutro, E., and Kazemi, E. (2006). Making sense of 'the boy who died': Tales of a struggling successful writer. *Reading and Writing Quarterly*, 22, 325–356.

Dyson, A. (2003). Popular literacies and the 'all' children: Rethinking literacy development for contemporary childhoods. *Language Arts*, 81(2), 100–109.

Dyson, A. (2020). 'This isn't my real writing': The fate of children's agency in too-tight curricula. *Theory into Practice*, 59(2), 119–127.

Edelsky, C. (2006). *With Literacy and Justice for All: Rethinking the Social in Language and Education* (3rd Ed.). Mahwah, NJ: Lawrence Erlbaum.

Eyres, I. (2017). Conceptualising writing and identity. In *Writer Identity and the Teaching and Learning of Writing*, Cremin, T., and Locke, T. (Eds.) (pp. 3–18). London: Routledge.

Fisher, T. (2006). Whose writing is it anyway? Issues of control in the teaching of writing. *Cambridge Journal of Education*, 36(2), 193–206.

Frank, C. (2001). 'What new things these words can do for you': A focus on one writing-project teacher and writing instruction. *Journal of Literacy Research*, 33(3), 467–506.

Gee, J. (1999). *An Introduction to Discourse Analysis: Theory and Method*. New York: Routledge.
Gonzalez, N., Moll, L. C., and Amanti, C. (2005). *Funds of Knowledge: Theorizing Practices in Households, Communities and Classrooms*. NJ: Lawrence Erlbaum Associates.
Graham, S., Liu, X., Bartlett, B., Ng, C., Harris, K.R., Aitken, A., and Talukdar, J. (2017). Reading for writing: A meta-analysis of the impact of reading and reading instruction on writing. *Review of Educational Research*, 88(2), 243–284.
Grainger, T., Goouch, K. and Lambirth, A. (2003). Playing the game called writing. *English in Education*, 37(2), 4–15.
Gaves, D. (1983). *Writing: Teachers and Children at Work*. Exeter, NH: Heinemann.
Gutiérrez, K. (2008). Developing a sociocritical literacy in the third space. *Reading Research Quarterly*, 43(2), 148–164.
Harwayne, S. (1992). *Lasting Impressions Weaving Literature into the Writing Workshop*. Portsmouth NH: Heinemann.
Hicks, J. (2008). *Writing identify and the writers' workshop: Looking back at my second grade* (USFSP Honors Program Theses) (Undergraduate) 83.
Hoewisch, A. (2001). 'Do I have to have a princess in my story?': Supporting children's writing of fairytales. *Reading and Writing Quarterly*, 17, 249–277.
Johnston, P., Woodside-Jiron, H., and Day, J. (2001). Teaching and learning literate epistemologies. *Journal of Educational Psychology*, 93(1), 223–233.
Kauffman, G. (2006). Authoring ourselves as readers and writers. *Language Arts*, 83(6), 502–504.
Laman, T., Davis, T., and Henderson, J. (2018). 'My hair has a lot of stories!': Unpacking culturally sustaining writing pedagogies in an elementary mediated field experience for teacher candidates. *Action in Teacher Education*, 40(4), 374–390.
Lazowski, R., and Hulleman, C. (2016). Motivation interventions in education: A meta-analytic review. *Review of Educational Research*, 86(2), 602–640.
Lensmire, T. (1998). Rewriting student voice. *Journal of Curriculum Studies*, 30(3), 261–291.
Leung, C., and Hicks, J. (2014). Writer identity and writing workshop a future teacher and teacher educator critically reflect. *Writing & Pedagogy*, 6(3), 583–605.
McCarthey, S., and Mkhize, D. (2013). Teachers' orientations towards writing. *Journal of Writing Research*, 5(1), 1–33.
McKeod, S. (1987). Some thoughts about feelings: The affective domains and the writing process. *College Composition and Communication*, 38(4), 426–435.
Moje, E., Luke, A., Davies, B., and Street, B. (2009). Literacy and identity: Examining the metaphors in history and contemporary research. *Reading Research Quarterly*, 44(4), 415–437.
Piazza, C., and Siebert, C. (2008). Development and validation of a writing dispositions scale for elementary and middle school students. *The Journal of Educational Research*, 101(5), 275–285.
Ray, K., and Laminack, L. (2001). *The Writing Workshop: Working through the Hard Parts*. Urbana, IL: National Council of Teachers of English.
Rosen, H. (1972). *Language & Class: A Critical Look at the Theories of Basil Bernstein*. London: Falling Wall Press.
Rowsell, J., and Pahl, K. (2007) Sedimented identities in texts: Instances of practice. *Reading Research Quarterly*, 42(3), 388–404.
Seban, D., and Tavsanli, Ö. (2015). Children's sense of being a writer: Identity construction in second grade writers workshop. *International Electronic Journal of Elementary Education*, 7(2), 217–234.
Subero, D., Vujasinović E., Esteban-Guitart, M., (2016). Mobilising funds of identity in and out of school. *Cambridge Journal of Education*, 47(2), 247–263.
Tarrés, E., Boix, G., Nadal, N., García, M. A., and Vila, I. (2012). El misterio de la biblioteca Millènium o cómo promover relaciones colaborativas desde la participación del alumnado [The mystery of the Millènium library: How to promote collaborative relationships through student participation]. *Revista de Educación*, 359, 102–119.

Vygotsky, L. S. (1978). *Mind in Society: The Development of Higher Psychological Processes* (M. Cole, V. John-Steiner, S. Scribner, & E. Souberman, Eds.). Cambridge, MA: Harvard University Press.

Young, R. (2019). *What is it 'Writing For Pleasure' teachers do that makes the difference?* The University of Sussex: The Goldsmiths' Company [Online] Available: www.writing4pleasure.com.

Young, R., and Ferguson, P. (2019). *Power English: Writing.* London: Pearson Education.

Young, R., and Ferguson, P. (2020). *Real-world writers: A Handbook for Teaching Writing with 7–11 Year Olds.* London: Routledge.

Young, R., Govender, N., and Kaufman, D. (in press). *Writing Realities.* Leicester: UKLA.

Zumbrunn, S., Ekholm, E., Stringer J.K., McKnight, K., and DeBusk-Lane, M. (2017). Student experiences with writing: Taking the temperature of the classroom. *The Reading Teacher*, 70(6), 667–677.

CHAPTER 10

The enduring principles of effective writing teaching

Introduction

The purpose of this chapter is to present 14 enduring principles of world-class writing teaching. These principles were identified by the authors through investigating:

- What for the past four decades educational researchers have repeatedly identified as effective practices in improving children's writing performance.
- What a number of high-profile case studies tell us about how the most effective teachers of writing improve children's academic progress.

Each of the 14 principles we describe in this chapter begins with a report on the meta-analyses carried out by Hillocks (1986); Graham and Perin (2007); Rogers and Graham (2008); Graham and Sandmel (2011); Graham et al. (2012); De Smedt and Van Keer (2014); Koster et al. (2015); Graham et al. (2016), and Graham and Harris (2019). For those who might not be familiar with the term, a meta-analysis is where a researcher will group many scientific studies on a particular subject, for example writing teaching, in order to identify recurring patterns.

The figure below lists the types of instruction that were identified by these meta-analyses and how they link to the principles of effective practice. The effect size tells us how powerful the type of instruction is found to be across the multiple studies analysed. Hattie (2009) suggests that anything at or above 0.4 can be considered to make a significant positive contribution towards children's learning, while anything at −0.32 or below should be considered to have a significant negative impact (Hillocks 1986; Graham and Perin 2007). Effect sizes can often be different across different meta-analyses. For example, setting writing goals was given an effect size of 0.80 by Graham, Harris, and Chambers (2016) but 2.03 by Koster et al. (2015). Readers should therefore treat such findings only as a broad indicator (Cheung and Slavin 2016; Van Weijen and Janssen 2018).

Type of instruction	Effect size	Links to principles
Setting writing goals	2.03	Chapter 16 *Set writing goals*
A contemporary writing workshop approach which includes self-regulation strategy instruction	1.75	Chapter 17 *Be reassuringly consistent* Chapter 20 *Teach mini-lessons*
Explicitly teaching the writing processes	1.26	Chapter 15 *Teach the writing processes*
Purposeful and authentic writing projects	1.07	Chapter 14 *Pursue authentic and purposeful class writing projects*
Working as a community of writers and reading, sharing, thinking, and talking about writing	0.89	Chapter 11 *Create a community of writers* Chapter 13 *Read, share, think, and talk about writing*
Feedback from teacher and peers	0.80	Chapter 13 *Read, share, think, and talk about writing* Chapter 22 *Pupil conference: meet children where they are*
Genre-study	0.76	Chapter 14 *Pursue authentic and purposeful writing projects* Chapter 16 *Set writing goals* Chapter 20 *Teach mini-lessons*
Time spent revising	0.58	Chapter 15 *Teach the writing processes*
Time spent generating ideas and planning	0.54	Chapter 15 *Teach the writing processes*
Children writing in response to their reading	0.50	Chapter 23 *Literacy for pleasure: connect reading and writing*
Functional grammar teaching	0.46	Chapter 20 *Teach mini-lessons*
Formal grammar teaching	−0.41	Chapter 20 *Teach mini-lessons*

Table shows the highest effect size recorded for each type of instruction using the following meta-analyses: Hillocks (1986), Graham (2006), Graham and Perin (2007), Graham and Sandmel (2011), Graham et al. (2012), Koster et al. (2015), Graham, Harris, and Chambers (2016), and Wyse and Torgerson (2017).

Whilst the experiments involved in these meta-analyses can be useful reading, they can also be far removed from the practical realities of day-to-day teaching and may not transfer across age range and school contexts (Hillocks 1986; Graham and Harris 2019). Therefore, we have also included case studies in which researchers have observed and described the daily practices of exceptional writing teachers (Medwell 1998; Langer 2001; Pressley et al. 2001; Pressley et al. 2006; Parr and Limbrick 2010; Dombey 2013; Grossman et al. 2013; Gadd 2014; Young 2019). What we can conclude is that researchers are affirming what these exceptional teachers do, and that the most exceptional teachers of writing are often confirming and applying many scientific findings practically and effectively across a variety of contexts.

From this reading, we have been able to identify 14 enduring principles of effective writing practice which encompass: the creation of a social environment and a positive culture for developing as a writer; high-quality teaching to produce authentic, confident, and independent writers; teachers writing, teaching, and giving feedback as writers, and teachers connecting writing with reading. These 14 principles which constitute a *Writing For Pleasure* pedagogy are summarised below, together with examples given of teachers' practices as observed in real classrooms.

Create a community of writers

Creating a safe and highly social environment in keeping with what feels like a contemporary writing workshop is conducive to children producing their best writing (De Smedt and Van Keer 2014; Graham and Harris 2019). High levels of pupil interaction, alongside conferencing with a teacher (Graham and Perin 2007; Graham and Sandmel 2011), also have significance for writing performance, with children seen as collaborators in the learning process (Graham et al. 2012). According to Morizawa (2014), the teacher should be flexible and allow children to rework their compositions if they feel they need to. Teachers simply must engage in highly responsive planning and teaching so as to meet their apprentice writers' learning needs as they emerge. Additionally, teachers have an instrumental role in creating links between children's writing, parents, and the local community (Hall and Harding 2003).

In their observations of the most effective writing teachers, Medwell et al. (1998) and Pressley et al. (2006) found that their writing environments were full of genuinely useful and well-used resources which helped children be more self-regulating. The teachers took time to produce posters in collaboration with their pupils and made resources, charts, graphic organisers and checklists which enabled children to write in largely independent and successful ways. Displays and posters were linked to the current class writing project and recent mini-lessons. Parr and Limbrick's (2011) exceptional teachers ensured children's published work was in the class library and that children's writing was everywhere in evidence in the classroom. Finally, children were aware of how much their teachers knew about them as writers and as people.

Treat every child as a writer

According to Medwell et al. (1998) and Dombey (2013), the most effective writing teachers do not confine their less experienced or lower-achieving pupils to mundane writing exercises or worksheets. Instead, all children are supported to participate in rich and relevant class writing projects. Parr and Limbrick (2011) observed that the exemplary teachers of writing in their case study would provide their less experienced writers with more pupil conferences, reteach any strategies taught during mini-lessons if required, encourage co-operative learning with peers, and give short additional mini-lessons through group teaching (Hall and Harding 2003).

Read, share, think, and talk about writing

Importantly, children need to collaborate and co-operate throughout a class writing project and support one another through peer assistance, peer-tutoring, and peer-evaluation (De Smedt and Van Keer 2014; Hillocks 1986; Grossman et al. 2013). Children learn from each other's developing compositions and from hearing how certain writing strategies, writerly techniques, literary devices or 'craft knowledge' are being applied by others (Graham et al. 2012; Graham and Harris 2019). According to Graham and Perin (2007), all these aspects have a strong positive impact on the quality of children's writing.

The case studies presented by Medwell et al. (1998), Langer (2001), and Gadd (2014) all showed that these practitioners promote co-regulation in their young writers by encouraging them to see writing as a social activity in which they can collaborate to improve each other's compositions or to help solve each other's writing problems. In addition, the teachers in Pressley et al. (1997) study ensured that children regularly read aloud their developing writing both to themselves and to others. Finally, Gadd and Parr's (2017) work suggests that children were encouraged to engage in rich conversation and deep discussion about writing and asked many 'how' and 'why' questions.

Pursue authentic and purposeful writing projects

Children's writing outcomes are improved if they engage in challenging and extended class writing projects where they write for authentic purposes and varied audiences which are well understood by them (Graham and Perin 2007; Dombey 2013; Grossman et al. 2013; Morizawa 2014). It is important that children feel they have personal responsibility for and ownership over their writing (Graham and Sandmel 2011). When engaged in a class writing project, children can sometimes be encouraged to get together in clusters and write on an idea of shared interest (Hillocks 1986).

The exceptional teachers observed by Gadd (2014) ensured that class writing projects were felt to be purposeful by the children. Across many case studies, exemplary teachers' practice promoted children's use of their existing funds of knowledge, interests, experiences, views, or opinions within class writing projects (Medwell et al. 1998; Langer 2001; Dombey 2013; Gadd and Parr 2017). Teachers also ensured that these projects were published in a number of different ways and reached a variety of genuine and responsive audiences (Pressley et al. 1997).

Pursue personal writing projects

Children become better writers by writing (Graham et al. 2012, 2015). Giving children additional daily time to work on self-chosen personal writing projects is shown to have a positive effect on writing development. Gadd (2014) observed that his case study teachers gave children ample time in which to produce their own personal writing projects, resulting in increased feelings of ownership and the sense of a writer-identity. Children were also able to continue such projects outside designated writing lessons. According to Dombey (2013), highly effective teachers link school and home writing and encourage children to regularly take their personal project books to and fro between home and school.

Teach the writing processes

In keeping with a contemporary writing-workshop approach (Young and Ferguson 2020), explicitly teaching children about the writing processes and how to use them in a self-regulating way is shown to be highly effective practice (Graham et al. 2012). Teachers should discuss the recursive nature of the writing processes (Graham and Perin 2007; Morizawa 2014) because, whilst young writers may initially benefit from a predictable and linear procedural routine for writing, eventually they will want to use the processes flexibly and in their own way (Dombey 2013; Morizawa 2014; Toria 2014).

Allowing young people time to generate their own ideas for class writing projects and to choose from a variety of planning techniques improves the quality of their writing (Graham and Perin 2007; Graham and Sandmel 2011; Graham et al. 2012; Morizawa 2014). In their survey and observations of effective teachers of writing, Pressley et al. (1997, 2006) noted that teachers took time to teach the writing processes and gave children ample time in which to plan, draft, revise, and attend to the mechanics and transcriptional aspects of their writing through proof-reading before publishing. Having access to visual aids, posters, and graphic organisers help children internalise these writing processes (Troia 2014). Allowing children to use word processors showed a consistent positive impact on young people's writing quality, and particularly so on the writing of those who are underachieving (Graham and Perin 2007; Graham et al. 2012; De Smedt and Van Keer 2014).

Set writing goals

Koster et al. (2015) state that goal setting is by far the most effective practice teachers can employ to improve children's writing outcomes. Setting **product goals** involves the teacher and their class coming together to discuss specific goals (critical characteristics, organisation, or elements they can use or apply within their writing) to make their writing meaningful and successful for its future audience. These goals have a broader reach than what is usually termed as 'success criteria' since they do not simply consist of a list of grammatical, literary, or linguistic features but also take into account the purpose and the receiving audience (Hillocks 1986; Graham and Perin 2007; Graham et al. 2012). Setting **process goals** involves the teacher and children knowing what part of the writing process they are going to be undertaking during that day's writing time. These 'writing deadlines' can be agreed by the whole class, or children can set their own (Morizawa 2014; Koster et al. 2015).

Parr and Limbrick (2010) state that the exemplary writing teachers in their study would always initially share the **distant goal** for a class writing project with their pupils and take time to explore and discuss the project with them. According to both Langer's (2001) and Gadd's (2014) studies, children made the greatest learning gains when their teachers invited them to develop product writing goals together as a whole class.

Teach mini-lessons

Writing study: teaching craft knowledge

Koster et al. (2015) record that strategy instruction has received the most attention from educational research and is therefore the most robust of effective writing practices. According to both Graham and Perin (2007) and Grossman et al. (2013), strategy instruction can have a dramatic effect on the quality of young people's writing. It involves teaching children strategies and techniques they can employ when they are generating ideas, planning, drafting, revising, editing, or publishing their writing (Morizawa 2014). The rationale here is that these kinds of lessons teach the generalities of writing, useful over the long term because strategies can be employed time and time again in an increasingly self-regulating way (Hall and Harding 2003; Graham and Perin 2007; Rogers and Graham 2008; Graham et al. 2012). Creating and giving children access to visual aids, posters, checklists, and graphic organisers is recommended alongside such teaching (Troia 2014).

Gadd's (2014) study of exceptional writing teachers showed that they regularly and systematically provided explicit instruction as described above. These teachers would demonstrate techniques and strategies live and would also explain how they had used them in texts they themselves had previously written. Effective teachers of writing taught these techniques as mini-lessons and invited children to use and apply what they had been taught in that day's writing time (Pressley et al. 2001; Dombey 2013; Young 2019). The exceptional teachers of Medwell et al. (1998), Langer (2001), and Pressley et al. (2006) were constantly promoting writing strategies and techniques that they knew would be useful to all their young writers in the long term.

Writing study: discussing exemplar texts

In all the studies they analysed, Koster et al. (2015) found that genre-study or 'text structure instruction' significantly improves children's writing performance (Hillocks 1986; Graham and Perin 2007; Graham et al. 2012). Exemplar texts are key here, studied and discussed by the whole class with product goals subsequently agreed upon (Graham and Perin 2007; Graham et al. 2012). In addition, Hillocks' (1986) analysis stated the usefulness of also discussing poor exemplars. Poor exemplars are texts which, for whatever reason, are not deemed to be successful or meaningful in achieving their purpose or attending to the needs of their audience. It was further recommended by Hillocks (1986) and Morizawa (2014) that children could be given a variety of exemplars and be asked to order them in terms of their success and meaningfulness.

The exceptional teachers of writing in Gadd's (2014) and Parr and Limbrick's (2011) case studies showed that they involved children in extended and high-level dialogic talk around exemplar texts, as described above. Talking about how the author had attended to their purpose and audience, and discussing the linguistic, literary, and textual features employed was vital. Discussion surrounding the overall success of the composition was seen as important for children's own later writing achievement.

Writing study: functional grammar lessons

Grammar lessons which are decontextualised result in negative writing performance (Hillocks 1986; Graham and Perin 2007; Graham et al. 2012; Wyse and Torgerson 2017). According to Koster et al. (2015), this is because children do not transfer what they are learning to real compositions. However, *functional* grammar mini-lessons attend to this problem efficiently and effectively and can have strong and positive effects on young people's writing (Rogers and Graham 2008; Myhill 2018). A particular grammatical or linguistic feature is discussed in terms of its function, and children are then invited to try it out in their writing that day. 'Sentence combining', how basic sentences can be combined into complex or compound sentences, can be taught in the same way, with children invited to try out the techniques during writing time (Graham and Perin 2007). The case studies of Medwell et al. (1998) and Langer (2001) show that this is what the best performing teachers do. They teach grammar or other writerly techniques within the context of authentic and meaningful writing and give direct instruction before inviting children to apply the technique during that day's writing time.

Pupil conference: meet children where they are

Hillocks (1986) found that excessive written feedback or extensive error correction had little or no positive impact on young writers' academic progress. Indeed, negative comments and heavy marking repeatedly resulted in children feeling less enthusiasm for writing, writing less, and having a low opinion of themselves as writers.

However, when children receive short, positive, and focused feedback from their teachers while they are actually engaged in writing, they revise their compositions to a significantly higher standard (Hillocks 1986; Dombey 2013). The combination of personalised instruction and immediate verbal feedback seem to be highly effective strategies (Graham and Perin 2007; Graham et al. 2012; Grossman et al. 2013; Morizawa 2014). In many of the case studies observing the most exceptional writing teachers, there is evidence of pupil conferencing being carried out in a serious and systematic way, with teachers employing both individual and group conferencing (Medwell et al. 1998; Langer 2001; Parr and Limbrick 2011; Young 2019).

Balance composition and transcription

Effective writing teachers balance their teaching of compositional strategies and techniques with transcriptional and technical skills (Graham and Harris 2019). For example, correcting spellings can be attended to when proof-reading rather than when composing, and punctuation should be used to indicate the intended meaning and how the writer wants their writing to be read (Dombey 2013). The observations of Pressley et al. (1997) of effective teachers of writing also show that they encouraged invented 'temporary' spelling during the compositional stages of writing.

Be a writer-teacher

Writing strategies, writerly techniques, and craft knowledge are best shared when they are modelled and legitimately used by teachers who write themselves (Hillocks 1986; Cremin and Oliver 2017). Essentially, a writer who teaches and a teacher who writes. Writer-teachers share their own writing products as mentor texts and discuss with their classes the structures, processes, literary techniques and linguistic features they used on their way to achieving a successful and meaningful piece (Parr and Limbrick 2011; Troia 2014). This is supported by Dombey (2013) and Medwell et al. (1998), who suggest that the most effective teachers of writing engage in writing for pleasure themselves. They model and share their own writing processes, problems and craft knowledge, and relate them to what the children are trying to achieve themselves in their compositions (Morizawa 2014). These teachers regularly sit and write among their pupils for short periods during daily writing time (Parr and Limbrick 2011).

Be reassuringly consistent

Having a reassuringly consistent and comprehensive approach to writing teaching improves the quality of children's writing (Hall and Harding 2003; Graham et al. 2012; Morizawa 2014). For example, teaching through the contemporary writing workshop approach (Young and Ferguson 2020), which is in keeping with the community orientation of writing discussed in Chapter 1, is shown to have a highly significant and positive effect on children's writing performance (Graham and Perin 2007; Graham and Sandmel 2011). The routine here is mini-lesson, writing time, and class sharing. Dombey's (2013) analysis of the most effective teachers of writing shows that their classrooms are highly organised, routines are made explicit, and expectations are clear. Gadd's (2014) study showed that exceptional writing teachers break down lessons into these clearly identifiable stages and allocate a consistent, substantial and sustained time for daily writing.

Literacy for pleasure: connect reading and writing

Hillocks (1986) notes that when children are invited to write in personal response to their reading, they produce better writing in general. A variety of evidence shows that effective teachers regularly read aloud in an engaging manner to their classes. This is an important way of helping children connect with what they are learning from texts and use it in their writing endeavours through the process of 'intertextuality' (Dombey 2013); children learn that they can take aspects of their reading and turn it into their own piece of writing (Hall and Harding 2003). Further, Dombey (2013) states that exceptional teachers of writing will adopt a *reading for pleasure* pedagogy (Cremin et al. 2014), and give children copious amounts of time in which to read high-quality and varied texts. Medwell et al. (1998), Langer (2001), and Parr and Limbrick (2011), noted that their case study teachers would often turn to, or ask the children to turn to, literature and other mentor texts to see how writers have employed certain writerly techniques, linguistic, or literary features and how they have used punctuation to clarify their meaning.

Interconnect the principles

Finally, analysis of educational research repeatedly shows the need for teachers who wish to teach writing effectively and create successful writers to blend all the above principles of practice (Graham and Perin 2007; De Smedt and Van Keer 2014). This matches what case studies of exceptional writing teachers do. Teachers employ the principles above in a rich combination, with Grossman et al. (2013), Gadd (2014), Morizawa (2014), and our own case study (Young 2019) all highlighting the importance of teaching being multidimensional. Throughout, this book describes what is meant by effective practice and successful writing in the broadest sense. For example, effective practices help writers to achieve the requirements of a curriculum. Successful writers write because they enjoy it or because it brings them a sense of satisfaction. They are knowledgeable about writing, they understand the writer's life, and they know themselves as writers. They live, read, talk, and work within a community of writers. They can write engaging, meaningful, and useful texts that others want to read. But ultimately, a successful writer is one who continues to write.

Conclusion

This chapter has shown that a *Writing For Pleasure* pedagogy is nothing less than the pursuit of world-class writing teaching. We have described the principles which have a proven track record for increasing children's progress and achievement in writing. However, what we cannot do is describe what many individual teachers have learnt about the teaching of writing through their own personal experiences, nor do we share the wisdom of professional or hobbyist writers (Cremin et al. 2017). Both of these, we would argue, also have a valuable role to play in the pursuit of great writing teaching.

We would like to point out that these principles are flexible and should be adapted to fit different school and classroom contexts. However, they have a very clear general application. Teachers would be wise to think carefully about whether they are creating a social environment and a positive culture for children to develop as writers. They should deliver high-quality teaching that aims to produce authentic, confident, and independent writers. Next, they should reflect on how their own writing can positively influence their writing *teaching* and how they give feedback as a writer. Finally, they must consider how they are creating conditions for their young apprentice writers to use their reading in the ways writers do.

Each of the chapters which follow will analyse each principle in depth. Again, we draw on the findings of specific scientific research and continue to provide illustrations from case studies of the practice of real teachers. In addition, we describe in detail what we ourselves observed outstanding teachers to be doing in their classrooms as they put each of the principles into operation. From this base, we then suggest practical strategies for teachers' immediate use and ask some thought-provoking questions.

References

Cheung, A., and Slavin, R. (2016). How methodological features affect effect sizes in education. *Educational Researcher*, 45(5), 283–292.

Cremin, T., and Oliver, L. (2017). Teachers as writers: A systematic review. *Research Papers in Education*, 32(3), 269–295.

Cremin, T., Mottram, M., Collins, F., Powell, S., and Safford, K. (2014). *Building Communities of Engaged Readers: Reading for Pleasure*. London: Routledge.

Cremin, T., Lillis, T., Myhill, D., and Eyres, I. (2017). Professional writers' identities. In *Writer Identity and the Teaching and Learning of Writing*, Cremin, T., and Locke, T. (Eds.) (pp. 19–36). London: Routledge.

De Smedt, F., and Van Keer, H. (2014). A research synthesis on effective writing instruction in primary education. *Procedia Social and Behavioral Sciences*, 112, 693–701.

Dombey, H. (2013). *Teaching Writing: What the Evidence Says UKLA Argues for An Evidence-informed Approach to Teaching and Testing Young Children's Writing*. London: UKLA.

Gadd, M. (2014). *What is Critical in the Effective Teaching of Writing?* Auckland: The University of Auckland.

Gadd, M., and Parr, J. (2017). Practices of effective writing teachers. *Reading & Writing* 30(6), 1551–1574.

Graham, S. (2006). Strategy instruction and the teaching of writing: A meta-analysis In *Handbook of Writing Research*, McArthur, C., Graham, S., and Fitzgerald, J. (Ed.) (pp. 187–207). New York: Guilford Press.

Graham, S., and Harris, K. (2019). Evidence-based practices in writing. In *Best Practices in Writing Instruction*, Graham, S., MacArthur, C., and Hebert, M. (Eds.) (3rd Ed.) (pp. 3–31). New York: The Guilford Press.

Graham, S., and Perin, D. (2007). *Writing Next: Effective Strategies to Improve Writing of Adolescents in Middle School & High Schools*. Washington, DC: Alliance for Excellent Education.

Graham, S., and Sandmel, K. (2011). The process writing approach: A meta-analysis. *Journal of Educational Research*, 104, 396–407.

Graham, S., McKeown, D., Kiuhara, S., and Harris, K. (2012). A meta-analysis of writing instruction for students in the elementary grades. In *Journal of Educational Psychology*, 104(4), 879–896.

Graham, S., Harris, K., Santangelo, T. (2015). Research-based writing practices and the common core. *Elementary School Journal*, 115(4), 498–522.

Graham, S., Harris, K., and Chambers, A. (2016). Evidence-based practice and writing instruction: A review of reviews. In *Handbook of Writing Research*, MacArthur, C., Graham, S., and Fitzgerald, J. (Ed.) (2nd Ed.) (pp. 211–227). New York: The Guilford Press.

Grossman, P.L., Loeb, S., Cohen, J., and Wyckoff, J. (2013). Measure for measure: The relationship between measures of instructional practice in middle school English Language Arts and teachers' value-added scores. *American Journal of Education*, 119(3), 445–470.

Hall, K., and Harding, A. (2003). *A Systematic Review of Effective Literacy Teaching in the 4 to14 Age Range of Mainstream Schooling*. London: Institute of Education.

Hattie, J. (2009). *Visible Learning: A Synthesis of over 800 Meta-Analyses Relating to Achievement*. London: Routledge.

Hillocks, G. (1986). *Research on Written Composition: New Directions for Teaching*. Urbana, IL: National Council of Teachers of English.

Koster, M., Tribushinina, E., De Jong, P.F., and Van de Bergh, B. (2015). Teaching children to write: A meta-analysis of writing intervention research. *Journal of Writing Research*, 7(2), 249–274.

Langer, J.A. (2001). Beating the odds: Teaching middle and high school students to read and write well. *American Educational Research Journal*, 38(4), 837–880.

Medwell, J., Wray, D., Poulson, L., and Fox, R. (1998). *Effective Teachers of Literacy. A Report Commissioned by the UK Teacher Training Agency*.

Morizawa, G. (2014). *Nesting the Neglected 'R' A Design Study: Writing Instruction within a Prescriptive Literacy Program* (Doctoral dissertation). University of California, Berkeley.

Myhill, D. (2018). Grammar as a meaning-making resource for improving writing. *L1-Educational Studies in Language and Literature* (Contribution to a special issue Working on Grammar at School in L1-Education: Empirical Research across Linguistic Regions), 18, 1–21.

Parr, J.M., and Limbrick, L. (2010). Contextualising practice: Hallmarks of effective teachers of writing. *Teaching and Teacher Education*, 26(3), 583–590.

Pressley, M., Yokoi, L., Rankin, J., Wharton-McDonald, R., and Mistretta, J. (1997). A survey of the instructional practices of grade 5 teachers nominated as effective in promoting literacy. *Scientific Studies of Reading*, 1(2), 145–160.

Pressley, M., Wharton-McDonald, R., Allington, R., Block, C., Morrow, L., Tracey, D., Baker, K., Brooks, G., Cronin, J., Nelson, E., and Woo, D. (2001). A study of effective first-grade literacy instruction. *Scientific Studies of Reading*, 5(1), 35–58.

Pressley, M., Gaskins, I., Solic, K., and Collins, S. (2006). A portrait of benchmark school: How a school produces high achievement in students who previously failed. *Journal of Educational Psychology*, 98(2), 282–306.

Rogers, L., and Graham, S. (2008). A meta-analysis of single subject design writing intervention research. *Journal of Educational Psychology*, 100, 879–906.

Toria, G. (2014). Evidence-based practices for writing instruction. In *CEEDAR*. Lansing, MI: Michigan State University.

Van-Weijen, D., and Janssen, T. (2018). High-quality writing instruction in Dutch primary education. A framework for national assessment. *L1 Educational Studies in Language and Literature*, 18, 1–41.

Wyse, D., and Torgerson, C. (2017). Experimental trials and 'what works?' in education: The case of grammar for writing. *British Educational Research Journal*, 43(6), 1019–1047.

Young, R. (2019). *What is it 'Writing For Pleasure' teachers do that makes the difference?* The University Of Sussex: The Goldsmiths' Company [Online]. Available: www.writing4pleasure.com.

Young, R., and Ferguson, F. (2020). *Real-World Writers: A Handbook for Teaching Writing with 7–11 Year Olds*. London: Routledge.

CHAPTER

11

Create a community of writers

The community or environmental approach to writing teaching as discussed in Chapter 1 has at its centre the conviction that young writers flourish more when they feel themselves part of a cohesive classroom group sharing common understandings, common ways of working, and similar aspirations for their writing. Research studies substantiate the belief in the importance of community. For example, Tompkins and Tway (2003, p. 502) have stated that 'classroom community is a more potent factor in students' academic success than any particular instructional method' while Brown et al. (1993, p. 39) say that 'little or no growth in student writing can take place in a superficial writing environment' (cited in Hoewisch 2001). It may be useful to remember that, as Young and Ferguson (2020) say, a community can be a class, a year group, or a whole school, and should even take in the locality.

Teachers who create and promote a community based on writing for pleasure will be as much concerned with developing the *writer* as with developing the writing (Frank 2001). They will respect the right of all children to be invited into the writer's life as members of the 'community of writers' (Cremin and Myhill 2012), the 'literacy club' (Smith 1988), or the 'writing collective' (Lewis and Heffernan 2008). The benefits are clear. According to Jonston et al. (2001), Flint and Fisher-Ari (2014), and Beach and Ward (2013), a true community environment enables all children to feel they have a place in the writing classroom. As participants in the practical and intellectual environment around them, they absorb its beliefs and values and, as Rowsell and Pahl (2007) and Rathmann et al. (2018) say, build personal theories of what they believe writing and being a writer means. By contrast, Beach and Ward (2013) give the serious warning that teachers who see their role as principally to provide material, cover curriculum content, and deliver instruction in a mechanical and detached way will in effect be preventing children from understanding the relevance of writing and from developing fully as writers.

Casey and Hemenway (2001, p. 74) paint a powerful picture of the ideal classroom community of writers envisioned by eight-year-old Page who took part in their study: 'neither a modern art studio nor a factory production line, the writing classroom created by Page's ideal teacher would provide time, support, and real audiences for writing; it would unite both fiction and nonfiction, process and product, content and form, and freedom and discipline; it would include talk about writing, global revision, opportunities for feedback and publication, and high, but realistic, teacher expectations'. As Page has articulated, and as Garrett and Moltzen (2011) comment, an important characteristic of the aspirational community classroom is how it feels as a place of *freedom* and *space*. Creating an atmosphere which incorporates both these elements is more than critical if children are to realise their writing talents. In Garrett and Motzen's view, primary schools are very suitable places in which to grow such writing communities. Primary classrooms, according to Tompkins and Tway (2003), should be 'enabling classrooms', arranged and organised to act as a self-regulatory tool in their own right. The environment will complement and reinforce strategies taught by the teacher and used by the children through the provision of working walls, posters, physical resources, graphic organisers, rubrics, checklists, and other artefacts which suggest and promote the idea that this is a space where writers write and where writers have access to the tools for writing.

Tompkins and Tway go on to observe that teachers in primary classrooms often use the eight strategies identified by Ralph Peterson (1992) to enrich their 'communities of learning'. We have adapted them for specific application to communities of writers:

- **Ceremonies.** Holding meetings to foster a collective writing identity for the class and discuss potential class writing projects together.
- **Rituals.** Activities which express value and commitment to writing and being writers.
- **Rights.** Children discuss and agree on their rights and responsibilities as writers within the writing community of the classroom.
- **Celebrations.** Festive celebration and performance highlights children's writing achievements. They can happen spontaneously or be more formal, celebrating publication or performance of children's finished writing.
- **Talk.** Writer-talk is an essential part of community life and an important learning tool.
- **Play.** Students engage in play when crafting writing, creating writing projects collaboratively, and experimenting with language and with the genres of writing.
- **Routines.** Students learn the procedures and behaviours for writing and being a writer. They take responsibility for regulating themselves as they write.
- **Residency.** Children begin to feel a sense of belonging to and membership of the writing community, where their writing identity and voice is valued, supported, and developed by teacher and peers alike. They feel at home.

The result is that, far from being an alien, mysterious, or unnatural activity, writing becomes an utterly normal and community-based pursuit done for the enjoyment and satisfaction it can bring.

Building writerly relationships

In a study comparing two very different classroom cultures, White (2000, pp. 20–21) writes engagingly that in one classroom 'pupils consistently confirmed that writing was an important cultural activity which was to be taken seriously', and that children were 'young craftspeople, serving their apprenticeship in a complex creative activity under the guidance of an expert'. The metaphor conveys what was obviously a supportive, serious, sympathetic, and highly productive relationship between the teacher and the pupils.

As we know, and as research studies consistently point out, relationships within the writing community have far-reaching effects on many aspects of learning. Burchinal et al. (2002) suggest, for example, that the social and emotional processes involved in establishing relationships have an influence on the acquisition of academic skills. According to Gadd (2014), studies discussing the relationship between teacher and learner often use terms such as positive, close, and caring, and they state that, when such relations exist, teachers are more likely to provide resources and instruction which encourage a sense of self-efficacy (Bruning and Horn 2000; Leung and Hicks 2014) and the expectation of writing *as* and *for* pleasure (Clark 2012; Young 2019). Bruning and Horn (2000) assert that a classroom which promotes a community of writers is one that nurtures functional and mastery beliefs about writing, provides a supportive context, and creates a positive emotional environment in which to talk about and engage in writing. Ruttle (2004) states further that building a community includes negotiating and constructing a reciprocal understanding of what a writer is, what writing is for, and why and how we engage in it. Finally, Tompkins and Tway (2003) observe that, when good relations prevail, there is a greater likelihood that children will become more actively involved in their own learning.

Graves (1991) believed that every writing session should take place in a kindly atmosphere of openness, trust, confidence, tolerance, understanding, and a feeling of belonging, together with a sense of high expectation, personal responsibility, order, and control. His summary reminds us in a timely way that we should never forget the social and human nature of all learning.

Getting to know each other

'Classrooms are spaces that can be infused with our students' identities' (Rowsell and Pahl 2007, p. 402). Among the most exciting examples of how teachers have capitalised on children's identities to enhance their classroom writing communities are those described by Subero et al. (2016). They describe children in multilingual settings writing dual-language books to share in school and with families outside school, and children collecting and rewriting fairy tales from their countries of origin to create an anthology of bilingual books. They also highlight the 'shoeboxes' project (Hughes and Pollard 2006), which involves children decorating 'all about me' shoeboxes and placing within them important artefacts, drawings, photographs, and other trinkets to represent who they are. The shoeboxes are then brought into school, and children are invited to produce writing in response. Another example of practice comes from Rosemberg and colleagues (2013) who describe how children from rural and urban populations were given audio and video recorders and were invited to document their lives outside of school; they then brought the recordings back into school as inspiration for writing.

In their book, Young and Ferguson (2020) suggest ways in which teachers can encourage children to write in personal response to literature and to what they are learning across the whole curriculum. They describe how children can undertake personal narrative (memoir) writing projects, write about or in response to local community or political events, and write 'people's history' and biography, interviewing and getting to know the people they admire or respect outside of school. These are all effective ways of strengthening communities through writing. As Subero et al. (2016) would agree, projects like these give teachers an opportunity to show that they value children's cultural capital by inviting them to bring their own experiences and elements of their linguistic and cultural heritages to their writing in school.

Writing as a social activity

As Frank Smith (1983, p. 564) wisely says: 'teachers must show the advantages that membership in the club of writers offers, and ensure that children can join'. Community-orientated classrooms are wonderfully social places, where teachers and children immerse themselves in writing, demonstrate aspects of their writing craft, expect each other to talk about their compositions, and feel a sense of responsibility for the quality of their final writing products. They experiment and play with writing and accept and give feedback about their own and others' developing works. A true community classroom will regard all children as authentic writers who can talk, teach, and learn from and with one another.

The role of the writer-teacher

Teachers can be the best role models for young writers to learn from (Nolen 2007; Beach and Ward 2013; Olthouse 2012).

Grainger et al. (2005, p. 161) write with feeling about how the passion and affective engagement of creative teachers can transform classrooms, filling them with 'pleasure, creativity, challenge and joy', and influencing children's attitudes and volition to write. A writer-teacher's passion for writing and being a writer, how writers talk, act, and think, and how writing is a social activity within a community communicates itself to the children, who begin to think and write with the same concerns in mind (Frank 2001).

Leung and Hicks (2014) write about a community which is focused on developing children's writerly identity through making connections with the real world. The classroom feels like a place where authentic writing is being undertaken by children who see themselves and their classmates as having the responsibility to be writers in the truest sense. The teacher is instrumental in constructing such a classroom, talking and writing alongside the children, sharing their own writing life and practices, and encouraging children to talk about and present their writing to others in positive and constructive ways (Dyson 2003; Fisher et al. 2010; Garrett and Moltzen 2011).

The affective domains

You know you are in a community of writers when the affective domains are being attended to (see Chapters 3–9). Children in such contexts are confident, motivated, driven, independent, responsible, identifying themselves as writers, and enjoying and getting a great deal of satisfaction from learning and writing together every day. They are writing for pleasure.

Examples of effective practice

In our research which observed *Writing For Pleasure* teachers (Young 2019), children noted that their teachers were extraordinarily positive, caring, strict, fun, calm, and interested in their lives and development as writers. This resulted in their classes being engaged in writing at a high level of progress and achievement. Their classrooms felt like a rich mixture of creative writers' workshop and the razor-sharp focus of a professional publishing house. For example, the teacher 'doesn't make it so fun that it isn't about getting the work done' and 'we can have fun with our writing but we also need to make it good'. Their classrooms were a place where important writing was done, where high quality was expected, and where children felt like genuine writers as opposed to simply being schooled in producing writing products for mainly evaluative purposes. They were communities of writers in which the teacher teaches and writes alongside their class and shares their own writing practices, strategies, and techniques. The children felt that they were being taught by an experienced and passionate writer-teacher who themselves loved writing, but who ensured that relationships between them remained reciprocal.

The children were taught how to talk and present their writing to others in positive and constructive ways. The community of writers took part in meaningful practices and writing projects they could identify with, and teachers supported and encouraged children to bring and use their own 'funds of knowledge' into their writing projects. Children could therefore write from a position of strength. Importantly, they were involved in actions, discussions and reflections that made a difference to how they were taught and how they undertook their writing. For example, they were able to take their personal writing project books to and from school and share them with the class community. The classrooms were entirely democratic spaces. The children talked of feeling confident and knowing that their teachers wanted them to try their best, take their time, and to focus specifically on making their written pieces the highest quality they could be for their future readership. One teacher, inspired by the National Writing Project (2011), had on display the writing community's rights and responsibilities.

Practical things you can do

- Identify yourself and the children in your class as *writers*. Talk about yourselves as being writers and your classroom as being your writing workshop.

- Try writing yourself in class and reflect on how easy it is (or not) to write in the environment you have created in your classroom. Is there the opportunity for both communal support and seclusion and quiet space?
- Continually keep an eye out for reasons why children cannot write well on their own and attend to them. Coach them in how to be as self-reliant and co-regulating as possible.
- Arouse children's interest in how to be a writer, how to live the writer's life, what it means to write, and what is involved in being a writer.
- Find out about children's existing writing lives – what they think writing is, how they do it outside school, how they feel about it, and what *moves* them to write.
- Draw on your knowledge as a writer and teacher when creating a positive writing workshop environment in your classroom.
- Ensure children get to engage with a whole host and variety of purposes and audiences throughout their time at school.
- Design and manage your classroom so that when children and adults enter it, they know it is a place where real writers get to work. Ensure it is organised and has clear structures and consistent routines which lead children to engage in writing regularly and easily.
- Emphasise collaboration, co-operation, sharing, personal responsibility, independence, and self-discipline.
- Be a warm, enthusiastic, and caring teacher who is interested in children's lives and listens deeply when children discuss their writing. Celebrate children's efforts and be their biggest supporter.
- Be a teacher who focuses on mastery through repeated meaningful practice, as opposed to being performance driven.
- Celebrate together when writing is published. This contributes significantly to a sense of community.
- Create your own school or class publishing house with its own statement of intent and logo (Young and Ferguson 2020).

QUESTIONS WORTH ASKING YOURSELF

- The texts children write reflect the environment in which they are crafted. What do your children's texts say about the writing environment in your classroom?
- From both a writer and a teacher's perspective, do you know how a writing workshop works? Have you attended a writer-teacher group? Do you attend writing institutes or retreats? Do you know how writers socialise and write when they attend these events? Does this reflect how your classroom works and how it feels?
- Does your writing classroom run like a well-oiled machine? Have children internalised the rituals, routines, rights, and responsibilities of the classroom?
- If someone walks into your classroom, would they think this is a place where writers work? How would they know? What would they feel, hear, and see to help them realise this is a community where writers learn and work alongside each other every day?

- Do you and the children in your class describe yourselves as published authors and writers?
- Do the practices, behaviours, and beliefs of your classroom mirror those of writers outside of school?
- Do you allow the outside community into the classroom writing community? Does children's home writing come into school? Do you have other recreational or professional writers from a range of disciplines visit and work in your classroom?
- Does your children's published writing ever bring them extra opportunities or responses from outside school?
- Could your school invite a local writer to be a 'writer in residence'?

References

Beach, S., and Ward, A. (2013). Insights into engaged literacy learning: Stories of literate identity. *Journal of Research in Childhood Education*, 27(2), 239–255.

Bruning, R., and Horn, C. (2000). Developing motivation to write. *Educational Psychologist*, 35(1), 25–37.

Burchinal, M., Peisner-Feinberg, E., Pianta R., and Howes, C. (2002). Development of academic skills from preschool through second grade: Family and classroom predictors of developmental trajectories. *Journal of School Psychology*, 40(5), 415–436.

Casey, M., and Hemenway, S. (2001). Structure and freedom: Achieving a balanced curriculum *The English Journal*, 90(6), 68–75.

Cremin, T., and Myhill, D. (2012). *Creating Communities of Writers*. London: Routledge.

Dyson, A. (2003). Popular literacies and the 'all' children: Rethinking literacy development for contemporary childhoods. *Language Arts*, 81(2), 100.

Flint, A.S., and Fisher, T. (2014). Writing their worlds: Young english language learners navigate writing workshop. *Writing & Pedagogy*, 6(3), 633–648.

Frank, C. (2001). 'What new things these words can do for you': A focus on one writing-project teacher and writing instruction. *Journal of Literacy Research*, 33(3), 467–506.

Garrett, L., and Moltzen, R. (2011). Writing because I want to, not because I have to: Young gifted writers' perspectives on the factors that 'matter' in developing expertise. *English Teaching: Practice and Critique*, 10(1), 165–180.

Grainger, T., Goouch, K., and Lambirth, A. (2005). *Creativity and Writing: Developing Voice and Verve in the Classroom*. London: Routledge.

Graves, D. (1991). *Build A Literate Classroom*. Portsmouth, NH: Heinemann.

Hoewisch, A. (2001). 'Do I have to have a princess in my story?': Supporting children's writing of fairytales. *Reading and Writing Quarterly*, 17, 249–277.

Hughes, M., and Pollard, A. (2006). Home-school knowledge exchange in context. *Educational Review*, 58, 385–395.

Johnston, P., Woodside-Jiron, H., and Day, J. (2001). Teaching and learning literate epistemologies. *Journal of Educational Psychology*, 93(1), 223–233.

Leung, C., and Hicks, J. (2014). Writer identity and writing workshop a future teacher and teacher educator critically reflect. *Writing & Pedagogy*, 6(3), 1756–5839.

Lewison, M., and Heffernan, L. (2008). Rewriting writers workshop: Creating safe spaces for disruptive stories. *Research in the Teaching of English*, 42(4), 435–465.

National Writing Project. (2011). *Ten rights of the writer*. https://thenationalwritingproject.weebly.com/uploads/5/7/5/2/57522719/poster_right_to_write2.pdf [Accessed 9th July 2019].

Olthouse, J. (2012). Why I write: What talented creative writers need their teachers to know. *Gifted Child Today*, 35(2), pp. 117–121.

Peterson, R. (1992). *Life in a Crowded Place: Making a Learning Community.* Portsmouth, NH: Heinemann.

Rathmann, K., Herke, M., Hurrelmann, K., and Richter, M. (2018). Perceived class climate and school-aged children's life satisfaction: The role of the learning environment in classrooms. *PLoS ONE*, 13(2): e0189335. Doi: 10.1371/journal.pone.0189335.

Rosemberg, C.R., Stein, A., and Alam, F. (2013). At home and at school: Bridging literacy for children from poor rural or marginalized urban communities. In *International Handbook of Research on Children's Literacy, Learning, and Culture*, Hall, K., Cremin, T., Camber, B., and Moll, L. (Eds.) (pp. 67–82). Oxford: Wiley-Blackwell.

Rowsell, J., and Pahl, K. (2007). Sedimented identities in texts: Instances of practice. *Reading Research Quarterly*, 42(3), 388–404.

Ruttle, K. (2004). What goes on inside my head when I'm writing? A case study of 8–9-year-old boys. *Literacy*, 38(2), 71–77.

Smith, F. (1983). Reading like a writer. *Language Arts*, 60(5), 558–567.

Smith, F. (1988). *Joining the Literacy Club.* Oxford: Heinemann.

Subero, D., Vujasinović E., and Esteban-Guitart, M. (2016). Mobilising funds of identity in and out of school. *Cambridge Journal of Education*, 47(2), 247–263.

Tompkins, G.E., and Tway, E. (2003). The elementary school classroom. In *Handbook of Research on Teaching the English Language Arts*, Flood, J., Lapp, D., Squire, J.R., and Jensen, J.M. (Eds.) (2nd Ed.) (pp. 501–511). Mahwah, NJ: Lawrence Erlbaum Publishers.

White, C. (2000). Strategies are not enough. *Education 3-13*, 28(1), 16–21.

Young, R. (2019). *What is it 'writing for pleasure' teachers do that makes the difference?* The University Of Sussex: The Goldsmiths' Company [Online]. Available: www.writing4pleasure.com.

Young, R., and Ferguson, F. (2020). *Real-World Writers: A Handbook for Teaching Writing with 7–11 Year Olds.* London Routledge.

CHAPTER 12

Treat every child as a writer

We cannot state strongly enough how essential it is that all children begin identifying themselves as genuine writers as early as possible and know that writing can be theirs as a life-long pursuit. All the principles of effective research-informed practice examined in this book are relevant to *every* child learning to be a writer, irrespective of individual or specific educational need. The practices they embody are inclusive because they are grounded in an approach which is oriented towards recognising strengths but is also capable of offering real support to struggling or inexperienced writers or those with additional needs (Graham et al. 2001; Gillespie and Graham 2014).

Every child is a member of the writing community

Teachers' expectations, the assumptions they might make about the future academic achievement of individual pupils, can often have the effect of distancing certain children from the practices and activities of the classroom writing community. Collier's study (2010, p. 152) warns that teachers' expectations, 'often influenced by perceptions of ability and identity markers such as gender, ethnicity, social class', can result in some children not being given the same experience as others of what it means to be a writer. She also makes the interesting comment that teachers should be careful not to pay more attention to children they perceive as being 'more like them'. According to Perl and Wilson (1986) and Hoewisch (2001), children who are viewed by their teachers as being linguistically lacking face barriers to participation in the writing community.

Research evidence suggests that the expectations teachers communicate in terms of how they want the whole community of writers to socialise, behave and achieve will positively affect children's self-efficacy and academic outcomes to an even greater degree than expectations formed for individual pupils (Miller and Satchwell 2006; Harris and Rosenthal 1985; Burchinal et al. 2002; Rubie-Davies 2010). The principle of *treat every child as a writer* essentially invites teachers to consider how to build and articulate a togetherness within the classroom, teaching first the writers then the writing (Fu and Shelton 2007; Olthouse 2012). Leung and Hicks (2014) insist that teachers simply must emphasise to the community members that they are all authors in possession of a rich variety of skills and strengths, and must set up a classroom which fosters exactly this sense of self-efficacy and a strong collective writer-identity; the sense of belonging and acceptance can be hugely motivating for children (Fu and Shelton 2007; Olthouse 2012). Of course, high expectations alone will not, in all likelihood, affect children's academic outcomes or their pleasure in writing. What is important, as Gadd (2014, p. 24) rightly says, is how these expectations impact on the planning and teaching decisions effective teachers of writing make.

Thompson (2018, p. 245) reminds us that 'sometimes approaches to teaching children facing extra challenges are grounded in deficit-models of teaching and learning that focus on what children cannot do. While the intention is well meaning, sometimes these approaches can become disconnected from the purposeful task of writing for meaning and enjoyment'. *Writing For Pleasure* teachers are unlikely to ally themselves to such a model and, according to Dombey's (2013) work, are unlikely to confine lower-achieving or less experienced writers to mundane writing tasks. Instead, these teachers see a 'struggling writer' as having a low sense of self-efficacy and self-regulation as the result of a long history of ineffective teaching decisions and an absence of instruction relevant to their needs. *Writing For Pleasure* teachers will regard children's writing struggles as interesting problems which can be solved through responsive mini-lessons (see Chapter 20) and pupil conferences (see Chapter 22). In this way, all children can be helped to believe themselves capable of becoming authentic writers (Glasswell et al. 2003).

Every child is connected to their writer-teacher

Writing For Pleasure teachers consider how they behave and talk in the classroom to make children understand they are genuine writers in the here and now. According to Cooper and Tom (1984) cited in Gadd (2014) they will give smiles, head nods, positive body language, eye contact, friendliness, clue giving, repetition, rephrasing, lots of praise and less criticism to all the children in their class. They see writing more as a mastery craft achieved through repeated purposeful practice, and so give children ample time, space, and opportunity to develop their writing (Rubie-Davies 2010). A variety of research has shown that these teachers are likely to set up mixed-ability interest-based groupings, where writing is often shared and discussed by all the members (Reutzel 2007; Paratore and McCormack 2009; Schumm and Avalos 2009). They also tend to believe more strongly than other colleagues that all learners can achieve if they receive appropriate support from their teacher (Rubie-Davies 2010). Parr and Limbrick (2010) note that exceptional teachers of writing work closely with struggling children, more usually in groups, and allow them to write collaboratively or co-operatively with their peers. Finally, Cornelius-White (2007) concludes that, as a result of these types of interactions and expectations, teachers will see an increase in children's volition and motivation to write, more satisfaction and pleasure in their learning, higher self-esteem and, finally, better social connections with their fellow writers.

Every child writes meaningfully

As we have so often said, effective writing teachers plan and teach to ensure every child in their class feels like a writer, writing with meaning, purpose, and pleasure. Leung and Hicks (2014) write engagingly about children having a sense of 'I'm an author!', a conviction that motivates and inspires them to pursue writing, possessing the confidence to use their own writing process and to write at their own pace. A plethora of studies, including Harris and Rosenthal (1985); Marchisan and Alber (2001); Rubie-Davies (2010); Olinghouse and Colwell (2013); Leung and Hicks (2014); and Satchwell (2019), all give useful advice to teachers seeking to create an environment where all, regardless of educational needs or experience, have the desire to write successfully. Most important are their suggestions that teachers:

- Ensure children get to write every day, with purpose and for a genuine audience. Graham and Harris (1994) state that too often children with additional needs are not afforded as much opportunity to write when compared with their peers.
- Monitor the expectations they communicate to their learners through pupil conferencing and responsive teaching on a daily basis.
- Create a supportive, positive, and social learning environment in which to write. Give all writers some ownership and agency over the class writing project, and ensure they are writing from a position of strength on a subject or idea which they are enthusiastic about and have expertise in.

It is hardly surprising to learn that, as Burchinal et al. (2002) found, children who feel emotionally secure and can communicate effectively with their teachers are better able to devote their energies and attention to writing. *Writing For Pleasure* teachers believe that children must be engaged socially with their classroom teachers so as to acquire the prerequisite knowledge and skills for learning within the classroom environment. The practices suggested above, entirely in keeping with the contemporary view of writing workshop, are particularly effective for children who are bilingual, multilingual, or learning English as a second language (Young and Ferguson 2020). As Laman (2014, p. 10) points out 'too often, students who speak languages other than English are marginalized for what they don't know rather than what they do know'. Therefore, a strength-based model of teaching and learning is needed to ensure that all children's identities are valued and that they all remain part of the community of writers.

Helping every child feel a sense of self-confidence and independence

As discussed in Chapter 11, whilst implicit teaching is a vital consideration, it is not nearly enough by itself (Graham and Harris 1994). All children, but particularly struggling or less experienced writers, need high-quality teaching and explicit instruction if they are to fulfil their potential as writers (Troia et al. 2009). The approach to explicit instruction which yields the strongest writing performance outcome for less experienced children or those with special educational needs is self-regulated strategy development (SRSD) instruction (Joseph and Konard 2009). Such instruction gives children confidence and encourages positive feelings about writing (Graham et al. 2000). This will be discussed in more detail in Chapter 20. Briefly, it involves building up children's confidence by having them:

- Set themselves writing goals.
- Generate their own to-do lists or 'self-instructions'.
- Write at a pace that suits them.
- Regularly evaluate how their writing is developing against class assigned product goals.
- Apply genuinely useful writing strategies and techniques that they feel make their writing more successful and meaningful.
- Use resources effectively.
- Know how and where to seek advice when they need it.
(Helsel and Greenberg 2007; Troia et al. 2009).

Each of these actions needs to be explicitly discussed and modelled by the teacher (ideally through a mini-lesson or pupil conference) before children are invited to try it out for themselves. If these strategies and techniques are well planned, then, over time, children internalise them and so become self-regulating.

Examples of effective practice

The following is a description of what was observed during our study of *Writing For Pleasure* teachers (Young 2019). These teachers held high expectations for all their writers in every way. They saw all children as writers and were always focused on teaching strategies and techniques that would lead to greater self-efficacy and self-regulation. All their children said they felt like independent writers who were achieving writing goals and regularly experiencing a sense of success. Teachers would positively praise the children for the goals they had achieved during the writing lesson and children commented that this helped them feel a sense of success in what they were doing. They ensured that all their writers remained part of the writing community. They taught what writing can do and positioned themselves as genuine readers of the children's compositions rather than simply evaluators. They would model and promote the social aspects of writing through their own manner, through pupil conferencing, and through sharing writerly advice and craft knowledge in their mini-lessons; these actions supported a culture where pupils would do the same for their peers.

Practical things you can do

- Ask any struggling writer what they feel they need instruction in and deliver it.
- Ensure children are aware that they can apply to their writing what you are teaching them during that day's mini-lesson or through a pupil conference.

- Allow a struggling or less experienced writer to write alongside two more experienced or confident writers and allow them to write in a highly social way.
- Consider being flexible with whole class writing deadlines, and so help children write to the best of their ability and at a pace that is better suited to them (Chapter 16).
- Make explicit to children how they can use their previous learning, strategies, or techniques in other writing projects too.
- Provide children with technology that can assist them in their writing, for example: dictation software, word prediction software, grammar assistance programs, electronic spell checkers, document reading software, word processing, and document sharing software.
- Increase less experienced writers' opportunities to write. For example, ensure they have access to personal writing project books.
- Ensure that your planning of mini-lessons and creation of resources and displays are always promoting and following the principles of self-regulated strategy development (Chapter 20). Resources can include picture/word prompts, graphic organisers, mnemonics, posters, rubrics, checklists, planning grids, procedural cue cards, to-do lists, and question cards. Ideally, these resources will be produced by the children themselves.
- Encourage children to create their own to-do lists and to set themselves a goal they wish to achieve during that day's writing time.
- Make pupil or group-conferencing with less experienced writers your priority during writing time (Chapter 22).
- Consider how you can take advantage of responsive teaching moments and conduct additional group mini-lessons for less experienced writers.

> **QUESTIONS WORTH ASKING YOURSELF**
>
> - How do you ensure that all children's progress is celebrated?
> - How can you help less experienced writers set their own goals and celebrate when achieved?
> - Do you know what less experienced writers worry about the most or feel least confident with? How can you teach a mini-lesson or create a resource that can help them feel more self-efficacy and self-regulation in dealing with these writing issues?
> - Do you spend lots of quality time engaged in conversation with less experienced writers to ensure that they feel valued and understood by you as their writer-teacher?
> - Do you have systems in place that allow children to learn and seek advice from their peers? Have you taught lessons on how writers collaborate, teach, or conference with their fellow writers?
> - Do less experienced writers have access to technology that can help them write with more ease and fluency?
> - Are less experienced writers feeling just as confident, happy, and successful as the other writers in your class? Are they catching up by having more instruction and by

engaging in writing more frequently than anyone else in class? Are they writing a lot both at home and at school?
- Have you encouraged parents or carers to be supportive and positive about writing and to make a happy and social environment for their child to write in? Could you suggest they write with their child at home (Young and Kaufman 2020)?

References

Burchinal, M., Peisner-Feinberg, E., Pianta R., and Howes., C. (2002). Development of academic skills from preschool through second grade: Family and classroom predictors of developmental trajectories. *Journal of School Psychology*, 40(5), 415–436.

Collier, D. (2010). Journey to becoming a writer: Review of research about children's identities as writers. *Language and Literacy*, 12(10), 147–164.

Cooper, H.M., and Tom, D.Y.H. (1984). Teacher expectation research: A review with implications for classroom instruction. *The Elementary School Journal*, 85(1), 76–89. doi:10.1086/461393.

Cornelius-White, J. (2007). Learner-centered teacher-student relationships are effective: A meta-analysis. *Review of Educational Research*, 77(1), 113–143.

Dombey, H. (2013). *Teaching Writing: What the Evidence Says UKLA Argues for an Evidence-Informed Approach to Teaching and Testing Young Children's Writing*. Leicester: United Kingdom Lubricants Association.

Fu, D., and Shelton, N. (2007). Including students with special educational needs in writing workshop. *Language Arts*, 84(4), 325–336.

Gadd, M. (2014). *What is Critical in the Effective Teaching of Writing?* Auckland: The University Of Auckland.

Gillespie, A., and Graham, S. (2014). A meta-analysis of writing interventions for students with learning disabilities. *Exceptional Children*, 80, 454–473.

Glasswell, K., Parr, J., and McNaughton, S. (2003). Working with William: Teaching, learning, and the joint construction of a struggling writer. *The Reading Teacher*, 56(5), 494–500.

Graham, S., and Harris, K.R. (1994). Implications of constructivism for teaching writing to students with special needs. *The Journal of Special Education*, 28(3), 275–289.

Graham, S., Harris, K.R., and Troia, G. (2000). Self-regulated strategy development revisited: Teaching writing strategies to struggling writers. *Topics in Language Disorders*, 20(4), 1–14.

Graham, S., Harris, K.R., and Larsen, L. (2001). Prevention and intervention of writing difficulties for students with learning disabilities, *Learning Disability Research & Practice*, 16, 74–84.

Harris, M.J., and Rosenthal, R. (1985). Mediation of interpersonal expectancy effects: 31 meta-analyses. *Psychological Bulletin* 97, 363–386.

Helsel, L., and Greenberg, D. (2007). Helping struggling writers succeed: A self-regulated strategy instruction program. *The Reading Teacher*, 60(8), 752–760.

Hoewisch, A. (2001). 'Do I have to have a princess in my story?': Supporting children's writing of fairytales. *Reading and Writing Quarterly*, 17, 249–277.

Joseph, L., and Konrad, M. (2009). Teaching students with intellectual or developmental disabilities to write: A review of the literature. *Research in Developmental Disabilities*, 30, 1–19.

Laman, T. (2014). Transforming literate identities: Writing and multilingual children at work. *Talking Points*, 26(1), 2–10.

Leung, C., and Hicks, J. (2014). Writer identity and writing workshop a future teacher and teacher educator critically reflect. *Writing & Pedagogy*, 6, 1756–5839.

Marchisan, M., and Alber, S. (2001). The write way: Tips for teaching the writing process to resistant writers. *Intervention in School and Clinic*, 36(3), 154–162.

Miller, K., and Satchwell, C. (2006). The effect of beliefs about literacy on teacher and student expectations: A further education perspective. *Journal of Vocational Education and Training*, 58(2), 135–150.

Olinghouse, N.G., and Colwell, R.P. (2013). Preparing students with learning disabilities for large scale writing-assessment. *Intervention in School and Clinic*, 49(2), 67–76.

Olthouse, J. (2012). Why I write: What talented creative writers need their teachers to know. *Gifted Child Today*, 35(2), 117–121.

Paratore, J.R., and McCormack, R.L. (2009). Grouping in the middle and secondary grades: Advancing content and literacy knowledge. In *Literacy Instruction for Adolescents: Research-Based Practice*, Wood, K. D., and Blanton, W.E. (Eds.) (pp. 420–441). New York: The Guilford Press.

Parr, J., and Limbrick, L. (2010). Contextualising practice: Hallmarks of effective teachers of writing. *Teaching and Teacher Education*, (26), 583–590.

Perl, S., and Wilson, N. (1986). *Through Teacher's Eyes*. Portsmouth, NH: Heinemann.

Reutzel, D.R. (2007). Organizing effective literacy instruction: Differentiating instruction to meet the needs of all children. In *Best Practices in Literacy Instruction*, Gambrell, L.B., Morrow, L.M., and Pressley, M. (Eds.) (pp. 313–434). New York: The Guilford Press.

Rubie-Davies, C.M. (2010). Teacher expectations and perceptions of student attributes: Is there a relationship? *British Journal of Educational Psychology*, 80(1), 121–135.

Satchwell, C. (2019). Collaborative writing with young people with disabilities: Raising new questions of authorship and agency. *Literacy*, 53(2), 77–85.

Schumm, J.S., and Avalos, M.A. (2009). Responsible differentiated instruction for the adolescent learner. In Literacy Instruction for Adolescents: Research-Based Practice, Wood, K.D., and Blanton, W.E. (Eds.) (pp. 144–169). New York: The Guilford Press.

Thompson, N. (2018). When learning to write isn't easy. In *Understanding and Supporting Young Writers from Birth to 8*, Mackenzie, N., and Scull, J. (Eds.) (pp. 245–265). London: Routledge.

Troia, G.A., Lin, S.C., Monroe, B.W., and Cohen, S. (2009). The effects of writing workshop instruction on the performance and motivation of good and poor writers. In *Instruction and Assessment for Struggling Writers*, Troia, G.A. (Ed.) (pp. 77–112). New York: Guilford Press.

Young, R. (2019). *What is it 'writing for pleasure' teachers do that makes the difference?* The University of Sussex: The Goldsmiths' Company [Online]. Available: www.writing4pleasure.com.

Young, R., and Ferguson, F. (2020). *Real-World Writers: A Handbook for Teaching Writers with 7–11 Year Olds*. London: Routledge.

Young, R., and Kaufman, D. (2020). *Writing With Children At Home* Available: https://writing4pleasure.com/supporting-children-writing-at-home.

CHAPTER

13

Read, share, think, and talk about writing

The value of talk in the writing community

The renowned linguist Michael Halliday (2013, p. 93) once wrote that 'when children learn language, they are not simply engaging in one type of learning among many; rather, they are learning the foundations of learning itself'. His words are reiterated in the many studies of children's classroom talk carried out over the past few decades. The present chapter considers how classroom talk about writing contributes to the sense of a community of writers and increases children's self-efficacy (Cremin 2006; Dyson 1989, 1997, 2000; Dix 2016), and particularly how in the *Writing For Pleasure* pedagogy it is important at every stage of a young writer's process.

James Britton (1970) famously said that writing takes place floating on a sea of talk, and Green et al. (2008) engagingly say that children must be allowed to talk their texts into being. Writing and talk blend together. For anyone involved in writing teaching to overlook this vital connection would be extremely concerning, since writing, like life, is an inherently social and communicative activity. It is a sociocultural process, taking place as it so often does in socially constructed establishments and contexts. It cannot be said to be a solitary activity even if apparently carried out alone, since the writer is always in some way involved with their implied or future readership, and will also, consciously or not, be employing the phenomenon called intertextuality, the continual referencing of and conversation with other texts, both spoken and written (Bourne 2002). Intertextuality helps us to see that all writing is in some sense collaborative. The specific nature and kinds of social collaboration through talk in the classroom is the focus of this chapter.

In the same way that, through language, knowledge is held, shared, and jointly constructed amongst members of a community (Mercer et al. 1999; Rojas-Drummond et al. 2008), so talk, used productively, can support and sustain our first principle of creating a writing community (see Chapter 11). Talk links the teacher, their apprentice writers and the writing, since the communal sharing and discussion of ideas encourages and satisfies the desire to be part of the larger literacy community (Parr et al. 2009; Leung and Hicks 2014; Dix 2016). It is important to remember, however, that thinking is an inherent part of the writing process. As Cremin and Myhill (2012) remind us, talking, thinking, and writing support each other. Thinking can be like talking to ourselves; we think as we write and writing can help us think through ideas and clarify our thoughts. They offer a discussion of how the (often naturally) applied strategy of 'oral rehearsal' – reading aloud your latest written paragraph or sentence to yourself or another person – provides time to think about and evaluate the quality or meaningfulness of what you have written, and a space for thinking how to continue. A *Writing For Pleasure* teacher will therefore be very concerned to give young writers strategies and ample time for thinking.

Dialogic teaching

The influential concept of dialogic teaching is informed by the ideas of Vygotsky (1978), Bakhtin (1986), and Bruner (1996). The most well-known contemporary exponent of the subject is Robin Alexander (2003). He considers dialogic approaches to teaching and learning in the classroom and defines them as:

- **Collective** – involving the group or class.
- **Reciprocal** – where ideas are shared on an equal basis.
- **Supportive** – where no one is afraid to seek or offer help.
- **Cumulative** – where ideas are exchanged and built on.

Reasoning, discussion, exchange of ideas, explaining, and reaching agreements are all components of dialogic talk and teaching. Both Mercer and Littleton (2007) and Rojas-Drummond et al. (2008) suggest that educational success – and failure – may be partly accounted for by the quality of the educational dialogues taking place in the classroom. In a number of research studies, for example in Mercer et al. (1999), dialogic talk has been shown to have a positive impact on children's problem-solving ability in the domains of maths, science, and logical reasoning, and some other studies have found that dialogic talk also has a positive influence on the quality of primary-aged children's writing. A report carried out by Jay et al. (2017) evaluated the effect of a dialogic approach to teaching on classroom talk and on raising attainment in maths, science, and literacy. The researchers concluded that, compared to control schools, children in dialogic teaching schools not only made gains in confidence, participation, and engagement but also showed two additional months' progress in English.

Exploratory talk

Exploratory talk, expounded by Mercer (1995, 2000) and Mercer et al. (1999), is embedded in dialogic teaching. It is essentially an interaction between peers which is both critical and constructive; it may contain challenge and counter-challenge, but the desired outcome is agreement and joint progress based on reasoned discussion and mutual consideration of different points of view. The social and collaborative nature of sharing knowledge, evaluating proposals, and considering options in a thoughtful and democratic way gives this type of talk and thinking significant educational value.

However, research studies consistently state that exploratory talk does not occur naturally but needs to be taught. The issue of *learning to collaborate* as well as collaborating to learn (Rojas-Drummond et al. 2008) will be discussed in the penultimate section of this chapter.

The kinds of talk expected in *Writing For Pleasure* classrooms

It will be easily understood why dialogic and exploratory talk is an integral part of the *Writing For Pleasure* pedagogy, which is based on the creation of an inclusive and respectful writing community where the contributions of all members, including those of the teacher, are shared, received, and discussed in a considerate, positive, and constructive way (Whittick 2020). Children will be regularly publishing their own texts and responding to their peers' on-going writing, sharing their techniques, strategies, and ways of negotiating the writing processes with their teacher and other members of the writing class (Dix 2016). These procedures are entirely in keeping with our second principle of creating a classroom where both teacher and students treat and define themselves and others as writers.

As we have said, writing is always in some sense collaborative, and markedly so in the primary classroom. Gibson (2008) and Dix (2016) state that teachers engage in collaboration with their pupils through the creation of apprenticeships which offer opportunities to learn through guided practice and participatory talk. It is important to say here that talk is necessary and relevant at all points in a writer's process (Young and Ferguson 2020). For example, children can talk to generate ideas (Gibson 2008; Fisher 2010), plan collaboratively, rehearse orally during drafting (Myhill 2010), and teach writing process strategies to other children (Gibson 2008). 'Author's chair' is an opportunity for writers to take centre stage when work is ready to be published or performed (Atwell 2014; Gibson 2008). The following sections of this chapter describe the different kinds of talk interactions and relationships between participants which happen in a *Writing For Pleasure* community.

Explicit and direct instruction

Gibson (2008) says all writers need instruction. Our own research (Young 2019) clearly showed that apprentice writers need and want high-quality instruction from knowledgeable writer-teachers. Explicit teaching is therefore an important part of *Writing For Pleasure* practice. Within a contemporary writing workshop structure (Young and Ferguson 2020), direct instruction from the teacher, planned according to the needs of the class, mostly takes place during mini-lessons and generally focuses on functional grammar study, writing techniques, the writer's craft, and strategies for managing the different processes, which children are then invited to try out in their writing that day (see Chapter 17). The teacher expertly models, often with the help of short written exemplars, and then withdraws to allow students to discuss and make decisions about how and when to apply the instruction's message that day, thus fostering self-efficacy and the independent application of taught skills and processes. Instruction in the mini-lesson is short, specific, and therefore efficient in terms of allowing children maximum time for writing, and is most effective when the intended learning is generalizable to future writing situations.

Interactions between writer-teacher and apprentice writers

Other types of teacher instruction will have a more dialogic nature as 'expertly delivered instructional conversations' (Gibson 2008, p. 324) in which the writer-teacher scaffolds the development of pupils' understanding and knowledge from the position of someone who, for the time being, is the most experienced writer, though not necessarily the best. This kind of dialogic teaching offers and promotes discussion of strategies and techniques derived from what writers actually do; for example, showing how intertextuality works to link reading and writing, or how writing is a process of design where the writer can first try out and then select from a number of structural and linguistic possibilities. Teachers are only able to take part in authentic dialogues and conversations about writing if they write themselves. Being a writer-teacher is of paramount importance in *Writing For Pleasure* practice and is discussed in Chapter 21. Another kind of conversation is the teacher–pupil conference, which will be given its own dedicated focus in Chapter 22.

Talk about writing between teacher and pupils is at its most social, community affirming, constructive and dialogic when it is also reciprocal; the talk is that of writer to writer and happens in *Writing For Pleasure* classrooms when teacher and pupils share their own writing products, processes, and writing problems with one another and recommend strategies which have helped them reach their writing goals in the past. As Paolo Freire (1996) observes, the teacher too will be taught by being in dialogue, and no one person is ever in authority all of the time. In his championing of the democratic classroom, Freire promotes the practical and pragmatic notion of pupils actively requesting the instruction they feel they need, ensuring that the teaching they receive is entirely relevant and will move their writing on.

Bringing metacognitive knowledge to consciousness: making the implicit explicit

Children's ability to reflect both on the written product and on the thinking behind their own writing processes is known to be important for attainment (Fisher et al. 2010). Metacognitive knowledge – the knowledge of oneself as a learner and in this context as a writer – must be brought to conscious awareness and a shared metalanguage developed, a vocabulary in which to think about, articulate, and communicate one's intentions to others (Larkin 2010). Employing the language of metacognition enables children to draw on their previous experiences of strategies which helped them achieve their writing goals, thereby increasing self-efficacy and self-regulation (Parr et al. 2009). There are many practical ways of helping children even as young as six develop metacognition and the associated linguistic terminology (Fisher et al. 2010). A major strategy is for the teacher to model the metalanguage and ways of talking, including:

- Using open questions: how, what, why did you ..., can you tell me more about ...
- Modelling the language of thinking: guess, know, believe, imagine, and think.
- Discussing themselves as writers, their writing processes, and sharing ideas about who and what a writer is.
- Collectively compiling lists of product goals and creating checklists, resources, displays, and rubrics (see Chapter 16).

Collaborative talking and writing between peers

Learners need opportunities to talk and write collaboratively and co-operatively with each other (Hoogeveen 2012; Whittick 2020). Working in this way not only helps them to engage more in writing projects, but also to become more self-regulated (Gibbs and Poskitt 2010). Collaborative talking broadly takes place between peers in the following situations:

- Joint collaborative writing when a text is co-authored.
- Pupil seeking support through peer conferencing from a response partner.
- Pupils sharing their writing with a peer group or the whole class.

Little research appears to have been done with regard to children cross-teaching or co-authoring texts. However, McQuitty (2014) points out that having two participants sharing authorship may facilitate generating ideas, building content, and evaluating the writing. In their study of how peer co-authorship can enhance classroom-based writing opportunities (story writing and poetry), Vass et al. (2008) report that, contrary to expectations, overlaps and interruptions between writers in fact indicated that a shared focus was being maintained on the writing processes and on the mutual goal. Recalling Britton, they use a child participant's analogy of 'ripple thinking' to describe how ideas build collaboratively on each other, becoming ever richer and ever expanding like ripples on water.

Research has tended to focus on the more frequently occurring critical and constructive interaction between peers, when a response partner or another class member supports an individual child in their writing, acting on behalf of the future reader (Nystrand et al. 1993; Bourne 2002). As Rojas-Drummond et al. (2008) have pointed out, collaborative talking and writing, if achieved productively, is essentially dialogic and intertextual since several participants are involved, each bringing unique insights and ideas to the construction of their friend's text. Cremin and Myhill (2012) have enumerated the things that may be happening during peer support, including:

- Learning strategies from each other.
- Gaining more thinking time to shape ideas and to consider and select from a number of sentences and vocabulary items.
- Reduction of the cognitive load.
- Adjusting their texts to the needs of their audience.
- Participants using a metalanguage to ensure mutual understanding.

One example of this can be found in Young and Ferguson's work (2020) where they recommend that children reread their developing compositions with their peers and ask them to act as 'future readers'. They suggest that the writer asks two questions: where does your 'reading tummy' rumble for more detail or information? Where might your tummy be too full? This is just one very small example of how children can work together to anticipate how their writing will be received by their audiences, where they need to provide more detail so as to avoid misunderstanding, and where less detail is required for the sake of the reader!

Myhill (2010) discusses oral rehearsal, the kind of inner conversation or review we have with ourselves when writing. This is something we as writers all do when we read aloud the phrase or sentence we have just written, giving ourselves pause to think, evaluate, and consider how to proceed. She describes how it is beneficial when used as a strategy to support paired writing in the classroom, becoming the means whereby the writer and others can hear the voice of the text. In their other work, Young and Ferguson (2020) discuss how children should be explicitly taught to read and talk about their developing compositions out loud to themselves or others at regular intervals during writing time until it becomes an utterly natural behaviour.

Lessons in talking

As we have said, sharing and talk should take place at all points in a writer's process, and so far, we have presented the most positive and constructive aspects of it. However, as Schneider (2003) points out, unskilful conferencing by a peer can result in a writer feeling vulnerable and alienated from the writing community. Therefore, talk must be used in a productive, exploratory, and dialogic way in order to avoid such scenarios, support writing, and maintain individual wellbeing and group cohesion. Dix (2016) places the responsibility firmly on the teacher to be the enabler and modeller of talk for thinking and learning. The need for pupils to be explicitly taught how to think and talk collaboratively is reiterated in many studies (Ruttle 2004; Rojas-Drummond et al. 2008; Dix 2016).

Investigating the influence of peer response, at a basic level, in a class of six-year-olds, Dix and Cawkwell (2011) found that introducing to children the system of a star (giving a compliment) and a wish (asking the author an open question) constructively helped writers to undertake revision of their pieces in a positive way. In an experimental teaching programme carried out with nine and ten-year-olds by Mercer et al. (1999), children were given lessons and explicit guidance from their teachers in how to engage in exploratory talk, which included the following elements:

- Discussing.
- Deep listening.
- Open questioning.
- Willingness to change one's mind.
- Thinking before speaking.
- Reaching a final agreement.

- Constructing a set of ground rules for exploratory talk to be displayed in the classroom as a poster.

While this study focused on children's reasoning skills, these techniques for dialogic talking can readily be applied in the area of collaborative writing. Finally, Cremin and Myhill (2012) have formulated EASE, a response framework which can be taught to pupils through discussion and teacher modelling and involves:

- **E**xpression of engagement.
- **A**ppreciation of the writer's achievements.
- **S**uggestion for improvement.
- **E**xtension ideas and strategies.

Sharing and Author's Chair

Sharing their writing every day ensures children are continually faced with the fact that they have to consider and attend seriously to readers' demands (Corden 2002). A particular sharing strategy employed in the classrooms observed in our own research (Young 2019) was entirely in keeping with the notion of a trusted community and was also very helpful for the young writers' writing process. Teachers simply asked children to find a page in their writing book which illustrated their successful achievement of a part of the writing process (generating an idea, a dabble, a page of revision, an example of editing, or a piece ready for publication). They then laid the open book on their table, and class members walked round and looked at each one. In this way, children showcased their own achievements and were able to learn from and be motivated by the successes of others.

In the contemporary writing workshop (Atwell 2014; Young and Ferguson 2020), Author's Chair takes place daily at the end of writing time and is an outlet for the desire and the need to share one's developing compositions. It provides a real and ready audience, an immediate response to the writing, allows writers to receive feedback, and celebrates achievement. As Cremin et al. (2005) note, the experience of receiving a genuine response from an interested reader makes a significant difference to reluctant writers, particularly boys, as does the satisfaction of having their work read aloud, shared, and enjoyed. Author's Chair also helps all writers develop awareness of their writer-identity and their own voice as authors through the prism of reading aloud and hearing others' responses. It creates an egalitarian space where all can contribute to the community. We found that it inspired confidence, encouraged social risk-taking, and strengthened social relations and group cohesion.

It is vital for all to know that negative and otherwise unproductive talk and responses to a child's shared writing is wholly unacceptable. In our vision of Author's Chair, a protocol for response is established and adhered to:

1. Give children time to consider what they might like to share.
2. Ask them to 'warm up the text' by explaining a little about the background behind it.

3   Ask the child whether there is anything in particular they would like the class to listen out for or any advice they would like to receive.
4   Allow the writer to read their whole piece or a particular extract from the writing.
5   Once the piece has been read out, invite someone in the class to explain briefly what they thought it was about.
6   Your last question should be whether anyone in the class feels they would like to give some feedback and advice. This is also an opportunity for you, as the writer-teacher, to give some advice on the written piece too.
7   It ends with applause for the writer.

(Young and Ferguson 2020, p. 72)

Interestingly, Chris White (2000) observed children in a strong writing community in a US elementary school having heated discussions during sharing sessions about the use of a preposition, the suitability of a phrase in a particular genre, and the credibility of a written account. His observation shows how many pathways can be opened up and explored through the sharing of written texts.

Examples of effective practice

In our research which observed *Writing For Pleasure* teachers (Young 2019), children were given ample opportunities to share and discuss with others (including their writer-teacher) their own and others' writing in order to give and receive constructive criticism, writerly advice, and celebrate achievement. One child reported 'he puts us in groups to help us understand how other people write'. Children often moved purposefully around the classroom to give support to a peer.

Writing was seen as a social act and talk was important at all stages of the writing process. Children were encouraged to talk to each other about the content of their writing, their writing processes, and to share any techniques or strategies they thought were working particularly well for them. The sophistication, maturity, and commitment children showed in their discussions about the developing compositions was striking. The writing communities had clearly developed their own metacognitive knowledge and metalanguage for talking and thinking as *writers*. Children discussed their planning, 'sticky bits', 'yawny bits', 'vomit drafts', 'paragraph piling', 'sentence stacking', and finding their 'diamond moments'. Sticky bits were parts that didn't sound quite right or didn't make sense. 'Yawny bits' were parts where the readers felt bored or were losing interest. 'Vomit drafts' were quick drafts which didn't slow down to attend to transcriptional issues. Instead, the children would revise and edit after completing the draft. 'Paragraph Pilers' drafted, revised, and edited each of their paragraphs before writing their next one. 'Sentence Stackers' did the same but focused on each sentence. Finally, 'Diamond moments' were the significant parts of their compositions. Whilst talk was an integral part of any writing time, so was maintaining a low level of noise so as not to disturb fellow writers.

Practical things you can do

- Give children ample opportunity to talk to one another and to you as writer-to-writer (Whittick 2020).
- Ensure that talk takes place throughout a writing project and not only during the production of idea generation or first drafts.
- Children can be encouraged to take notes of anything their peers have recommended to be changed or attended to.
- It's important that you model how to talk about writing through pupil conferencing (see Chapter 22).
- Encourage children to reflect together on how their developing compositions are attending to the distant and product goals for the class writing project (see Chapter 16).
- Allow children opportunities to read, respond, and be inspired by each other's published works.
- Discuss ground rules for talking and make these rules into a poster.
- Encourage periodic reading aloud to selves, teacher, or peer during writing time.
- Establish Author's Chair (Harris 2020).
- Teach a metalanguage for talking about writing.
- Give young writers an opportunity to observe, listen in and take notes as they hear two or more people read and discuss their writing.
- Provide books for the class library about writing and how to write.
- Agree and display protocols for yourself and children for response and sharing.

QUESTIONS WORTH ASKING YOURSELF

- Do you ever invite an unpublished 'writer' in? Could you use resources drawn from school staff, other school personnel, and the local community?
- Do children get a chance to 'talk their text into being'? Do they share ideas, use ideas from others (heard or read), and adapt them for themselves?
- Are there opportunities for dialogic talk? Keep a one-day diary of how long and how often talk was led by you.
- Do you encourage oral rehearsal as a strategy? Do you ever talk aloud as you write?
- How independent are the children during writing?
- Do all children engage in talk while writing? Is the talk always supportive?

References

Alexander, R. (2003). Oracy, literacy and pedagogy: International perspectives. In *Classroom Interactions in Literacy*, Bearne, E., Dombey, H., and Grainger, T. (Eds.). London: Open University Press.

Atwell, N. (2014). *In the Middle* (3rd Ed.). Portsmouth, NH: Heinemann.
Bakhtin, M. (1986). The problem with speech genres (V. McGee, Trans.). In *Speech Genres and Other Late Essays: M.M. Bakhtin*, Emerson, C., and Holquist, M. (Eds.) (pp. 60–102). Austin: University of Texas Press.
Bourne, J. (2002). Oh, what will Miss say!: Constructing texts and identities in the discursive processes of classroom writing. *Language and Education*, 16(4), 241–259.
Britton, J. (1970). *Language and Learning*. Harmondsworth, UK: Penguin.
Bruner, J. (1996). *The Culture of Education*. Massachusetts: Harvard University Press.
Corden, R. (2002). Developing reflective writers in primary schools: Findings from partnership research. *Educational Review*, 54(3), 249–276.
Cremin, T. (2006). Creativity, uncertainty and discomfort: Teachers as writers. *Cambridge Journal of Education*, 36(3), 415–433.
Cremin, T., and Myhill, D. (2012). *Creating Communities of Writers*. London: Routledge.
Cremin, T., Grainger, T., Goouch, K., and Lambirth, A. (2005). *Creativity and Writing: Developing Voice and Verve in the Classroom*. London: Routledge.
Dix, S. (2016). Teaching writing: A multilayered participatory scaffolding practice. *Literacy*, 50(1), 23–31.
Dix, S., and Cawkwell, G. (2011). The Influence of peer group response: Building a teacher and student expertise in the writing classroom. *English Teaching: Practice and Critique*, 10(4), 41–57.
Dyson, A.H. (1989). *Multiple Worlds of Child Writers: Friends Learning to Write*. New York: Teachers College Press.
Dyson, A.H. (1997). *Writing Superheroes: Contemporary Childhood, Popular Culture and Classroom Literacy*. New York: Teachers College Press.
Dyson, A.H. (2000). Writing and the sea of voices: Oral language in, around and about writing. In *Perspectives on Writing: Research Theory and Practice*, Indrisano, R., and Squires, J.R. (Eds.) (pp. 45–65). Newark, DL: International Reading Association.
Fisher, R. (2010). Talk to generate ideas. In *Using Talk to Support Writing*, Fisher, R., Myhill, D., Jones, S., and Larkin, S. (Eds.). London: Sage.
Fisher, R., Myhill, D., Jones, S., and Larkin, S. (2010). *Using Talk to Support Writing*. London: Sage.
Freire, P. (1996). *Pedagogy of the Oppressed* (2nd Ed.). London: Penguin Press.
Gibbs, R.S., and Poskitt, J.M. (2010). *Student Engagement in the Middle Years of Schooling (Years 7–10): A Literature Review*. Wellington, NZ: Ministry of Education. Retrieved from https://nzcurriculum.tki.org.nz/content/download/4911/70679/file/940_Student%20Engagement.pdf
Gibson, S. (2008). An effective framework for primary-grade guided writing instruction. *The Reading Teacher*, 62(4), 324–334.
Green, J., Yeager, B., and Castanheira, M. (2008). Talking texts into being: On the social construction of everyday life and academic knowledge in the classroom. In *Exploring Talk in School: Inspired by the Work of Douglas Barnes*, Mercer, N., and Hodgkinson, S. (Eds.) (pp. 115–130). London: Sage.
Halliday, M. (2013). *Introduction to Functional Grammar* (4th Ed.). London: Routledge.
Harris, B. (2020). *Author's chair* Available: https://writing4pleasure.com/authors-chair.
Hoogeveen, M. (2012). *Writing with Peer Response Using Genre Knowledge*. Thesis University of Twente. Available: https://ris.utwente.nl/ws/portalfiles/portal/6062163/thesis_M_Hoogeveen.pdf.
Jay, T., Taylor, R., Moore, N., Burnett, C., Merchant, G., Thomas, P., Willis, B., and Stevens, A. (2017). *Dialogic Teaching: Evaluation Report and Executive Summary*. London: Education Endowment Foundation.
Larkin, S. (2010). Talk for reflecting on writing. In *Using Talk to Support Writing*. London: Sage.
Leung, C., and Hicks, J. (2014). Writer identity and writing workshop a future teacher and teacher educator critically reflect. *Writing & Pedagogy*, 6(3), 1756–5839.

McQuitty, V. (2014). Process-oriented writing instruction in elementary classrooms: Evidence of effective practices from the research literature. *Writing & Pedagogy*, 6(3), 467–495.

Mercer, N. (1995). *The Guided Construction of Knowledge: Talk Amongst Teachers and Learners.* Clevedon, UK: Multilingual Matters.

Mercer, N. (2000). *Words and Minds: How We Use Language to Think Together.* London: Routledge.

Mercer, N., and Littleton, K. (2007). *Dialogue and the Development of Children's Thinking: A Sociocultural Approach.* London: Routledge.

Mercer, N., Wegerif, R., and Dawes, L. (1999). Children's talk and the development of reasoning in the classroom. *British Educational Research Journal*, 25, 95–111.

Myhill, D. (2010). Writing aloud: The role of oral rehearsal. In *Using Talk to Support Writing*, Fisher, R., Myhill, D., Jones, S., and Larkin, S. (Eds.). London: Sage.

Nystrand, M, Greene, S., and Wiemelt, J. (1993). Where did composition studies come from? An intellectual history. *Written Communication*, 10, 267–333.

Parr, J., Jesson, J., and McNaughton, S. (2009). Agency and platform: The relationships between talk and writing. In *The SAGE Handbook of Writing Development*. London: Sage.

Rojas-Drummond, S.M., Albarr'an, C.D., and Littleton, K.S. (2008). Collaboration, creativity and the co-construction of oral and written texts. *Thinking Skills and Creativity*, 3(3), 177–191.

Ruttle, K. (2004). What goes on inside my head when I'm writing? A case study of 8–9-year-old boys. *Literacy*, 38(2), 71–77.

Schneider, J. (2003). Contexts, genres, and imagination: An examination of the idiosyncratic writing performances of three elementary children within multiple contexts of writing instruction. *Research in the Teaching of English*, 37, 329–379.

Vass, E., Littleton, K., Miell, D., and Jones, A. (2008). The discourse of collaborative creative writing: Peer collaboration as a context for mutual inspiration. *Thinking Skills and Creativity*, 3(3), 192–202.

Vygotsky, L.S. (1978). *Thought and Language.* Cambridge, MA: MIT Press.

White, C. (2000). Strategies are not enough. *Education 3-13*, 28(1), 16–21.

Whittick, L. (2020). *Write a little – share a little* [Available: https://writing4pleasure.com/write-a-little-share-a-little/]

Young, R. (2019). *What is it 'writing for pleasure' teachers do that makes the difference?* The University of Sussex: The Goldsmiths' Company [Online]. Available: www.writing4pleasure.com.

Young, R., and Ferguson, F. (2020). *Real-World Writers: A Handbook for Teaching Writing with 7–11 Year Olds.* London: Routledge.

CHAPTER 14

Pursue authentic and purposeful writing projects

What is authentic, purposeful, and meaningful writing?

In her article aptly entitled *Keeping It Real*, Whitney (2017, p. 21) writes 'I want the life in my classroom to be lived. I want us to be a group of real people doing real work. I pray that nothing we do in my classroom is "as good as it's going to get." Instead I want what we do with students to be just a beginning. To be a provocation toward full engagement with themselves and their world'. So what is this 'real work', and what do we mean when we say that children should be writing authentically?

Behizadeh (2014) offers a definition of authentic writing as being the outcome of a child's judgement of the connection between a writing project and their life. A significant number of research studies on the subject express a broad but compelling consensus of opinion. For example:

- Splitter (2009) argues that authenticity is subjective and that children deserve to understand and be in agreement with why they are undertaking a class writing project.
- Bruning and Horn (2000) state that, although much theory and practical research strongly recommends authentic writing projects, teachers do not often inquire as to what the students themselves would wish a class project to be and for whom. They suggest that teachers should not assume that their own conceptions of authentic writing will always be the same as those of the pupil-writers in their class.
- Wiggins (2009) states that writing is authentic when it makes a difference, achieves a real-world result, has consequences, and is written with a very specific audience in mind.
- Purcell-Gates et al. (2007) claim that it is the genre and purpose of writing which determine its authenticity. Specifically, a project is authentic if the genre exists in the world outside the classroom, and when the purpose is the same as if the child were writing outside of school.

- Locke (2015 suggests that if a writing project is to be meaningful and motivating, it must be relevant to the student's world, have reference to previous writing projects, and have a legitimate purpose and a genuine anticipated audience at its end. Gadd and Parr (2016) add that projects such as these contribute to children's present and future writing development.
- Gambrell et al. (2011) claim that authentic writing projects are similar to those people encounter in their daily lives. 'Schooled' activities, for example completing worksheets or answering teacher-posed questions, they claim, have no such authenticity.
- Behizadeh (2018) asserts that both genre and purpose must have real-world relevance and be valued outside of school. To be meaningful, a writing project must allow children to make a connection in some way with their own lives – their experiences, culture, interests, knowledge, and goals.

Finally, Whitney's answer to the question is that 'authenticity means not pretending' (2017, p. 16).

Authentic and purposeful writing projects have the power to secure young writers' engagement and significantly contribute to positive academic achievements (Frank 2001; Gadd and Parr 2016; Behizadeh 2018; Boscolo and Gelati 2019). These outcomes are the result of the projects' capacity to bring together the rigour and objectives of a school curriculum and children's personal and social interests and knowledge. Children who are able to write on topics they are interested in, personally committed to, and knowledgeable about write better and pay more attention to learning about writing (Solsken et al. 2000; Hidi and Renninger 2006; Boscolo and Hidi 2006; McCutchen 2011; Olinghouse et al. 2015). If writing projects do not take advantage of pupils' resources, funds of knowledge, identities, and interests the result may be that they underachieve academically and are less likely to enjoy writing (Maloch 2005; Clark and Teravainen 2017; Young 2019; Dyson 2020).

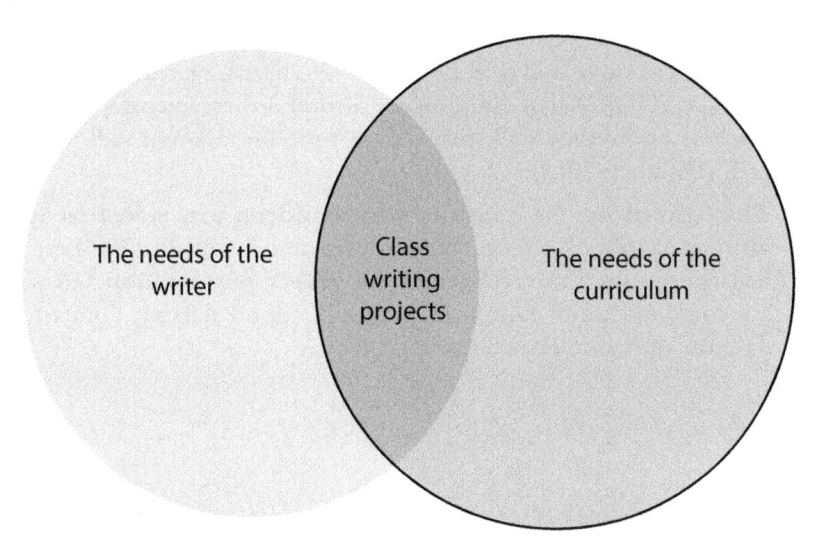

FIGURE 14.1 What the authors call a sincere writing curriculum where whole class writing projects are driven by the needs of the curriculum but are supported by the knowledge, identity, interests and needs of the young writer too. Ultimately, these two circles completely overlap, becoming one.

Authentic class writing projects

Writing For Pleasure teachers ensure projects are authentic in a number of ways:

- **They give children agency over choice of topic.** Leung and Hicks (2014) state that giving children agency over choosing subjects for writing stimulates their very natural desire to express themselves and their identities (Graves 1983; Calkins, 1994; Szczepanski 2003). *Writing For Pleasure* teachers will help children by suggesting and offering strategies for generating ideas (Grainger et al. 2005; Young and Ferguson 2020). It is expected that topics will sail around the class, and groups of ideas will begin to emerge through sharing, writing, and conversations. Agency is discussed in more detail in Chapter 6.

- **They welcome children's own funds of knowledge into the classroom.** In Garrett and Moltzen's (2011) study, high-achieving writers reported high levels of satisfaction, enjoyment, volition, and motivation when they were afforded the opportunity to write about their 'funds of knowledge' and 'funds of identity'. The writers wrote about personal experiences, knowledge, urges, concerns, passions, and their issues of significance from an early age. *Writing For Pleasure* teachers know that all children benefit from drawing on their funds of knowledge and identity.

- **They allow children to construct their own imaginative writing projects.** For example, Young and Ferguson (2020) suggest ways in which children can be encouraged to consider and create for themselves their own 'faction', storytelling and other imaginative projects.

- **They involve children in the construction of a project.** According to Gadd and Parr (2016), the most effective teachers of writing know that children find pleasure in class writing projects when they are able to participate meaningfully in their conception and production, and when they know that their writing has value and will be used, seen, heard, or read by genuine audiences (Hickey 2003). When children are afforded these writing opportunities, their teachers know they will spend more time on task and will enjoy writing as a craft (Dombey 2013).

- **They promote the reasons why children are *moved* to write.** In their writing handbook for teachers, Young and Ferguson (2020, pp. 4–7) suggest that reasons such as: teach, entertain, reflect, give opinion and persuade, make a record, and 'paint with words' provide good starting points for teachers to develop authentic class writing projects.

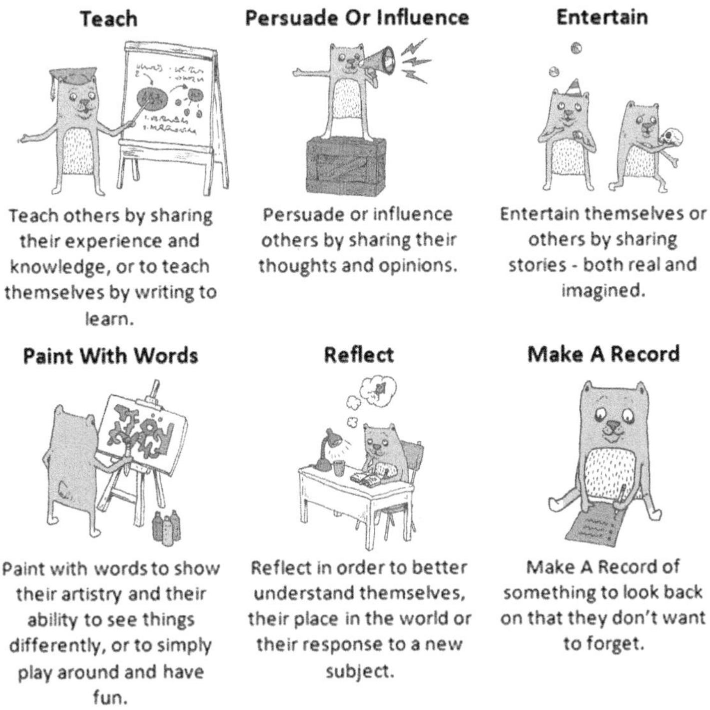

Teach

Teach others by sharing their experience and knowledge, or to teach themselves by writing to learn.

Persuade Or Influence

Persuade or influence others by sharing their thoughts and opinions.

Entertain

Entertain themselves or others by sharing stories - both real and imagined.

Paint With Words

Paint with words to show their artistry and their ability to see things differently, or to simply play around and have fun.

Reflect

Reflect in order to better understand themselves, their place in the world or their response to a new subject.

Make A Record

Make A Record of something to look back on that they don't want to forget.

FIGURE 14.2 The reasons children are moved to write as realised by Young and Ferguson (2020, pp. 4–7).

■ **They highlight for children the features of meaningful texts.** According to Breetvelt et al. (1994) and Halliday (2013), good writers are able to understand writing projects from a purpose and audience perspective, and Flower and Hayes (1981) found that the best young writers were those who wrote with a clear audience in mind. They also noted that poorer writers tended to concentrate on the content material. Therefore, *Writing For Pleasure* teachers remind children of the following important considerations as they engage in authentic and purposeful class writing projects. Children's attention to these features is essential if they are to write meaningfully, with purpose, and to realise their intentions. We describe these features in more detail in Chapter 16 but include them below not only because they are relevant but also because they demonstrate the interconnectedness of setting writing goals and writing authentically and purposefully.

1. **Pragmatics** – We know that the context in which we are writing affects in profound ways what we write and how we write it, and we are continually attentive to this fact as we craft.

- **Field** – We think about the subject matter of our piece and what content our future readership is likely to want, respond to, appreciate, or need.

- **Tenor** – We think about the relationship between ourselves as the writer, and our future audience, the readers. Are they more or less powerful than us? Are they younger or older? Are they more or less experienced or knowledgeable? Do their tastes, interests, opinions, and experiences match ours, or not? Are our cultures and terms of reference vastly different or the same? How does this affect what I'm crafting?
- **Mode** – We think about the aesthetics of our writing. How will it be laid out? Will we use other artefacts to supplement the writing? Will we use other devices such as tables, illustrations, photographs, or film? Will it be published electronically? Will it be performed?
2 **Semantics and syntax** – We consider carefully the words and phrases we use to ensure we get our meaning across to our audience.
3 **Graphophonics** – We are conscious of how our writing sounds and what it looks like.

Lack of authentic and purposeful writing in schools

Inauthentic writing, as set by many practitioners who have unfortunately misunderstood or ignored the concept of true authenticity, is writing which has no purpose or audience beyond compliance on the part of the students and is intended solely for the teacher's evaluation. Edelsky and Smith (1984) also question the belief that children are able to transfer what they learn from these inauthentic writing tasks into future real writing.

Writing in school is often arbitrarily harnessed to a task or a text chosen by the teacher, or in some cases even by the writers of a purchased scheme (Knight 2009; Dutro 2010). Many research studies agree that teacher-assigned topics which work against authentic writing have serious consequences. John Dixon warns that 'ideally, no pupil should be given an assignment which does not yield them enough fruit in their own terms, so that he can feel it is worth doing' (1967, p. 78). Children must value and have investment in their writing. Bereiter and Scardamalia (1987, p. 360) reflect that 'an arbitrarily assigned topic, with an error-hunting teacher as the sole audience, may do little for the writer, whereas a topic the writer cares about and an audience responsive to what the writer has to say are the essential ingredients for a profitable experience'. Children too often see themselves as passive receivers of writing subjects and as a result become disengaged and feel disenfranchised (Hoewisch 2001; Langer 2001; Grainger et al. 2003; Dyson 2020). In 1982, Donald Graves warned that when we *assign* topics, we do no less than create a welfare system, putting children, our students, on to writers' welfare. Willinsky (1990, p. 209) goes as far as to say that 'to diminish the potential for individual meaningfulness in students' work is a denial of their basic humanity', while Gutiérrez (2008) concludes that the imposition of such writing tasks can be acts of linguistic oppression.

Another key finding is the remarkable strength of feeling voiced by children about freedom and autonomy when writing. In a study by Grainger et al. (2003), pupils described experiencing pleasure and enjoyment when a degree of choice and personal responsibility was offered. As is discussed in Chapter 15, when given choice *and* a level of self-regulation over their writing processes, children's attitudes can change significantly. Children's desire for more control over content, form, and writing approach is repeated in many studies such as those of Graves (1982), Pollard et al. (1994), and Grainger et al. (2003). Our own research (Young 2019) notes that agency and self-regulation feature highly in pupils' views about the optimal conditions for learning and are closely related to writing for pleasure. However, despite the evidence, choice and the chance to write authentically are still rare commodities in schools.

In 1988, Wray and colleagues made the claim that children had little motivation to write because:

- They had been made to feel that they had nothing to say.
- They had been made to feel they did not write well and were discouraged by their final writing products.
- They did not engage in writing regularly enough to see it as a natural and powerful progression from talking.
- They were tired of repeating the same tasks without a meaningful purpose.
- They felt that interesting events and learning in school were often turned into arbitrary writing tasks with little opportunity for voice or personal response.
- They felt that, after all their efforts, nobody took real notice of what they had written.

Over 30 years later, these claims are still worth reflecting on.

Writing For Pleasure teachers will concur with Graves' (1983) view that, if children feel that their writing is their personal *property*, they are far more likely to take care of it than if they are in the position of having to *rent* a writing task from the authority figure of the classroom. They understand that children will pay more attention to the compositional and transcriptional aspects of the writing process when they have invested a part of themselves in it (Edelsky and Smith 1984; Grainger et al. 2005; Young and Ferguson 2020). They know children want their writing to be the best it can be.

Whitney (2017, p. 19) warns teachers against creating pseudo-authentic writing tasks with ill-defined and contrived goals. As she explains, 'we've all heard the advice to have students write for authentic audiences. But the truth is that too many times, even when we try to follow that advice, we accidentally end up just having students pretend to write for someone other than us. So our students write letters to the school board about lunch or the parking lot, but do we really deliver the letters? Is there a conversation with members of the board afterward?' Beard (2000, p. 89) adds: 'children can write letters to the man on the moon. They can write a diary of the classroom hamster. They can write warning notices designed for sites of nuclear waste. The outcomes from such tasks may look effective and may provide useful practice in following conventions. Nevertheless, without the use of an underlying rationale … such writing may only have short-term value'. Young and Ferguson (2020) point out that the main issue with these types of projects is not the imaginative aspect, as writers write imaginatively all the time, but rather who conceived the imaginative idea and why. If the topic is solely the brainchild of a teacher or scheme, it can result in feelings of 'enforced fun'. The alternative of course is to uphold the principle of inviting children to put forward their own imaginative ideas for class writing projects and for teachers to be responsive to them.

Links to building a writing community

By creating a community of writers, teachers promote children's writing voices and their motivation to write (White 2000; Flint and Fisher 2014). A writing community empowers children to share more about their lives, beliefs, interests, and expertise with one another and enables each one to feel that they have a place and a valuable contribution to make to the class (Dyson 2003; Flint and Fisher 2014; Subero et al. 2016). This feeling can increase children's understanding of social power, cultural capital, and what it is to be a recognised participant in classroom culture (Maloch 2005, Young et al. *in press*). Gadd (2014) suggests that the sense of membership can manifest itself practically, with teachers generating and agreeing upon a class writing project idea with the whole class community. In such a community, and with opportunities for purposeful writing, explicit instruction given by teachers is felt to be more relevant, and thus the teaching–learning process is improved (Flint and Fisher 2014). White (2000) suggests that effective writing teaching involves teachers sharing a common starting point before giving children room to claim ownership over the project. In this way, teachers and children can learn, teach, and write in partnership; teachers maintain an acceptable amount of structure and order in which to teach whilst children have sufficient ownership and agency in which to learn. Flint and Laman (2012) also conclude that by offering this kind of authentic, meaningful, and sincere writing curriculum, real differences are seen in children's academic outcomes. However, despite this being well known, it is unfortunate and a missed opportunity that, for many teachers and commercial providers, there continues to be a gap between what is understood as best practice and what is actually implemented in classrooms.

Finally, we suggest that authentic and purposeful class writing projects are ultimately an apprenticeship for undertaking personal writing projects. The knowledge and skills acquired through authentic and purposeful whole-class projects generates in children an individual interest in pursuing personal writing projects (Hidi and Renninger 2006; Young and Ferguson 2020). For more information about personal writing projects, go to Chapter 18.

Examples of effective practice

In our research which reported on exceptional teachers of writing (Young 2019), it was observed that they carefully considered the meaningfulness, future audience, and purpose for their class writing projects. Children were given the opportunity to generate their own ideas and there was a clear distant goal for the writing to be published, with a strong sense of a real reader at the end of the project. For example, children in one class were writing their own anthology of short stories which would be published and placed in their class library for others to read. Given these circumstances, writers remained focused on developing their compositions over time, maintained a strong personal agency over and commitment to their writing, and so produced something significant for themselves and in keeping with their teacher's expectations. In short, the children cared about their writing and wanted it to do well. These writing projects were worked on by the class over an extended period of time. One teacher in particular took great pains to ensure the writing projects reflected as closely as possible the kinds of projects undertaken by writers outside of the classroom (Young and Ferguson 2020). Their classes had access to a variety of audiences over the course of the year and the children's writing escaped the confines of the classroom and was 'put to work' out in the world.

Agency played an important role within these writing projects, with children stating 'we don't have to write what the teacher says. It's actually better if you choose what you're going to write because you know what you're going to write about' and 'there is a day where we do idea generation and we think of loads of ideas and then we pick one we want to write about. It's not really strict that you have to write about that one. You can choose'. The teachers varied where they gave children agency, with one teacher exposing their class to a genre, discussing its typical purpose and potential audiences, and then allowing children to consider how they would like to use it for their own purposes. Other teachers gave children scope within a set topic or theme to choose what they would write about. However, it was understood by everyone that having responsibility over the topic for writing gave children a greater sense of self-efficacy; they were more confident using ideas from their existing 'funds of knowledge' and ones they had a personal commitment to, in contrast to having a topic chosen for them by the teacher. This is evidenced in comments such as 'mainly what we are writing is about our world and I love it'. The classes were encouraged to either generate their own individual ideas, share and work on ideas in clusters, or as a whole class generate an idea that they could all pursue together.

Teachers regularly refocused the children on considering the future readership of their piece throughout the project. Children were encouraged to look forward to the publishing of their pieces. 'I normally share my writing and I want it to be reader-ready and really good for them; when we publish it, it is put in our library in the classroom and that's cool … when we had free reading time, everyone went to the published writing – not the proper books'.

Practical things you can do

- Discuss with children what they believe to be authentic reasons for writing and find out what class writing projects children would like to pursue.
- Plan class writing projects around a future purpose, audience, and the production of a handwritten or electronic writing product or performance. Ensuring there is time to sit down and discuss the project with your class is an effective teaching strategy and can result in young writers producing better quality texts (van den Bergh and Rijlaarsdam 2001).
- Begin to see writing projects as being on an 'authenticity continuum' rather than either/or. This might help you consider how you could make a writing project *more* authentic. You can also give more 'leeway' to children when they are generating ideas and allow them to go off topic if it appears that a particular line of enquiry could be fruitful.
- Ensure there is variety in who children publish for. They should publish both for people they will meet and those they will never meet. Younger audiences and older ones, informed audiences, and ignorant ones, readers in authority and positions of power and those who need support and a voice.

- Ensure that children's published writing is accessible in the class or school library or elsewhere in the school and local community. Make sure the writing isn't simply there for display purposes but is actually going to 'get to work' and meet readers.
- Reflect on whether you are actually setting pseudo-authentic tasks which don't need a real audience. How might you be able to adapt these tasks to serve a legitimate purpose and audience?
- Allow children to use their 'funds of knowledge' from outside school in their class writing projects instead of always providing the 'funds of knowledge' yourself (see Chapter 23).
- Encourage children to notice where they see people writing outside of school.
- Understand that children will need to be taught the strategies and techniques writers employ when generating ideas for themselves, particularly if they have been brought up on a diet of 'back to basics' writing instruction (Young and Ferguson 2020). Create a community of writers where these writing ideas can be generated collaboratively as a whole class, in groups, pairs, or as individuals, and make them publicly available to be taken up and used as children wish.
- The best authentic writing experiences, as discussed in Chapter 2, are ones which merge writing as a pleasurable experience with writing for the pleasure of gaining satisfaction in sharing a final written product. This involves the writing having an impact on others. As we see in Chapter 2, if young writers know there is an authentic outcome for their writing, they will engage in the writing processes in an authentic and focused way too (Behizadeh 2018).
- Begin to reflect on the erroneous assumption that although children might enjoy authentic writing more, they won't learn and demonstrate the skills required in the curriculum. The reality is that, when children's desire for authentic writing is honoured, they write with much greater commitment, care, and attention and so are more likely to succeed in any high-stakes writing assessments. Research demonstrates that authentic writing instruction is effective writing instruction (Graham and Perin 2007; Dombey 2013; Morizawa 2014; Gadd and Parr 2016).

QUESTIONS WORTH ASKING YOURSELF

- Are your class writing projects sincere? Do they have a final destination? Do they serve a real purpose and reach an audience?
- Are your writing projects teacher-assigned, teacher-directed, or teacher-suggested? Do your class writing projects begin with a class discussion about the purpose and future audience for the finished pieces? Are children asked for their thoughts about the project's aims and outcomes? Do they have a say?
- Do children feel they have ownership over their writing ideas and their writing processes?
- Is idea generation part of your class' writing process? Are children allowed to use their own ideas within a class project?

- Do children know what the term 'publishing' means?
- Is publication or performance part of your class' writing process?
- Does children's published writing meet a variety of audiences and serve a variety of purposes over the course of their time with you?

References

Beard, R. (2000). *Developing Writing 3–13*. London: Hodder & Stoughton.

Behizadeh, N. (2014). Xavier's take on authentic writing: Structuring choices for expression and impact. *Journal of Adolescent & Adult Literacy*, 58(4), 289–298.

Behizadeh, N. (2018). Aiming for authenticity: Successes and struggles of an attempt to increase authenticity in writing. *Journal of Adolescent & Adult Literacy*, 62(4), 411–419.

Bereiter, C., and Scardamalia, M. (1987). *The Psychology of Written Composition*. London: Routledge.

Boscolo, P., and Gelati, C. (2019). Motivating Writers. In *Best Practices in Writing Instruction*, Graham, S., MacArthur, C., and Hebert, M. (Eds.) (3rd Ed.) (pp. 51–78). New York: The Guilford Press.

Boscolo, P., and Hidi, S. (2006). *Writing & Motivation*. Holland: Elsevier Science.

Breetvelt, I., van den Bergh, H., and Rijlaarsdam, G. (1994). Relations between writing processes and text quality: When and how? *Cognition and Instruction*, 12(2), 103–123.

Bruning, R., and Horn, C. (2000). Developing motivation to write. *Educational Psychologist*, 35(1), 25–37.

Clark, C., and Teravainen, A. (2017). *Writing for Enjoyment and Its Link to Wider Writing*. London: National Literacy Trust.

Dixon, J. (1967). *Growth in English*. London: Oxford University Press.

Dombey, H. (2013). *Teaching Writing: What the Evidence Says UKLA Argues for an Evidence-Informed Approach to Teaching and Testing Young Children's Writing*. Leicester: United Kingdom Lubricants Association.

Dutro, E. (2010). What 'hard times' means: Mandated curricula, class-privileged assumptions, and the lives of poor children. *Research in the Teaching of English*, 44(3), 255–291.

Dyson, A. (2003). Popular literacies and the 'all' children: Rethinking literacy development for contemporary childhoods. *Language Arts*. 81(2), 100.

Dyson, A. (2020). 'This isn't my real writing': The fate of children's agency in too-tight curricula. *Theory Into Practice*, 59(2), 119–127.

Edelsky, C., and Smith, K. (1984). Is that writing: Or are those marks just a figment of your curriculum. *Language Arts*, 61(1), 24–32.

Flint, A.S., and Fisher, T. (2014). Writing their worlds: Young English language learners navigate writing workshop. *Writing & Pedagogy*, 6(3), 1756–5839.

Flint, A.S., and Laman, T.T. (2012). Where poems hide: Finding reflective, critical spaces inside writing workshop. *Theory Into Practice*, 51(1), 12–19.

Flower, L., and Hayes, J. (1981). The pregnant pause: An inquiry into the nature of planning. *Research in the Teaching of English*, 15, 229–243.

Frank, C. (2001). 'What new things these words can do for you': A focus on one writing-project teacher and writing instruction. *Journal of Literacy Research*, 33(3), 467–506.

Gadd, M. (2014). *What is Critical in the Effective Teaching of Writing?* Auckland, NZ: The University of Auckland.

Gadd, M., and Parr, J. (2016). It's all about Baxter: Task orientation in the effective teaching of writing. *Literacy*, 50(2), 93–99.

Gambrell, L.B., Hughes, E.M., Calvert, L., Malloy, J.A., and Igo, B. (2011). Authentic reading, writing and discussion: An exploratory study of a pen pal project. *The Elementary School Journal*, 112(2), 23–258.

Garrett, L., and Moltzen, R. (2011). Writing because I want to, not because I have to: Young gifted writers' perspectives on the factors that 'matter' in developing expertise. *English Teaching: Practice and Critique*, 10(1), 165–180.

Grainger, T., Goouch, K., and Lambirth, A. (2003). Playing the game called writing. *English in Education*, 37(2), 4–15.

Grainger, T., Goouch, K., and Lambirth, A. (2005). *Creativity and Writing: Developing Voice and Verve in the Classroom.* London: Routledge.

Graham, S., and Perin, D. (2007). *Writing Next: Effective Strategies To Improve Writing Of Adolescents In Middle School & High Schools.* New York: Alliance For Excellent Education.

Graves, D. (1982). Break the welfare cycle: Let writers choose their topics. The English Composition Board, 3(2), 75–78.

Graves, D. (1983). *Writing: Teachers and Children at Work.* Porstmouth, NH: Heinemann.

Gutiérrez, K. (2008). Developing a sociocritical literacy in the third space. *Reading Research Quarterly*, 43(2), 148–164.

Halliday, M. (2013). *Introduction to Functional Grammar* (4th Ed.). London: Routledge.

Hickey, D.T. (2003). Engaged participation versus marginal nonparticipation: A stridently sociocultural approach to achievement motivation. *The Elementary School Journal*, 103(4), 401–429.

Hidi, S., and Renninger, K.A. (2006). The four-phase model of interest development. *Educational Psychologist*, 41, 111–127.

Hoewisch, A. (2001). 'Do I have to have a princess in my story?': Supporting children's writing of fairytales. *Reading and Writing Quarterly*, 17, 249–277.

Knight, A. (2009). Re-engaging students disengaged with English: A unit of work on Othering. *English Teaching: Practice & Critique*, 8(1), 112–124.

Langer, J.A. (2001). Beating the odds: Teaching middle and high school students to read and write well. *American Educational Research Journal*, 38(4), 837–880.

Leung, C., and Hicks, J. (2014). Writer identity and writing workshop a future teacher and teacher educator critically reflect. *Writing & Pedagogy*, 1756–5839.

Locke, T. (2015). *Developing Writing Teachers.* London: Routledge

Maloch, B. (2005). Moments by which change is made: A cross-case exploration of teacher mediation and student participation in literacy events. *Journal of Literacy Research*, 37(1), 95–142.

McCutchen, D. (2011). From novice to expert: Implications of language skills and writing-relevant knowledge for memory during the development of writing skill. *Journal of Writing Research*, 3(1), 51–68.

Morizawa, G. (2014). *Nesting the Neglected 'R' A Design Study: Writing Instruction within a Prescriptive Literacy Program* Unpublished. Berkeley, CA: University of California.

Olinghouse, N., Graham, S., and Gillespie, A. (2015). The relationship of discourse and topic knowledge to fifth graders' writing performance. *Journal of Educational Psychology*, 107(2), 391–406.

Pollard, A., Broadfoot, P., Croll, P., Osborn, M., and Abbott, D. (1994). *Changing English in Primary Schools? The Impact of the Education Reform Act at KS1.* London: Cassell.

Purcell-Gates, V., Duke, N.K., and Martineau, J.A. (2007). Learning to read and write genre-specific text: Roles of authentic experience and explicit teaching. *Reading Research Quarterly*, 42(1), 8–45.

Solsken, J., Willett, J., and Wilson-Keenan, J. (2000). Cultivating hybrid texts in multicultural classrooms: "Promise and challenge". *National Council of Teachers of English*, 179–212.

Splitter, L.J. (2009). Authenticity and constructivism in education. *Studies in Philosophy and Education*, 28, 135–151.

Subero, D., Vujasinović E., and Esteban-Guitart, M. (2016). Mobilising funds of identity in and out of school. *Cambridge Journal of Education*, 47(2), 247–263.

Szczepanski, S. (2003). Writing workshop: Three ingredients that work. *Michigan Reading Journal*, 35(2), 13–15.

van den Bergh, H., and Rijlaarsdam, G. (2001). Changes in cognitive activities during the writing process and relationships with text quality. *Educational Psychology*, 21(4), 373–385.

Walshe, R. (2015). Writing as process. In *Teaching Writing in Today's Classrooms: Looking Back to Look Forward*, Turbill, J., Barton, G., and Brock, C. (Eds.) (pp. 13–26). Adelaide, SA: Australaian Literacy Educators' Association.

White, C. (2000). Strategies are not enough. *Education 3-13*, 28(1), 16–21.

Whitney, A.E. (2017). Keeping it real: Valuing authenticity in the writing classroom. *English Journal*, 6(106), 16–21.

Wiggins, G. (2009). Real-world writing: Making purpose & audience matter. *English Journal*, 98(5), 29–37.

Willinksy, J. (1990). *New Literacy: Redefining Reading and Writing in Schools*. London: Routledge.

Wray, D., Beard, R., Raban, B., Hall, N., Bloom, W., Robinson, A., Potter, F., Sands, H., and Yates, I. (1988). *Developing Children's Writing*. Leamington Spa, UK: Scholastic.

Young, R. (2019). *What is it 'writing for pleasure' teachers do that makes the difference?* The University of Sussex: The Goldsmiths' Company [Online]. Available: www.writing4pleasure.com.

Young, R., and Ferguson, F. (2020). *Real-World Writers: A Handbook for Teaching Writing with 7–11 Year Olds*. London: Routledge.

Young, R., Govender, N., and Kaufman, D. (in press) *Writing Realities*. Leicester: UKLA.

CHAPTER

15

Teach the writing processes

The recursive and creative nature of the writing process

A writer's process is a recursive, flexible, and sometimes spontaneous undertaking which can, depending on the context of the writing, include a set of processes such as generating ideas, planning (prewriting), drafting, revising (evaluating), editing (proof-reading), publishing, or performing (Flower and Hayes 1981; Smith 1982; Smagorinsky and Smith 1992; Dyson and Freedman 2003; Hayes 2012; Sharp 2016). We know that it is not the straightforwardly linear undertaking that the producers of many teaching materials would have us believe (Schneider 2003; Morizawa 2014). It is highly unlikely to look like this:

LINEAR MODEL

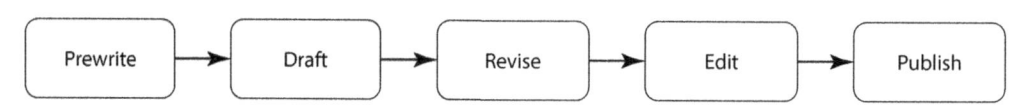

Prewrite → Draft → Revise → Edit → Publish

FIGURE 15.1 A common misconception of 'the' writing process – reproduced from Young and Ferguson (2020b, p. 47).

but much more like this:

Idea Generation → Planning → Drafting → Revising → Editing → Publishing & Performing

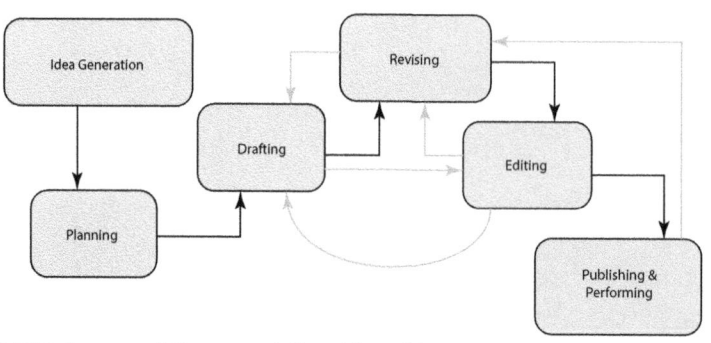

FIGURE 15.2 A more realistic representation of the writing processes.

We would argue that there are also processes like playing, abandoning, reimagining, returning, and updating. For example, younger writers will abandon pieces, reimagine old writing, return to crafting unfinished compositions, and will update already published material to create new editions or versions. And whilst any piece of writing might have gone through many or all of these processes, no two writers will use them in the same way, in the same order, and with the same levels of attention or priority (van den Bergh and Rijlaarsdam 2001). One model does not fit all.

The current orthodoxy of what makes successful writing means that instruction in the classroom is mainly directed towards children producing a very specific written piece, in a very specific way, primarily for evaluation. Preoccupation with this type of presentation-oriented teaching means that teachers often neglect to give more generalised instruction in the writing processes so essential to achieving long-term writing success. According to Lipson et al. (2000), many teachers fail to see the relevance of attention to the writing processes in the development of writing competency. For example, they may:

- Omit or pay only cursory attention to some of the processes.
- Focus only briefly (if at all) on idea generation.
- Insist on high-stakes first drafts.
- Demand that children attend to composition and transcription at the same time.
- Deny time or opportunity for revision.
- Set rigid deadlines that the whole class must meet at the same time.
- Only allow a short time for checking spelling and grammar.
- Not provide time or opportunity for publication or performance.

As Bloodgood (2002) says, these practices work to the detriment of children's developing craft knowledge and the quality of their written pieces. However, schools achieving dramatic writing progress ensure children understand writing to be a multi-step process which involves taking a germ of an idea and seeing it through to publication or performance (Pressley et al. 2006). Children need time to generate ideas, plan their writing, draft freely, and conference with their peers and teacher. They need time in which to reflect and attend to their initial drafts through revision and proof-reading until the manuscript is as accurate as possible before publication or performance. In time, they will internalise and then personalise the processes, procedures, and tactics that good writers employ when crafting texts (Berninger and Winn 2006; Kellogg 2008; Kellogg et al. 2013).

Explicitly teaching the writing processes and techniques writers employ

It is sometimes assumed that professional writers possess a mysterious gift, perhaps bestowed by some kind of higher power. Some writers may even subscribe to this idea themselves, though it is more likely that most will remember only too well the hard graft, the wrestling with words lamented by T.S. Eliot. We believe that writing is a craft which children learn through a combination of high-quality instruction, attention to the affective domains, and repeated and meaningful practice (Young 2019).

An essential part of instruction in the processes of writing is to make visible and overt what may otherwise be covert or implicit (Englert et al. 1991; Kellogg 1987, 2008, Kellogg et al. 2013). *Writing For Pleasure* teachers simply do not allow writing to be a mystery. Displaying and making explicit, through systematic instruction, the variety of strategies and techniques writers use to navigate the writing processes is vital to children's academic success. This is one of the most robust, validated, and effective teaching practices writer-teachers can employ in their classrooms (see Chapter 10), and without such instruction, children run the very real risk of academic underachievement (Koster et al. 2015). Many studies suggest that teachers can give children this essential craft knowledge through the medium of daily mini-lessons and pupil conferencing (Danoff et al. 1993; Lipson et al. 2000; Schneider 2003; Pritchard and Honeycutt 2006; Graham and Sandwell 2011; Levitt et al. 2014; McQuitty 2014). Finally, Jasmine and Weiner (2007) and Levitt (2014) argue convincingly that children as young as six can successfully learn about and use the writing processes.

It is our strong view that teachers should move away from spending too much lesson-time teaching the stimulus for a writing task, which, according to Hoogeveen (2012), is a far too common occurrence in schools, and instead should focus their attention on explicitly teaching the craft of writing and the writing processes. This could be done by the writer-teacher through the following strategies:

- Modelling live how they use a particular writing strategy.
- Allowing time for children to ask questions and reflect on their own strategies.
- Using an exemplar taken from their own writing.
- Coaching children in how to apply the strategy.
- Creating resources to encourage self-regulation.

If, in keeping with the contemporary and highly collaborative writing-workshop approach (Young and Ferguson 2020b), this instruction is coupled with giving children daily and sustained time to manage the writing processes in class and personal projects, then teachers will have what researchers and case studies consider to be a powerful base for highly effective writing teaching (Langer 2001; Pritchard and Honeycutt 2006; Graham and Perin 2007; Hmelo-Silver et al. 2007; Graham and Sandwell 2011; McQuitty 2014; Wyse and Torgerson 2017; Young 2019).

The role of the writer-teacher

Below, Frank (2001, p. 469) describes a teacher from her study who identifies herself as a writer-teacher:

> Because she is a writer, her underlying premises about writing instruction are grounded in what authors do as they write … The underlying belief system of her classroom is based on what writers know about writing … Her practice is grounded in her experiences as an author, which means that her students are

concerned with the social and cultural practices of authors: how writers talk, act, and think, as well as issues concerning the content and mechanics of writing. Because she is a writer, Lois encourages her students to place editorial decisions about spelling and punctuation in the final stages of the writing process while at the same time uses these editing opportunities to teach writing skills.

Here we see that, when writer-teachers like Lois make their writing processes visible and discuss them with their pupils through modelling, classroom talk, or in pupil conferencing, children get to see and hear what writers do as they craft texts. Studying and asking questions about the teacher's mentor texts is an important way for children to learn about a host of new strategies they can apply in their own writing process (Beach and Friedrich 2006; Morizawa 2014). The role of the writer-teacher and pupil conferencing in effective instruction is discussed in more detail in Chapters 21 and 22.

Agency over process

The goal of engaging children in the process of writing is to help them gain control over the types of recursive activity characteristic of mature authors (Lipson et al. 2000, p. 212). Here we see how children's knowledge and subsequent use of the writing processes is intrinsically linked to their writer-identity (Kauffman 2006; Collier 2017). It is easy to see the attraction, in terms of classroom management and teacher control, of teaching a linear writing process and having everyone write at much the same pace, particularly in a class of early writers. However, as we have said, to produce their best writing children need to work at their own pace and use the writing processes in a combination and in a way that best suits them (Lipson et al. 2000; Schneider 2003; Dutro et al. 2004; Collier 2017). It will ultimately be more efficient and instructionally beneficial to encourage children's self-regulation and the development of their own writing process as soon as possible (Frank 2001; Schneider 2003; Dutro et al. 2004; Harris et al. 2006; Kellogg 2008; Collier 2017). Therefore, part of teaching about the writing processes involves giving children personal responsibility for how they write once they are competent and experienced enough (Lipson et al. 2000; McQuitty 2014). This is what Calkins (2013, p. 26) neatly terms the 'demonstrate, scaffold and release' approach.

Generating ideas

With the exception of copying out an existing text, all writing is original and in some way creative. When visual images, ideas, and schemas in our heads become transformed into words and sentences on paper or screen, it is always a creative process.

When we are speaking, thinking, and daydreaming, we are composing. These sorts of chats, soliloquies, and dreams are writing 'gold'. In such circumstances, a dedicated writer of any age has a 'writerself' hovering nearby, notepad in hand, grasping at anything that might be good for writing down. The 'writerself' will always be watching and taking notes. It wears virtual reality goggles, has huge bat ears, and a quivering comical nose. It picks up, inspects, and tries out a sip, lick, bite, or slice of everything that comes its way. It knows that subjects for writing are everywhere. In a more sober vein, Moffett and Wagner (1992, p. 198) say, 'if you can help your students regard their inner speech as something they can in some edited form transcribe any time to paper, they will take a giant step toward becoming fluent writers'. However, whilst everything *can* be a subject for writing, we leave most of our 'lived compositions' untranscribed. We are discriminating; not everything we experience, think, or discuss is worth the energy, time, and effort of putting on paper. Writers, both professional and recreational, are selective about which ideas to turn into texts, and the strategies and techniques they use can be shared and used by children too (Young and Ferguson 2020b).

According to Sharples (1999), writers generate ideas by setting themselves parameters. Without parameters, writers can all too easily come to feel paralysed by the sheer volume of possibilities that the whole of human creativity, knowledge, and experience affords them. However, having too many parameters restricts the ability to create visual images or schemas in the mind's eye. Either situation can result in 'writer's block', and so it is necessary to proceed with caution. Parameters that writers set themselves include: creating, finding, or being presented with a writing situation; choosing a genre in which they would like to write; identifying a topic they wish to write about; or deciding to engage in 'free writing' and see what may surface. Teachers could set children similar parameters for class writing projects:

- **A writing situation**. A genuine purpose and anticipated audience for a particular situation is thought about and discussed. For example, the class will produce an anthology of writing for the local care home. Children will participate and respond within the context of the writing situation by generating ideas for individual pieces.
- **A genre**. Children can be taught about a particular genre and then consider how they themselves would like to use it, imaginatively subverting and manipulating it if they wish. An example might be to write an information or explanation text on a personally chosen topic and contribute it to a class encyclopaedia of knowledge for everyone to read.
- **A topic**. A topic can be a concept, theme, text, subject, or experience. Children search and filter their opinions, memories, knowledge, and experiences to generate ideas in response to that topic. For example, children are asked to write something about 'temptation', write something in response to a book they've liked, or write something in response to what they've learnt in the science lesson today.
- Begin with **reflecting and thinking** through free writing (Elbow 1998). Children write freely for a short, sustained period, either whatever is in their mind or on a suggested topic, and then mine their writing for ideas worth developing.

Young writers can play around within the parameters set and will often create something new and unexpected.

Writing ideas can be generated as a whole class, in groups, or individually. A well-known technique is inviting children to brainstorm around a situation, genre, or topic. By generating ideas in this social and dynamic way, ideas always spark further ideas (Young and Ferguson 2020b). Children can find ideas through volitional reading (Parry and Taylor 2018) and through drawing. Interestingly, MacKenzie (2011) states that children in classrooms where drawing is valued and given priority as a meaning-generating device go on to create longer and more complex texts. Finally, some teachers undertake 'a writing register', where children in turn call out and share their ideas, thus opening up the possibility of inspiring and being inspired by others in the classroom (Frank 2001; Young and Ferguson 2020b).

As Sharples (1999) has noted, and as we know, teachers often formulate writing ideas on children's behalf. In our chapter Pursue Authentic and Purposeful Writing Projects, we argue that leaving children with little agency over topics for writing is a serious instructional mistake. Hoewisch's (2001, p. 250) perspective is that 'children resent the imposition of having to write on preselected or teacher-selected topics about which they are not familiar or interested', going on to say: 'while some teachers use "story starters" or "creative writing topics" as imaginative ploys to motivate students to begin writing, when used too often, children can begin to rely on their teachers for topics'. Rosen (2017) also suggests that when teachers regularly choose topics derived from their own interests and cultures they are only ever helping children who are most 'like them'. Graves (1982, p. 77) says simply that 'independence begins for writers when they choose their topics'. Other studies focus on the consequences of children being required to write on subjects not of their choosing, which they have only recently acquired knowledge about. Heller (1999, p. 73) tells us that 'research findings indicate that composition is impaired if a writer lacks sufficient background knowledge about topics and ideas', while Stein (1983) points out that children are being subjected to an additional and unnecessary cognitive demand, that of having to assimilate newly acquired subject matter while at the same time managing the process and craft of writing. Both these views are supported by Kellogg (2001, 2008) and Graham (2006), who show that when children are allowed to choose and access a topic they are familiar and emotionally connected with, their writing performance improves and they produce higher quality texts. Lack of trust in children's collective and individual ability to find good writing ideas remains a particular problem for teachers. However, our experience is that children who are part of a community of writers and who write meaningfully every day seldom struggle to generate them.

Planning

Planning becomes important when ideas need to be captured on paper or screen as external representations. Plans discover, make visible, and organise our insights and ideas. Children who spend time planning have been shown to produce more complete stories and improve their writing performance (Graham et al. 2012; Limpo and Alves 2013). They understand more about the writer's craft and are able to use these techniques successfully in future writing projects (Harris et al. 2006).

Planning strategies are many and varied and can include: talking, drawing, physical and dramatic play, thinking, daydreaming, observing, reading, gathering notes from the internet, mind mapping, webbing, drawing diagrams or maps, tables, lists, notes and possible phrases, writing an outline, creating or filling in a planning grid, free writing, or discovery drafting.

Planning is a matter of personal preference. Children may benefit from drawing rather than talking when they are undertaking an early attempt at a composition (Fu and Shelton 2007; Mackenzie 2011), whilst others like to arrive at a plan through talking to peers (Schneider 2003). Some children like planning grids while others prefer to undertake what is in effect a discovery draft (Lipson et al. 2000; Schneider 2003). Some children like to use post-it notes creatively (Harmey 2020). As Sharples (1999) reminds us, plans are also there to be altered and updated. What is important is that the child has a general idea of where their writing is going, while planning at a more micro level is unlikely to be useful (Kellogg 2008). Finally, Shanahan's research (2016) claims that the quality of children's writing is improved when their planning is informed by an explicit final goal and a defined and definite audience in mind.

Drafting

As children put fingers to keyboard or pen to paper, they organise schemas (packages of images and information inside the brain) and translate them into phrases of written language (Clay 2001; Kellogg 2008; Halliday 2013; Fayol 2016). Drafting, then, is about finding out and seeing, perhaps for the first time, *what* it is we want to say.

According to Schneider's (2003) observations of young writers, children have open to them a variety of ways in which to draft. Schneider notes that some children like to orally rehearse and then draft a sentence quickly, returning later to revise or edit it as they deem necessary, while some will prefer to stop at intervals to reread their developing compositions, checking that the flow of the writing is maintained. Other children may adopt a less methodical and more interactive approach. They work on a discovery basis, outlining or making a rough draft of their piece before returning to it, redrafting, and shaping it until it emerges as a final composition ready for proof-reading. This type of approach is similar to Peter Elbow's (1998) strategy of 'free-writing'. According to Murray (1982), experienced writers actually review and adjust their planning while drafting. Young writers are no different; they will try things out, draw, and talk about their writing as they draft. We therefore recommend that children have access to a 'trying things out' page in their books (Young and Ferguson 2020b).

Interestingly, when Pressley and his colleagues (2006) were observing a high-achieving 'benchmark' school working in challenging circumstances, they noted that children were taught when drafting to underline any words whose spelling they were unsure of, and were then given dedicated time to attend to and check them later during editing. Influenced by the work of Kellogg (2008), Young and Ferguson (2020, p. 53) offer a set of proven 'drafting rules' to help children maintain fluency whilst drafting and to reduce the cognitive demands of composing (Chenoweth and Hayes 2001).

Drafting Rules	
Got a sticky or a yawny bit? - Put a line under the bit you are unsure about. - Carry on.	**Don't know how to spell a word?** - Invent the spelling. - Put a circle around it. - Carry on.
Don't know what to write next? - Read it to a partner. - Get your partner to ask you questions.	**Not sure of punctuation?** - Put a box where the punctuation might need to go. - Carry on.
Think you have finished? Start or continue with a personal writing project!	

FIGURE 15.3 Drafting rules taken from Real-World Writers (Young and Ferguson 2020b, p. 53).

Revising

If drafting is finding out *what* it is we want to say, revising is about *how best* to say it. Revising is about re-seeing, rethinking, reviewing, and transforming drafted writing. It should be considered as a form of play. Revision stands out from all the processes because it offers writers the chance to be at their most creative and dynamic. As Hayes (2004) asserts, revision is not about hunting for errors nor, as Becker (2006) says, is it all about correcting 'bad' writing. Since these are misconceptions commonly held in the classroom, it appears that ideas about revision are in need of being revised! What should happen during the process is that writers reread, discover new insights, and take this precious second chance to add, remove, replace, rewrite completely, and say what they mean as fluently, clearly and engagingly as they would wish. And, of course, revising can afford immense satisfaction and be entirely enjoyable, as the much-quoted Hemingway claimed.

An ability to revise whilst planning or drafting is part of becoming an expert writer (Scardamalia and Bereiter 1991; Hacker 1994; McCutchen 1996). According to Hayes (2004), there are a number of ways in which we reread and improve our developing drafts or plans:

- **Reread to comprehend** – rereading to hear how the composition sounds, how easily the text reads and for the pleasure of hearing your own words and voice.

- **Reread to discover opportunities** – rereading with another to see how they are responding to your developing plan or composition, and to discover new insights.
- **Reread to evaluate** – rereading to detect any issues that may need attention and improvement.
- **Reread to fix problems** – rereading in an attempt to resolve any cohesive or other higher-level transcriptional issues.

For interest, Scardamalia and Bereiter (1983) illustrate the cognitive processes underlying the act of revising with a strategy entitled CDO (Compare, Diagnose, Operate). First, the young writer can **compare** their drafted text against what they wish their text to be or against a generated list of product goals (see Chapter 16). Next, **diagnose** involves the child scanning their draft for opportunities to make changes in response. Finally, **operate** involves the young writers making their desired changes.

Studies such as those of De La Paz et al. (1998), Holliway and McCutchen (2004), and Shanahan (2016) show how children revise more successfully when they keep a focus on what they want the future readership to understand and take from the text. The inspirational work of Hayes and Flower (1980) and Halliday (2013) shows how taking on a reader's perspective can help children to revise on several levels:

- **Field** – How will my reader respond to the content/knowledge I've chosen to share? Will they comprehend what I'm trying to say and get across? How might they read it differently?
- **Tenor** – Am I addressing my audience correctly? How involved are they in my text?
- **Mode** – Is the writing organised, cohesive, and appropriately presented?
- **Semantics** – Are my linguistic choices making for a successful and meaningful text?
- **Lexis** – Have I used appropriate vocabulary choices in relation to my future readership? Am I being too wordy? Am I using vocabulary my readers will understand? Will they understand key vocabulary in the context of my work or do certain words warrant specific definition?

We can now clearly see the importance of teachers planning, defining, and discussing class writing projects with their class in terms of purpose and future audience (Dix and Cawkwell 2011). Indeed, Allal (2004) and Young and Ferguson (2020b) suggest that through taking an active part in creating an authentic and purposeful writing project, children are motivated to invest more time and energy into their texts. They are more likely to revise and edit their writing to a high standard to make sure it will satisfy their readers' needs and be 'reader-ready' in terms of transcriptional accuracy and adherence to conventions.

According to Becker (2006), MacArthur et al. (2004), and Chanquoy (2001), apprentice writers need instruction in how to make effective revisions (for more information, see Chapter 20). It is worth noting the studies conducted by Hayes (2004) and Sharples (1999), which suggest that less experienced and younger writers tend when revising to focus on making semantic changes at word level, whereas more experienced writers will also focus on making semantic changes but at text level (Hayes 2004; Sharples 1999). As Myhill and Jones (2007) and Young (2019) both say, younger children can make text level revisions if they know what to do and how to do it. This is best achieved through writing-study mini-lessons. A particularly effective way of providing instruction is to give children access to a co-constructed revision checklist (Young and Ferguson 2019, 2020a) or set of product goals which highlight in a broad way what their text should achieve if it is to be successful and meaningful. If children are able to discuss, reflect on, and assess their writing with the help of these resources, the accuracy and the power of their revisions skyrockets (Andrade 2019). We suggest that, just as the craftsman throws his pot then adds detail and decoration, children must first be allowed to draft quite freely and then be given ample time to revise with the help of co-constructed rubrics and checklists (Young and Ferguson 2020b).

Below is a revision checklist used by a class of nine to ten-year-olds when writing a memoir. It is an excellent example of how teachers can 'blur the distinction between assessment and instruction' and so 'transform classroom assessment into a moment of learning' (Andrade and Brooke 2010, p. 84).

Memoir revision checklist

	I gave it a try!
Think. What do you want your readers to feel?	☐
Have you fixed any 'sticky' bits and 'yawny' bits? Ask a friend to read your draft with you. Do you have any sticky bits? Do you have any bits that don't make sense? Do they think you have any boring bits? If so, change them.	☐
Write the title last Think about your title once you have finished. Make a list of titles and check with a partner which one they think is best.	☐
Underline your best line Underline the best line and think about why you like it so much. Can you turn that sentence into a whole paragraph?	☐
Use your senses At the top of the page, write a list of at least three of the seven writer's senses: seeing, hearing, touching, tasting, smelling, imagining, and remembering. Think about where you could use these senses in your writing.	☐

Crack open boring words ☐
Find some of the most boring words you have used and turn them into more interesting ones – particularly your nouns and verbs!

Show don't tell ☐
When we tell readers something we often use *is, was, have, had,* and *did*. Replace them and you'll find yourself showing your readers rather than telling them.

- Don't tell your readers where the setting is – show them by using your senses.
- Don't name the emotion someone is feeling – show them by describing it.

Describe new characters and settings to your readers ☐
Read through your draft and highlight where you introduce a new place or character. It is sometimes good to add some description here for your readers.

Body language ☐
What facial expressions, gestures, or movements will your character use? How will these help to tell readers what they are really like?

How does your character talk? ☐
What is the tone of your character's voice? What do they sound like? Do they speak in short or long sentences? Do they have an accent? Do they use slang?

Powerful and thoughtful ending ☐
Try writing a shock, question, action, speech, or description ending.

Figure: an example of a revision checklist taken from Young and Ferguson (2020a).

Beliefs and opinions about revision differ. For example, some question whether it is always appropriate to ask children, particularly the younger ones, to revise their piece (Schneider 2003). Others suggest that children as young as five can do it quite successfully if they are taught how (Dix and Cawkwell 2011; Horn and Giacobbe 2007). There can be no doubt that more research is needed, especially with the youngest children in mind, to describe and explain this profoundly interesting writing process.

Editing

Revising and editing (also known as proof-reading) are two very different cognitive processes. Revising involves reviewing drafted text to consider its compositional impact on the reader, whereas editing is when the writer considers transcriptional accuracy and conventions. They are highly demanding processes, and it would be inappropriate to expect children to deal with them both at exactly the same time (McCutchen 1996; Chanquoy 2001; MacArthur et al. 2004). Indeed, professional writers regularly call on a copy editor to undertake at least some of this work on their behalf. Anderson (2007) encourages teachers to actively and systematically teach children how editing is done and suggests they should teach copy editors' procedures and how and why they make certain decisions. He claims that if such instruction was underpinned by the constant reminder that the work is being prepared for a real audience, children would be well placed to edit meaningfully, accurately, and thoroughly.

Through repeated practice, the processes involved in editing can become automated and children can even proof-read as they write, yet even the most accomplished writers also need a specific and sustained period in which to proof-read. In his paper, Hayes (2004) points out that young writers can only correct problems if they are able to identify them in the first place. There would, therefore, seem to be a need for specific instruction in how proof-readers go about detecting problems and how they correct them. An effective strategy is to teach children the CUPS process (Young and Ferguson 2020b). CUPS stands for capitalisation, use of vocabulary, punctuation, and spelling. Modelling how to read a text four times, once for each category in turn, and then inviting children to practise this technique in their own compositions could be a fruitful way of teaching them to be proof-readers. It is well worth pursuing this kind of instruction since, as Lipson et al. (2000) observed, once children are explicitly taught strategies and techniques for editing, they enjoy taking responsibility for proof-reading their own works. Myhill and Jones (2007) support this view, suggesting that while teachers may decide to highlight transcriptional errors, they should invite the child to correct them.

Frank (2001) states that teachers employing a contemporary writing-workshop approach hold transcriptional accuracy in the highest regard and consider it to be as important as other writing processes. She describes how the children in her study were given a checklist of words and were asked to look back at their drafts and correct any 'invented spellings', which they had circled when drafting. They were praised enthusiastically for the number of invented spellings which turned out to be correctly spelt but also for the number they had corrected as part of the proof-reading process. A strategy which celebrates success is always the best one.

For the writer, familiarity with their own text can make detecting errors difficult. Sharing a manuscript with someone who has little or no prior knowledge of the text seems to help the writer identify transcriptional issues (Alber-Morgan et al. 2007). Another strategy often employed in classrooms is to set up a variety of 'editing stations', each with a different focus, where children can work in collaboration to proof-read their writing. Children can also be given significant time away from their compositions before undertaking proof-reading. However teachers decide to help their children manage this process, it is clear that successful proof-reading by pupils depends on their prior conviction that they have written a quality piece which is destined to reach a defined audience and so be put to work. Children have to believe that they have crafted something worth proof-reading.

Publishing and performing

The process of publishing or performing their writing is extremely important to children (Frank 2001; Rowe 2003), and published pieces should be more than 'neat copies' of a first draft. Writers need to feel that their writing is serving a legitimate purpose and reaching real audiences. Publishing is a time for celebration (Frank 2001). It is also an intelligent instructional decision since it can increase students' motivation and their interest in revising and editing their compositions, and it contributes to better writing performance (MacArthur et al. 1991, 1995). However, as Murray (1985, p. 192) tells us: 'there is simply no comparison between the artificial, academic situation of classroom publication and the chance to achieve a readership of real people'. Instead of gathering dust on classroom walls, finished pieces can be published in myriad forms and can 'get to work' as big books that circulate round classroom or school libraries, as audio recordings or podcasts, as items printed in the school newspaper, or as selections published in a class magazine or posted on the internet (Bloodgood 2002). There are of course many other opportunities for recorded or public performances of writing. In their book *Real-World Writers*, Young and Ferguson (2020b, pp. 41–42) enumerate just some of them:

- Read it out during class sharing times (in your own or in another class).
- Have a live debate or political discussion evening centred around the writing.
- Read it out during assembly.
- Have a slam poetry evening.
- Have a lunchtime or after school 'coffee house' read-aloud club.
- Have a publishing party or a writers' picnic.
- Hold special writing celebration evenings or exhibitions where the community can be invited in to read, hear, or see live or videoed performances.
- Put it in a frame or give it as a gift.
- Put it on your bedroom wall.
- Put it in the bathroom for people to read on the loo or while they're in the bath.
- Leave it in the car to read during traffic jams.
- Turn it into a presentation.
- Turn it into a film.
- Turn it into a piece of artwork.
- Add it to the class or school library.
- Send it to another school either here or abroad.
- Send it in the post to a friend or a family member.
- Take it home to share with the family.
- Mail it to a person who needs to read it.
- Send it to an expert, charity, or association to see what they think.
- Collect it together with other pieces to make an anthology.
- Share it with another class.
- Enter it in a year group, school, local, or national writing competition.
- Send it to a local or national newspaper, magazine, or fanzine.
- Publish it online.

- Publish it in the school newsletter or newspaper.
- Have a 'lecture day' where people can sign up to hear different speakers discuss what they've learnt during class topics.
- Put on a book or poetry sale. You can sell your writing – especially if people know it's going to a good cause. It can feel good knowing your thoughts, passions, and ideas are worth money.
- Make an audio recording for the class library or school website.
- Suggest that it be used as an 'exemplar-text', when the writing is kept by your teacher to help teach next year's class.
- Ask if it can be placed anonymously in local establishments such as libraries, places of worship, local history centres, museums, art galleries, train stations, bus stops, bookshops, corner shop windows, on lamp posts, gates or fences, in takeaways, retirement homes, cafes, coffee houses, pubs, sports clubs, dentists' or doctors' surgeries, or on buses or trains.

Examples of effective practice

Our research (Young 2019) observed that *Writing For Pleasure* teachers gave explicit instruction in strategies and techniques for the different components of the writing process (how to generate an idea, plan, draft, revise, edit, publish). They scaffolded children's understanding of these processes through demonstration, resources, displays, discussion, modelling, sharing exemplars which they had written themselves and showing techniques used by children. As a result, the children were made to feel incredibly knowledgeable about the writing process and felt able to navigate it on their own.

These teachers were utterly committed to helping their children relinquish dependency on these scaffolds and to allowing children to develop a writing process that suited them. As one child put it 'he lets us write the way we write best'. The children were able to use the writing processes recursively and were not tied to a linear model. For example, children in one class were able to identify what kind of writing process they liked using the most. These included being a discoverer, planner, vomiter, paragraph piler, and sentence stacker (Hayden 2020; Young and Ferguson 2020b). A 'discoverer' is someone who favours drafting, which resembles Peter Elbow's free-writing technique (1998). A planner, in contrast, likes to plan their writing in detail before attempting their first draft. The children were given a variety of ways in which they could plan their writing, including 'planning grids', 'dabbling' (a mixture of drawing and notes), and of course 'discovery drafting'. They were also encouraged to use the following rules when drafting, for example, to circle any unsure spellings and to carry on writing, underline any parts that need work or do not make sense, and to put a box where they might be unsure of punctuation. The children would then attend to these issues later. They were also given specific techniques to consider using when revising their initial drafts, linked to the purpose, audience, and distant goal for the writing. Finally, they were given checklists of transcriptional items to attend to when proof-reading and getting their compositions what the teachers called 'reader-ready'. Again, children were explicitly taught techniques for proof-reading, for example, checking for one type of error at a time. Alternatively, children would proof-read their writing in clusters at editing stations.

Practical things you can do

- Have on display a poster which shows the flexible, creative, and recursive nature of the writing process.
- Regularly teach writing strategies through mini-lessons and invite children to try the strategy during that day's writing time (see Chapter 20).
- Once they are experienced enough, allow children to use a writing process and a set of strategies that they know helps them craft their best writing.
- Allow children to write at their own pace and to set their own process goals (deadlines). See Chapter 16 for more details.
- Provide children with a variety of planning strategies and techniques and give them ample time to plan. Children should also feel confident to return and make adjustments to their initial plans if they feel a need to.
- Encourage fluency whilst drafting and don't overburden children as they undertake the difficult task of translating their ideas into sentences, paragraphs, and a whole text for the first time.
- As a class, set your product goals for the class writing project. Children can then use these goals to help them when crafting their writing but particularly when revising. See Chapter 16 for more details.
- Encourage separate and dedicated time for children to revise and then proof-read their compositions in preparation for publishing and/or performance.
- Ensure that publishing or performing is part of any class writing project.

> **QUESTIONS WORTH ASKING YOURSELF**
>
> - Do your children know that the writing process is flexible, creative, and recursive?
> - Does your class or school have a shared vocabulary for the writing processes and their associated strategies?
> - Do you regularly provide strategy instruction through mini-lessons?
> - Do you share examples of your writing processes with your class and the strategies you employ as you craft your writing?
> - Do children feel like they have ownership over their writing process?
> - Do children have a variety of writing strategies they can choose from?
> - Are children given enough time and opportunity to attend to all the processes of writing?
> - Do children change their writing process depending on the context for their writing?

- Do children generate their own ideas for writing?
- As well as encouraging children to regularly reread as they craft, do you set aside specific time for them to revise, edit, publish, and perform their compositions?
- When revising, do children know what they are looking to achieve?
- Are children revising, editing, and publishing their writing with a real audience in mind?

References

Alber-Morgan, S., Hessler, T., and Konrad, M. (2007). Teaching writing for keeps. *Education and Treatment of Children*, 30, 107–128.

Allal, L. (2004). Integrated writing instruction and the development of revision skills. In *Revision of Written Language: Cognitive and Instructional Processes*, Allal, L., Chanquoy, L., and Largy, P. (Eds.) (pp. 139–155). Philadelphia, PA: Kluwer.

Anderson, J. (2007). *Everyday Editing*. Portsmouth, NH: Stenhouse.

Andrade, H. (2019). A critical review of research on student self-assessment. *Frontiers in Education*, 4(87), 1–13.

Andrade, H., and Brooke, G. (2010). Self-assessment and learning to write. In *Writing: Processes, Tools and Techniques*, Mertens, N. (Ed.) (pp. 74–89). New York: Nova Science Publishers.

Beach, R., and Friedrich, T. (2006). Response to writing. In *Handbook of Writing Research*, Macarthur, C., Graham, S., and Fitzgerald, J. (Eds.) (pp. 222–234). New York: Guilford.

Becker, A. (2006). A review of writing model research based on cognitive processes. In *Revision: History, Theory and Practice*, Horning, A., and Becker, A. (Eds.) (pp. 25–49). Herndon, VA: Clearinghouse.

Berninger, V.W., and Winn, W. (2006). Implications of advancements in brain research and technology for writing development, writing instruction, and educational evolution. In *Handbook of Writing Research*, MacArthur, C., Graham, S., and Fitzgerald, J. (Eds.) (pp. 96–114). New York: Guilford Press

Bloodgood, J. (2002). Quintilian: A classical educator speaks to the writing process. *Reading Research and Instruction*, 42(1), 30–43.

Calkins, L. (2013). *A Guide to the Writing Workshop: Intermediate Grades*. Portsmouth, NH: Heinnaman.

Chanquoy, L. (2001). How to make it easier for children to revise their writing: A study of text revision from 3rd to 5th grades. *British Journal of Educational Psychology*, 71(1), 15–41.

Chenoweth, A., and Hayes, J. (2001). Fluency in writing. *Written Communication*, 18(1), 80–98.

Clay, M. (2001). *Change Over Time in Children's Literacy Development*. Auckland: Heinemann.

Collier, D.R. (2017). What kind of writer are you?: Glancing sideways at writers becoming. In Cremin, T., and Locke, T. (Eds.) *Writer Identity and the Teaching and Learning of Writing* (pp. 169–182). London: Routledge.

Danoff, B., Harris, K.R., and Graham, S. (1993). Incorporating strategy instruction within the writing process in the regular classroom: Effects on the writing of students with and without learning disabilities. *Journal of Reading Behavior*, 25(3), 295–322.

De La Paz, S., Swanson, P., and Graham, S. (1998). The contribution of executive control to the revising by students with writing and learning difficulties. *Journal of Educational Psychology*, 90(3), 448–460.

Dix, S., and Cawkwell, C. (2011). The influence of peer group response: Building a teacher and student expertise in the writing classroom. *English Teaching Practice & Critique*, 10(4), 41–57.

Dutro, E., Kazemi, E., and Balf, R. (2004). Children writing for themselves, their teachers, and the state in an urban elementary classroom. Paper presented at the annual meeting of the American Educational Research Association, San Diego, CA.

Dyson, A.H., and Freedman, S.W. (2003). Writing. In *Handbook of Research on Teaching the English Language Arts*, Flood, J., Jensen, J. Lapp, D., and Squire, R.J. (Eds.) (pp. 967–992). Mahwah, NJ: Erlbaum.

Elbow, P. (1998). *Writing Without Teachers*. USA: Oxford University Press.

Englert, C. S., Raphael, T. E., Anderson, L. M., Anthony, H. M., and Stevens, D. D. (1991). Making strategies and self-talk visible: Writing instruction in regular and special education classrooms. *American Educational Research Journal*, 28(2), 337–372.

Fayol, M. (2016). The development and learning of translation. In *Handbook of Writing Research*, MacArthur, C., Graham, S., and Fitzgerald, J. (Eds) (2nd Ed.) (pp. 130–143). New York: The Guilford Press.

Flower, L., and Hayes, J.R. (1981). A cognitive process theory of writing. *College Composition and Communication*, 32(4), 365–387.

Frank, C. (2001). 'What new things these words can do for you': A focus on one writing-project teacher and writing instruction. *Journal of Literacy Research*, 33(3), 467–506.

Fu, D., and Shelton, N. (2007). Including students with special needs in a writing workshop. *Language Arts*, 84, 325–336.

Graham, S. (2006). Writing. In *Handbook of Educational Psychology*, Alexander, P. and Winne, P. (Eds.) (pp. 900–927). Mahwah, NJ: Erlbaum.

Graham, S., and Perin, D. (2007). *Writing Next: Effective Strategies to Improve Writing of Adolescents in Middle School & High Schools*. Washington, DC: Alliance For Excellent Education.

Graham, S., and Sandmel, K. (2011). The process writing approach: A metaanalysis. *Journal of Educational Research*, 104, 396–407.

Graham, S., McKeown, D., Kiuhara, S., and Harris, K. (2012). A meta-analysis of writing instruction for students in the elementary grades. *Journal of Educational Psychology*, 104, (4), 879–896.

Graves, D. (1982). Break the welfare cycle: Let writers choose their topics. The English Composition Board, 3(2), 75–78.

Hacker, D.J. (1994). Comprehension monitoring as a writing process. In Advances in Cognition and Educational Practice, Butterfield, E.C., and Carlson, J.S. (Eds.) (Vol. 2, pp. 143–172). *Children's Writing: Toward a Process Theory of the Development of Skilled Writing*. Greenwich, CT: JAI Press.

Halliday, M. (2013). *Introduction to Functional Grammar* (4th Ed.). London: Routledge.

Harmey, S. (2020). Co-constructing writing: Handing over the reins to young authors. *Education*, 3-13, 3–11.

Harris, K.R., Graham, S., and Mason, L. (2006). Improving the writing, knowledge, and motivation of struggling young writers: Effects of self-regulated strategy development with and without peer support. *American Educational Research Journal*, 43, 295–337.

Hayden, T. (2020) *No More Draft Dodging: The Advantages of a Flexible Approach*. [Available: https://writing4pleasure.com/no-more-draft-dodging/]

Hayes, J. (2004). What triggers revision. In *Revision of Written Language: Cognitive and Instructional Processes*, Allal, L., Chanquoy, L., and Largy, P. (Eds.) (pp. 9–20). Philadelphia, PA: Kluwer.

Hayes, J. (2012). Modeling and remodeling writing. *Written Communication*, 29, 369–388.

Hayes, J.R., and Flower, L. (1980). Identifying the organization of writing processes. In *Cognitive Processes in Writing: An Interdisciplinary Approach*, Gregg, L.W., and Steinberg, E.R. (Eds.) (pp. 3–30). Hillsdale, NJ: Lawrence Erlbaum.

Heller, M. (1999). *Reading-Writing Connections: From Theory to Practice*. London: Routledge.

Hmelo-Silver, C.E., Duncan, R.G., and Chinn, C.A. (2007). Scaffolding and achievement in problem-based and inquiry learning: A response to Kirschner, Sweller, and Clark (2006). *Educational Psychologist*, 42(2), 99–107.

Hoewisch, A. (2001). 'Do I have to have a princess in my story?': Supporting children's writing of fairytales. *Reading and Writing Quarterly*, 17, 249–277.

Holliway, D., and McCutchen, D. (2004). Audience perspective in young writers' composing and revising. In *Revision of Written Language: Cognitive and Instructional Processes*, Allal, L., Chanquoy, L., and Largy, P. (Eds.) (pp. 87–101). Philadelphia, PA: Kluwer.

Hoogeveen, M. (2012). *Writing with Peer Response Using Genre Knowledge*. Thesis University of Twente Available: https://ris.utwente.nl/ws/portalfiles/portal/6062163/thesis_M_Hoogeveen.pdf.

Horn, M., and Giacobbe, M. (2007). *Talking, Drawing, Writing: Lessons for Our Youngest Writers* Portsmouth, NH: Heinnaman.

Jasmine, J., and Weiner, W. (2007). The effects of writing workshop on abilities of first grade students to become confident and independent writers. *Early Childhood Education Journal*, 35(2), 131–139.

Kauffman, G. (2006). Authoring ourselves as readers and writers. *Language Arts*, 83(6), 502–504.

Kellogg, R.T. (1987). Effects of topic knowledge on the allocation of processing time and cognitive effort to writing processes. *Memory & Cognition*, 15(3), 256–266.

Kellogg, R.T. (2001). Competition for working memory among writing processes. *American Journal of Psychology*, 114(2), 175–191.

Kellogg, R.T. (2008). Training writing skills: A cognitive developmental perspective. *Journal of Writing Research*, 1(1), 1–26.

Kellogg, R.T., Whiteford, A.P., Turner, C.E., Cahill, M., and Mertens, A. (2013). Working memory in written composition: An evaluation of the 1996 model. *Journal of Writing Research*, 5(2), 159–190.

Koster, M., Tribushinina, E., De Jong, P.F., and Van de Bergh, B. (2015). Teaching children to write: A meta-analysis of writing intervention research. *Journal of Writing Research*, 7(2), 249–274.

Langer, J.A. (2001). Beating the odds: Teaching middle and high school students to read and write well. *American Educational Research Journal*, 38(4), 837–880.

Levitt, R., Kramer-Vida, L., Palumbo, A., and Kelly, S. (2014). Professional development: A skills approach to a writing workshop. *The New Educator*, 10(3), 248–264.

Limpo, T., and Alves, R. (2013). Teaching planning or sentence-combining strategies: Effective SRSD interventions at different levels of written composition. *Contemporary Educational Psychology*, 38, 328–341.

Lipson, M., Mosenthal, J., Daniels, P., and Woodside-Jiron, H. (2000). Process writing in the classrooms of eleven fifth-grade teachers with different orientations to teaching and learning. In *Elementary School Journal*, 101(2), 209–231.

MacArthur, C.A., Schwartz, S.S., and Graham, S. (1991). Effects of a reciprocal peer revision strategy in special education classrooms. *Learning Disabilities Research and Practice*, 6, 201–210.

MacArthur, C.A., Graham, S., Schwartz, S.S., and Schafer, W.D. (1995). Evaluation of a writing instruction model that integrated a process approach, strategy instruction, and word processing. *Learning Disability Quarterly*, 18, 278–291.

MacArthur, C., Graham, S., and Harris, K. (2004). Insights from instructional research on revision with struggling writers. In *Revision of Written Language: Cognitive and Instructional Processes*, Allal, L., Chanquoy, L., and Largy, P. (Eds.) (pp. 125–137). Philadelphia, PA: Kluwer.

Mackenzie, N. (2011). From drawing to writing: What happens when you shift teaching priorities in the first six months of school? *Australian Journal of Language and Literacy*, 34: 322–340.

McCutchen D. (1996). A capacity theory of writing: Working memory in composition. *Educational Psychology Review*, 8(3), 299–325.

McQuitty, V. (2014). Process-oriented writing instruction in elementary classrooms: Evidence of effective practices from the research literature. *Writing & Pedagogy*, 6(3), 467–495.

Moffett, J., and Wagner, B. (1992). *Student Centered Language Arts K-12* (4th Ed.). Portsmouth, NH: Heinemann.

Morizawa, G. (2014). *Nesting the Neglected 'R' A Design Study: Writing Instruction within a Prescriptive Literacy Program* University of California, Berkeley. [Available: https://digitalassets.lib.berkeley.edu/etd/ucb/text/Morizawa_berkeley_0028E_14961.pdf]

Murray, D. (1982). *Learning by Teaching*. Princeton, NJ: Boynton Cook.

Murray, D. (1985). *A Writer Teaches Writing* (2nd Ed.). Boston, MA: Houghton Mifflin.

Myhill, D., and Jones, S. (2007). More than just error correction: Students' perspectives on their revision processes during writing. *Written Communication*, 24(4), 323–343.

Parry, B., and Taylor, L. (2018). Readers in the round: Children's holistic engagements with texts. *Literacy*, 52(2), 103–110.

Pressley, M., Gaskins, I., Solic, K., and Collins, S. (2006). A portrait of benchmark school: How a school produces high achievement in students who previously failed. *Journal of Educational Psychology*, 98(2), 282–306.

Pritchard, R.J., and Honeycutt, R.L. (2006). Best practices in implementing a process approach to teaching writing. In *Best Practices in Writing Instruction*, Graham, S., MacArthur, C.A., and Fitzgerald, J. (Eds.) (pp. 28–49). New York: Guilford Press.

Rosen, H. (2017). The politics of writing. In *Harold Rosen Writings on Life, Language and Learning 1958–2008*, Richmond, J. (Ed.) (pp. 347–361). London: UCL IOE Press.

Rowe, D. (2003). The nature of young children's authoring. In *Handbook of Early Childhood Literacy*, Hall, N., Jarson, J., and Marsh, J. (Eds.) (pp. 258–270). London: Sage.

Scardamalia, M., and Bereiter, C. (1983). The development of evaluative, diagnostic, and remedial capabilities in children's composing. In *The Psychology of Written Language: Development of Educational Perspectives*, Martlew, M. (Ed.) (pp. 67–95). London: Wiley.

Scardamalia, M., and Bereiter, C. (1991). Literate expertise. In *Toward a General Theory of Expertise*, Ericsson, K.A., and Smith, J. (Eds.) (pp. 172–194). Cambridge, MA: Cambridge University Press.

Schneider, J. (2003). Contexts, genres, and imagination: An examination of the idiosyncratic writing performances of three elementary children within multiple contexts of writing instruction. *Research in the Teaching of English*, 37, 329–379.

Shanahan, T. (2016). Relationships between reading and writing development. In *Handbook of Writing Research*, MacArthur, C., Graham, S., and Fitzgerald, J. (Eds.) (2nd Ed.) (pp. 194–207). New York: The Guilford Press.

Sharp, L. (2016). Acts of writing: A compilation of six models that define the processes of writing. *International Journal of Instruction*, 9, 77–90.

Sharples, M. (1999). *How We Write: Writing as Creative Design*. London: Routledge.

Smagorinsky, P., and Smith, M. (1992). The nature of knowledge in composition and literary understanding: The question of specificity. *Review of Educational Research*, 62(3), 279–305.

Smith, F. (1982). *Writing and the Writer*. New York: HEB.

Stein, N. (1983). On the goals, functions, and knowledge of reading and writing. *Contemporary Educational Psychology*, 8(3), 261–292.

van den Bergh, H., and Rijlaarsdam G. (2001). Changes in cognitive activities during the writing process and relationships with text quality. *Educational Psychology*, 21(4), 373–385.

Wyse, D., and Torgerson, C. (2017). Experimental trials and 'what works?' In education: The case of grammar for writing. *British Educational Research Journal*, 43(6), 1019–1047.

Young, R. (2019). *What is it 'writing for pleasure' teachers do that makes the difference?* The University of Sussex: The Goldsmiths' Company [Online]. Available: www.writing4pleasure.com.

Young, R., and Ferguson, F. (2019). *Power English Writing: Teacher's Guide Year 6*. Oxford: Pearson.

Young, R., and Ferguson, F. (2020a). *Class Writing Projects* Accessed at: www.writing4pleasure.com/class-writing-projects.

Young, R., and Ferguson, F. (2020b). *Real-World Writers: A Handbook for Teaching Writing with 7–11 Year Olds*. London: Routledge.

CHAPTER 16
Set writing goals

Koster et al. (2015) claimed that the setting of writing goals is by far the most effective teaching instruction teachers can employ. In his study of the most exceptional writing teachers, Murray Gadd (2014) noted that they scaffolded class writing projects by setting *distant*, *product*, and *process* orientated writing goals within a social, community, inquiry, and mastery based writing environment. As discussed in Chapter 14, teacher and pupils together will consider the nature of a class writing project and its distant goal (its purpose and future audience). Having a distant goal gives children a sense of motivation (Young 2019). They know what they want their writing to do and they keep that goal in mind throughout. Product goals follow, established through genre-study and the examination and discussion of mentor texts. These goals will be items the children have identified as likely to be important for the success of their written pieces. Product goals help provide children with a sense of self-regulation (I know what to do and how to do it) and self-efficacy (I am being successful). Finally, process goals or 'writing deadlines', will be set. As children become more experienced, they will be able to set their own deadlines and so write at a pace and use a writing process that best suits them. Again, process goals help children feel a sense of self-efficacy and self-regulation (Young 2019).

Distant goals

Authentic and purposeful class writing projects are fundamental to children's success in writing and becoming writers. According to the research, participating in the formulation of goals and having some agency over them has a positive effect on the subsequent quality of children's texts (Ames and Archer 1988; Covington 2000; van den Bergh and Rijlaarsdam 2001; Timperley and Parr 2009; Rooke 2013 Bradford et al. 2016). This is what Wiggins (2009) terms 'backward curriculum design'. In this way, the community of writers establish together what they are going to learn before being taught about it. Discussion of the distant goal for a project not only increases children's motivation and engagement in the act of writing but also helps them clarify what they have to do to be successful, and so builds their sense of self-efficacy and self-regulation (Bandura and Schunk 1981; Latham and Locke 1991; Butler and Winnie 1995; Schunk, 1990, 1996; Timperley and Parr 2009; Rooke 2013). According to Shanahan (2016) and Breetvelt et al. (1994), young writers craft better texts when they have time to consider and discuss their future readers' needs before getting on to generating ideas.

Teachers might ask their classes some of the following questions:

Purpose

- Why do you think we are undertaking this writing project? What do we want this writing to achieve or do when we are finished?
- What do you think we should do with this writing once it's ready for publication and performance?
- Why might this project be important for your development as writers? What is it helping you learn about?

Audience

- Who do you think we should write for? Who do you want to write for?
- What do we know about the audience? What do we need to find out?
- Let's draw our audience! Who might they be? What might they look like? What might they be interested in? What might they want from us?

You will note the questions above include the pronoun 'we'. This is because *Writing For Pleasure* teachers will actively participate in class writing projects too (Englert and Raphael 1991; Paris and Winograd 2003). This practice is discussed in more detail in Chapter 21.

Teaching about genre

The setting of distant goals cannot be separated from the study and discussion of genre. The linguist and genre theorist James Martin (2009) defines genre as nothing less than how we use language to live, while Lucy Calkins (1998) states that teachers should regard genre-study as fundamental enough to shape their curriculum, claiming it to be life giving. Genre-study requires the setting of goals because it connects a young apprentice writer's desires with their knowledge about certain structures and textual features that can help them make their writing intentions successful and meaningful (Kress 1994; Purcell-Gates et al. 2007; Rose 2008; Olinghouse et al. 2015). As discussed in Chapter 1, researchers see genre-study in school as a social justice issue since it gives children full access to purposes and audiences for writing they may not otherwise have the chance to encounter, or which are deliberately withheld from them.

Genre-based approaches to teaching writing have been widely adopted across the world and have achieved spectacular improvements in student outcomes, with Rose (2008, pp. 151–152) claiming such approaches achieve 'twice to over four times expected rates' of learning whilst at the same time 'closing the gap between the most and least successful students'. Bloodgood (2002), Englert and Raphael (1991), Martin and Rothery (1993), Schneider (2003), and Eltringham et al. (2018) all suggest that if teachers understand and use genre study intelligently to help children match writing style to purpose and audience, they expand children's writing repertoire and choices, improve their knowledge of texts, and so support their creative experimentation. Genre teaching, when used skilfully, helps *Writing For Pleasure* teachers fulfil many of the affective domains of writing for pleasure and supports a contemporary writing workshop approach (Corden 2002; Young and Ferguson 2020a).

Genre and goal setting

In terms of children learning to be writers, a genre is a social, goal-orientated, and staged process (Hyland 2007; Martin 2009).

- **Social** – because every genre has an audience in mind, even if that audience is only yourself. There are certain conventions and social expectations that come with certain genres of writing. These can be conformed to or else actively and imaginatively manipulated, subverted, or hybridized by writers.
- **Goal-orientated** – because it helps us fulfil the reasons we are *moved* to write. Learning to write involves learning to use writing for your own purposes and goals. We identify these goals by reading, examining, and discussing mentor texts before trying to construct our own.
- **Staged** – because you usually have to move through a variety of processes to achieve your final writing intentions.

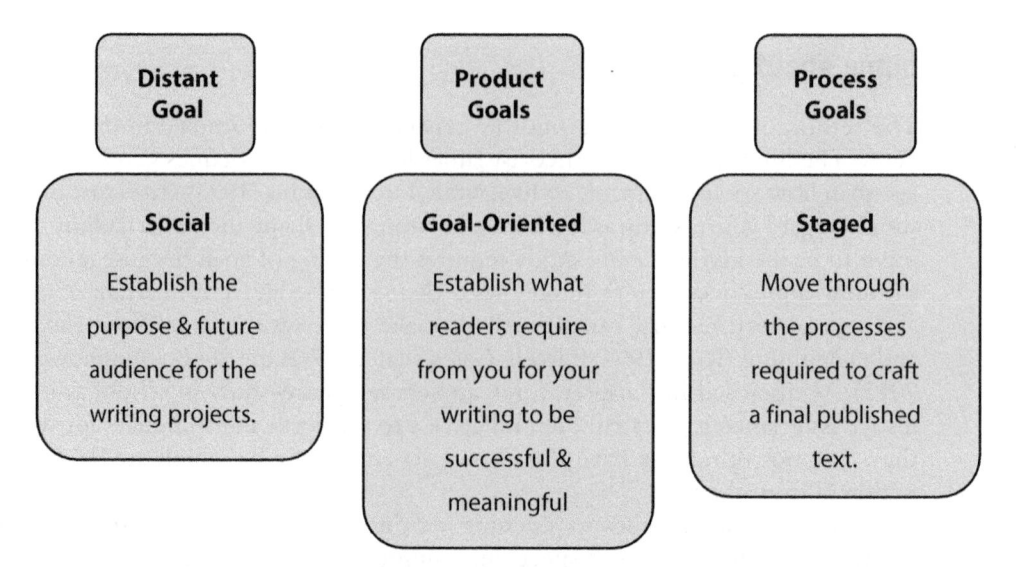

Distant Goal	Product Goals	Process Goals
Social	**Goal-Oriented**	**Staged**
Establish the purpose & future audience for the writing projects.	Establish what readers require from you for your writing to be successful & meaningful	Move through the processes required to craft a final published text.

FIGURE 16.1 Showing the relationship between authentic and purposeful writing projects, goal setting, and genre teaching.

Michael Halliday (2013) suggests that genres are made up of three interrelated meanings or 'metafunctions' which affect the type of language we use in our writing: ideational, interpersonal, and textual.

- **Ideational** is our interest in expressing a reality or topic (whatever it may be).
- **Interpersonal** is about negotiating this topic with our audience.
- **Textual** is about how to best manage and present what it is we want to share.

These metafunctions can be mediated for children through Halliday's concept of 'register', which is composed of field, tenor, and mode. Each genre has its own register. In their work, Young and Ferguson (2020a, 2020b) recommend that teachers use the register features of a genre as the means of helping children consider the distant goal and then the product goals for a project, and to generate rich conversation and discussion with their classes when reading mentor texts.

- **Field** is about sharing and discussing the type of activity children will be engaging in within the class writing project. The 'what is going on' and what ideas and topics are usually discussed or used within the genre. It involves the writer having knowledge, opinion, thoughts, creative artistry, stories, and/or reflections to share.
- **Tenor** is about sharing and discussing with children their role as the writer and how they will relate to and interact with their reader.
- **Mode** is about discussing how best to share their information in terms of structure, visual devices, modality, and organisation, and how best to publish or perform their writing.

According to Martin (2009, p. 24) children 'are generally more conscious of the meanings associated with register and genre once you point them out'. *Writing For Pleasure* teachers take a top-down perspective on writing, starting with the social functions of a class writing project. Before any of the features of register are discussed, the purpose of the project is agreed, and the future audience identified and considered (Eltringham et al. 2018; Young 2019). By these means, the community of writers will better understand the reason for the type of writing, its potential, and how they might like to use it for their own purposes by generating their own writing ideas (see Chapter 15).

Martin and Rose (2007, p. 4) support such an approach. They state that, although 'traditional approaches assume that language must be taught as it is described in school grammars as a set of decontextualized systems', what children actually need is the skill to be able to recognise language patterns 'at each level as they read real texts', to discuss a text's function in relation to the goals of the genre, and then to use what they have learnt about these language patterns (or grammar) authentically, for their own chosen purposes in their very own writing (Purcell-Gates et al. 2007).

According to Frank Smith, 'writing requires an enormous fund of specialised knowledge that cannot possibly be acquired from lectures, drill or even from the exercise of writing itself'. He continues with 'much more is required to become a competent and adaptable author of letters, reports, journals, poems or pieces of fiction', concluding that 'to learn how to write for newspapers you must read newspapers; to write poetry, read it' (1988, pp. 17–20). His words lead us perfectly into the discussion of mentor texts and the identification and setting of product goals in the next section.

Product goals

'To become writers children must read like writers. To read like writers they must see themselves as writers. Children will read stories, poems, and letters differently when they see these texts as things they themselves could produce' (Smith 1983, p. 565). Through the establishment of distant goals, *Writing For Pleasure* teachers create the desire to investigate other texts in keeping with the genre children are looking to use for themselves (Young 2019). They provide mentor texts to help the community identify the typical conventions of a genre and make them visible to their pupil-writers. They attend to children's self-efficacy and self-regulation by clarifying what children will have to do and how it can be done to make their writing meaningful, or, as Timperley and Parr (2009) put it, to 'reveal the secrets of how to be successful'. By sharing mentor texts, teachers allow children, whether formally or informally, to learn from and discuss high-quality contextualised examples (Martin and Rose 2007; Hoogeveen 2012; Gallagher 2014; Andrade 2019). Frank Smith (1982, p. 201) sums it up beautifully when he says: 'the environment in which a child will want to write is an environment of demonstrations, not just of "this is the way we do things" but also "these are things that can be done"'. Academic research also supports this position (Hillocks 1986; Andrade et al. 2008; Koster et al. 2015; Andrade 2019) and shows that it is advantageous to decide as a class what the product goals are going to be by reading a variety of mentor texts. On a practical level, Young and Ferguson (2020, p. 43) share the following advice with teachers:

- First, give out and read an example written by you. Talk with your children about why and how you went about writing it. Ask them their opinion of it. What do they think makes it a strong or weak piece of writing?
- It is then really important that children get to see and discuss a variety of good examples written by other children in previous years. Therefore, it is always good to store away excellent examples for future use.
- It is also important that children discuss authentic examples from the world outside school. Give out a variety of examples (maybe four or five) and allow the children to discuss which they think is the strongest piece of writing. The reasons they give will be a good starting point for setting the product goals for the project. You may even want to ask that they put them in rank order.

According to Hillocks (1986), a good strategy when establishing product goals is to explore writing which has failed to achieve its intentions; it may be particularly helpful for inexperienced writers to see what *not* to do when they start writing.

The *Writing For Pleasure* teachers observed as part of Young's (2019) study would ensure that the final product goals were put on display, converted into child-friendly rubrics or 'revision checklists' (see Chapter 15), were well known by the children, and were regularly referred to. By providing exemplar texts and identifying product goals together, teachers can develop children's confidence, self-esteem, and self-efficacy in writing and being a writer (Corden 2003; Bradford et al. 2016; Andrade 2019). Using Halliday's (2013) theory of field, tenor, and mode as their foundation, Young and Ferguson (2020, p. 43) suggest what the writing community could consider when formulating a list of product goals. It is important to emphasise that goals will be purpose driven and will focus on the crucial, meaningful, and significant qualities of writing rather than on easily quantifiable linguistic features (Andrade and Brooke 2008; Myhill 2008; Crossley 2020). In other words, product goals should help children consider the 'big picture' (Eltringham et al. 2018).

Purpose

- What would be helpful to remember about writing a …?
- What would be helpful to remember when reading a …?
- What do we intend this writing to do?

Content and topics (*field*)

- What sorts of topics are typically used in a …?
- How could we play around with this type of writing? Can we include people or topics that are too often ignored?
- How are you sure the topic you've chosen will appeal to your reader?
- How can you take advantage of your reader's passions, interests, or concerns?

We as the writers (*tenor*)

Do we need to come across as an expert, inquisitor, thinker, historian, scientist, aggressor, defender, critic, champion, salesperson, influencer, storyteller, memoirist, or artist? Do we need to be more than one of these?

The audience (*tenor*)

- Are we writing to one person or many?
- What do we know about our audience(s)? What are they going to want from this writing?
- What does the relationship between the writer and reader have to be like? Do we know them? Are they strangers? Are we close to them? Are we going to be friendly, formal, intimate, detached, or colloquial?
- What sort of reaction do we want our readers to have to our writing?
- How do you ensure the reader finds you, as the writer, appealing?
- What might we be able to copy from the mentor texts we've read that our readers might appreciate in our texts too?

How it looks (*mode*)

- How can the writing be presented? What other modalities might be useful or required?

Style and features

- What would be helpful to remember about writing in general?
- What sort of literary, linguistic, or grammatical features are going to be useful?
- What sort of vocabulary might be useful?

Gadd's (2014) work notes that the teachers he observed had quite open-ended interpretations of product goals. He suggests that they can be:

- Single goals for all learners or multiple writing goals for learners to select from.
- Worked on by learners at varying times or simultaneously.
- Designed to generate one intended outcome or a range of possible outcomes.
- Designed for class writing projects or personal projects.
- Devised by the teacher, the children, or collaboratively.

Writing For Pleasure teachers will allow their learners to attend to writing goals at their own level and at their own pace (Pollard et al. 1994; Reutzel 2007; Paratore and McCormack 2009; Schumm and Avalos 2009; Rubie-Davies 2010; Garrett and Moltzen 2011; Wyse and Torgerson 2017). In Young's (2019) study, because the teachers explained the genre fully, their pupils had considerable freedom to determine how they were to realise their own piece of writing. The product goals were not a set of success criteria or a mechanical formula which, as Martin (2009) rightly says, stands in the way of a child's creativity or self-expression, but were a genuinely useful tool to help children monitor their own progress and feel success. Additionally, Englert and Raphael (1991) make the attractive suggestion that product goals can free children up to show more of their personality, wit, and voice. Below, Young and Ferguson (2020, p. 44) provide an example of product goals set for a class writing project on the topic of *Advocacy Journalism*.

What we will have to do to make our advocacy journalism articles effective:

- Raise awareness for your chosen charity and encourage people to donate.
- Charities typically involve people, animals, or the environment.
- Your writing voice will want to persuade, sound knowledgeable, and share a touching personal story.
- The examples used photographs, maps, contact details, information boxes, and subheadings.
- Pick a charity you can identify with.
- Come across as enthusiastic and earnest – pull at your reader's heartstrings. *Don't* sound desperate or aggressive though!
- The following will be useful: specific verbs, the subjunctive, subordination, and quotations for interviews.
- A variety of modal verbs.
- Explain any technical terms using simple vocabulary.

Teachers will teach mini-lessons based on product goals, giving contextualised and responsive instruction which children will welcome and which will directly impact their writing (Bradford et al. 2016). This is discussed in more detail in Chapter 20. A list of product goals provides an explicit resource and a point of reference when children are receiving high-quality peer and teacher feedback through pupil conferencing (see Chapter 22). Finally, research suggests that children need specific time to evaluate their writing against the agreed product goals and to revise their developing compositions, using a child-friendly rubric which matches the goals the children themselves have identified with the teacher (Andrade et al. 2008; Bradford et al. 2016; Andrade 2019). See Chapter 15 for more information on revising and the use of rubrics.

Process goals

Achieving process goals (meeting writing deadlines) is what professional writers are often required to do. In school, *Writing For Pleasure* teachers seek to encourage in their apprentice writers the same disciplined ways of thinking, working, and organising themselves (Langer 2001; Pressley et al. 2006).

According to Ames and Archer (1988) and Vanderburg (2006), a focus on setting process goals results in children:

- Leading themselves successfully towards publication or performance.
- Having a greater understanding of writing processes and becoming more metacognitive.
- Having greater intrinsic desire and motivation to produce writing that is reader focused and academically successful.
- Having a contextualised understanding of what is gained by writing and being a writer.
- Moving from dependence to independence by improving their sense of self-regulation (knowing what they have to do and how to do it).
- Preferring more cognitively challenging writing projects.

Timperley and Parr (2009) suggest that mastery learning of the writing processes through regular and meaningful practice has one of the largest effects reported for a teaching strategy. The idea of mastery learning is based on a child's effort and attitude in applying and practising the processes involved in producing writing and being a writer. Research studies have found that children who write under such conditions achieve better academically, have higher levels of motivation, and find more meaning in their learning than children taught through a skills, performance, or otherwise presentational approach (Hillocks 1986; Ames and Archer 1988; Schunk and Swartz 1993; Butler and Winnie 1995; Covington 2000; Langer 2001; Hmelo-Silver et al. 2007).

Teachers setting process goals

Research into the effectiveness of learning goals generally concludes that an emphasis on process benefits learners more than an emphasis on outcomes alone (Ames and Archer 1988; Schunk 1996; Covington 2000; Seijts et al. 2004; Hmelo-Silver et al. 2007; Rooke 2013). In our own study (Young 2019), *Writing For Pleasure* teachers set specific writing goals in an environment and atmosphere of inquiry which was scaffolded and directed towards mastery of particular writing strategies or processes (Ames and Archer 1988; Timperley and Parr 2009). Distant goals for a class writing project, for example 'let's write flash-fiction pieces for a class anthology', were subdivided into more manageable 'chunks', which allowed not only for long-term progress to be monitored clearly and regularly, but also allowed children to feel the sense of satisfaction that comes from frequently reaching their goals (Bandura and Schunk 1981; Butler and Winnie 1995; Hmelo-Silver et al. 2007). The cognitive load involved in creating a published writing product was shared out across the writing processes, making a writing project feel more accessible and manageable and increasing children's sense of self-efficacy.

The teacher's own ultimate goal is that, over time, children will be able to navigate these cognitively challenging writing projects independently, set their own process goals and use their own authentic process (Whitney 2017). Lipson et al. (2000) suggest that children be given plenty of time in which to write through the different processes, setting themselves deadlines which can be recursive, revisited if required, and therefore flexible. They continue by observing that *Writing For Pleasure* teachers could hand over to children considerable responsibility for setting process goals whilst still providing structure and holding pupils accountable for meeting deadlines. Young and Ferguson (2020, pp. 69–70), show how goals might change over time as children become more experienced:

Examples of process goal setting in LKS2 (seven to nine-year-olds):

- Over the next couple of writing sessions, you will need to work on a plan for your instructional text.
- Using your plan to help you, you will have the next few writing sessions to draft your instructions.
- I am giving you this writing session to work with your partner on revising your instructional text ready for publication. If you feel that you may need another session because you have a lot of revisions to do, please let me know.
- If you feel ready, I have put aside this writing session (and tomorrow's session if we need it) so that you can proof-read and edit your instructional texts to make sure they are 'reader-ready'.
- Today is the day! This writing session is for you to publish your instructional texts into the class library.

Examples of process goal setting in UKS2 (nine to eleven-year-olds):

- You have 12 writing sessions to write your short stories and prepare them for publication.
- It's day three of 12. I would suggest that many of you start drafting today if you are going to meet our publishing deadline.

- You have two days left until publication day. Make sure your manuscripts are 'reader-ready'.
- This is your last day. Your short stories must be ready for publication tomorrow. If you don't think you are going to make the deadline, come and speak with me.

Children setting goals for personal writing projects

The importance of children having opportunities to pursue their personal writing projects and their own social writing goals cannot be underestimated (Ames and Archer 1988; Covington 2000). *Writing For Pleasure* teachers teach writing processes with a view to children applying them to personal projects and for individual mastery of them (Young 2019). Therefore, the connection between setting writing goals and pursuing personal writing projects, as discussed in Chapter 18, is profound. Because a *Writing For Pleasure* pedagogy allows more time for writing, children who achieve their process goal for that day should have the opportunity to continue with any personal writing topics in the time that remains in the session. In this way, children will be in what Young and Ferguson (2020, p. 64) call 'a constant state of composition'.

Examples of effective practice

The following is a description of what we observed during our study of *Writing For Pleasure* teachers (Young 2019). To maintain children's commitment and motivation during a class writing project, the teachers ensured that their classes knew the 'distant goal' for the project, that is to say the future audience and purpose for their finished writing. The class, as a community, also had a say in setting the 'product goals' for their project. This was achieved in discussion about what they would have to do and what it was writers did to ensure their writing was successful and meaningful. The teachers would often share an exemplar of their own piece of writing which was in keeping with the writing project. They would then discuss the decisions they had made and what they had tried to achieve in the piece. The children would use the outcomes of the discussion to help set product goals for their own writing. In one class, they even discussed what *not* to do by looking at ineffective examples. The product goals were similar to success criteria, but they also included more overarching goals which were linked directly to the purpose and audience of the writing; for example, one teacher used Durran's 'boxed resource' (2019). Product goals were put on display and were repeatedly referred to by the children and the teachers throughout the class writing project. The teachers gave pupils the knowledge they needed so that they could be empowered to see their own writing idea through to successful publication.

Teachers set loose 'process goals' for writing time (e.g. generating an idea/planning/drafting/revising/editing/publishing). These goals kept their classes on track as a whole without forcing them to keep to a certain pace or writing process. This meant the children felt they could write happily and to the best of their abilities. In interview, some children stated that having the writing project's 'to-do' list and keeping to a schedule was helpful, with one child noting the satisfaction she experienced when reaching a goal set by the teacher. Interestingly, another pupil expressed the excitement of being set a challenging product goal, 'I get pushed off my level and I do enjoy to do that – it just feels exciting'.

Whilst distant, product, and process goals were being set by or with the children during class writing projects, the same was not seen for personal writing projects, which often lacked direction as a result. The children were not always encouraged to have the same expectations for their personal projects, nor were they always given the opportunity to fulfil the distant goals they may have had for some of their personal projects.

Some of the teachers were able to elicit high levels of enjoyment from their classes as a result of regular, systematic, and enthusiastic praise of product goals achieved; children commented on the enjoyment and satisfaction in writing which came from pleasing their teacher. Other teachers elicited high levels of enjoyment from their classes by giving them greater agency over the subjects for their writing, their writing processes, and deadlines. Some children expressed intrinsic motivation leading to enjoyment and satisfaction in writing. Unfortunately, teacher focus on external and internal motivation was not observed in rich combination.

Practical things you can do

- Whenever you are planning a class writing project, consider whether you have exemplar texts from the world outside school. As Whitney (2017, p. 17) explains, 'rule of thumb: if you can't find it, your students probably shouldn't be writing it'.
- Have on display the distant goal for a writing project to remind children why they are writing and who they are writing for.
- Construct product goals for a project in conjunction with your class and in response to effective and ineffective exemplar texts.
- Make sure your product goals are not simply a list of 'success criteria'.
- Make sure the product goals for a project are on display and can be read or understood by the class.
- Plan mini-lessons which will help children in their pursuit of the class product goals (see Chapter 20 for more details).
- Create a child-friendly rubric based on the class product goals which children can use whilst revising their compositions.
- Set realistic process goals (writing deadlines) as milestones for children to achieve on their way towards formal publication or performance of their writing. Regularly remind children of these deadlines but be flexible to their needs.
- Encourage children to keep a process log – where they set and log process goals they want to achieve by a certain time. Alternatively, consider keeping a class 'writing register' (Young and Ferguson 2020).
- Have in place a clear routine of what children are to do once they have completed a writing deadline. Make a decision as to whether you wish children to

continue towards preparing their writing for publication or performance or else to carry on with personal writing projects.

- When assessing children's writing, be sure you are looking at the overall effectiveness, success, and meaningfulness of the child's piece. Avoid limiting assessment solely to the number of product goals achieved. In addition, don't regard active subversion or manipulation of the product goals as a weakness if the child has fulfilled the objective of creating something that is suitable for their audience.

QUESTIONS WORTH ASKING YOURSELF

- Before you start a writing project, do you discuss the final goal for the project with your class? Do you take time to discuss the purpose and, importantly, the future audience for a writing project with your class?
- Do you refer back to the ultimate goal for the project throughout a writing project?
- Do you construct the product goals for a class writing project with your class? Do your product goals look at the 'big picture' rather than read as a list of genre, linguistic, or grammatical features for inclusion in the text?
- Do you use mentor texts, which match the volume and type of writing you're asking the children to engage in, to help aid the construction of class product goals?
- Do you examine ineffective exemplar texts to help you consider what *not* to do when writing your own compositions?
- Do you put product goals on display in the class, and are you and the children continually referring back to them?
- Do you plan to teach mini-lessons which enable children to attend to the product goals for the project? (see chapter 20 for more details).
- Do you provide children with resources and do you use your working wall to help children achieve the product goals set?
- Do you create child-friendly rubrics for children to use whilst revising their developing compositions? Do these rubrics match the constructed product goals? (see Chapter 15 for more details).
- Are you flexible with your writing deadlines so as to ensure all children, regardless of the writing process, have enough time to achieve their best writing?
- Have you put in place a routine of what children are to do if they reach a writing deadline early? Do they go on to the next stage in their process, or perhaps continue with their personal writing projects? (see Chapter 18 for more details).
- Do you allow children to pursue their own social goals by giving them time and opportunity to develop their personal writing projects and see some of these through to formal publication or performance?
- When assessing children's finished writing products, do you look beyond the list of product goals and consider the 'big picture'?
- Are you able to acknowledge and celebrate any active and creative manipulation, subversion, and disregard for the product goals if the writing has proven itself to be successful, meaningful, and effective?

References

Ames, C., and Archer, J. (1988). Achievement goals in the classroom: Students' learning strategies and motivation processes. *Journal of Educational Psychology*, 80(3), 260–267.

Andrade, H. (2019). A critical review of research on student self-assessment. *Frontiers in Education*, 4(87), 1–13.

Andrade, H., Du, Y., and Wang, X. (2008). Putting rubrics to the test: The effect of a model, criteria generation, and rubric-referenced self-assessment on elementary school students' writing. *Educational Measurement: Issues and Practice*, 27, 3–13.

Bandura, A., and Schunk, D.H. (1981). Cultivating competence, self-efficacy and intrinsic interest through proximal self-motivation. *Journal of Personality and Social Psychology*, 41(3), 586–598.

Bloodgood, J. (2002). Quintilian: A classical educator speaks to the writing process. *Reading Research and Instruction*, 42(1), 30–43.

Bradford, K., Newland, A., Rule, A., and Montgomery, S. (2016). Rubrics as a tool in writing instruction: Effects on the opinion essays of first and second graders. *Early Childhood Education*, 44, 463–472.

Breetvelt, I., van den Bergh, H., and Rijlaarsdam, G. (1994). Relations between writing processes and text quality: When and how? *Cognition and Instruction*, 12(2), 103–123.

Butler, D.L., and Winne, P.H. (1995). Feedback and self-regulated learning: A theoretical synthesis. *Review of Educational Research*, 65(3), 245–274.

Calkins, L. (1998). *The Art of Teaching Writing*. Portsmouth, NH: Heinemann.

Corden, R. (2002). developing reflective writers in primary schools: Findings from partnership research. *Educational Review*, 54(3), 249–276.

Corden, R. (2003). Writing is more than 'exciting': Equipping primary children to become reflective writers. *Reading Literacy and Language*, April, pp. 18–26.

Covington, M.V. (2000). Goal theory, motivation, and school achievement: An integrative review. *Annual Review of Psychology*, 51, 171–200.

Crossley, S.A. (2020). Linguistic features in writing quality and development: An overview. *Journal of Writing Research*, 11(3), 415–443.

Durran, J. (2019). Re-thinking 'success criteria': a simple device to support pupils' writing. [Accessed 9th July 2019 https://jamesdurran.blog/2019/01/24/re-thinking-success-criteria-asimple-device-to-support-pupils-writing/]

Eltringham, K., Hawe, E., and Dixon, H. (2018). Checking, highlighting, adding and ticking off: Year 6 students' understandings of and responses to the use of goals in New Zealand writing classroom. *Education 3-13*, 46(7), 851–866.

Englert, C., and Raphael, T. (1991). Making strategies and self-talk visible: Writing instruction in regular and special education classrooms. *American Educational Research Journal*, 28(2), 337–372.

Gadd, M. (2014). *What is Critical in the Effective Teaching of Writing?* Auckland: The University of Auckland.

Gallagher, K. (2014). Making the most of mentor texts. *Writing: A Core Skill*, 71(7). 28–33.

Garrett, L., and Moltzen, R. (2011). Writing because I want to, not because I have to: Young gifted writers' perspectives on the factors that 'matter' in developing expertise. *English Teaching: Practice and Critique*, 10(1), 165–180.

Halliday, M. (2013). *Introduction to Functional Grammar* (4th Ed.). London: Routledge.

Hillocks, G. (1986). *Research on Written Composition: New Directions for Teaching*. Urbana, IL: National Council of Teachers of English.

Hmelo-Silver, C., Duncan, R., and Chinn, C. (2007). Scaffolding and achievement in problem-based and inquiry learning: A response to Kirschner, Sweller, and Clark (2006). *Educational Psychologist*, 42(2), 99–107.

Hoogeveen, M. (2012). *Writing with Peer Response Using Genre Knowledge*. Thesis University of Twente. Available: https://ris.utwente.nl/ws/portalfiles/portal/6062163/thesis_M_Hoogeveen.pdf.

Hyland, K. (2007). Genre pedagogy: Language, literacy and L2 writing instruction. *Journal of Second Language Writing* 16, 148–164.

Koster, M., Tribushinina, E., De Jong, P.F., and Van de Bergh, B. (2015). Teaching children to write: A meta-analysis of writing intervention research. *Journal of Writing Research*, 7(2), 249–274.

Kress, G. (1994). *Learning to Write* (2nd Ed.). London: Routledge.

Langer, J.A. (2001). Beating the odds: Teaching middle and high school students to read and write well. *American Educational Research Journal*, 38(4), 837–880.

Latham, G.P., and Locke, E.A. (1991). Self-regulation through goal setting. *Organizational Behavior and Human Decision Processes*, 50(2), 212–247.

Lipson, M., Mosenthal, J., Daniels, P., and Woodside-Jiron, H. (2000). Process writing in the classrooms of eleven fifth-grade teachers with different orientations to teaching and learning. *Elementary School Journal*, 101(2), 209–231.

Martin, J.R. (2009). Genre and language learning: A social semiotic perspective. *Linguistics and Education*, 20(1), 10–21.

Martin, J., and Rose, D. (2007). Interacting with text: The role of dialogue in learning to read and write. Foreign Languages. *Foreign Languages in China*, 4(5), 66–80.

Martin, J.R., and Rothery, J. (1993). Grammar: Making meaning in writing. In *The Powers of Literacy: A Genre Approach to Teaching Writing*, Cope, B., and Kalantzis, M. (Eds.) (pp. 137–153). Pittsburgh, PA: University of Pittsburgh Press.

Myhill, D. (2008). Towards a linguistic model of sentence development in writing. *Language & Education*, 22(5), 271–288.

Olinghouse, N., Graham, S., and Gillespie, A. (2015). The relationship of discourse and topic knowledge to fifth graders' writing performance. *Journal of Educational Psychology*, 107(2), 391–406.

Paratore, J.R., and McCormack, R.L. (2009). Grouping in the middle and secondary grades: Advancing content and literacy knowledge. In *Literacy Instruction for Adolescents: Research-Based Practice*, Wood, K.D., and Blanton, W.E. (Eds.) (pp. 420–441). New York: The Guilford Press.

Paris, S. G., and Winograd, P. (2003). *The role of self-regulated learning in contextual teaching: Principles and practices for teacher preparation* (CIERA Report). Retrieved from https://files.eric.ed.gov/fulltext/ED479905.pdf.

Pollard, A., Broadfoot, P., Croll, P., Osborn, M., and Abbott, D. (1994). *Changing English in Primary Schools? The Impact of the Education Reform Act at KS1*. London: Cassell.

Pressley, M., Gaskins, I., Solic, K., and Collins, S. (2006). A portrait of benchmark school: How a school produces high achievement in students who previously failed. *Journal of Educational Psychology*, 98(2), 282–306.

Purcell-Gates, V., Duke, N. K., and Martineau, J. A. (2007). Learning to read and write genrespecific text: Roles of authentic experience and explicit teaching. *Reading Research Quarterly*, 42(1), 8–45.

Reutzel, D.R. (2007). Organizing effective literacy instruction: Differentiating instruction to meet the needs of all children. In *Best Practices in Literacy Instruction*, Gambrell, L.B., Morrow, L.M., and Pressley, M. (Eds.) (pp. 313–434). New York: The Guilford Press.

Rooke, J. (2013). *Transforming Writing: Final Evaluation Report*. London: National Literacy Trust.

Rose, D. (2008). Writing as linguistic mastery: The development of genre-based literacy pedagogy. In *Handbook of Writing Development*, Myhill, D., Beard, R., Nystrand, M., and Riley, J. (Eds.) (pp. 151–166). London: Sage.

Rubie-Davies, C.M. (2010). Teacher expectations and perceptions of student attributes: Is there a relationship? *British Journal of Educational Psychology*, 80(1), 121–135.

Schneider, J. (2003). Contexts, genres, and imagination: An examination of the idiosyncratic writing performances of three elementary children within multiple contexts of writing instruction. *Research in the Teaching of English*, 37, 329–379.

Schumm, J.S., and Avalos, M.A. (2009). Responsible differentiated instruction for the adolescent learner. In *Literacy Instruction for Adolescents: Research-Based Practice*, Wood, K.D., and Blanton, W.E. (Eds.) (pp. 144–169). New York: The Guilford Press.

Schunk, D.H. (1990). Goal setting and self-efficacy during self-regulated learning. *Educational Psychologist*, 25, 71–86.

Schunk, D.H. (1996). Goal and self-evaluative influences during children's cognitive skill learning. *American Educational Research Journal*, 33(2), 359–382.

Schunk, D.H., and Swartz, C.W. (1993). Goals and progress feedback: Effects on self-efficacy and writing achievement *Contemporary Educational Psychology*, 18(3), 337–354.

Seijts, G.H., Latham, G.P., Tasa, K., and Latham, B.W. (2004). Goal setting and goal orientation: An integration of two different yet related literatures. *Academy of Management Journal*, 47(2), 227–239.

Shanahan, T. (2016). Relationships between reading and writing development. In *Handbook of Writing Research*, MacArthur, C., Graham, S., and Fitzgerald, J. (Eds.) (2nd Ed.) (pp. 194–207). New York: The Guilford Press.

Smith, F. (1982). *Writing and the Writer*. Oxford: Heinemann.

Smith, F. (1983). Reading like a writer. *Language Arts*, 60(5), 558–567.

Smith, F. (1988). *Joining the Literacy Club*. Oxford: Heinemann.

Timperley, H., and Parr, J. (2009). What is this lesson about? Instructional processes and student understandings in writing classrooms *The Curriculum Journal*, 20(1), 43–60.

van den Bergh, H., and Rijlaarsdam, G. (2001). Changes in cognitive activities during the writing process and relationships with text quality. *Educational Psychology*, 21(4), 373–385.

Vanderburg, R. (2006). Reviewing research on teaching writing based on Vygotsky's theories: What we can learn. *Reading & Writing Quarterly*, 22(4), 375–393.

Whitney, A.E. (2017). Keeping it real: Valuing authenticity in the writing classroom. *English Journal*, 6(106), 16–21.

Wiggins, G. (2009). Real-world writing: Making purpose & audience matter. *English Journal*, 98(5), 29–37.

Wyse, D., and Torgerson, C. (2017). Experimental trials and 'what works?' In education: The case of grammar for writing. *British Educational Research Journal*, 43(6), 1019–1047.

Young, R. (2019). *What is it 'writing for pleasure' teachers do that makes the difference?* The University of Sussex: The Goldsmiths' Company [Online]. Available: www.writing4pleasure.com.

Young, R., and Ferguson, F. (2020a). *Real-World Writers: A Handbook for Teaching Writing with 7–11 Year Olds*. London: Routledge.

Young, R., and Ferguson, F. (2020b). *Class Writing Projects*. [Available: https://writing4pleasure.com/class-writing-projects/]

CHAPTER

17

Be reassuringly consistent

Writing workshop: mini-lesson, writing time and class sharing

A contemporary writing workshop approach (Young and Ferguson 2020), which ensures attention is given to what research and case studies say are the most effective writing practices (Wyse and Torgerson 2017; Wyse 2019; Young 2019), provides teachers and pupils with a reassuringly consistent routine for individual writing lessons.

The writing workshop approach was first introduced by Donald Graves (1983) and at the time was more in keeping with the naturalistic and self-expressionist approach to writing (described in Chapter 1) than are contemporary manifestations (Calkins et al. 2013; Atwell 2014; Shubitz and Dorfman 2019 (USA); Young and Ferguson 2020 (UK)). As is the case now, children were treated and taught as genuine apprentices learning a craft, choosing what to write about, and writing daily. The notion of a workshop was particularly suited to the approach in which writers took the germ of an idea and crafted it through the writing processes towards some kind of publication. As now, too, the teacher was encouraged to create a supportive and social writerly environment, teach daily mini-lessons, and give regular feedback through pupil conferencing to help children on their writing journey. Teachers planned mini-lessons in response to what they felt their class needed instruction in the most, additionally informed by the pupil conferencing they carried out each day.

As you will have noticed in Chapter 10 of this book, Graves' writing workshop approach, even in its earliest form, enacts many of the principles of best practice established by contemporary academic research and case studies (Graham et al. 2016; Graham and Harris 2019; Wyse 2019; Young 2019). It was and is still regarded as a highly effective pedagogy (Hillocks 1986; Strech 1994; Martin et al. 2005; Hachem et al. 2008). Contemporary manifestations have built on this success, but have taken greater account of the crucial role of genre teaching (Chapter 16), explicit and direct strategy instruction (Chapter 20), and the critical and community aspects of learning to write (Chapter 1).

Experimental and random control trials, systematic reviews, meta-analyses and case studies (Graham et al. 2016; Graham and Harris 2019; Wyse 2019) together with research into what the most effective schools do (Applebee 2002; Troia 2011; Hamel 2017) all point to the efficacy of a contemporary writing workshop approach for conducting daily writing lessons. An essential component is the reassuringly consistent routine of mini-lesson, writing time, and class sharing. What is innovative here is that, after the mini-lesson, children are invited to immediately apply the taught skills in a way that is relevant to their own writing. Teaching, meaningful application and review happen daily. We can see in the table below why this consistent approach is so useful and effective.

Writing workshop routine	Research and case study findings into effective writing teaching
Mini-lessons Daily explicit and direct instruction.	Children need regular and explicit strategy instruction if they are to develop their craft (see Chapter 20).
Writing time Daily time to write and to meaningfully and repeatedly apply taught knowledge, skills, and processes.	If children are to become better writers, they need ample, sustained, and daily time in which to enact the processes involved in writing and to develop their writing craft (see Chapter 15).
Pupil conferencing and class sharing Daily formative assessment, additional bespoke instruction, peer assessment, and informed next-day responsive teaching.	Children need responsive teaching based on formative assessment, regular feedback, and additional bespoke instruction if they are to become better writers (see Chapter 22).

In this way, children learn something about writing every day, they have an opportunity to write every day, and every day their teacher learns what their class needs to know about next.

Ensuring a consistent amount of time for writing

In exceptional writing classrooms 'effective writing instruction and practice happen every day' (Zumbrunn and Krause 2012, p. 349). Children need time for deliberate, spaced, extensive and repeated practice in the craft of writing (Konrad et al. 2011; Graham et al. 2012; Graham and Harris 2019). According to Applebee and Langer (2011), Kellogg et al. (2013), and Bazerman et al. (2017), writing sessions in school are often so sporadic and irregular that children are not spending enough overall time writing, and are therefore not internalising the processes involved in crafting texts as thoroughly as they should. Kellogg (2008) tells us that professional writers have a thoroughly consistent and daily writing routine and recommends that children experience the same. Children become more fluent and better writers by writing.

Efficient timetabling and scheduling by the teacher is an essential condition for effective classroom organisation and management. *Writing For Pleasure* teachers ensure that their apprentice writers have sufficient time and opportunity every day to acquire or consolidate new skills and knowledge in mini-lessons, and then have dedicated time to participate in writing (Lipson et al. 2000; Langer 2001; Pressley et al. 2001; Hall and Harding 2003; Paris and Winograd 2003; Hachem et al. 2008). As Reutzel, cited in Gadd (2014, p. 45), explains 'while teaching the critical components of the literacy process is important, so too is allocating sufficient time for writing each day'.

Behaviour whilst writing

As discussed in our chapter *Build A Community Of Writers*, teachers need to think carefully about their writing environments. For example, the maximum noise level allowed during different periods of the writing sessions might be made plain to the class, with Hicks (2008, p. 6) suggesting there should be a time where children are 'seated, silent and self-reliant'. *Writing For Pleasure* teachers understand that, if a classroom is characterised by predictability and a clear structure, they are better able to focus on providing instruction and pupil conferences instead of having to manage behaviour (Graham et al. 2011; Konrad et al. 2011). Classroom rights, rules, consequences, and schedules are expected to be visible so learners know what is expected of them.

Organisation, access to resources, and routines

Writing For Pleasure teachers aim to create enabling and efficient classrooms which promote a sense of self-efficacy, independence, and personal and collective responsibility (Pressley et al. 2001; Whittick 2020). They establish and communicate clear guidelines and goals for writing projects (Chapter 16) and for the processes involved in achieving high-quality writing (Hall and Harding, 2003; Konrad et al. 2011; Langer, 2001; Reutzel, 2007; Rooke 2013; Graham and Harris 2019).

A reassuringly consistent writing classroom settles learners and helps them maintain focus during a lesson. According to both Reutzel (2007) and Hmelo-Silver (2006), learners benefit from the security of a clear and explicit framework that allocates space and determines rights, rules, directions, schedules, and familiar routines. Children will know what both the long-term and short-term goals of a writing project are, be given enough time to complete their writing processes, and know where to access resources which will aid them in being self-regulatory. Young and Ferguson (2020) make the suggestion that teachers start the year with 'welcome projects' which are directed towards making children feel comfortable and secure in these routines of the writing classroom.

Writing For Pleasure teachers ensure their lessons have just such predictable routines and procedures. However, they also understand that consistency does not mean rigidity. They will construct their writing lessons as 'chunks' of time so that children keep their attention and have frequent and regular periods of practice (Paris and Winograd 2003; Toppino et al. 2009). Konrad et al. (2011) note the importance of explicit identification and communication of class learning goals as another way to ensure a smooth and efficient learning environment. Visitors to *Writing For Pleasure* classrooms would see opportunities for daily writing time within a mastery styled approach (Konrad et al. 2011). Finally, Langer (2001) states that exceptional writing schools typically communicate strategies, procedures, and resources across year groups, thereby bringing even more reassuring consistency to their learners.

Examples of effective practice

Our research investigating the practices of exceptional *Writing For Pleasure* teachers (Young 2019) showed that they have excellent classroom organisation. There was strong emphasis on routines, promoting self-regulation, behavioural expectations and focused collaborative learning among the children in their classes. Interview data showed that this enhanced children's feelings of self-efficacy and self-regulation because, each day, they knew what to do and how to do it. As one child put it 'he doesn't make you worry as a student because you've done it so often'. Having these routines also saved the teachers time. Their classrooms were set up to direct children to the act of writing quickly, daily, and largely independently. Resources and working walls were made visible and were focused on sharing self-regulation strategies.

The teachers established a consistent routine of mini-lesson, writing time, and class sharing/Author's Chair. In mini-lessons lasting between ten and 20 minutes they gave a short instruction on an aspect of writing which was likely to be useful to the children that day. The teachers taught from their own craft regularly – sharing their writing 'tips, tricks and secrets' before that day's writing time. They would also share examples of a particular aspect of craft taken from books in the class library.

During writing time, the teachers either wrote amongst their children for a short while or proceeded straight into pupil conferencing with groups and/or individuals. A number of the teachers set up the routine that, once finished with that day's crafting of the class project, the children could work on their personal projects. For example, there was a box readily accessible on each table where children would deposit their personal writing notebooks from their school bags each day. Writing time lasted between 30 and 40 minutes.

Finally, the teachers made time for class sharing and/or Author's Chair. Firstly, the children would share their developing pieces and discuss the writing goals they had achieved that day with their peers. This would be followed by Author's Chair. Author's Chair is when one or two children come up to the front to address the class about their writing. The routine was for the children to give a little background information about their piece and explain what they would like feedback on before reading it out. The class would then respond, first saying what strengths they thought the piece had before giving their opinion and suggestions about how it could be developed further. The teachers would also occasionally give their feedback too. This usually lasted between ten and 15 minutes.

Practical things you can do

- Plan your writing lessons so that they are in keeping with the writing workshop routine.
- Ensure children have plenty of daily writing time in which to craft their texts.
- Ensure you have clear expectations about when and how children can discuss their developing compositions with each other and when silent working is required (see Chapter 11).

- Always look for ways in which children can be more independent during writing time.
- Consider setting out your expectations and sharing procedures and routines with your class at the beginning of the year as part of a class 'welcome project' (Young and Ferguson 2020).
- Make expectations, procedures, routines, and resources consistent across year groups when possible.
- Co-construct with your class a set of rules, rights, and responsibilities for writing and put them on display.

QUESTIONS WORTH ASKING YOURSELF

- Do you ensure your explicit instruction is short, concise, and doesn't eat into your class' writing time? (see Chapter 20)
- Do you ensure that children get to write every day?
- Do children know how to move around the classroom and access resources?
- Do children know how to set writing out on paper (or screen) when planning, writing, revising, editing, or publishing?
- Do they know how to use resources and other study aids independently?
- Are you always on the lookout for things your class is unable to do independently? When you notice such things, are you conducting a mini-lesson in response?
- Do they know how to talk to their peers in an efficient way that doesn't disturb the rest of the class?
- Is there a time for talking and sharing writing and a time for silent engagement?
- Are your children independent enough for you to be able to focus on pupil conferencing?
- Does your school, where appropriate, encourage you to communicate strategies, procedures, and resources across year groups?

References

Applebee, A. (2002). Engaging students in the disciplines of English: What are effective schools doing? *English Journal*, 91(6), 30–36.

Applebee, A., and Langer, J. (2011). A snapshot of writing instruction in middle and high schools. *English Journal*, 100, 14–27.

Atwell, N. (2014). *In the Middle* (3rd Ed.). Portsmouth, NH: Heinemann.

Bazerman, C., Applebee, A.N., Berninger, V.W., Brandt, D., Graham, S., Matsuda, P.K., and Schleppegrell, M. (2017). Taking the long view on writing development. *Research in the Teaching of English*, 51, 351–360.

Calkins, L. (2013). *A guide to the Writing Workshop: Intermediate Grades*. Portsmouth, NH: Heinnaman

Graham, S., and Harris, K. (2019). Evidence-Based Practices in Writing. In *Best Practices in Writing Instruction*, Graham, S., MacArthur, C., and Hebert, M. (Eds.) (3rd Ed.) (pp. 3–31). New York: The Guilford Press.

Graham, S., Bollinger, A., Booth Olson, C., D'Aoust, C., MacArthur, C., McCutchen, D., and Olinghouse, N. (2012). *Teaching Elementary School Students to be Effective Writers: A Practice Guide.* Washington, DC: U.S. Department of Education, Institute of Education Sciences, National Center for Education Evaluation and Regional Assistance.

Graham, S., Harris, K., and Chambers, A. (2016). Evidence-based practice and writing instruction: A review of reviews. In *Handbook of Writing Research*, MacArthur, C., Graham, S., and Fitzgerald, J. (Eds.) (2nd Ed.) (pp. 211–227). New York: The Guilford Press.

Graves, D. (1983). *Writing: Teachers and Children at Work.* Portsmouth NH: Heinemann Educational.

Hachem, A., Nabhani, M., and Bahous, R. (2008). 'We can write!' The writing workshop for young learners, Education 3–13, 36(4), 325–337.

Hall, K., and Harding, A. (2003) A systematic review of effective literacy teaching in the 4 to 14 age range of mainstream schooling (Tech. Rep.). Research Evidence in Education Library London Social Science Research Unit, Institute of Education.

Hicks, J. (2008). *Writing identity and the writers' workshop: Looking back at my second grade* [USFSP Honors Program Theses (Undergraduate)], 83. Retrieved from: https://digital.stpetersburg.usf.edu/cgi/viewcontent.cgi?article=1082&context=honorstheses

Hillocks, G. (1986) *Research on Written Composition: New Directions for Teaching.* Urbana, IL: National Council of Teachers of English.

Kellogg, R.T. (2008). Training writing skills: A cognitive developmental perspective. *Journal of Writing Research*, 1(1), 1–26.

Kellogg, R.T., Whiteford, A.P., Turner, C.E., Cahill, M., and Mertens, A. (2013). Working memory in written composition: An evaluation of the 1996 model. *Journal of Writing Research*, 5(2), 159–190.

Konrad, M., Helf, S., and Joseph, L.M. (2011). Evidence-based instruction is not enough: Strategies for increasing instructional efficiency. *Intervention in School and Clinic*, 47(2), 67–74.

Langer, J.A. (2001). Beating the odds: Teaching middle and high school students to read and write well. *American Educational Research Journal*, 38(4), 837–880.

Lipson, M., Mosenthal, J., Daniels, P., and Woodside-Jiron, H. (2000). Process writing in the classrooms of eleven fifth-grade teachers with different orientations to teaching and learning. *Elementary School Journal*, 101(2), 209–231.

Martin, L., Segraves, R., Thacker, S., and Young, L. (2005). The writing process: Three first grade teachers and their students reflect on what was learned. *Reading Psychology*, 26, 235–249.

Paris, S.G., and Winograd, P. (2003). The role of self-regulated learning in contextual teaching: Principles and practices for teacher preparation (CIERA Report). Retrieved from https://files.eric.ed.gov/fulltext/ED479905.pdf.

Pressley, M., Wharton-McDonald, R., Allington, R., Block, C., Morrow, L., Tracey, D., Baker, K., Brooks, G., Cronin, J., Nelson, E., and Woo, D. (2001) A study of effective first-grade literacy instruction. *Scientific Studies of Reading*, 5(1), 35–8.

Rooke, J. (2013). *Transforming Writing: Final Evaluation Report.* London: National Literacy Trust.

Shubitz, S., and Dorfman, L. (2019). *Welcome to Writing Workshop.* Portsmouth, NH: Stenhouse.

Strech, L. (1994). *The implementation of writing workshop: A review of the literature.* Non-journal. Available at: https://eric.ed.gov/?id=ed380797.

Toppino, T.C., Cohen, M.S., Davis, M.L., and Moors, A.C. (2009). Metacognitive control over the distribution of practice: When is spacing preferred? *Journal of Experimental Psychology, Learning, Memory, and Cognition*, 35, 1352–1358.

Troia, G. (2011). A year in the writing workshop: Linking writing instruction practices and teachers' epistemologies and beliefs about writing instruction. *Elementary School Journal*, 112(1), 155–182.

Whittick, L. (2020). *Write a little – share a little* [Available: https://writing4pleasure.com/write-a-little-share-a-little/]

Wyse, D. (2019). Choice, voice and process: Teaching writing in the 21st century: Revisiting the influence of donald graves and the process approach to writing. *English in Australia*, 53(3), 82–92.

Wyse, D., and Torgerson, C. (2017). Experimental trials and 'what works?' In education: The case of grammar for writing. *British Educational Research Journal*, 43(6), 1019–1047.

Young, R. (2019). *What Is It Writing for Pleasure Teachers Do That Makes the Difference?* University of Sussex: The Goldsmiths' Company:.

Young, R., and Ferguson, F. (2020). *Real-World Writers: A Handbook for Teaching Writing with 7–11 Year Olds*. London: Routledge.

Zumbrunn, S., and Krause, K. (2012). Conversations with leaders: Principles of effective writing instruction. *The Reading Teacher*, 65(5), 346–353.

CHAPTER 18

Personal writing projects

It is vitally important that children be provided with time and opportunity to construct and follow their own learning agendas and not simply be required to respond to the day-to-day demands of their teacher (Bereiter and Scardamalia 1987; Chamberlain 2015; Brady 2017; Collier 2017; Schultz et al. 2017). Only in this way do children come to know what they are capable of doing on their own. However, the most potent reason for making the pursuit of personal writing projects both possible and essential is because they are precisely the arena where children can engage in writing as they will do in the world beyond school and in their present and future lives.

The earliest versions of writing workshop, pioneered by Moffett (1968), Graves (1983), Murray (1984), Calkins (1986), and Atwell (1987), were heavily based on the self-expressionist orientation towards the teaching of writing, and personal writing projects were the central part of the writing curriculum. At that time, the approach stressed the essentially creative nature of writing, seeing it as the means by which writers discover and express themselves in a natural way. The apprentice writer was of paramount importance and was accorded much personal freedom and responsibility. As this chapter will show, contemporary writing workshop approaches have, over time and in several ways, reconfigured this early conception (Atwell 2014; Turbill et al. 2015; Wyse 2019; Calkins 2020; Young and Ferguson 2020) which, at the time, was subject to many criticisms levelled at its so-called 'romantic' philosophy. These criticisms have been explored in Chapter 1 of this book.

Personal projects remain central to the contemporary writing workshop approach, with teachers providing the opportunity for children to choose their own topic, genre, process, purpose, and audience, and to write in their own way, at their own pace, and with their own goals and intentions. In this chapter, we see that personal writing projects can have a prominent and important place within a writing curriculum and be accorded the status and value equal to that given to class writing projects.

Affective benefits of personal writing projects

Goouch and Lambirth (2006) state that choice and autonomy profoundly engage the affective.

If children write from what they know, have experienced, heard, read, or are deeply interested in, they will have an emotional investment in the writing and be motivated to make it the best they can because they care about it. To return to Donald Graves' metaphor, having your own self-chosen writing topic rather than one assigned to you by your teacher is the difference between owning and renting a property (1982). You will be more committed to looking after the house and tending the garden if it's yours.

Goouch and Lambirth (2006) confirm that there is clear evidence in many research studies and writings (for example, Graves 1983; Calkins 1986; Corden 2000; David et al. 2000) that the factors influencing children's affective engagement and motivation in writing both in and out of school include, among others, authentic contexts and choice over content, genre, and audience. Agency and genuine choice are seen by Grainger et al. (2005) as important in fostering creativity and what they describe as 'innovation and enterprise '(p. 18) in children's writing; Rief (2006, p. 37) is in agreement, adding that 'when writers care, they write with passion and voice'. Grainger et al. (2005) also recall Dyson's (2000) warning that too much teacher control results in children losing hold of what they are doing and why, becoming detached from their writing and losing the sense of themselves *as writers*. Finally, we would add that students simply will not be writing frequently enough to ensure they develop if they are only ever allowed to write under their teachers' control and surveillance.

In her inquiry into young writers' motivation, Nolen (2007) draws attention to the work of Hidi et al. (2002), Pajares (2003), and Walker (2003), whose research projects found that, when children are able to pursue their own interests in writing, the prior knowledge they hold of their topic helps them produce successful texts. The experience of success then increases the writer's self-efficacy and gives rise to positive emotions. Nolen goes on to cite Pekrun et al. (2002), whose study concludes that children are motivated not only through interest in their subject but also as a result of the positive feelings created by the opportunity for self-expression and self-determination in the writing processes. Frank (2001) reiterates these conclusions in a slightly different way, pointing out the potential satisfaction to be had when writers take on the responsibility for directing their own writing, choosing what to do, when to do it, and how to do it. As Moffett and Wagner (1992) suggest, this of course mirrors what writers do out in the world, writing for and as pleasure, and therefore children are helped to see themselves as writers. Finally, Vygotsky (2004) warns that pupils are denied knowledge of the true purposes of writing when they are required to respond to teacher-assigned writing topics which very often fail to connect with their interests and emotions.

The importance of positive feelings should never be underestimated, particularly in a pedagogy which foregrounds writing for pleasure. In many research studies, the majority of children expressed anticipation and pleasure at the prospect of writing on self-chosen subjects and having control of form, purpose, audience, and process (Abbott 2000; Grainger et al. 2005; Nolen 2007; Cremin 2010; Cremin and Myhill 2012; Young 2019). Interestingly, a DfE research report (2012) identified a gender gap in writing achievement, with the lack of ownership over their writing named as a key factor behind boys' underperformance.

Voice and the sense of self

In her thesis describing her personal experience as a pupil in a writers' workshop classroom, Hicks (2008) writes that she gained 'a sense of myself as someone who writes that has become a cornerstone of my identity' (p. 3). This is a strong statement about the deep connection between writing and a sense of selfhood, as discussed in more detail in Chapter 9. It will come as no surprise that the development of a child's writing identity is greatly helped by the classroom environment in which they undertake their writing. Dutro et al. (2006), Goouch and Lambirth (2006), Hicks (2008), Jeffrey (2008), and Collier (2010) agree that communities of writers, in which 'writerly' interactions and collective responsibility take place between peers and an engaged writer-teacher, coupled with choice, time, authentic contexts and real audiences for writing, are the best conditions for helping children construct strong writer-identities. Hicks (2008) further asserts that the construction of a writer-identity should be a crucial goal of the writing curriculum. There can be no doubt that personal writing projects as understood in a *Writing For Pleasure* pedagogy, when children have agency over what they wish to write and how to write it, offer the best opportunities for identities to be shaped and confirmed, and for the individual voice to be heard, connecting the writer with the reader in a personal way. Both Graves (1983) and Rosen (1998) claim that, in so many teacher-assigned writing tasks, the authentic 'thinking' and communicative voice of the writer is diminished and may even be removed from the writing; when this happens there will be a resulting lack of motivation on the part of the writer and a less engaged and affective response from the reader. Grainger et al. (2005) state that different voices should be welcomed and considered by teachers as a valuable resource, while Lensmire (1998, p. 6) gives us the serious warning that: 'to not affirm and respect student voices is both morally wrong, because it disparages who students are and what they know, and strategically a mistake, because students will resist becoming active partners in teaching and learning'. Personal writing projects allow these individual voices to be heard.

Funds of knowledge and funds of identity

As was discussed in Chapter 9, refusing or diminishing children's identities is an act of social injustice. Moll et al. (1992, p. 134) rightly view children's households 'as containing ample cultural and cognitive resources with great potential utility for classroom instruction ... a view which contrasts sharply with prevailing and accepted perceptions of working-class families as somehow disorganized, socially and deficient intellectually; perceptions that are well accepted and rarely challenged in the field of education and elsewhere'. Subero et al. (2016) distinguish between the more generalised *funds of knowledge,* drawn from family routines and activities, social interactions, popular culture, and community practices, and *funds of identity* – which include 'significant people, institutions, artefacts, passions and interests encrusted in a learner's self-definition' (p. 7). Teachers making the effort to learn about and appreciate the home cultures of all their children and particularly those of minority groups, acting as a bridge between pupils' worlds and the classroom experience, and, crucially, allowing unique and individual funds of knowledge and identity to be used as resources in the classroom has a significant positive impact on children's writing (Dyson 2000; Solsken et al. 2000; Hull & Schultz 2001; Duke and Purcell-Gates 2003; Ranker 2009; Carbone and Orellana 2010; Dutro 2010; Subero et al. 2016). As Young and Ferguson (2020) have written, educators must acknowledge children's thoughts, interests, and experiences as valid and valuable subjects for writing personal projects. Further, teachers may come to 'know' their pupils in a deeper way, be moved to relinquish stereotypical beliefs and so begin the journey of encouraging a culturally sustaining writing community (Compton-Lilly 2006; Yandell 2016; Kinloch 2017; DeStiger 2019; Young et al. *in press*).

Agency supported by self-efficacy and self-regulation

It is crucial for practitioners to understand that, as Young's (2019) research clearly showed, agency *alone* does not guarantee that personal writing will be pleasurable or academically successful, a fact not generally articulated in other research studies. Alongside agency, writers need the solid foundation of feelings of self-efficacy and knowledge of self-regulation strategies gained from high-quality instruction and whole-class writing projects. This need was strongly identified by some of the children in Young's study. The consequence of the absence of such a bedrock is that children find themselves struggling to stay upright on what feels like shifting sands, and so the enjoyment, significance, and purpose that can come from personal writing projects are not realised. It would appear that self-efficacy and self-regulation are the key foundations that allow children's agency to flourish. In this way, children can appropriate the knowledge, skills, projects and texts of the school curriculum and of class writing projects and blend them with their own writing topics and their personal and social desires (Solsken et al. 2000; Duke and Purcell-Gates 2003).

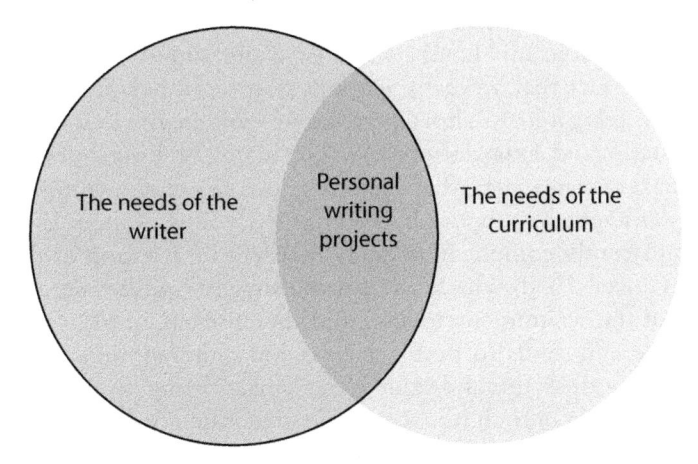

FIGURE 18.1 Personal writing projects are driven by the needs of the young writer but are often supported by what they've learnt through the curriculum and from class writing projects.

Personal writing on the periphery

Anne Haas Dyson (2020) shares with us an anecdote of a seven-year-old African-American writer discussing his writing with her. He talks with her enthusiastically about a piece he is writing in his personal writing project book including guidance on how to play the guitar, how he plays music with his grandma, and what he's learnt from her about blues guitarists. However, he is quick to tell Anne that this isn't his *real* writing. He goes on to explain that real writing is the assigned writing he does for evaluation by his teacher. We must ask: how did it come about that this seven-year-old had thoroughly internalised such a limited view of what writing and being a writer means ? The answer has to be that the establishment which should be educating him in exactly these things has not been set up to do so.

Writing is about making your mark on the world, both literally and figuratively. It is a sign that you exist. As studies and this chapter have shown, through writing personally and sharing their texts, children gradually develop voice and identity. Collier (2010) states that identity is always in a process of becoming, and that 'children need to have room to create new narratives or occupy new positions as writers' (p. 149). Personal writing projects, freed from teacher-placed constraints, offer this potential; through intertextuality, pupils are enabled to 'remix' texts, create hybrids, write communally, and make new resources and artefacts (this is discussed in more detail in Chapter 23).

Writing journals, though not always in evidence in current UK classrooms, are a place in which children can produce self-initiated independent writing. Graham and Johnson (2012) counted among the benefits of writing journals that children would write freely – and, if they wished, privately – with motivation and commitment, using their own cultural capital in their texts. Parry and Taylor (2018, p. 107) reported that: 'children were invited to use a free choice, independent writing journal. They were given time and space in their classrooms to write in the journals and were encouraged to take them home. Participants were also surveyed about their reading habits and preferences. Children chose to write in a remarkable range of genres and styles, including narrative, prose, non-fiction, poetry, labelled illustrations, comics, lists, personal accounts and songs'.

While Goouch and Lambirth (2006) applauded such initiatives, they also deplored the fact that, in many schools, writing in personal journals had become ghettoised, relegated to short periods of 'golden time' and thus accorded low teacher status and expectations. As they stated, 'telling ourselves, as academics, policy makers or teachers, that small portions of creative, autonomous opportunities are sufficient to support lively, engaged young writers is woefully mistaken and complacently compliant' (p. 152). A recent incarnation of this is 'Free Writing Friday' (Cowell 2018) which, as its name suggests, pushes personal writing to the margins of the writing curriculum and therefore, as an idea, is tokenistic, of little significance and sends to both teachers and children alike a dangerously wrong message about the status and value of personal writing. In the face, therefore, of the ineffectual nature of such initiatives, and given the positive findings of the research studies into agency described in this chapter and beyond, we must ask ourselves why it is that practices which help children write better texts, promote writing for pleasure, offer agency, and enlist pupils' feelings of self-efficacy and self-regulation through instruction, are not where they should be – at the very centre of the writing curriculum.

A time for play

Another important message that children receive through personal writing projects is that not everything we write works out (Young and Ferguson 2020). It is important too that children learn about writing processes which occur much less frequently in traditional curriculum-controlled class writing projects, for example, playing, dabbling, abandoning, reimagining, returning, and updating. Children need space and time to simply experiment, try things out and sometimes even fail (Cremin and Myhill 2012).

Personal writing projects in the *Writing For Pleasure* classroom

Writing For Pleasure teachers know that 'children want to write' (Graves 1983, p. 1), that they want to write on their own topics and that they all have something to say. According to Young's study (2019), these teachers understand the vital importance of allowing children daily time to pursue both class and personal writing projects, with personal writing time often following directly after work on class writing has been completed for that day. Young and Ferguson (2020) suggest that routines and skills learnt in class writing projects are assumed and applied at a high level of sophistication in dedicated personal writing project weeks. They share how teachers can support pupils in pursuing their personal writing by:

- Providing children with a sustained period of daily personal writing sessions.
- Keeping to a routine of mini-lesson, writing time, and class sharing.
- Reminding them of strategies for generating ideas.
- Displaying lists of genres for reference and inspiration.
- Writing alongside.
- Offering conferences, giving responsive advice, and helping with goal setting.
- Encouraging the social aspect of writing.

Personal writing takes on a new meaning and momentum in *Writing For Pleasure* classrooms. Called 'projects' for a good reason, personal pieces are valued, held in high esteem by all, and have a central place in the writing curriculum. As with class writing projects, these teachers rightly have high expectations for the quality of the texts produced, and anticipate that the writing processes will be seen through from beginning to end, from original idea to potential publication and performance (Ranker 2009; Vasques 2020).

Yandell (2016, p. 21) suggests that through personal writing projects, an intimate relationship can develop 'between the learners' lifeworlds and English as a school subject'. Class writing projects are ultimately an apprenticeship and preparation for children to craft something completely from themselves and for it to be successful. In them, children have acquired procedures for navigating the writing processes, learnt how to write for different purposes using a variety of structures, and internalised much fundamental craft knowledge. They have gained the skills and the affective qualities they need to be able to produce effective and meaningful texts. In a personal writing project, they utilise everything they know and have as full an agency as possible, writing in their own way, at their own pace, and for their own reasons, as other writers out in the world do.

A third space: technology and personal writing projects

Timothy Lensmire (1994) described the writing classroom as being like a carnival. A place that encourages explosions of possibility, creativity, and maybe even controlled risk and danger! This potential for carnival can also be found increasingly in online spaces. Teachers like Nicola Izibili at The Writing Web (2020) are taking the principles of *Writing For Pleasure,* and specifically the concept of personal writing projects, online through class blogging platforms. Through platforms like The Writing Web, Google Classroom, and Kidblog, whole classes are able to talk, craft, support, co-create, and publish in what feels like a safe 'writing playground'. Writing on these platforms leads to more writing. The community of writers which was once only accessible at school is now open to children all the time. According to Kucirkova et al. (2019) the online space can actually be a place where some children feel most at home and best able to achieve from a position of expertise, although of course questions remain about children's access to the technology required to participate in such online community work.

Examples of effective practice

The example below is taken from Young's (2019) study of *Writing For Pleasure* teachers. These teachers appreciated how essential it is that children are given time to write for a sustained period every day and to work on both class and personal writing projects. Time for working solely on personal projects was timetabled, and children were given at least an hour a week to spend on them. However, the teachers also encouraged personal writing to be pursued in any little pockets of time throughout the week. Some teachers set up a routine that allowed personal writing project books to travel to and fro between school and home every day; the books were always freely available to the children, kept either in their trays or on their desks. Personal projects were seen by these teachers as an important part of the writing curriculum since it was here, through exercising their own choice of subject, purpose, audience, and writing process, that their class had true agency and came to see writing as an empowering and pleasurable activity to be used now and in the future. Teachers were also fully aware that personal writing projects provided them with insights into their children's personalities and identities, helped build relationships, and were useful evidence in the assessment of children's development as independent writers. Whilst all the teachers showed an interest in their children's personal projects, there was regrettably only one who had the same high expectations for them as he had for class projects. He ensured that any personal writing that the children wanted to publish had been rigorously considered by them, with revision and proof-reading taking place before publication.

Practical things you can do

- Give each child a personal project book (or writer's notebook). Have a system in place where it can go between school and home freely.
- Consider where you can timetable regular and sustained personal project sessions (Young and Ferguson 2020). Ensure these sessions still follow the routine of mini-lesson, writing time, and class sharing (see Chapter 17).
- Provide a consistent expectation that children know they are to continue with their personal writing projects once their class writing is finished for the day.
- Have on display and remind children of idea generation strategies.
- Invite children to bring in artefacts from home to spark a writing idea.
- Think of different ways of publishing and presenting pieces: for example, as anthologies, performances, videos, or podcasts.
- Make published pieces accessible in the classroom, around the school, and beyond.
- Allow children to abandon personal pieces and start new ones.
- Consider the possibility that children's published personal projects could contribute towards a portfolio of assessed writing.
- Share your personal notebook with your class and write alongside them where possible.
- Ensure you have available a variety of examples of personal writing project books for reference. This can help children see how different people manage a writer's notebook.
- Continue to discuss problems and successes experienced by all writers, including yourself and your class.
- Continue to offer conferences to children if they request them during personal project times.

> **QUESTIONS WORTH ASKING YOURSELF**
>
> - Are you timetabling ample time for personal writing projects?
> - Do children understand the routine of pursuing personal projects after they have finished working on class projects for that day, and of working on personal pieces in any other small pockets of time?

- Can the school provide a space for children to pursue their personal writing projects during breaks, lunch times, and after school?
- Do you hold personal writing projects in high regard, accepting children's chosen topics as valid and valued subjects for writing?
- Do you establish that writing project books, along with reading books, go between home and school each day? This allows the momentum of the writing to be sustained, and helps children be in a constant state of composition (Young and Ferguson 2020).
- Can you suggest a variety of audiences, both in and out of school, near and far, people children will meet, and those they will never meet?
- Do children have an opportunity to work collaboratively on their personal projects?
- Do you critically question your own assumptions about your pupils, their funds of knowledge, and their funds of identity?

References

Abbott, J. (2000). 'Blinking out' and 'having the touch' two fifth-grade boys talk about flow experiences in writing. *Written Communication*, 17(1), 53–92.

Atwell, N. (1987). *In the Middle* (1st Ed.). Portsmouth, NH: Heinemann.

Atwell, N. (2014). *In the Middle* (3rd Ed.). Portsmouth, NH: Heinemann.

Bereiter, C., and Scardamalia, M. (1987). An attainable version of high literacy: Approaches to teaching higher-order skills in reading and writing. *Curriculum Inquiry*, 17(1), 19–30.

Brady, J. (2017). Being in the world: Students' writing identities beyond school. In *Writer Identity and the Teaching and Learning of Writing*, Cremin, T., and Locke, T. (Eds.) (pp. 151–169). London: Routledge.

Calkins, L. (1986) *The Art of Teaching Writing*. Portsmouth, NH: Heinemann.

Calkins, L. (2020). *Teaching Writing*. Portsmouth, NH: Heinemann.

Carbone, P.W., and Orellana, M.F. (2010). Developing academic identities: Persuasive writing as a tool to strengthen emergent academic identities. *Research in the Teaching of English*, 44(3), 292–316.

Chamberlain, L. (2015). *Exploring the out-of-school writing practices of three children aged 9–10 years old and how these practices travel across and within the domains of home and school* (PhD thesis). The Open University.

Collier, D. (2010). Journey to becoming a writer: Review of research about children's identities as writers. *Language and Literacy*, 12(1), 147–164.

Collier, D. (2017). Glancing sideways at young writers becoming. In *Writer Identity and the Teaching and Learning of Writing*, Cremin, T., and Locke, T. (Eds.) (pp. 169–183). London: Routledge.

Compton-Lilly, C. (2006). Identity, childhood culture, and literacy learning: A case study. *Journal of Early Childhood Studies*, 6(1), 57–76.

Corden, R. (2000). *Literacy and Learning Through Talk: Strategies for the Primary Classroom*. Buckingham: Open University Press.

Cowell, C. (2018). *Free Writing Friday: Cressida Cowell's Top Writing Tips for Primary Pupils* [Online]. Available: https://literacytrust.org.uk/resources/free-writing-friday-resource/.

Cremin, T. (2010). Motivating children to write with purpose and passion. In *The Literate Classroom*, Goodwin, P. (Ed.) (2nd Ed.) (pp. 131–141). London: Routledge.

Cremin, T., and Myhill, D. (2012). *Creating Communities of Writers*. London: Routledge

David, T., Raban, B., Ure, C., Goouch, K., Jago, M., Barriere, I., and Lambirth, A. (2000). *Making Sense of Early Literacy: A Practitioner's Perspective*. Stoke on Trent, UK: Trentham Books.

DeStigter, T. (2019). Culturally sustaining pedagogy and the problem of poverty. In *The Future of English Teaching Worldwide*, Durrant, C., Sawyer, W., Scherff, L., and Goodwyn, A. (Eds.) (pp. 227–241). London: Routledge.

DfE. (2012). *What is the Research Evidence on Writing? Education Standards Research Team*. London: Department for Education.

Duke, N., and Purcell-Gates, V. (2003). Genres at home and at school: Bridging the known to the new. *The Reading Teacher*, 57(1), 30–37.

Dutro, E. (2010). What 'hard times' means: Mandated curricula, class-privileged assumptions, and the lives of poor children. *Research in the Teaching of English*, 44(3), 255–291.

Dutro, E., Kazemi, E., and Balf, R. (2006). Making sense of "the boy who died": Tales of a struggling successful writer. *Reading and Writing Quarterly*, 22(4), 325–356.

Dyson, A. (2000). Writing and the sea of voices: Oral language in, around and about writing. In *Perspectives on Writing: Research Theory and Practice*, Indrisano, R., and Squires, J.R. (Eds.) (pp. 45–65). Newark, DL: International Reading Association.

Dyson, A. (2020). 'This isn't my real writing': The fate of children's agency in too-tight curricula. *Theory Into Practice*, 59(2), 119–127.

Frank, C.R. (2001). 'What new things these words can do for you': A focus on one writing-project teacher and writing instruction. *Journal of Literacy Research*, 33(3), 467–506.

Goouch, K., and Lambirth, A. (2006). Golden times of writing: The creative compliance of writing journals. *Literacy*, 40(3), 146–152.

Graham, L., and Johnson, A. (2012). *Children's Writing Journals*. Royston: United Kingdom Literacy Association.

Grainger, T., Goouch, K., and Lambirth, A. (2005). *Creativity and writing: Developing voice and verve in the classroom*. London: Routledge.

Graves, D. (1982). Break the welfare cycle: Let writers choose their topics. The English Composition Board, 3(2), 75–78.

Graves, D. (1983). *Writing: Teachers & Children at Work*. Portsmouth, NH: Heinemann.

Hicks, J. (2008). *Writing identity and the writers' workshop: Looking back at my second grade classroom* [USFSP Honors Program Theses (Undergraduate)], 83.

Hidi, S., Berndorff, D., and Ainley, M. (2002). Children's argument writing, interest and self-efficacy: An intervention study. *Learning & Instruction*, 12(4), 429–446.

Hull, G., and Schultz, K. (2001). Literacy and learning out of school: A review of theory and research. *Review of Educational Research*, 71, 575–611.

Jeffrey, B. (2008). Creative learning identities. *Education*, 36(3), 253–263.

Kinloch, V. (2017). 'You ain't making me write': Culturally sustaining pedagogies and black youths' performance of resistance. In *Culturally Sustaining Pedagogies*, Paris, D., and Alim, S. (Eds.) (pp. 25–42). New York: Teachers' College Press.

Kucirkova, N., Rowe, D., Oliver, L., and Piestrzynski, L. (2019). Systematic review of young children's writing on screen: What do we know and what do we need to know. *Literacy*, 53(4), 216–225.

Lensmire, T. (1994). Writing workshop as carnival: Reflections on an alternative learning environment. *Harvard Educational Review*, 64(4), 371–392.

Lensmire, T. (1998). Rewriting student voice. *Journal of Curriculum Studies*, 30(3), 261–291.

Moffett, J. (1968). *Teaching the Universe Of Discourse*. Portsmouth NH: Boynton/Cook.

Moffett, J., and Wagner, B. (1992). *Student-Centered Language Arts K-12* (4th Ed.). Portsmouth NH: Boynton/Cook.

Moll, L., Amanti, C., Neff, D., and Gonzalez, N. (1992). Funds of knowledge for teaching: Using a qualitative approach to connect homes and classrooms: Theory into practice. *Qualitative Issues in Educational Research*, 31(2), 132–141.

Murray, D. (1984). *Write to Learn*. New York: Rinehart & Winston.

Nolen, S. (2007). Young children's motivation to read and write: Development in social contexts. *Cognition and Instruction*, 25(2–3), 219–270.

Pajares, F. (2003). Self-efficacy beliefs, motivation, and achievement in writing: A review of the literature. *Reading and Writing Quarterly*, 19(2), 139–158.

Parry, B., and Taylor, L. (2018). Readers in the round: children's holistic engagements with texts. *Literacy*, 52(2): 103–110.

Pekrun, R., Goetz, T., Titz, W., and Perry, R. (2002). Academic emotions in students' self-regulated learning and achievement: A program of qualitative and quantitative research. *Educational Psychologist*, 37(2), 91–105.

Ranker, J. (2009). Student appropriation of writing lessons through hybrid composing practices: Direct diffuse, and indirect use of teacher-offered writing tools in an ESL classroom. *Journal of Literacy Research*, 41, 393–431.

Rief, L. (2006). What's right with writing. *Voice From the Middle*, 13(4), 32–39.

Rosen, M. (1998). *Did I Hear You Write?* (2nd Ed.). London: Five Leaves Publications.

Schultz, K., Hull, G., and Higgs, J. (2017). After writing, after school. In *Handbook of Writing Research*, MacArthur, C., Graham, S., and Fitzgerald, J. (Eds.) (2nd Ed.) (pp. 102–115). New York: Guilford Press.

Solsken, J., Willett, J., and Wilson-Keenan, J. (2000). Cultivating hybrid texts in multicultural classrooms: "Promise and challenge". *National Council of Teachers of English*, 179–212.

Subero, D., Vujasinović E., and Esteban-Guitart, M. (2016). Mobilising funds of identity in and out of school. *Cambridge Journal of Education*, 47(2), 247–263.

Turbil, J., Barton, G., and Brock, C. (2015). *Teaching Writing in Today's Classrooms: Looking Back to Look Forward*. St Leonards, Australia: ALEA.

Vasques, M. (2020). *Setting Up Personal Writing Project Books In KS1*. Available: https://writing4pleasure.com/setting-up-personal-writing-project-books-in-ks1.

Vygotsky, L. (2004). Imagination and creativity in childhood. *Journal of Russian and Eastern European Psychology*, 42(1), 7–97.

Walker, B.J. (2003). The cultivation of student self-efficacy in reading and writing. *Reading & Writing Quarterly*, 19(2), 173–187.

Wyse, D. (2019). Choice, voice and process: Teaching writing in the 21st century: Revisiting the influence of donald graves and the process approach to writing. *English in Australia*, 53(3), 82–91.

Yandell, J. (2016). Growth and the category of experience. *English in Australia*, 51(3), 19–26.

Young, R. (2019). *What is it 'Writing For Pleasure' teachers do that makes the difference?* University of Sussex: The Goldsmiths' Company [Online]. Available: www.writing4pleasure.com.

Young, R., Govender, N., and Kaufman, D. (in press) *Writing Realities*. Leicester: UKLA

Young, R., and Ferguson, F. (2020). *Real-World Writers: A Handbook for Teaching Writing with 7–11 Year Olds*. London: Routledge.

CHAPTER

19

Balance composition and transcription

Let us be clear. If children do not learn and internalise the essential transcriptional skills involved in crafting writing – spelling, handwriting, and punctuation – then their attempts to share meaning with others may be compromised or even fruitless. *Writing For Pleasure* teachers care deeply about children's transcriptional accuracy because they want the writing to do well once it is out there in the world. Therefore, in the *Writing For Pleasure* pedagogy, the call to teach fundamental writing skills is always welcome (Berninger and Amtmann 2003; Chuy et al. 2011; McCutchen 2011; Graham et al. 2012; Limpo and Alves 2013; Graham & Santangelo 2014). However, it is not intended that transcriptional skills be taught in isolation, away from the craft of meaning making and sharing (Richardson 1998; Harmey 2020) and at the expense of developing writers' processes as discussed in Chapter 15. Teaching and practising transcriptional skills is only part of developing a writer. According to Kent and Wanzek (2016, p. 573), transcriptional skills 'influence, or supplement, the process and product of writing' and are acquired developmentally. Corden (2002, p. 252) claims that sentence level work, for example, can only improve 'if it genuinely and continually connects with real purposeful writing'. Finally, Harmey (2020, p. 3) warns against adopting a 'first and then' sequence of teaching, adding that: 'while control of transcription skills is essential, there is a danger, particularly for children who struggle with transcription skills, that the instructional focus over time may remain fixed on accuracy versus the quality of their written message'. Basically, teachers who do not achieve a balance between teaching composition and transcription fail to give children the apprenticeship they need for writing or being a writer.

Alongside transcription is composition. According to Harmey (2020), composition is the most demanding aspect of writing. For example, when composing, children have to find and formulate what it is they want to say and which they believe is worth time and effort to commit to paper or screen. It can be an exciting but challenging task. Yet composition does not always receive the instructional attention from teachers that children require (see Chapter 15).

In summary so far, evidence from the best writing teaching suggests that learning is achieved most effectively and efficiently when teachers adopt a balanced approach to the teaching of composition and transcription (Knapp et al. 1995;

Medwell et al. 1998; Casey and Hemenway 2001; Louden et al. 2005; Daffern and Mackenzie 2015; Graham and Harris 2019). As Warrington et al. (2006, p. 145) put it, teaching writing means 'providing a balance between helping young writers develop a personal voice and ensuring that they also know how to present well-structured and accurately written texts'.

The writer and the secretary

In his book *Writing and the Writer* (1982), Frank Smith uses the analogy of a writer and her secretary to describe composition and transcription as if they were performed by two different people. His analogy is a useful one, helping us visualise the different processes that take place if one is writing alone.

The writer (*composition*) has to attend to the following:

- Generating ideas.
- Turning thoughts, opinions, and feelings into words/sentences.
- Making grammatical, punctuation, and linguistic decisions.
- Vocabulary and tone choice.
- Maintaining cohesion.
- Considering the purpose of the text.
- Keeping the needs of the reader in mind throughout.
- How it might look (including multimodality).

The secretary (*transcription*) has to attend to the following:

- Physical effort of writing.
- Handwriting.
- Spelling.
- Capitalisation.
- Ensuring adherence to the conventions of punctuation.

A contemporary writing-workshop approach acknowledges the importance of developing both the 'writer' and the 'secretary' within an apprentice writer (Young and Ferguson 2020).

Kellogg et al. (2013) and Berninger and Amtmann (2003) in particular offer us a perspective of the fundamental or basic processes involved in crafting a text; indeed Berninger and Amtmann (2003) call their model the 'Simple View Of Writing'. They show how a child's working memory has to accommodate aspects of composition, executive function, and transcription. Composition is about formulating text by planning and composing it on a mental writing 'sketch pad'. Transcription is about physically producing the text on paper or screen and includes spelling and punctuation. Executive function is how we regulate ourselves as we write, for example by monitoring our attention, setting goals, making plans, reviewing, revising, and using other self-regulating strategies (Santangelo and Graham 2016; Kim and Schatschneider 2017). See Chapter 5 for more on self-regulation.

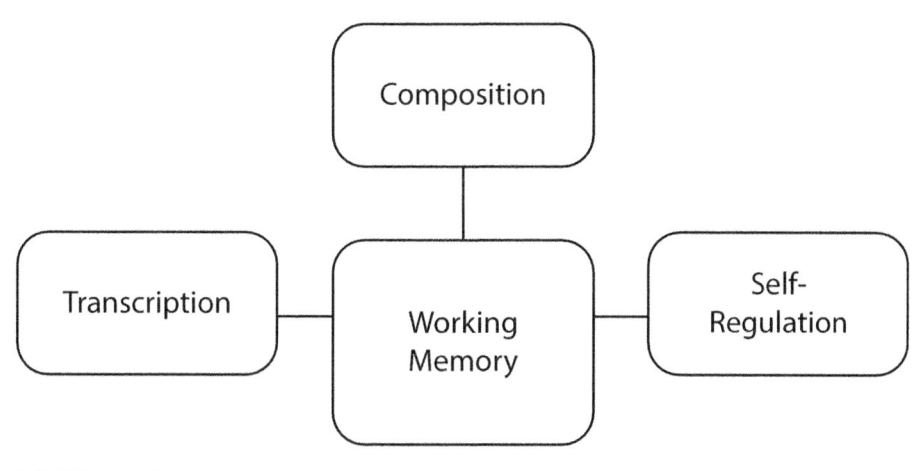

```
          Composition
              │
Transcription ─ Working ─ Self-
              Memory     Regulation
```

FIGURE 19.1 Writing and its fundamental processes.

When children are learning to write, composition and transcription can interfere with each other. The more attention they try to give to one, the more the other is likely to suffer. The problem is essentially a competition for attention (Breetvelt et al. 1994; Kellogg 2008; McCutchen 2011; Kellogg et al. 2013). If thoughts are coming too fast, then the quality of children's handwriting, spelling, or punctuation can suffer. If they concentrate on the transcription, or the physical appearance of the writing, then the quality of their composition can be impaired, and children may well produce 'perfect drivel'.

Too often teachers will ask inexperienced writers to engage in both these cognitively demanding acts simultaneously before they are ready. Kellogg et al. (2013), Bereiter and Scardamalia (1987), and Berninger and Amtmann (2003) suggest that overloading a child's working memory can have a detrimental impact on the young writer and their ability to craft great texts. To avoid this occurrence, teachers should encourage children to shift between the two processes, which over time and through repeated practice become automatic and internalised (Kellogg et al. 2013). Young and Ferguson (2020, p. 60) recommend discussing with children a variety of common 'writing habits' which they can choose from, adapt, or switch between, depending on personal preference or the type of writing they are undertaking.

Adventurer	Planner	Vomiter	Paragraph piler	Sentence stacker
Likes to write a draft first before looking at it and using it as a plan for a second draft.	Likes to plan in great detail, working out exactly what will be written and where it will go before they begin their draft.	Likes to write their piece out from a plan, before attending to revision and editing separately.	Likes to write a paragraph, reread it, revise it, and edit it before moving on to drafting their next paragraph.	Likes to write a sentence and ensure it is revised and edited just how they want it before moving on to the next sentence.

Table shows the typical writing habits children employ when they are crafting texts (Young and Ferguson 2020, p. 60).

Children care about transcription

Children can feel motivated to produce well-transcribed writing. If young writers value their writing and want to share it publicly, the desire to present an accurate and aesthetically pleasing text is increased. McQuitty (2014) writes about how children in an effective writing teacher's class improved their writing at the revision and editing stage of the process because they wanted their compositions to look and sound right when they entered the public space of the class library. Calkins (1980) found that in classrooms where writing was purposeful and attention was focused on how the reader would be affected, children used a wider variety of punctuation and used it more effectively than did children in classrooms where writing was more regulated and punctuation was learned by rote and practised through skill exercises. Finally, Young and Ferguson (2020) state that the act of publishing is an incentive for children to attend more closely to spelling and is also a legitimate and intrinsically worthwhile handwriting activity.

Attending to transcription at the right time

'As teachers we need to develop children's knowledge about genres of writing and we will need to set targets which relate to punctuation and spelling for example, but these also need to be balanced by targets which focus on making an impact upon the reader, and writing to persuade, to amuse or to shock for example, so that children are recognised as authors, communicators and meaning makers' (Cremin 2010, p. 122). A misguided focus on testing and on performance-based rather than meaning-based writing objectives can lead teachers to overemphasise conventions and the transcriptional elements of writing *at the wrong stages* of a young writer's process (Grainger et al. 2005; Cremin and Myhill 2012; Lambirth 2016).

The consequences of a teacher's ill-timed insistence on perfecting the secretarial aspects of writing receive serious attention in some studies. According to Bloodgood (2002) for example, it can impair the capturing of ideas, consideration of an audience, attention to detail, risk taking, and creative expression. Grainger et al. (2005, p. 91) memorably claim that teachers too often send children 'off on the road to writing with the songs of how to fulfil measurable technical requirements ringing in their ears, drowning perhaps any sense of the text's tune and meaning or the author's voice or intention'. Frank Smith (1982, p. 24) states that 'transcription skill is obviously achieved at too high a price if the cost is reluctance or inability to compose anything in the first place'. His warning is given colour by Corden (2003), who observed in his study some children who, when asked to focus and attend to transcription too early into their process, reported feeling physically sick, confused, and in a state of mental agony. Therefore, a dynamic approach to writing which allows children to shift focus, change activity, and give different aspects of their writing process their dominant attention when most appropriate, would seem to be rather sensible (van den Bergh and Rijlaarsdam 2001).

Writing For Pleasure teachers know that children value both the compositional and transcriptional aspects of writing (Calkins 1998; Tompkins 2011; Atwell 2014). They appreciate what Calkins came to realise in her work, that 'the most important thing we can do for our students is to help them write freely and unselfconsciously. No one learns well while feeling afraid and ashamed. Our students need to realise that it's okay to make editorial errors as they write; all of us do, but we always correct them when we edit' (1998, p. 290). *Writing For Pleasure* teachers will uphold the principles outlined in Chapter 15 by ensuring children focus on composition and transcription at the right time, the time which suits them best. They will accord their teaching of transcriptional skills and self-regulation strategies a high priority and teach them in a systematic and integrated way (Troia et al. 2009). Finally, they know that a balanced approach to the teaching of composition and transcription will help children to internalise and ultimately use both skills concurrently (Berninger and Winn 2006; Berninger and Chanquoy 2012; Drijbooms 2016).

Embedding transcriptional skills at the editing stage

Research suggests that the most effective way to embed transcriptional skills is during the editing stage of a child's real writing process, and not through the completion of punctuation or skill exercises (Fearn and Farnan 1998, 2007). The use of rubrics whilst revising and editing checklists whilst proof-reading is effective in helping children be independent and confident writers (see Chapter 15).

Spelling

Harold Rosen once famously said to Donald Graves that any idiot can tell a genius they've made a spelling mistake (Graves 1983, p. 188). We are sure there are many who have experienced ridicule or been made to feel unintelligent simply because they were unable to spell conventionally. Unfortunately, these negative views still persist in society and have serious long-term consequences for an individual's confidence and desire to write.

Ways in which teachers can improve children's spelling include:

- Prolific opportunities to write.
- Prolific opportunities and time to read.
- Explicit instruction in how to proof-read.
- Explicit spelling instruction. It is suggested that children be exposed to a balanced approach to instruction which includes teaching phonology, morphology, orthography and etymology in combination and at the earliest of stages.

(Adoniou 2014; Alves et al. 2019)

Writing For Pleasure teachers are likely to promote the strategy of inventing spellings (which Frank (2001) calls *temporary* spelling) because, in the early phases of learning to spell, the most productive ways of helping children make progress appear, not surprisingly, to be encouragement, a safe learning environment, and ample purposeful writing opportunities (Bissex 1980). Invented spelling, which contributes to feelings of self-efficacy and self-regulation in composing, has been shown to benefit children's long-term spelling abilities (Ouellette and Sénéchal 2017). Without the opportunity to invent spellings, children avoid using ambitious vocabulary, do not write as much and write more tentatively (Summer et al. 2016). It should be noted that children are likely to focus on correcting invented spellings when texts are being edited in preparation for publication, rather than during the composition process when, according to Knapp et al. (1995), composition must be their prime concern.

Handwriting

Children, parents, and teachers attach much importance to the 'neatness' of handwriting (Limpo and Alves 2013; Santangelo and Graham 2016). When children see their handwriting as poor, slow, and not automatised, they may lose confidence, interest, and enjoyment in writing (Pajares 2003; Olinghouse and Graham 2009). However, through authentic use of the writing processes and by writing every day, handwriting, and keyboard skills can also be practised every day (Graham 2009; Malpique et al. 2020). In addition, handwriting can be taught in a meaningful context when children are publishing (Graham 2009; Dombey 2013).

Writing For Pleasure teachers will know that children who can handwrite and type easily and happily tend to write better texts (Graham et al. 1997; Medwell and Wray 2007; Santangelo and Graham 2016). They will provide explicit handwriting instruction when children first learn to write, with a continued focus on speed, automaticity, and the development of an individual style, freeing children up to deal with the cognitive demands of composing (McCutchen 2011; Hayes 2012; Santangelo and Graham 2016).

Time and space just to compose

It is imperative that children be given time simply to compose: generating ideas, considering the purpose and audience for the text, making decisions on choice of tone, maintaining cohesion, and also attending to text structure decisions, sentence construction, and vocabulary choices (Smith 1982; Daffern and Mackenzie 2015; Young and Ferguson 2020).

Examples of effective practice

In our own research (Young 2019), it was clear that *Writing For Pleasure* teachers focused on direct instruction in the 'generalities' of good writing. They taught lessons in such a way that what the children were learning was not applicable only to that particular piece of writing or to a specific writing task. These were writing lessons which would work and be applied across future writing projects too. They regularly taught what good writing is (through technique and strategy teaching) as opposed to giving instructional, technical, or administrative lessons which were *only* relevant to completing that particular task on that particular day.

They also ensured that they taught the right lessons at the right time, focusing on teaching more compositional lessons at the beginning of a writing project and moving their focus later towards teaching strategies and techniques related to good transcription. The teachers had high expectations for transcriptional accuracy, spelling, and handwriting and wanted the children to take pride in their final written products. To do this, they encouraged children to concentrate on composing their piece (or part of their piece) before giving their attention to transcriptional accuracy or particular grammatical or linguistic features. They allocated specific time for children to revise their pieces, followed by specific time for editing. They also gave children time within a writing session to stop and regularly reread and share their work with their peers and to revise and edit what they had composed so far. Finally, there was a good balance between discussion of what the content of the class writing project might be, how the writing might be organised and structured, and the explicit teaching of different writing processes.

The *Writing For Pleasure* teachers accepted invented spellings during the composition stage. It was also accepted that children's handwriting skills were best practised when publishing their completed pieces. Spelling and punctuation were largely self-monitored by the children as they wrote, marking their texts for items to be checked and corrected by them at the editing stage. The teachers were very aware that, if grammar is to be understood in a meaningful way, it must be taught functionally and applied and examined in the context of crafting real composition.

Practical things you can do

- When discussing product goals, ensure children know which goals are best to focus on at different times in their process (see Chapter 16).
- Ensure that your mini-lessons are relevant to where the majority of your class are at in terms of their writing process. Focus your mini-lessons on compositional aspects of writing at the start of class or personal writing projects weeks before shifting focus towards the more transcriptional aspects of writing (see Chapter 20).
- Ensure that your pupil conferences take into account where the child is in the process of crafting their writing, focusing on the composition of their piece during the early stages of their writing before giving more feedback and instruction on transcription towards the end of the project (see Chapter 22).
- When developing rubrics or revision checklists, ensure they not only match the product goals discussed at the beginning of the project but that they focus on improving the compositional aspects of the writing (see Chapter 15).
- When developing editing checklists, ensure they focus children on attending to spelling and transcriptional conventions (see Chapter 15).

> **QUESTIONS WORTH ASKING YOURSELF**
>
> - Does your class try to attend to composition *and* transcription simultaneously as they draft? How successful are they? Does either suffer?
> - Do children have ample time to revise and edit their drafted pieces?
> - Do children know what writers do when they proof-read? Have they been given strategies and resources to help them successfully attend to transcriptional accuracy and conventions?
> - Do you use publishing as a contextualised way in which to teach about handwriting and typing?

References

Adoniou, M. (2014). What should teachers know about spelling. *Literacy*, 48(3), 144–153.
Alves, R., Limpo, T., Salas, N., and Joshi, R. (2019). Handwriting and spelling. In *Best Practices in Writing Instruction*, Graham, S., MacArthur, C., and Hebert, M. (Eds.) (3rd Ed.) (pp. 211–240). New York: Guilford Press.
Atwell, N. (2014). *In the Middle* (3rd Ed.). Portsmouth, NH: Heinemann.
Bereiter, C., and Scardamalia, M. (1987). *The Psychology of Written Composition*. Mahwah, NJ: Lawrence Erlbaum Associates.
Berninger, V.W., and Amtmann, D. (2003). Preventing written expression disabilities through early and continuing assessment and intervention for handwriting and/or spelling problems: Research into practice. In *Handbook of Learning Disabilities*, Swanson, H.L., Harris, K.R., and Graham, S. (Eds.) (pp. 345–363). New York: Guilford Press.
Berninger, V.W., and Chanquoy, L. (2012). What writing is and how it changes across early and middle childhood development: A multidisciplinary perspective. In *Writing: A Mosaic of Perspectives and Views*, Grigorenko, E., Mambrino, E., and Preiss, D. (Eds.) (pp. 65–84). Brandon, VT: Psychology Press.
Berninger, V.W., and Winn, W. (2006). Implications of advancements in brain research and technology for writing development, writing instruction, and educational evolution. In *Handbook of Writing Research*, MacArthur, C., Graham, S., and Fitzgerald, J. (Eds.) (pp. 96–114). New York: Guilford Press.
Bissex, G. (1980). *Gnys at Wrk: A Child Learns to Write and Read*. Cambridge, MA: Harvard University Press.
Breetvelt, I., van den Bergh, H., and Rijlaarsdam, G. (1994). Relations between writing processes and text quality: When and how? *Cognition and Instruction*, 12(2), 103–123.
Calkins, L. (1980). When children want to punctuate: Basic skills belong in context. *Language Arts*, 57, 567–573.
Calkins, L. (1998). *The Art of Teaching Writing*. Portsmouth, NH: Heinemann.
Casey, M., and Hemenway, S. (2001). Structure and freedom: Achieving a balanced writing-curriculum. *The English Journal*, 90(6), 68–75.
Chuy, M., Scardamalia, M., and Bereiter, C. (2011). Development of ideational writing through knowledge building: Theoretical and empirical bases. In *Handbook of Writing: A Mosaic of New Perspectives*, Grigorenko, E., Mambrino, E., Preiss, E. (Eds.) (pp. 175–190). New York: Psychology Press.
Corden, R. (2002). Developing reflective writers in primary schools: Findings from partnership research. *Educational Review*, 54(3), 249–276.
Corden, R. (2003). Writing is more than 'exciting': Equipping primary children to become reflective writers. *Literacy*, 37(1), 18–26.
Cremin, T. (2010). Motivating children to write with purpose and pleasure. In *The Literate Classroom*, Goodwin, P. (Ed.) (pp. 131–141). London: Routledge.
Cremin, T., and Myhill, D. (2012). *Creating Communities of Writers*. London: Routledge.
Daffern, T., and Mackenzie, N. (2015). Building strong writers: Creating a balance between the authorial and secretarial elements of writing. *Literacy Learning*, 23(1), 23–32.
Dombey, H. (2013). *Teaching Writing: What the Evidence Says UKLA Argues for an Evidence-Informed Approach to Teaching and Testing Young Children's Writing*. Leicester: United Kingdom Lubricants Association.
Drijbooms, E. (2016). *Cognitive and linguistic factors in writing development* (thesis). Radboud Universiteit Nijmegen, Nijmegen.
Fearn, L., and Farman, N. (1998). *Writing Effectively: Helping Students Master the Conventions of Writing*. London: Pearson.
Fearn, L., and Farnan, N. (2007). When is a verb? Using functional grammar to teach writing. *Journal of Basic Writing*, 26(1), 63–87.

Frank, C. (2001). 'What new things these words can do for you': A focus on one writing-project teacher and writing instruction. *Journal of Literacy Research*, 33(3), 467–506.

Graham, S. (2009). Want to improve children's writing?: Don't neglect their handwriting. *American Educator*, 33, 20–40.

Graham, S., and Harris, K. (2019). Evidence-based practices in writing. In *Best Practices in Writing Instruction*, Graham, S., MacArthur, C., and Hebert, M. (Eds.) (3rd Ed.) (pp. 3–31). New York: The Guilford Press.

Graham, S., and Santangelo, T. (2014). Does spelling instruction make students better spellers, readers, and writers? A meta-analytic review. *Reading and Writing: An Interdisciplinary Journal*, 27, 1703–1743.

Graham, S., Berninger, V., Abbot, R., Abbott, S., and Whittaker, D. (1997). The role of mechanics in composing of elementary school students: A new methodological approach. *Journal of Educational Psychology*, 89(1), 170–182.

Graham, S., McKeown, D., Kiuhara, S., and Harris, K. (2012). A meta-analysis of writing instruction for students in the elementary grades. *Journal of Educational Psychology*, 104(4), 879–896.

Grainger, T., Goouch, K., and Lambirth, A. (2005). *Creativity and Writing: Developing Voice and Verve in the Classroom*. London: Routledge.

Graves, D. (1983). *Writing: Teachers & Children at Work*. Portsmouth, NH: Heinemann.

Harmey, S. (2020). Co-constructing writing: Handing over the reins to young authors. *Education 3-13*, 3–11.

Hayes, J. (2012). Modeling and remodeling writing. *Written Communication*, 29, 369–388.

Kellogg, R. (2008). Training writing skills: A cognitive developmental perspective. *Journal of Writing Research*, 1, 1–26.

Kellogg, R., Whiteford, A., Turner, C., Cahill, M., and Mertens, A. (2013). Working memory in written composition: An evaluation of the 1996 model. *Journal of Writing Research*, 5(2), 159–190.

Kent, S.C., and Wanzek, J. (2016). The relationship between component skills and writing quality and production across developmental levels: A meta-analysis of the last 25 years. *Review of Educational Research*, 86(2), 570–601.

Kim, Y., and Schatschneider, C. (2017). Expanding the developmental models of writing: A direct and indirect effects model of developmental writing (DIEW). *Journal of Educational Psychology*, 109(1), 35–50.

Knapp, M.S., and Associates. (1995). *Teaching for Meaning in High-Poverty Classrooms*. New York: Teachers' College Press.

Lambirth, A. (2016). Exploring children's discourses of writing. *English in Education*, 50(3), 215–232.

Limpo, T., and Alves, R. (2013). Modeling writing development: Contribution of transcription and self-regulation to Portuguese students' text generation quality. *Journal of Educational Psychology*, 105, 401–413.

Louden, W., Rohl, M., Barrat-Pugh, C., Brown, C., Cairney, T., Elderfield, J., House, H., Meiers, M., Rivaland, J., and Rowe, K.J. (2005). In teachers' hands: Effective literacy teaching practices in the early years of schooling. *Australian Journal of Language and Literacy*, 28(3), 173–252.

Malpique, A., Pino-Pasternak, D., and Sofia Roberto, M. (2020). Writing and reading performance in Year 1 Australian classrooms: Associations with handwriting automaticity and writing instruction. *Reading & Writing*, 33, 783–805.

McCutchen, D. (2011). From novice to expert: Implications of language skills and writing-relevant knowledge for memory during the development of writing skill. *Journal of Writing Research*, 3(1), 51–68.

McQuitty, V. (2014). Process-oriented writing instruction in elementary classrooms: Evidence of effective practices from the research literature. *Writing & Pedagogy*, 6(3), 467–495.

Medwell, J., and Wray, D. (2007). Handwriting: What do we know and what do we need to know? *Literacy*, 41(1), 10–16.

Medwell, J., Wray, D, Poulson, L., and Fox, R. (1998). *Effective Teachers of Literacy*. Exeter, UK: The University of Exeter for the Teacher Training Agency.

Olinghouse, N., and Graham, S. (2009). The relationship between the discourse knowledge and the writing performance of elementary-grade students. *Journal of Educational Psychology*, 101, 37–50.

Ouellette, G., and Sénéchal, M. (2017). Invented spelling in kindergarten as a predictor of reading and spelling in grade 1: A new pathway to literacy, or just the same road, less known? *Developmental Psychology*, 53(1), 77–88.

Pajares, F. (2003). Self-efficacy beliefs, motivation, and achievement in writing: A review of the literature. *Reading and Writing Quarterly*, 19(2), 139–158.

Richardson, P. (1998). Literacy, learning and teaching, *Educational Review*, 50(2), 115–134.

Santangelo, T., and Graham, S. (2016). A comprehensive meta-analysis of handwriting instruction. *Educational Psychology Review*, 28, 225–265.

Smith, F. (1982). *Writing and the Writer*. New York: HEB.

Summer, E., Connelly, V., and Barnett, A. (2016). The influence of spelling ability on vocabulary choices when writing for children with dyslexia. *Journal of Learning Disabilities*, 49(3), 293–304.

Tompkins, G.E. (2011). *Teaching writing: Balancing Process and Product*. Upper Saddle River, NJ: Merrill.

Troia, G.A., Lin, S.C., Monroe, B.W., and Cohen, S. (2009). The effects of writing workshop instruction on the performance and motivation of good and poor writers. In *Instruction and Assessment for Struggling Writers*, Troia, G.A. (Ed.) (pp. 77–112). New York: Guilford Press.

van den Bergh, H., and Rijlaarsdam G. (2001). Changes in cognitive activities during the writing process and relationships with text quality. *Educational Psychology*, 21(4), 373–385.

Warrington, M., Younger, M., and Bearne E. (2006). *Raising Boys' Achievement in Primary Schools*. Buckingham: Open University Press.

Young, R. (2019) *What is is 'Writing For Pleasure' teachers do that makes the difference*. The University Of Sussex: The Goldsmiths' Company

Young, R., and Ferguson, F. (2020). *Real-World Writers: A Handbook for Teaching Writing with 7–11 Year Olds*. London: Routledge.

CHAPTER 20

Teach mini-lessons

Young writers learn to write by learning about writing. They perform better when they are knowledgeable about the strategies, processes, procedures, techniques, the role of audience, literary and linguistic features, and the textual structures involved in writing and in being a writer (Saddler and Graham 2017). Therefore, instruction that is aimed at improving children's writerly knowledge improves their writing performance. Mini-lessons are 'an efficient way to teach a wide range of writing skills' and knowledge (Alber-Morgan et al. 2007, p. 116). They are essentially short, lasting between five and 15 minutes, should precede daily sustained writing time, and are repeatable (Calkins 2013; Atwell 2014; Shubitz and Dorfman 2019; Young and Ferguson 2020a).

Writing study: teaching about the craft

Writing study (Young and Ferguson 2020a), also known as teaching 'craft knowledge' (Cremin and Myhill 2012), 'writing knowledge' (Saddler and Graham 2017), 'knowledge relevant to writing' (McCutchen 2011) or 'strategy and technique instruction' (Graham and Perin 2007l Graham et al. 2014), is, according to a great many studies, the single most effective practice a teacher of writing can employ (Graham and Perin 2007; Graham et al. 2012; Grossman et al. 2013; Koster et al. 2015). As the name suggests, writing study is when teachers share the 'how to' knowledge, characteristics, and habits of good writers and the techniques, strategies, and procedures they use. Children are then invited to apply these craft strategies and techniques in the class or personal projects they are currently engaged in (Paris and Winograd 2003; Pressley et al. 2006; Hmelo-Silver et al. 2007; Hicks 2008). As Pressley et al. (2006, p. 298) say: 'teachers make clear that students are learning to write as excellent writers write, and the students can choose to use the strategies being learned whenever they write'. So what might a knowledge-rich writing curriculum look like? It is likely that teacher will teach:

- **Craft knowledge** involved in creating texts, including:
  - **Process knowledge**, knowledge about the processes, procedures, strategies, and techniques writers employ as they go through their writing process, generating ideas, planning, drafting, revising, editing, publishing, and performing.
  - **Genre knowledge**, the typical textual, linguistic, literary, and grammatical features genres employ to be at their most meaningful and successful.
  - **Goal knowledge**, how writers set themselves goals and manage their writing deadlines.
  - **Knowledge about their reader**, how writers will meditate on the purpose for their writing, gather information about and consider their future readership.
  - **Knowledge about a writerly environment**, how writers live and work with others, and the conditions which are conducive to writing productively and happily.
- **Transcriptional knowledge**, including spelling and punctuation conventions and keyboard and handwriting skills.
- **Knowledge of how writers use their reading**, including how they read to enhance their craft knowledge and search for content material.
- **Knowledge of technology** and other modalities.
- **Knowledge of the affective domains** used by writers as they craft and publish texts. This includes giving attention to their confidence, motivation, desire, competence and their personal and collective responsibilities.

Kellogg (2008) claims it takes around 20 to 30 years to acquire and use all this knowledge and its associated skills and processes. We prefer to see writing as a pursuit in progress over a whole lifetime!

Writing For Pleasure teachers are determined to elucidate and demystify the writing processes and strategies through relevant and explicit teaching. Under their instruction, children begin slowly to realise that writing development is recursive and strategic, understand how to manage the cognitive load involved, and see writing more in terms of the gradual mastery of a craft than simply as a high stakes do-or-die performance task (Paris and Winograd 2003; Kellogg 2008). To give a practical example, when children see that their use of a taught strategy or technique has paid dividends in terms of process or product, they are more likely to use it again in their future writing (Graham and Harris 2000).

Writing For Pleasure teachers know that if they teach such craft knowledge, they give children access to the highly valuable and transferable 'generalities' of writing (Englert et al. 1991; Graham 2006; Alber-Morgan et al. 2007; Hmelo-Silver et al. 2007; Graham et al. 2011). Unfortunately, the usual procedural instruction seen in classrooms is often only applicable to the piece of writing being currently undertaken and what is taught is not easily transferable to future writing (Paris and Winograd 2003). The result of teaching writing-study lessons however is that children are more able to carry over learning from one project to another, feel greater pleasure when crafting, and have a better understanding and ownership over their writing and writing process (Graham et al. 2011). They will also make greater than expected academic learning gains, particularly if the school adheres to the principles of being reassuringly consistent across year groups (Chapter 17), teaching the writing processes (Chapter 15) and setting writing goals (Chapter 16), and if their teachers engage in daily pupil conferencing and responsive teaching (Chapter 22) (Butler and Winnie 1995; Paris and Winograd 2003; Graham 2006; Kellogg 2008; McQuitty 2014).

Young and Ferguson (2020a) state that it is essential for teachers to plan writing-study lessons in a responsive way, identifying what instruction is needed through observing children while writing amongst them, and through information gained when pupil conferencing. This, according to Pressley et al. (2001) and Corden (2003) is what the most effective teachers of writing do.

Writing study: functional grammar lessons

Graham and Perin's (2007) meta-analysis into effective writing practices, together with other research (Kolln 1996; Fearn and Farnan 1998; Andrews et al. 2006; Weaver et al. 2006; Wyse and Torgerson 2017; Hudson 2017; Myhill 2018) makes it clear that the formal teaching of grammar has continually impacted negatively on children's writing. In contrast, functional grammar teaching (also known as embedded or contextualised grammar teaching) and sentence combining are more promising. Both involve showing children what literary, linguistic, and grammatical features or structures can 'do' for and in a composition.

Research shows that effective teachers of writing do teach grammar functionally, always with the expectation that their instruction will be meaningful to children during that day's writing time (Medwell et al. 1998; Cremin 2010; Myhill et al. 2012; Limpo and Alves 2013; Drijbooms 2016; Young 2019). Young and Ferguson (2020a, p. 66) have taken into account all these findings and recommend that teachers consider the following when planning and teaching about grammar:

- Teach one item at a time and invite children to apply it that same day in their developing writing.
- In literature-based mini-lessons (see Chapter 23 for more information), share short examples from high-quality literature. Encourage children to look out for and squirrel away good examples of literary, linguistic, and grammatical features which they have found in their own reading.
- Share both your writing and children's own writing to showcase great craft.
- Effective teachers have a 'let's see what this does' as opposed to a 'right/wrong rule' attitude towards grammar.
- Do not have the expectation that children transfer knowledge from formal grammar exercises into their own writing.
- Functional grammar lessons are not only the key to good writing, but teaching in this way results in a deeper understanding of grammar for formal testing.

Sentence combining

According to Flower and Hayes (1981), every time we write a sentence, we are enacting all the writing processes or, as they say, creating a 'composition in miniature'. When crafting texts, children go through this process of miniature composition time and time again. They gradually become syntactically fluent and better able to consider other aspects of quality composition as they craft sentences, for example textual features and cohesiveness (Berninger et al. 2011). They are able to contemplate what will come next and reference what has come before. Saddler (2019) states that children require direct and explicit instruction in sentence combining as part of a stimulating overall writing programme; it should not be taught as a separate entity nor be seen as a complete programme in itself.

When constructing sentences orally, children are utilizing their knowledge of syntax acquired when learning to talk and read. They then transfer this knowledge to their early writing endeavours. However, written language requires particular organisational skills. For the purposes of effective communication, children need to be able to use a variety of sentence types, understand their functions, and know how to combine them. It is our belief that these skills are best taught through functional grammar mini-lessons aiming to show children how they can 'paint with words' or 'put the best words for the job in the best order'. Painting with words and putting the best words in the best order is what writers spend a lot of their time thinking about and doing, so why not teach their techniques to children? As Saddler (2019) makes clear, a high-quality lesson should focus on how types of sentence combining can clarify meaning, serve the intended purpose, and give the writing rhythmic appeal. Syntactic complexity should not be considered a virtue in itself. Finally, Young and Ferguson (2020a) suggest that, to teach grammar and sentence combining effectively, teachers employ a routine similar to the self-regulated strategy development model explained below.

Mini-lessons and self-regulated strategy development instruction

'The most effective learners are self-regulating' (Butler and Winne 1995, p. 245). According to McQuitty (2014 p.485) 'self-regulated strategy development (SRSD) has an empirical foundation that clearly supports its effectiveness, and it is notable that this is a specific structured approach to implementing the writing process'. Both research and literature about SRSD is compelling, consistently demonstrating its effectiveness within a contemporary writing-workshop approach (Danoff et al. 1993; McQuitty, 2014; Young and Ferguson 2020a). Graham's (2006) meta-analysis of 39 studies indicated that SRSD significantly improves the writing of *all* writers (Zumbrunn and Bruning 2013), including those with learning disabilities (Lane et al. 2010; Johnson et al. 2012). The average effect size for strategy instruction was 1.15 (0.32 is typically seen as significantly effective), far exceeding the effectiveness of writing workshop taught in a naturalistic or self-expressive way (Graham and Perin 2007; Graham and Sandmel 2011). In addition, studies show that a combination of SRSD instruction and writing workshop can increase children's pleasure in writing (Englert et al. 1991; Sexton et al. 1998; Graham, Harris and Mason 2011; Harris et al. 2006). *Writing For*

Pleasure teachers are therefore likely to teach self-regulation development strategies (SRSD) when teaching writing study and functional grammar mini-lessons. They understand how adherence to the mini-lesson structure is instrumental in helping children undertake writing projects independently (Pressley et al. 1997, 2001).

Young and Ferguson (2020a), inspired by the work of Harris and Graham (1996) and McQuitty (2014), suggest that effective teachers of writing use the following process to teach mini-lessons:

Introduce → Share → Provide information → Invite

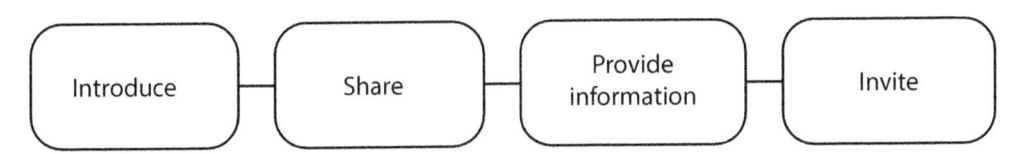

FIGURE 20.1 A recommended approach to teaching mini-lessons.

1. *Introduce the topic and its purpose* – The mini-lesson is directed towards giving children writerly knowledge, critical to their growth as writers (Perry and VandeKamp 2000; Graham et al. 2011). Children need to know *what* writing strategies are, *how* they can be used, and *when* is the best time to use them. As discussed in Chapter 15, *Writing For Pleasure* teachers will begin by discussing what good writers tend to do when engaging in the different processes of writing. They will talk about a writing strategy or a technique in a general way so that children understand they can use them in future writing projects. Discussions are therefore framed in a 'mastery' perspective which enhances children's aspirations and motivation (Paris and Winograd 2003; Perry et al. 2008; Graham et al. 2011).

2. *Share examples* – As we discuss in more detail in Chapter 21, Graham et al. (2011, p. 24) suggest that 'teacher modelling is critical for establishing the metacognitive processes needed for effective strategy use'. The teacher does this by talking about their use of a strategy, asking for children's opinions, and discussing when best to use the strategy (Regan and Berkeley 2012). For example, the teacher might say 'once I've drafted my short story, I often read through it and look for the moments when I introduce my characters for the first time. I then try to revise into my piece some description to develop my character more for my reader'.

3. *Provide information* – *Writing For Pleasure* teachers will provide resources, prompts, and/or visual displays to support children's use of the strategy. These can be discussed and constructed in collaboration with the children and so adjustments can be made if suggested. Children can then be invited to try out the strategy or technique during that day's writing time.

4. *Invite to try out strategies and assess learning* – As we know very well, and as Cremin (2010, p. 137) says: 'skills transfer more easily if they are embedded in a meaningful framework and are employed for real outcomes and purposes'. Therefore, *Writing For Pleasure* teachers will create a writing environment where children feel encouraged to try out a newly taught strategy and comment on how it has benefited their composition. Because the writing community is a

social environment, children will be able to discuss and practise the strategy collaboratively (Paris and Winograd 2003; Hmelo-Silver et al. 2007). For example, during class sharing and Author's Chair, the teacher can invite children to share how they felt about the effect of using the strategy that day (see Chapter 13). Finally, several texts have been written sharing practical examples of types of mini-lessons described in this chapter, including the authors' own online resources (Young and Ferguson 2020b and others Fletcher and Portalupi 2001, 2007; Serravallo 2017).

The role of the writer-teacher

In order to be successful, teachers must be reflective and analytical about their own writing practices and must acquire a deep understanding of the cognitive and motivational aspects of learning to write (Paris and Winograd 2003). Teachers should therefore themselves engage in reflective writing and gain a powerful insight into the writing strategies, techniques and processes they employ. They are then enabled to better communicate self-regulating strategies to their class and to recommend effective writerly strategies (Hillocks 1984, 1986; Englert et al. 1991). The kinds of reflective writing practice we would expect to see include teachers writing collaboratively with the children and constructing texts (at different stages of the writing process) alongside their learners. As writer-teachers they will also provide exemplars written by themselves, other writers, or by children in previous years to show the application of certain techniques (Hayden 2020).

Young and Ferguson (2020a, p. 68) suggest that teachers will know they are teaching a good mini-lesson if they find themselves saying things like:

- When I write …
- Yesterday, I couldn't help but notice that …
- When some writers … they'll …
- Why do authors use …
- I've noticed recently that …
- I wanted to show you how …
- I thought today we could try …
- We need to show that we can …
- Remember when we wrote our … well now I think we are ready to …
- I know that last year you … well this year …

The link between mini-lessons and writing goals

Product goals give teachers and pupils a clear vision of the strategies, processes, and literary and linguistic techniques most needed to produce successful and meaningful writing. Mini-lessons that explicitly address the identified product goals for a class writing project are particularly effective (Zumbrunn and Krause 2012; Bradford et al. 2016; Hayden 2020).

The link between mini-lessons and the community of writers

When observing a high-achieving benchmark school working in challenging circumstances, Pressley et al. (2006) recorded that writing study and functional grammar mini-lessons were a dominant teaching practice. They noted especially that lessons would be converted into, for example, posters or other kinds of resources such as graphic organisers, checklists, or rubrics, which were regularly adjusted to reflect the project and the current stage in the writing process. The community of the classroom in which these writers worked every day was full of artefacts and resources which reflected how they were deciding to craft meaningful and successful texts.

Lave and Wenger (1994, cited in Paris and Winograd 2003) discuss how learning is situated in domains of expertise and social interactions, which they label 'legitimate participation'. It is here we see links between mini-lessons and the first principle of growing a community of writers. Children who take on the identity of the writing community will be keen to learn, through mini-lessons, the skills and writerly knowledge of that community too (Perry and Drummond 2002; Hayden 2020).

The importance of daily writing time

According to Tolchinsky (2017, p. 149), 'the principal source of knowledge for understanding writing is writing itself. It is by using writing that children will learn to master it'. Newly acquired writing strategies and processes (writing study) and linguistic techniques (functional grammar) taught through mini-lessons can only be internalised and retained in a child's writerly repertoire if there is a daily and sustained period in which to write (Pressley et al. 2006; Alber-Morgan et al. 2007; Kellogg 2008; Zumbrunn and Krause 2012). For example, Ranker (2009) found this to be true in his study of six-year-old writers: they continued to use learned strategies in their daily writing over many days and weeks.

Examples of effective practice

In our research which observed *Writing For Pleasure* teachers (Young 2019), the teachers regarded self-regulation strategies as vital to the way they taught writing. It was clear from the student data that self-regulation had a positive impact on children writing with self-efficacy and independence. For example, one student notes: 'when I know what I'm going to write about and I've thought about it and when I start writing it just calms me down; I just felt like I knew what I was doing – I knew how to do it'.

Children were taught numerous strategies and techniques that they could employ independently. They were taught strategies for generating ideas, planning, drafting, revising, editing and publishing, and they knew how to employ these strategies across all their writing projects – both class and personal. They were taught how to draw as a means of generating ideas and of planning, using story maps, planning grids, discovery drafts, proof-reading marks, peer conferencing, and revision and editing checklists. The classes also had ready access to resources for editing and publishing such as electronic spell-checkers, dictionaries, common word mats, guidelines, papers, laptops, and other stationery. These teachers made use of their working walls for sharing self-regulation strategies which were linked to recent mini-lessons taught. One teacher also had baskets which contained advice and strategies for being more self-regulating. For example, sentence starters, common word lists, vocabulary lists, types of story openings and endings, and planning grids. This provided pupils with the knowledge they needed and empowered them to see their own writing idea through to successful publication. Children were taught to keep space available on the right-hand side of their writing notebooks for 'trying things out' or for making major revisions to their developing pieces.

These self-regulation strategies and resources were introduced carefully and given dedicated instructional time. Via a mini-lesson, the teachers would discuss the benefits of a writing strategy or resource before modelling and encouraging its use that day. The strategies and techniques were offered in the spirit of a writer-teacher sharing their own writerly knowledge and their 'tricks'. Part of this was explaining the benefits the strategy or resource had on their own writing development. Finally, through peer conferencing and class sharing, these teachers helped children teach others about their own developing writerly knowledge, strategies, and techniques. For example, one child in the study explained: 'well at first I will try to think about it and what I'm going to do about it. I'll probably be sitting there looking like I'm doing nothing but I'm thinking about it. Sometimes I'll ask my friends and they will give me ideas of how to change things around – sometimes they're not very helpful but most of the time we can get it fixed'.

Practical things you can do

- Teach both writing-study and functional grammar mini-lessons and teach mini-lessons every day.
- Make sure your mini-lessons are generalisable, promote self-regulation, and are genuinely useful to children's development as writers.
- Make sure your mini-lessons are useful to children during that day's writing time. Ensure mini-lessons are kept short and to the point. Protect children's access to daily and sustained writing time. Developing a reassuringly consistent routine can help. See Chapter 17 for more details.
- Match your mini-lessons to your class writing goals. See Chapter 16 for more details.
- Make sure you're planning your mini-lessons in response to what you're seeing and hearing your children need help with most. Undertaking daily pupil conferencing can help. See Chapter 22 for more details. Ask children what they feel they need instruction in most and deliver it.
- Take advantage of spontaneous moments during daily writing time in which to teach a responsive mini-lesson.
- See your mini-lessons as encouraging children's mastery over process and techniques rather than as procedural instruction in how to complete a very specific writing task.

- During your writing study mini-lessons, make sure you're teaching children what excellent writers do as they craft their texts.
- As much as possible, use your own writing and your own use of writing strategies, techniques, features, processes, and procedures to help you teach your mini-lessons.
- Share examples of great craft with your pupils.
- Teach functional grammar lessons always with a view the children can be invited to try out the linguistic or literary features discussed during that day's writing time.
- Turn your mini-lessons into posters, graphic organisers, and other resources to help promote children's future use and self-regulation.

QUESTIONS WORTH ASKING YOURSELF

- Are you knowledgeable about the craft, habits, processes, procedures, techniques, and strategies you and other writers employ when crafting texts?
- Are you knowledgeable about the literary and linguistic features that make for great writing?
- Are you knowledgeable about the function of grammar in use and not just the conventions and rules of punctuation?
- Do you invite children to try out what you teach them during your mini-lessons? Do you have a routine in place that allows you to teach mini-lessons every day before children engage in daily writing? (see Chapter 17).
- Do you share craft-knowledge, strategies, and techniques for all parts of a writer's process?
- Do you turn your mini-lessons into usable posters and or resources?
- Are you continually looking to increase children's craft knowledge?
- Do your mini-lessons generally match what children are currently undertaking in their writing and so are of practical use to them?
- Do you plan your mini-lessons in response to what you're seeing your children do during writing time? Are you planning mini-lessons that your children clearly feel they need? Do you ask what your children feel they need mini-lessons on?
- Can children use the strategies you teach without needing your help and are the strategies you teach useful in lots of writing situations?

References

Alber-Morgan, S., Hessler, T., and Konrad, M. (2007). Teaching writing for keeps. *Education and Treatment of Children*, 30, 107–128.

Andrews, R., Torgerson, C., Beverton, S., Locke, T., Low, G., Robinson, A., and Zhu, D. (2006). The effect of grammar teaching on writing development. *British Educational Research Journal*, 32(1), 39–55.

Atwell, N. (2014). *In the Middle* (3rd Ed). Portsmouth, NH: Heinemann.

Berninger, V., Nagy, W., and Beers, S. (2011). Child writers' construction and reconstruction of single sentences and construction of multi-sentence texts: Contributions of syntax and transcription to translation. *Reading and Writing*, 24, 151–182.

Bradford, K., Newland, A., Rule, A., and Montgomery, S. (2016). Rubrics as a tool in writing instruction: Effects on the opinion essays of first and second graders. *Early Childhood Education*, 44, 463–472.

Butler, D.L., and Winne, P.H. (1995). Feedback and self-regulated learning: A theoretical synthesis. *Review of Educational Research*, 65(3), 245–274.

Calkins, L. (2013). *A guide to the writing workshop: Intermediate grades*. Portsmouth, NH: Heinnaman.

Corden, R. (2003). Writing is more than 'exciting': Equipping primary children to become reflective writers. *Literacy*, 37(1), 18–26.

Cremin, T. (2010). Motivating children to write with purpose and pleasure. In *The Literate Classroom*, Goodwin, P. (Ed.) (2nd Ed.) (pp. 131–141). London: Routledge.

Cremin, T., and Myhill, D. (2012). *Writing Voices: Creating Communities of Writers*. London: Routledge.

Danoff, B., Harris, K. R., and Graham, S. (1993). Incorporating strategy instruction within the writing process in the regular classroom: Effects on the writing of students with and without learning disabilities. *Journal of Reading Behavior*, 25(3), 295–322.

Drijbooms, E. (2016). *Cognitive and linguistic factors in writing* development (thesis). Radboud Universiteit Nijmegen, Nijmegen.

Englert, C.S., Raphael, T.E., Anderson, L.M., Anthony, H.M., and Stevens, D.D. (1991). Making strategies and self-talk visible: Writing instruction in regular and special education classrooms. *American Educational Research Journal*, 28(2), 337–372.

Fearn, L., and Farman, N. (1998). *Writing Effectively: Helping Students Master the Conventions of Writing*. London: Pearson.

Fletcher, R., and Portalupi, J. (2001). *Non-Fiction Craft Lessons: Teaching Information Writing K-8*. New York: Stenhouse.

Fletcher, R., and Portalupi, J. (2007). *Craft Lessons: Teaching Writing K-8* (2nd Ed.). New York: Stenhouse.

Flower, L., and Hayes, J. (1981). A cognitive process theory of writing. *College Composition and Communication*, 32, 365–387.

Graham, S. (2006). Strategy instruction and the teaching of writing: A meta-analysis. In *Handbook of Writing Research*, McArthur, C., Graham, S., and Fitzgerald, J. (Eds.) (pp. 187–207). New York: Guilford Press.

Graham, S., and Harris, K. R. (1996). Self-regulation and strategy instruction for students who find writing and learning challenging. In *The Science of Writing: Theories, Methods, Individual Differences, and Applications*, Levy, C. M. and Ransdell, S. (Eds.) (pp. 347–360). Lawrence Erlbaum Associates, Inc.

Graham, S., and Harris, K. (2000). The role of self-regulation and transcription skills in writing and writing development. *Educational Psychologist*, 35(1), 3–12.

Graham, S., and Perin, D. (2007). *Writing Next: Effective Strategies to Improve Writing of Adolescents In Middle School & High Schools*. Washington, DC: Alliance For Excellent Education.

Graham, S. and Sandmel, K. (2011). The process writing approach: A meta-analysis. *Journal of Educational Research*, 104: 396–407.

Graham, S., Harris, K., and Mason, L. (2011). Self-regulated strategy development for students with writing difficulties. *Theory Into Practice*, 50(1), 20–27.

Graham, S., McKeown, D., Kiuhara, S., and Harris, K. (2012). A meta-analysis of writing instruction for students in the elementary grades. *Journal of Educational Psychology*, 104(4), 879–896.

Graham, S., Harris, K., and Mason, L. (2014). Improving the writing performance, knowledge, and self-efficacy of struggling young writers: The effects of self-regulated strategy development. *Contemporary Educational Psychology*, 30(2), 207–241.

Grossman, P.L., Loeb, S., Cohen, J., and Wyckoff, J. (2013). Measure for measure: The relationship between measures of instructional practice in middle school English language arts and teachers' value-added scores. *American Journal of Education*, *119*(3), 445–470.

Harris, K., Graham, S., and Mason, L. (2006). Improving the writing, knowledge, and motivation of struggling young writers: effects of self- regulated strategy development with and without peer support. *American Educational Research Journal*, 43(2), 295–340.

Hayden, T. (2020). *'Mr Hayden! How do writers start their stories?'* [Available: https://writing4pleasure.com/mr-hayden-how-do-writers-start-their-stories-2/]

Hicks, J. (2008). *Writing identify and the writers' workshop: Looking back at my second grade* [USFSP Honors Program Theses (Undergraduate)], 83.

Hillocks, G. (1984). What works in teaching composition: A meta-analysis of experimental studies. *American Journal of Education*, 93(1), 133–170.

Hillocks, G. (1986). *Research on Written Composition: New Directions for Teaching*. Urbana, IL: National Council of Teachers of English.

Hmelo-Silver, C., Duncan, R., and Chinn, C. (2007). Scaffolding and achievement in problem-based and inquiry learning: A response to Kirschner, Sweller, and Clark (2006). *Educational Psychologist*, 42(2), 99–107.

Hudson, R. (2017). Grammar instruction. In *Handbook of Writing Research*, MacArthur, C., Graham, S., Fitzgerald, J. (Eds.) (pp. 288–300) (2nd Ed.). New York: Guildford Press..

Johnson, E., Hancock, C., Carter, D., and Pool, J. (2012). Self-regulated strategy development as a tier 2 writing intervention. *Intervention in School and Clinic*, 48(4), 218–222.

Kellogg, R.T. (2008). Training writing skills: A cognitive developmental perspective. *Journal of Writing Research*, 1(1), 1–26.

Kolln, M. (1996). Rhetorical grammar: A modification lesson. *English Journal*, 85(7), 25–31.

Koster, M., Tribushinina, E., De Jong, P.F., and Van de Bergh, B. (2015). Teaching children to write: A meta-analysis of writing intervention research. *Journal of Writing Research*, 7(2), 249–274.

Lane, K., Graham, S., Harris, K., Little, M., Sandmel, K., and Brindle, M. (2010). The effects of self-regulated strategy development for second-grade students with writing and behavioral difficulties. *The Journal of Special Education*, 44(2), 107–128.

Limpo, T., and Alves, R. (2013). Teaching planning or sentence-combining strategies: Effective SRSD interventions at different levels of written composition. *Contemporary Educational Psychology*, 38, 328–341.

McCutchen, D. (2011). From novice to expert: Implications of language skills and writing-relevant knowledge for memory during the development of writing skill. *Journal of Writing Research*, 3(1), 51–68.

McQuitty, V. (2014). Process-oriented writing instruction in elementary classrooms: Evidence of effective practices from the research literature. *Writing & Pedagogy*, 6(3), 467–495.

Medwell, J., Wray, D., Poulson, L., and Fox, R. (1998). *Effective teachers of literacy. A report commissioned by the UK Teacher Training Agency*.

Myhill, D. (2018). Grammar as a meaning-making resource for improving writing (Contribution to a special issue Working on Grammar at School in L1-Education: Empirical Research across Linguistic Regions). *L1-Educational Studies Language and Literature*, 18, 1–21.

Myhill, D., Jones, S., Lines, H., and Watson, A. (2012). Re-thinking grammar: The impact of embedded grammar teaching on students' writing and students' metalinguistic understanding. *Research Papers in Education*, 27(2), 139–166.

Paris, S.G., and Winograd, P. (2003). *The role of self-regulated learning in contextual teaching: Principles and practices for teacher preparation* (CIERA Report). Retrieved from https://files.eric.ed.gov/fulltext/ED479905.pdf

Perry, N.E., and Drummond, L. (2002). Helping young students become self-regulated researchers and writers. The Reading Teacher, 56(3), 298–310.

Perry, N.E., and VandeKamp, K. J. O. (2000). Creating classroom contexts that support young children's development of self-regulated learning. *International Journal of Educational Research*, 33(7), 821–843.

Perry, N.E., Hutchinson, L., and Thauberger, C. (2008). Talking about teaching self-regulated learning: Scaffolding student teachers' development and use of practices that promote self-regulated learning. *International Journal of Educational Research*, 47(2), 97–108.

Pressley, M., Yokoi, L., Rankin, J., Wharton-McDonald, R., and Mistretta, J., (1997) A survey of the instructional practices of grade 5 teachers nominated as effective in promoting literacy. *Scientific Studies of Reading*, 1:2, 145–160.

Pressley, M., Wharton-McDonald, R., Allington, R., Block, C., Morrow, L., Tracey, D., Baker, K., Brooks, G., Cronin, J., Nelson, E., and Woo, D. (2001). A study of effective first-grade literacy instruction. *Scientific Studies of Reading*, 5(1), 35–58.

Pressley, M., Gaskins, I., Solic, K., and Collins, S. (2006). A portrait of benchmark school: How a school produces high achievement in students who previously failed. *Journal of Educational Psychology*, 98(2), 282–306.

Ranker, J. (2009). Student appropriation of writing lessons through hybrid composing practices: direct diffuse, and indirect use of teacher-offered writing tools in an ESL classroom. *Journal of Literacy Research*, 41, 393–431.

Regan, K., and Berkeley, S. (2012). Effective reading and writing instruction: A focus on modelling. *Intervention in School and Clinic*, 47(5), 276–282.

Saddler, B. (2019). Sentence combining. In *Best Practices in Writing Instruction*, Graham, S., MacArthur, C., and Hebert, M. (3rd Ed.) (pp. 240–261). New York: Guildford Press.

Saddler, B., and Graham, S. (2017). The relationship between writing knowledge and writing performance among more and less skilled writers. *Reading & Writing Quarterly*, 23(3), 231–247.

Serravallo, J. (2017). *The Writing Strategies Book*. Portsmouth NH: Heinemann

Sexton, M., Harris, K., and Graham, S. (1998). Self-Regulated Strategy Development and the Writing Process: Effects on Essay Writing and Attributions. *Exceptional Children*, 64(3), 295–311.

Shubitz, S., and Dorfman, L. (2019). *Welcome to Writing Workshop*. Portsmouth, NH: Stenhouse.

Tolchinsky, L. (2017). From text to language and back. In *Handbook of Writing Research*, MacArthur, C., Graham, S., and Fitzgerald, J. (Eds.) (2nd Ed.) (pp. 144–159). London: Guildford

Weaver, C., Bush, J., Anderson, J., and Bills, P. (2006). Grammar intertwined throughout the writing process: An inch wide and a mile deep. *English Teaching: Practice & Critique*, 5(1), 77–101.

Wyse, D., and Torgerson, C. (2017). Experimental trials and 'what works?' In education: The case of grammar for writing. *British Educational Research Journal*, 43(6), 1019–1047.

Young, R. (2019). *What is it 'Writing For Pleasure' teachers do that makes the difference?* The University Of Sussex: The Goldsmiths' Company [Online]. Available: www.writing4pleasure.com.

Young, R., and Ferguson, F. (2020a). *Real-World Writers: A Handbook for Teaching Writing with 7–11 Year Olds*. London: Routledge.

Young, Y., Young, R., and Ferguson, F. (2020b). *Class writing projects* [Available: https://writing4pleasure.com/class-writing-projects/]

Zumbrunn, S., and Bruning, R. (2013). Improving the writing and knowledge of emergent writers: The effects of self-regulated strategy development. *Reading and Writing: An Interdisciplinary Journal*, 26(1), 91–110.

Zumbrunn, S., and Krause, K. (2012). Conversations with leaders: Principles of effective writing instruction. *The Reading Teacher*, 65(5), 346–353.

CHAPTER

21

Be a writer-teacher

'I immersed myself in writing for pleasure, and I brought my pleasure into the classroom. The effect was palpable' (Kaufman 2002, p. 53). A writer-teacher is simultaneously a writer who knows how to teach writing and a teacher who identifies as a writer. As we have seen in other chapters, being a *Writing For Pleasure* teacher is about creating and modelling for children the environment and behaviours of a writer, or, as Kaufman says, how to live a literate life (2009). It involves teaching and demonstrating from a position of expertise the processes, procedures, craft knowledge, strategies, and techniques writers use to fulfil their writing intentions and feel themselves to be successful. A teacher can be the passionate writer every child should be entitled to meet and learn from.

What writer-teachers do

Crafting and role modelling	Teaching and demonstrating
In our chapter **Create a community of writers**, we conclude that writer-teachers write to better understand how to build a community of writers in their classrooms – a community which reflects how writers live and work together (Graves 1991; Frank 2001; Kaufman 2002; Grainger 2005; Andrews 2008).	In our chapter **Teach the writing processes**, we show that teachers write to gain a better understanding of the processes, procedures, and craft knowledge children require if they are to produce meaningful and successful writing (Andrews 2008; Kaufman 2009; Watts 2009; Dix and Cawkwell 2011).
In our chapter **Read, share, think, and talk about writing**, we find that teachers write to ensure they can read, think, and talk authentically to children about writing and being a writer from a position of empathy and expertise (Cremin 2006; Andrews 2008; Whitney 2009; Dix and Cawkwell 2011; Rooke 2013).	In our chapter **Teach daily mini-lessons**, we see that teachers write to build up a repertoire of useful and responsive writing study mini-lessons (Watts 2009; Cremin and Baker 2010; Morgan 2010).

(Continued)

Crafting and role modelling	Teaching and demonstrating
In our chapter **Pursue personal writing projects**, we note that teachers write to share their own writing goals and ambitions, and that they write to showcase for their class the power and satisfaction of personal writing projects (Graves 1983; Calkins 1994; Grainger 2005; Andrews 2008; Atwell 2014; Gardner 2014).	In our chapter **Set writing goals**, we find that teachers write to produce excellent mentor texts which help students better understand the goals for a class writing project. In addition, they undertake their own writing within the class writing project and write alongside their pupils towards publication or performance (Kaufman 2002; Andrews 2008; Young and Ferguson 2020).
In our chapter **Pupil conference: meet children where they are**, we explain that teachers write in order to give effective pupil conferences whilst children are in the act of writing (Frank 2001; Andrews 2008; Atwell 2014).	In our chapter **Literacy for pleasure: connect reading and writing,** we discuss how teachers write in order to show how writers use their own reading as inspiration and mentor (Hansen 1987; Harwayne 1992; Murray 1993; Barrs and Cork 2001; Frank 2001).
Finally, they write because of the pleasure it affords them (Kaufman 2002; Brooks 2007; Andrews 2008; Young and Ferguson 2020).	

Whilst Cremin and Oliver's (2017) systematic review of research into writer-teachers is inconclusive about whether children benefit *academically* from a teacher who writes, the body of work we have drawn on in this book suggests that delivering effective writing instruction most effectively requires teachers to be writers. Whyte et al. (2007), for example, show that when teachers are writers *and* employ research-informed teaching practices, their students' achievement in writing increases significantly. However, the reality is that, as Whitney (2008, 2009) points out, too many writer-teachers feel a strong tension between what they know to be true about developing children as writers and the classroom practices they are required to employ.

Be a role model

Young and Ferguson (2020, p. 135) note that 'being a writer-teacher does not mean you have to be good at writing, but it does mean that you join and become a member of your community of writers, writing alongside the children when possible'. Writer-teachers need to be passionate learners. They believe that the best way to teach pupil-writers is to create a classroom writing community in which they can embody and model for children the way writers work (Frank 2001; Kaufman 2009; Vasques 2020). Children then come to see their teacher as a genuine writer who writes legitimately alongside them.

'Personal beliefs about writing are very important … they spill over into the classroom in ways that we probably don't even understand' (Zumbrunn and Krause 2012, p. 347). Grainger et al. (2005) express the same view with considerable emotion. They perceive passion and affective engagement to be both critical and underrated components of a creative teacher's repertoire and, citing Hargreaves, claim that *Writing For Pleasure* teachers are 'emotional, passionate beings who connect with their students and fill their work and their classes with pleasure, creativity, challenge and joy' (Grainger et al. 2005, p. 161). We would certainly expect to see

Writing For Pleasure teachers' enthusiasm motivating their apprentice writers and impacting the community in a supportive way (Street 2003), and how, as Cremin and Oliver (2017, p. 286) suggest: 'teachers who perceive themselves as writers offer richer classroom writing experiences and generate increased enjoyment, motivation and tenacity among their students than non-writers'.

Demonstrate what writers do

'If I were to give a tip to teachers, I'd tell them to take out a sheet of paper and start writing. I'd also tell them to share what they write with students. I think we (as teachers) provide the type of demonstration that students need to see and be around. There's power in making yourself as vulnerable as the students you're teaching' (Zumbrunn and Krause 2012, p. 347). This is a bold and challenging statement which is in line with our own assertion in Chapter 20, and with that of Kaufman (2009) and Regan and Berkeley (2012), that honest and explicit demonstration of what writers do is a part of effective writing instruction. Taylor (2000, p. 49) gives us a picture of demonstration in action, describing how a writer-teacher she observed would place herself 'as an expert directly in the midst of her readers and writers, directing their activity', and would use her energy to demonstrate writing as whole-class instruction. In individual pupil conferences, she would also discuss 'what works and doesn't' and would, as writer to writer, collaborate with the child on developing their manuscript.

The two examples described above show how demonstrating what writes do can take different forms. These are not mutually exclusive; a teacher can take both these stances on different occasions.

Share your writing

In his customary shrewd, direct, and logical way, Frank Smith points out that: 'there is no way of helping children to see themselves as writers if they themselves are not interested. That is why the first responsibility of teachers is to show children that writing is interesting, possible, and worthwhile. But there is also no way of helping children to write if the teacher does not think writing is interesting, possible, and worthwhile. Teachers who are not members of the club cannot admit children to the club' (Smith 1983, p. 566).

Writer-teachers sharing their writing can help create a feeling of involvedness amongst the members of the writing community (Frank 2001; Young and Ferguson 2020; Vasques 2020). A teacher's writing can be an exemplar for a class writing project, but it can also be discussed in a way that allows the author to share their vital 'tips, tricks and secrets'. Children might ask questions along the lines of:

- How and why did you craft this text?
- How did you come up with your idea?
- How did you plan it?
- How did you get started?
- How did you come up with that part?
- Can we see your draft?

- Why did you decide to revise that part?
- How can we write like that?
- Can you show us how you did that part?

This is fundamentally different from the situation where teachers share a pre-prepared one-off text, with intentions already predetermined and often at a cool distance away from what the children actually feel they need instruction in. It would appear that being *responsive* is the vital part of *sharing* writing, because, as Murray explains (1990, p. 5), 'good writing does not reveal its making. The problems are already solved, the scaffolding has been removed, and the discarded building materials have been hauled away'. However, if we invite children to ask questions about how we constructed our text, we can reveal the secrets of how it was made, and children will lean in, listen, and learn.

Shared writing and think-aloud

It is widely accepted that teachers modelling writing live with their class is a part of good instruction if the aim is clearly understood and kept in mind. Research strongly suggests that live writing is most effective when: it is short; the teacher names and explains what it is they are about to showcase; they model a single strategy, process or literary technique; they invite children to use the strategy that day, and the strategy can be used by their apprentice writers time and time again. (Block and Israel 2004; Grainger 2005; Regan and Berkeley, 2012; Rooke 2013). We know that, when crafting writing and at all stages of the process, writers carry on an inner dialogue with themselves. Teachers writing live and sharing their writing with the class have the opportunity to make this dialogue and the underlying thought processes visible (Grainger et al. 2005; Regan and Berkeley 2012; Rooke 2013). Through thinking aloud, they model and make visible 'the normally invisible cognitive processes related to planning, drafting and revising text' (Englert et al. 1991, p. 339). Essentially, they make explicit for children what writers think and do. This, of course, is the objective of shared writing.

According to Young and Ferguson (2020), writer-teachers stand to gain the respect of pupils when they put pen to paper in the classroom and craft a genuine text, becoming active participants in the class project from idea generation to publishing. They model all the processes rather than simply privileging drafting or proof-reading, as is so often the case in 'demonstration writing'. When conducted with the right intentions, shared writing as a practice becomes a consistent learning tool, supplying artefacts which are open to discussion and change throughout the project, and responding to what children feel they need to see modelled at the right time (Mercer et al. 1988; Aulls 2002).

As we have considered in Chapters 13 and 22, how teachers talk with their pupils is of paramount importance. A teacher's approach and tone are crucial to the effectiveness of the instruction; they also of course reflect the reciprocal relationships which teachers are careful to establish so children will learn, and their writing will flourish. In their book *Real-World Writers,* Young and Ferguson (2020, p. 68) suggest what writer-teachers might hear themselves saying when crafting live for children. It is easy to see how this kind of address can create feelings of involvedness and inclusiveness and also promote the brisk practical character of writing workshop:

- When I write, I often …
- Yesterday, I couldn't help but notice that …
- When some writers want to … they'll …
- The other day, you all said you wanted to know why writers …
- I've noticed recently that …
- I wanted to show you how …
- I thought today we could try …
- We need to show that we can …
- Yesterday, some of you asked me how to …
- Remember when we wrote our … well now I think we are ready to …
- I know that last year you … well, this year let's …

Finding the time

Kaufman (2002) and Alford and Early (2017) acknowledge that teachers may feel they lack time to write for and with their pupils. The evidence shared in the opening of this chapter would argue that, in fact, teachers cannot afford *not* to write. Kaufman (2002) challenges teachers to remove from their workload and teaching instruction the things that do not help children develop as writers and replace them with the research-based writing practices described in this book.

Writer-teachers as investigators

'Teachers need to write in order to become effective writing teachers' (Morgan, 2010, p. 352). As we have described and as research has suggested, being an effective teacher of writing has several different facets. It is certain that, beyond the pleasure gained and transferred to their pupils, *Writing For Pleasure* teachers write so as to better understand writing processes and strategies and know how to see them from their pupils' perspective (Kaufman 2002; Grainger 2005; Gardner 2014; Cremin and Locke 2017 Bean 2020). Interestingly, they will also be motivated to investigate the writing of others when away from the classroom, use what they discover to enrich their writing instruction, and add to the self-regulatory strategies they share with pupils (Grainger 2005; Gennrich and Janks 2013; Woodard 2015). This is discussed in more detail in Chapter 24.

Living the writer's life: writer-teachers writing for pleasure

'The idea that teaching and writing not only could be compatible but could actually be complementary pursuits comes as a revelation' (Faust 1998, p. 191). In this chapter, we have spoken in the main about teachers writing as a way to improve their instruction, feedback, and classroom environments. However, to paraphrase Faust (1998, p. 181), a good teacher of writing needs also to be a good learner of writing. He goes on to say that by connecting their teaching of writing to their own learning of writing teachers can enhance the quality of their lives in profound ways. Engaging in writing which is not simply for teaching purposes but is a recreational and volitional act of lifelong learning can offer enormous benefits personally but also, in unexpected ways, for one's teaching. Faust (1998) suggests that writing for personal pleasure can give teachers renewed energy and enthusiasm for their day-to-day work of teaching writing. Ings (2009) agrees that teachers simply writing for their own pleasure may also find that it benefits their teaching. This is demonstrated in the figure below taken from Baker and Cremin's (2010) work.

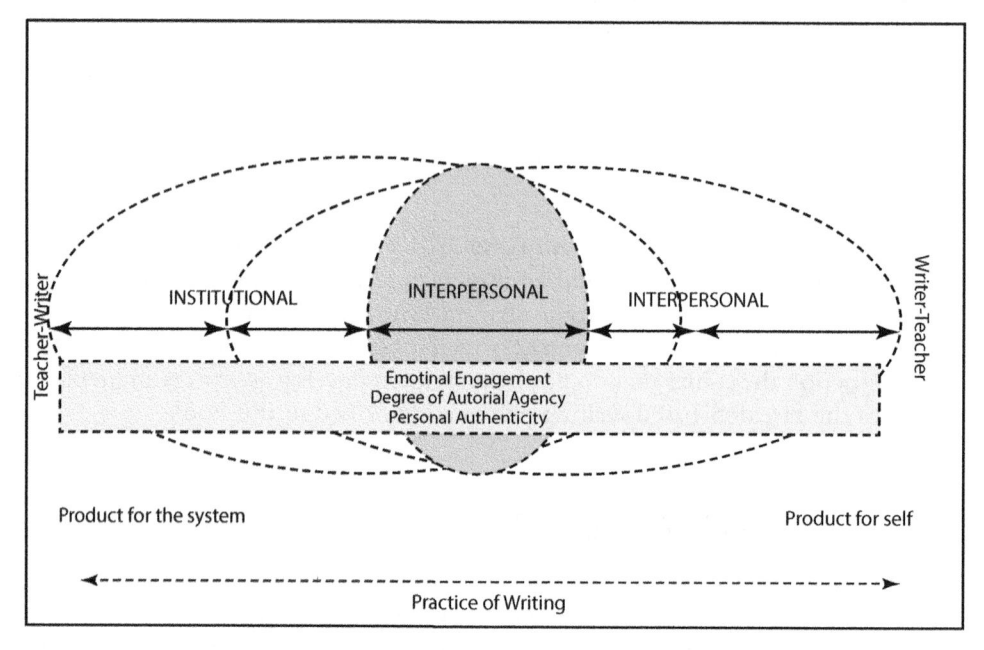

FIGURE 21.1 Diagram to represent a teacher-writer, writer-teacher continuum (Baker and Cremin 2010, p. 99). Reproduced by permission of Taylor and Francis, a division of Informa PLC.

The challenges involved in nurturing writer-teachers

According to Whitney (2018, p. 130), you can 'ask almost any adult about writing in school. You may hear a success story or two, but almost all can also tell a story of feeling deep shame in a writing classroom'. This depressing picture is only too clearly reflected in Paul Gardner's (2014) survey of over 100 trainee teachers. He found that only 1.8% wrote with and for pleasure, while half stated that they had never found and never do find any pleasure at all in it. Much has been written about the fact that many trainees enter the profession with negative views of writing and negative memories of being taught or learning to write (Graham et al. 2001; Street 2003; Gardner 2014; Cremin et al. 2019). These views are well established even before they begin their initial teacher training and are highly resistant to change (Parker 1988; Hall and Grisham-Brown 2011). The danger is that teachers' beliefs about writing may influence their pedagogical decisions. The worst scenario, and a surprising irony, is that teachers may reproduce in their classroom exactly the same teaching experience they were given themselves (Frank 2003; McCarthey et al. 2014; Dobson 2016; Yoo 2018).

It appears that many adults, including teachers, carry certain mistaken assumptions about how writers work and how writing is crafted (Graham 1999; Frank 2003; Gusevik 2020). It has also been noted that a great many teachers come to teaching with a love of reading and not writing (Gannon and Davies 2007; Cremin and Myhill 2012; Cremin et al. 2019; Cushing 2019). We are told that, despite the importance of learning about writing instruction, it seems to be the case that many ITE (Initial Teacher Education) courses place little emphasis on how to teach writing (and writers) effectively (Graham 1999; Norman and Spencer 2005; Kaufman 2009; Myers et al. 2016; Cushing 2019), whereas it has been observed that trainee teachers spend much of their time focused on how to teach reading (Domaille and Edwards 2006; Andrews 2008; Cremin and Locke 2017). Given this information, it is hardly surprising to learn that teachers do not typically feel confident in teaching writing (Andrews 2008; Morgan 2010; Morgan and Pytash 2014). A final irony is that there are confident teachers who wish to teach using the evidence-based effective writing practices described in this book, but find themselves prevented from doing so because of ill-informed interpretations of school curricula or poorly designed governmental policy (Cremin 2006; Bifuh-Ambe 2013; Dobson 2016; Yoo 2018). We might describe this situation as an absurdist's perfect storm and a classic *Catch-22*. Please see our concluding chapter for more on this issue.

We think it is necessary for teachers to engage in some introspection and consider what is their attitude towards writing and themselves as a writer, reflect on their own experience of learning to write and come to terms with how this must affect their teaching. Hayler (2011 and McKinney and Giorgis 2009) usefully talks about the professional and affective benefits of teachers writing about their lives, their school experiences and themselves as teachers, and Deegan's (2008) study included student teachers, who were encouraged to write personal narratives or meditations on what it means to teach and be a teacher, but also to reflect on their experience of being taught.

We propose that teachers then try to gain an understanding of how writers live and work together in a community of writers by participating in writer-teacher groups. There are ample opportunities to do this: for example, through the National Writing Project (Whyte et al. 2007; Andrews 2008; Locke et al. 2011), by establishing school-based writing groups (Smith and Wrigley 2012; Young and Ferguson 2020), through participating in teacher writing retreats (Young 2020a), or through joining online groups such as #WritersByNight (Young 2020b). The experience of writing and receiving verbal feedback in a community of writers, one that is in keeping with a contemporary writing workshop approach, is invaluable for gaining the 'craft knowledge' needed to radically influence pedagogy and so bring about positive changes for themselves as teachers of writing and for the experiences of their young apprentice writers. In their chapter *A guide to becoming a writer-teacher*, Young and Ferguson (2020) suggest very practical ways in which teachers, schools, and even universities could achieve such transformations.

Examples of effective practice

In his study, Young (2019, p. 37) observed that teachers wrote for pleasure in their own lives outside the classroom. They used their literate lives and their writerly 'craft knowledge' as an educational tool. It appears that children gained from knowing that their teacher was a teacher who also writes. 'He has had years and years of practice. I like that because like you have to practise writing because otherwise what are you going to know what to write about? and how are you going to know what writing means?'

Through mini-lessons and pupil conferences, children not only understood that their teacher faces the same writing challenges that they do but that they can also share their writerly knowledge to help them improve their developing compositions. The teachers wrote and shared their writing with their class with regularity. They would share their own pieces in relation to the projects they were asking the children to engage in. There was use of dialogic talk and the teachers maintained genuine reciprocal relations when modelling their own writing processes and discussing their exemplar texts. For example, 'he spoke to us about him writing his poems and like how difficult it can be – not everything is going to be easy. He gave us tips yesterday like the "show don't tell" one – I've done that in my diary and it really worked. He's been showing his writing more recently – he definitely speaks about his writing and what he is finding difficult as well and he gives us help when it's difficult because it relates to him'.

The teachers would readily draw on their knowledge of effective teaching and also their knowledge of writing and of being a writer, and shared the 'tricks, tips and secrets' strategies that they employed in their own writing, inviting children to give them a try too. From the student data, it appeared that the children respected the advice, opinions, and instruction given by teachers whom they saw as genuine and 'good' writers. The children would very often appropriate the social practices of their writer-teacher too.

Practical things you can do

- Don't share an exemplar text you have written at home without spending time explaining the processes, procedures, strategies, and techniques you employed to craft it.
- Invite children to ask questions about the mentor texts you're crafting and have crafted.
- Make sure that 'live' writing is genuinely live and not copied from a text you have written beforehand. This kind of pretence is utterly unproductive and potentially damaging, giving children the impression that writing comes easily and fully formed at the first attempt.
- Keep writing-study mini-lessons short – between 10 and 20 minutes. Make sure that the writing you've crafted and modelled goes on to be finally published or performed, just as children's pieces will be at the project's conclusion.
- It is important to model all the writing processes and not simply drafting or editing. Model idea generating, planning, dabbling, revising, abandoning, revisiting, publishing, and performing. It's also best practice to model a single strategy,

process or literary technique rather than overwhelm your pupils with a whole host of processes all at once.
- Identify yourself as a fellow writer, and at the start of the session sit and write for a brief time amongst the children.
- Model your writing community on one you yourself participate in. For example, the National Writing Project, your school's writer-teacher group, or a writer-teacher retreat.
- Read, share, talk, and think about writing alongside your class. Talk together, exchange anecdotes, discuss the exhilaration, enjoyment, satisfaction, pleasure, apprehension, and uncertainty that comes from crafting writing.
- Invite children to share the difficulties they experience when crafting and use this information to provide responsive mini-lessons tailored to what they are telling you they need.
- Consider making a classroom display of the variety of writing processes and strategies you and the members of your class use to craft your texts.

QUESTIONS WORTH ASKING YOURSELF

- Can you define yourself as a particular type of writer?
- Do you share your writer-identity with your class?
- Do you own a writer's notebook?
- Have you reflected on how you were taught to write and its impact on how you teach it now?
- How often do you write? How and when do you share this writing with your class?
- Do you use your writing as a tool for teaching about writing?
- Do you share your writing at different parts of the writing process?
- Do you use your writing to enhance your writing study mini-lessons and pupil conferences?
- Do you take part in class writing projects alongside your pupils?
- Do you take time to read, think, and talk as well as share your writing with your class?
- Do you publish your writing into the class library alongside your pupils?
- Do you model how to live the writer's life?

References

Alford, K., and Early, J. (2017). Take time to write!: A teacher's story of writing within a community of teacher writers. *English Leadership Quarterly*, 40, 2–5.

Andrews, R. (2008). *The Case for a National Writing Project for Teachers*. Reading: CfBT Educational Trust.

Atwell, N. (2014). *In the Middle* (3rd Ed). Portsmouth, NH: Heinemann.

Aulls, M.W. (2002). The contributions of co-occurring forms of classroom discourse and academic activities to curriculum events and instruction. *Journal of Educational Psychology*, 94(3), 520–538.

Baker, S., and Cremin, T. (2017). Teachers' identities as writers. In *Writer Identity and the Teaching and Learning of Writing*, Cremin, T., and Locke, T. (Ed.)(pp. 98–114). London: Routledge.

Barrs, M., and Cork, V. (2001). *The Reader in the Writer Case Studies in Children's Writing*. London: CLPE.

Bean, B. (2020). *Tens minutes a day – a writer I'll stay* [Available: https://writing4pleasure.com/ten-minutes-a-day-a-writer-ill-stay/]

Bifuh-Ambe, E. (2013). Developing successful writing teachers: Outcomes of professional development exploring teachers' perceptions of themselves as writers and writing teachers and their students' attitudes and abilities to write across the curriculum. *English Teaching*, 12, 137–156.

Block, C.C., and Israel, S.E. (2004). The ABCs of performing highly effective think-alouds. *The Reading Teacher*, 58(2), 154–167.

Brooks, G.W. (2007). Teachers as readers and writers and as teachers of reading and writing. *The Journal of Educational Research*, 100(3), 177–191.

Calkins, L.M. (1994). *The Art of Teaching Writing*. Portsmouth, NH: Heinemann.

Cremin, T. (2006). Creativity, uncertainty and discomfort: Teachers as writers. *Cambridge Journal of Education*, 36(3), 415–433.

Cremin, T., and Baker, S. (2010). Exploring teacher-writer identities in the classroom: Conceptualising the struggle. *English Teaching: Practice and Critique*, 9(3), 8–25.

Cremin, T., and Myhill, D. (2012). *Creating Communities of Writers*. London: Routledge.

Cremin, T., and Oliver, L. (2017). Teachers as writers: A systematic review. *Research Papers in Education*, 32(3), 269–295.

Cremin, T., Myhill, D., Eyres, I., Nash, T., Wilson, A., and Oliver, L. (2019). Teachers as writers: Learning Together with Others. *Literacy* 54(2), 49–59. doi.org/10.1111/lit.12201.

Cushing, I. (2019). Grammar policy and pedagogy from primary to secondary school. *Literacy*, 53(3), 170–179.

Deegan, J. (2008). Teacher-writer memoirs as lens for writing emotionally in a primary teacher education programme. *Teaching Education*, 19(3), 185–196.

Dix, S., and Cawkwell, G. (2011). The influence of peer group response: Building a teacher and student expertise in the writing classroom. *English Teaching: Practice and Critique*, 10(4), 41–57.

Dobson, T. (2016). 'Just because I'm not a published author does not mean that I'm not a writer': Primary trainee teachers' identities as creative writers. *Writing in Practice: The Journal of Creative Writing Research*, 2. [Retrieved at: https://www.nawe.co.uk/DB/current-wip-edition-2/articles/just-because-im-not-a-published-author-does-not--2.html]

Domaille, K., and Edwards, J. (2006). Partnerships for learning: Extending knowledge and understanding of creative writing processes in ITT year. *English in Education*, 40(2),71–84.

Englert, C.S., Raphael, T.E., Anderson, L.M., Anthony, H.M., and Stevens, D.D. (1991). Making writing strategies and self-talk visible: Cognitive strategy instruction in writing in regular and special education classrooms. *American Educational Research Journal*, 28, 337–372.

Faust, M. (1998). Foucault on care of the self: Connecting writing with life-long learning. *International Journal of Leadership in Education Theory and Practice*, 1(20), 181–193.

Frank, C. (2001). 'What new things these words can do for you': A focus on one writing-project teacher and writing instruction. *Journal of Literacy Research*, 33(3), 467–506.

Frank, C. (2003). Mapping our stories: Teachers' reflections on themselves as writers. *Language Arts*, 80(3), 185–195.

Gannon, S., and Davies, C. (2007). For love of the word: English teaching, affect and writing. *Changing English*, 14(1), 87–98.

Gardner, P. (2014). Becoming a teacher of writing: Primary student teachers reviewing their relationship with writing. *English in Education*, 48(2), 128–148.

Gennrich, T., and Janks, H. (2013). Teachers' literate identities. In *International Handbook of Research on Children's Literacy, Learning and Culture*, Hall, K., Cremin, T., Comber, B., and Moll, L. (Eds.) (pp.456–468). Oxford: Wiley.

Graham, R. (1999). The self as writer: Assumptions and identities in the writing workshop. *Journal of Adolescent & Adult Literacy*, 43(4), 358–364.

Graham, S., Harris, K.R., Fink, B., and MacArthur, C.A. (2001). Teacher efficacy in writing: A construct validation with primary grade teachers. *Scientific Studies of Reading*, 56, 177–202.

Grainger, T., Goouch, K., and Lambirth, A. (2005). *Creativity and Writing: Developing Voice and Verve in the Classroom*. London: Routledge.

Graves, D. (1983). *Writing: Teachers and Children at Work*. Portsmouth, NH: Heinemann.

Graves, D. (1991). *Build A Literate Classroom*. Portsmouth, NH: Heinemann.

Gusevik, R. (2020) *Writing for Pleasure and the Teaching of Writing at the Primary Level: A Teacher Cognition Case Study* Unpublished dissertation University of Stavanger [Available: https://writing4pleasuredotcom.files.wordpress.com/2020/08/gusevik_rebeccamarie.pdf]

Hall, A., and Grisham-Brown, J. (2011). Writing development over time: Examining preservice teachers' attitudes and beliefs about writing. *Journal of Early Childhood Teacher Education*, 32, 148–158.

Hansen, J. (1987). *When Writers Read*. Portsmouth, NH: Heinemann.

Harwayne, S. (1992). *Lasting Impressions. Weaving Literature into the Writing Workshop*. Portsmouth, NH: Heinemann.

Hayler, M. (2011). *Autoethnography, Self-Narrative and Teacher Education*. Rotterdam: Sense.

Ings, R. (2009). *Writing is Primary: Action Research on the Teaching of Writing in Primary Schools*. London: Esmee Fairburn Trust.

Kaufman, D. (2002). Living a literate life: Revisited. *English Journal*, 91(6), 51–57.

Kaufman, D. (2009). A teacher educator writes and shares: Student perceptions of a publicly literate life. *Journal of Teacher Education*, 60, 338.

Locke, T., Whitehead, D., Dix, S., and Cawkwell, G. (2011). New Zealand teachers respond to the 'national writing project' experience. *Teacher Development*, 15(3), 273–291.

McCarthey, S., Woodard, R., and Kang, G. (2014). Elementary teachers negotiating discourses in writing instruction. *Written Communication*, 31(1), 58–90.

McKinney, M., and Giorgis, C. (2009). Narrating and performing identity: Literacy specialists' writing identities. *Journal of Literacy Research*, 41, 104–149.

Mercer, N., Edwards, D., and Maybin, J. (1988). Putting context into oracy: The construction of shared knowledge through classroom discourse. In *English Language and Education*, Maclure, M., Phillips, T., and Wilkinson, A. (Eds.) (pp. 122–132). Philadelphia, PA: Open University Press.

Morgan, D. (2010). Preservice teachers as writers. *Literacy Research and Instruction*, 49, 352–365.

Morgan, D., and Pytash, K. (2014). Preparing preservice teachers to become teachers of writing: A 20-year review of the research literature. *English Education*, 47(1), 6–37.

Murray, D. (1990). *Learn to Write* (3rd Ed.). New York: Rinehart & Winston.

Murray, D. (1993). *Read to Write* (3rd Ed.). San Diego, CA: Harcourt.

Myers, J., Scales, R.Q., Grisham, D.L., Wolsey, T.D., Dismuke, S., Smetana, L., Kreider, K., Ikpeze, Y., Ganske, K., and Martin, S. (2016). What about writing: A national exploratory study of writing instruction in teacher preparation programs. *Literacy Research & Instruction*, 55, 309–330.

Norman, K., and Spencer, B. (2005). Our lives as writers: Examining preservice teachers' experiences and beliefs about the nature of writing and writing instruction. *Teacher Education Quarterly*, 32(1), 25–40.

Parker, R. (1988). Theories of writing instruction: Having them, use them, change them. *English Education*, 20(1), 18–40.

Regan, K., and Berkeley, S. (2012). Effective reading and writing instruction: A focus on modelling. *Intervention in School and Clinic*, 47(5), 276–282.

Rooke, J. (2013). *Transforming Writing: Final Evaluation Report*. London: National Literacy Trust.

Smith, F. (1983). Reading like a writer. *Language Arts*, 60(5), 558–567.

Smith, J., and Wrigley, S. (2012). What has writing ever done for us? The power of teachers' writing groups. *English in Education*, 46(1), 69–84.

Street, C. (2003). Pre-service teachers' attitudes about writing and learning to teach writing: Implications for teacher educators. *Teacher Education Quarterly* Summer, 30(3), 33–50.

Taylor, M. (2000). Nancie Atwell's "in the middle" and the ongoing transformation of the writing workshop. *The English Journal*, 90(1), 46–52.

Vasques, M. (2020). *Writing like a writer in the classroom* [Available: https://writing4pleasure.com/writing-like-a-writer-in-the-classroom/]

Watts, J. (2009). Teachers as writers. *Kappa Delta Pi Record*, 45(4), 154–155.

Whitney, A. (2008). Teacher transformation in the national writing project. *Research in the Teaching of English*, 43(2), 144–187.

Whitney, A. (2009). Writer, teacher, person: Tensions between personal and professional writing in a national writing project summer institute. *English Education*, 41(3), 236–259.

Whitney, A. (2018). Shame in the writing classroom. *English Journal*, 107(3), 130–132.

Whyte, A., Lazerte, A., Thomson, I., Ellis, N., Muse, A., and Talbot, R. (2007). The national writing project, teachers' writing lives, and student achievement in writing. *Action in Teacher Education*, 29(2), 5–16.

Woodard, R. (2015). The dialogic interplay of writing and teaching writing: Teacher writers' talk and textual practices across contexts. *Research in the Teaching of English*, 50(1), 35–59.

Yoo, J. (2018). Teachers as creative writers: Needs, desires and opportunities for growth. *New Writing*, 15(3), 300–310.

Young, R. (2019). *What is it 'Writing For Pleasure' teachers do that makes the difference?* The University Of Sussex: The Goldsmiths' Company [Online]. Available: www.writing4pleasure.com.

Young, R. (2020a). Training, CPD & School Improvement. Available: www.writing4pleasure.com/cpd-training-school-improvement.

Young, R. (2020b). #WritersByNight. Available: www.writing4pleasure.com.

Young, R., and Ferguson, F. (2020). *Real-World Writers: A Handbook for Teaching Writing with 7–11 Year Olds*. London: Routledge.

Zumbrunn, S., and Krause, K. (2012). Conversations with leaders: Principles of effective writing instruction. *The Reading Teacher*, 65(5), 346–353.

CHAPTER

22

Pupil conference

Meet children where they are

'Feedback has been a powerful shaper of who you are and what you believe, or do not believe, about yourself in the many facets of your life' (McGee 2017, p. 15). We know, and research confirms, that feedback is an essential part of teaching and learning (Hattie 2009; Zumbrunn et al. 2016; Allal 2019). Research specific to the teaching of writing shows that consistently high-quality feedback delivered to individual writers leads to academic improvement and higher attainment (Hattie and Timperley 2007; Popham 2011; Wiliam 2011; Rooke 2013; Elliott et al. 2016).

Teachers should be aware that they bear a huge responsibility towards their young apprentice writers when they offer them feedback, since, as McGee (2017) observes, what teachers say about our writing and how they decide to deliver it has a profound and lasting effect on our writer-identities. As Taggart and Laughlin (2017, p. 6) say: 'accepting and processing feedback in one's work is one of the greatest challenges a writer can face'. Children's affective responses to feedback have an effect on their attainment, as Zumbrunn et al. (2016) showed in their research project. They reported the findings of Cleary and Zimmerman (2004) who demonstrated how feedback can be influential in increasing self-efficacy, motivation, and self-regulation, all of which we know to have a significant influence on children's writing performance. Their own findings showed that most pupils had positive feelings about receiving feedback, believing that if it were constructively critical and even challenging, and useful and operational in their developing composition, then it helped them learn, think, and improve their writing over the long-term. Such feedback also gave them more confidence and pride as writers and they reported greater feelings of happiness, warmth, and self-esteem.

Zumbrunn et al. (2016) also stated that some feedback was not perceived as helpful; when teachers focused only on the weaknesses and errors within a written piece, children repeatedly experienced sadness, nervousness, anxiety, and decreased motivation to work on their writing. Taggart and Laughlin (2017, p. 1) preface their interesting study of negative responses to feedback with the following hypothetical situation: 'A student gets "tough" feedback from a teacher who is trying to push her, who sees in her the possibility of excellence. The student feels challenged. How to bridge the gap between her negative feeling and the teacher's sense of how strong a writer she might be?' While in this instance the teacher's motivation is positive, the authors imply that she also needs to be sensitively attuned to the writer's self-esteem, emotional investment in and control of the writing. This vital issue is applicable to all situations where feedback is given.

What constitutes high-quality feedback to young writers?

Wolfe and Alexander (2008) and Wiliam (2011) claim that feedback which guides children whilst they are actually engaged in their learning is the most significant assessment because it promotes and supports high-level thinking; it means that children cannot help but learn something and cannot help but apply it in their writing (Young and Ferguson 2020). We therefore propose that high-quality writing feedback be:

- **Writer-centred** – moving writers and their writing forward and making children more knowledgeable about the craft and processes involved in writing.
- **Goal-centred** – relating to the product goals that have been identified (see Chapter 16).
- **Useful** – the emphasis being that the child will learn something that is not only useful to them for that writing project but will be useful in the future too.
- **Encouraging self-regulation** – the feedback always encourages the writer to make the changes for themselves.

Verbal or written feedback?

As early as 1986, Hillocks noted with irony that 'traditions in the teaching of English hold that compositions must be marked and commented upon – the more thoroughly, the better'. His meta-analysis revealed that 'such feedback has very little effect on enhancing the quality of student writing regardless of frequency or thoroughness' (1986, p.252). Indeed, such relentess feedback resulted in pupils feeling less enthusiasm for writing, writing less, and having a low opinion of themselves as writers. Fox Tree and Clark (2013) found spoken feedback to be more effective than written. Finally, Elliott et al. (2016) found that written feedback can be beneficial if it makes specific actionable recommendations, but only with the proviso that pupils will be given time to discuss, consider, and apply these recommendations to their compositions while they are still in process.

Pupil conferencing

According to Sims (2001, p. 28), 'the writing conference has been one of the most effective and efficient methods of improving underachieving students' writing'. Calkins (1994, p. 223) claims that 'teacher-student and peer conferences are at the heart of teaching writing. Through them, students learn to interact with their own writing'. Too often, as teachers, we do not show enough interest in the writer and what they are writing about. Instead, we only focus on what has been written. This feels like both a human and an instructional mistake. The idea of pupil conferencing, so much a part of the *Writing For Pleasure* pedagogy, has attracted considerable research interest (Bayraktar 2012; Young 2019; Fisher et al. 2010). It has been given many definitions which attempt to reflect its different functions, among them: conversations, problem-solving sessions, interactive dialogues, focused instructional sessions, meaningful contact, and even 'rove and assist' sessions (Lipson et al. 2000; Bayraktar 2012; Parr 2016). Pupil conferencing is seen in all the research writings as the integration of formative assessment and instruction. This is by no means to say that learners have no part to play in the conference except to act on the instruction. On the contrary, they are fully involved in a collaborative and interactive way. Pupil conferencing, then, is an ideal way of offering effective, writer-centred, self-regulating, and useful feedback (Ebsworth 2014).

Glasswell et al. (2003), in a very engaging paper entitled '*Four Ways to Work against Yourself When Conferencing with Struggling Writers*', emphasise that the unique benefit of a conference is that it allows the teacher to provide individualised instruction based on the particular needs of different writers, also with the intention of leading them towards independence through the development of self-efficacy and particularly self-regulation (Timperley and Parr 2009; Neitzel and Davis 2014). Timperley and Parr (2009) draw a distinction between 'minimal' learning (surface, related to correctness, and content) and 'deep' learning (knowledge development); they state that the most efficacious feedback is directed at deep learning and fosters autonomy, self-control, self-direction, and self-discipline. As we have indicated, 'deep' learning is a principal aim of the conference. Neitzel and Davis (2014) describe the strategy of 'help seeking' as being a self-regulatory behaviour as children learn to seek the assistance, advice, or information they know they need. This makes the teacher's job of giving feedback highly efficient and effective as, on these occasions, the teacher responds to the learning need already identified by the child. Help of this kind is less likely to be effectively requested and obtained through any kind of written feedback, which is not immediate, is not constructed alongside the writer, may be restricted to giving superficial praise, and will therefore often miss being responsive to the needs of the child.

Responsive teaching and pupil conferencing: a match made in heaven

Glasswell and Parr (2009) state that what many teachers refer to as 'teachable moments' occur in the arena of the conference. For them, a teachable moment is 'an episode that is a dynamic blend of interactive formative assessment and needs based teaching' (2009, p.355). They urge teachers to adopt a responsive teaching approach that makes the most of each teachable moment, giving timely specific instruction acting as a temporary scaffold and, most importantly, offering a strategy or craft knowledge which will lead to further learning that day and eventual independence. It is hard to imagine written feedback being able to take advantage of such moments. The responsive nature of teaching, both in the mini-lesson and in conferencing, leads us to propose that in the contemporary writing workshop (Young and Ferguson 2020) 'assessment for learning' be replaced by the more comprehensive 'assessment for responsive teaching'. Hansen (1987, p. 165) claims that in this way, the teacher's role 'is to find out what students know, affirm for them what they know' but then, and importantly, 'ask what they want to know next, and teach it'.

In summary, it is vital that children receive feedback which is short, positive, focused, and occurs while they are actually engaged in crafting their writing. With this in mind, it is of little surprise that high-quality writer-focused interaction and verbal feedback and instruction was at the centre of the *Writing For Pleasure* teachers' practice which we observed, and specifically their use of pupil conferencing (Young 2019).

Pupil conferencing: what *Writing For Pleasure* teachers do

The art of teaching writing is realised in the conferencing between teachers and students (Lipson et al. 2000, p. 211). Conducting an effective conference with a pupil is a skill which is learned through practice and having a clear conception of what a conference is and what are its aims. Several helpful texts have been written about how to conduct a conference in the classroom, notably *How's it Going?* (Anderson 2000), *Conferences & Conversations* (Kaufman 2000) and *Feedback that Moves Writers Forward* (McGee 2017). In her book, Patty McGee describes in practical terms the different ways of incorporating into any school or curriculum the transformative type of feedback and teaching we have described in this chapter. In this final section we will show how a good conference proceeds, and how the theory and practice of effective feeding back are clearly connected.

Donald Murray has said: 'conferences are not mini lectures but the working talk of fellow writers sharing their experience with the writing process' (1985, p. 148). We can add that effective writing conferences, as carried out by *Writing For Pleasure* teachers, are:

- Specific, positive, and frequent.
- Writer-to-writer.
- Timely, brief and relevant.
- Related to goals and goal setting.
- Forward-looking, centred on the writer's learning and future independence.
- Part of the reassuringly consistent classroom routine (see Chapter 17).

And are *not*:

- Error focused.
- Overly focused on transcription during the early stages of composing.
- Solely evaluative.
- Punitive.
- Intended to 'fix' the writing.
        (Heward 2009; Konrad et al. 2011; Young and Ferguson 2020)

In their book *Real-World Writers*, Young and Ferguson (2020), describe how a teacher can engage their young writer in conversation, assess the developing composition with the child, and respond with a teaching point which can immediately be applied to the writing, thereby adding to the child's thinking and writerly knowledge, and crucially moving the composition on too. In a conference, the pupil will benefit from the insight of a real audience, will be enabled to keep their purpose and goals firmly in mind, and will develop a meta-language (language about language and writing), the art of reflection, and self-assessment through identifying the help they need (Graham et al. 2011).

Frequent conferences with individuals (in practice a few times a week) help the teacher develop a knowledge of each one as a writer. The importance of this is emphasised in McQuitty's (2014) study. Equally necessary for the effectiveness of conferences is the environment of the classroom in which they take place, by which we mean the community of writers we would expect to see in *Writing For Pleasure* classrooms (see Chapter 11). Most important of all is to keep in mind the affective impact of feedback, which we have noted earlier in this chapter. There is no doubt that the tone of a conference will be crucial to its effectiveness. If the teacher can meet their young writers with warmth, patience, openness, and a sense of investment in what they are trying to achieve, then the conference has a much greater chance of success. We are certain that the key is for the teacher to practise 'deep listening', discover more about the writing identity of their writers, and be genuinely interested in and care about their lives. In these circumstances, the teacher is motivated (beyond just performance measures) by their desire for the child's writing to fulfil the intentions they have and for it to be a success.

We find Anderson's (2000) outline of the structure of a live individual conference helpful and clear. He identifies two parts: first, joint talking about what the child is currently doing as a writer, and second, using this information to make and share with the pupil a specific teaching decision that will help them become a better writer. Conferences should take place throughout the writing process. A conference begins with the most potentially productive open question one could ever ask: 'how's it going?', 'how can I help you?', or 'what are you doing in your writing today?' thereby paving the way for the pupil to set the agenda for the conference. In setting the agenda, pupils are engaged in assessing their own writing; the teacher's role is to connect with the writer's intended meaning and intention, which Glasswell and Parr (2009, p. 355) have called a 'meeting of minds'. In practical terms, the teacher may have to ask more 'research' questions and use the writer's responses to help construct a mutual understanding of their intentions. The second part of the conference now takes place, with the teacher developing a 'line of thinking' with the pupil, that is to say, making a decision about what to teach which will help the writer to move the piece forward and give them something to take and use independently in future writing. This is the nub of the conference. As Lucy Calkins reminds us, 'if a piece of writing gets better but the writer has learned nothing that will help him or her on another piece, then the conference was a waste of everyone's time' (1994, p. 228).

Pupil conferencing as a writer-teacher

Teachers should, according to Anderson (2000) and Sims (2001), show pupils what other writers do to solve particular problems or to enhance their drafts. The writer can of course be the teacher – a further instance where it is invaluable to be a writer-teacher, well-placed to give advice and support grounded in personal experience (see Chapter 21). This can include the teacher demonstrating and modelling their own writing process strategies as part of the pupil conference before inviting the child to do it for themselves. In addition, the teacher can teach responsively by reminding their class in a timely way of relevant instruction previously given in mini-lessons; mini-lessons can in turn be informed by what the teacher learns in the course of conferring with pupils (see Chapter 20). The conference ends with the teacher leaving the pupil to act on the advice given, returning later in the writing session or in class sharing to check on their progress.

Examples of effective practice

The *Writing For Pleasure* teachers we observed in our 2019 study believed that a rich response to children's writing was crucial. Whilst they used both written and verbal feedback, they particularly emphasised the usefulness of 'live' verbal feedback, which they felt was immediate, relevant, and allowed the child to reflect on and attend to learning points raised while still actually engaged in their writing. Their conferences were short, friendly, supportive, and incredibly positive. The children looked forward to them as they knew they would get genuine praise for and celebration of the writing goals they were achieving, but also good advice about how they could improve their developing compositions. This had a major impact on children's sense of self-efficacy. The teachers' advice had an 'enabling' feeling about it; the children felt they could enact the feedback on their own (increasing their feelings of self-regulation) and that it would make a genuine difference to the quality of their writing. One of the children interviewed described her teacher's conferencing clearly: 'I think she helps a lot. If we do something good she'll pick up on that and tell us how good we are doing and if we haven't done something good she won't tell us off for it but she'll help us understand how to get better at it and say things like "you could do that …" and this is good. She isn't saying all the bad things or all the good things – it's constructive criticism'. Another child added, 'I've shown [my writing] to Mr Harding and he's shown me so much other things I could do and I'm like oh yeah … I think I will do that maybe tomorrow'.

Interestingly, the children in these classes were also heard giving each other feedback and advice similar to the pupil conferences they engaged in with their teachers, meaning that they were internalising their learning and then teaching each other. Finally, if the teachers found themselves repeatedly giving the same advice, they would stop the class and teach an additional mini-lesson on the issue before inviting the children to continue with their writing.

The teachers were able to undertake pupil conferencing in a systematic way and were successful because their children and classrooms were settled, focused, highly organised, and self-regulating. Behavioural expectations were also very clear. They would give feedback to those who were most in need of assistance first and would visit children at their tables as opposed to having children come to them. This meant that other children could benefit from any discussion as 'over-hearers'. As writer-teachers, they were better able to advise and give feedback because they seemed to understand the issues children encountered when writing themselves, and could share their writing 'craft knowledge' (Cremin and Oliver 2017). This certainly influenced the way they delivered their conferences and gave their feedback.

Practical things you can do

- Respond first and foremost as a genuine reader. Use phrases such as: as your reader I…Keep a simple record of when you have conferred with each child.
- Keep mental or brief written notes of repeated whole-class or individual writing issues. This can then inform your future planning of mini-lessons (see Chapter 20).
- Ensure that resources which enable children to work independently are readily accessible.
- Ensure your working wall is regularly updated for children's reference.
- Disruptions can negatively impact on pupil conferencing during writing time. Share the expectation with your class that you are not to be disturbed during conferencing and that the atmosphere must be quiet and orderly. You will therefore need to ensure that children know exactly what to do during writing time, where resources can be found, and what to do if they run into difficulties. In addition, children should know that once they have finished their class writing for the day, they are to continue with any personal writing projects in progress or begin a new one.
- Ensure that any adult helpers or assistant teachers are trained in delivering pupil conferences.
- Over time, model and train your children on how to peer conference.
- Continue to engage in your own writing and so boost your ability to provide effective pupil conferences from a position of expertise and understanding.
- Keep a note of anything you hear in a pupil conference which could be useful for discussion during class sharing/Author's Chair (see Chapter 13).

QUESTIONS WORTH ASKING YOURSELF

- Can you recall feedback from another person which helped you to grow or which had a negative effect? How can remembering this help when you conduct a conference as a teacher?
- In a conference, who speaks more, you or the child?
- Do you find yourself 'fixing' their writing on their behalf?
- Do you tend to focus disproportionately on children's transcriptional errors?
- Do your conferences go on for too long? They should not last longer than a few minutes.
- Do the other children understand that interrupting you in a conference is not acceptable?
- Do you end each conference by asking 'was that helpful?'

References

Ackerman, K., and McDonough, J. (2016). *Conferring with Young Writers*. Portsmouth, NH: Stenhouse.

Allal, L. (2019). Assessment and the co-regulation of learning in the classroom. *Assessment in Education: Principles, Policy & Practice*, 27(4), 332–349. DOI: 10.1080/0969594X.2019.1609411.

Anderson, C. (2000). *How's It Going*. Portsmouth, NH: Heinemann.

Anderson, C. (2018). *A Teacher's Guide to Writing Conferences*. Portsmouth, NH: Heinemann.

Bayraktar, A. (2012). Teaching writing through teacher-student writing conferences. *Procedia – Social and Behavioral Sciences*, 51, 709–713.

Calkins, L. (1994). *The Art of Teaching Writing*. Portsmouth, NH: Heinemann.

Cleary T.J., and Zimmerman B.J. (2004). Self-regulated empowerment program: A school-based program to enhance self-regulated and self-motivated cycles of student learning. *Psychology in the Schools*, 41(5), 537–550.

Cremin, T., and Oliver, L. (2017). Teachers as writers: A systematic review. *Research Papers in Education*, 32(3), 269–295.

Ebsworth, M. (2014). The many faces of feedback on writing: A historical perspective. *Writing & Pedagogy*, 6(2), 195–221.

Elliott, V., Baird, J., Hopfenbeck, T.N., Ingram, J., Thompson, I., Usher, N., Zantout, M., Richardson, J., and Coleman, R. (2016). *A marked improvement? A review of the evidence on written marking*. Education Endowment Foundation. https://educationendowmentfoundation.org.uk/public/files/Publications/EEF_Marking_Review:April_2016.pdf.

Fisher, R., Myhill, D., Jones, S., and Larkin, S. (2010). *Using Talk to Support Writing*. London: Sage.

Fox Tree, J., and Clark, N. (2013). Communicative effectiveness of written versus spoken feedback. *Discourse Processes*, 50(5), 339–359.

Glasswell, K., and Parr, J. (2009). Teachable moments: Linking assessment and teaching in talk around writing. *Language Arts*, 86(5), 352–361.

Glasswell, K., Parr, J., and McNaughton, S. (2003). Four ways to work again yourself when conferencing with struggling writers. *Language Arts*, 80(4), 299–309.

Graham, S., Harris, K., and Hebert, M.A. (2011). *Informing Writing: The Benefits of Formative Assessment. A Carnegie Corporation Time to Act Report*. Washington, DC: Alliance for Excellent Education.

Hansen, J. (1987). *When Writers Read*. Portsmouth, NH: Heinemann.

Hattie, J. (2009). *Visible Learning: A Synthesis of over 800 Meta-Analyses Relating to Achievement*. London: Routledge.

Hattie, J., and Timperly, H. (2007). The power of feedback. *Review of Educational Research*, 77(1), 81–112.

Heward, W.L. (2009). *Exceptional Children: An Introduction to Special Education* (9th Ed.). Upper Saddle River, NJ: Merrill/Prentice Hall.

Hillocks, G. (1986). *Research on Written Composition: New Directions for Teaching*. Urbana, IL: National Council of Teachers of English.

Kaufman, D., (2000). *Conferences and Conversations*. Portsmouth NH: Heinemann.

Kissel, B. (2017). *When Writers Drive the Workshop*. Portsmouth, NH: Stenhouse.

Konrad, M., Helf, S., and Joseph, L.M. (2011). Evidence-based instruction is not enough: Strategies for increasing instructional efficiency. *Intervention in School and Clinic*, 47(2), 67–74.

Lipson, M., Mosenthal, J., Daniels, P., and Woodside-Jiron, H. (2000). Process writing in the classrooms of eleven fifth-grade teachers with different orientations to teaching and learning. *Elementary School Journal*, 101 (2), 209–231.

McGee, P. (2017). *Feedback that Moves Writers Forward*. Thousand Oaks, CA: Corwin Literacy.

McQuitty, V. (2014). Process-oriented writing instruction in elementary classrooms: Evidence of effective practices from the research literature. *Writing & Pedagogy*, 6(3), 467–495.

Murray, D. (1985). *A Writer Teaches Writing*. Boston, MA: Houghton Mifflin.

Neitzel, C., and Davis, D. (2014). Direct and indirect effects of teacher instruction and feedback on student adaptive help-seeking in upper-elementary literacy classrooms. *Journal of Research in Education*, 24(1), 53–68.

Parr, J. (2016). Accelerating student progress in writing: Examining practices effective in new zealand primary school classrooms. *Writing Instruction to Support Literacy Success* (Literacy Research, Practice and Evaluation, Vol. 7), 41–64.

Popham, W.J. (2011). *Classroom Assessment: What Teachers Need to Know*. Boston, MA: Allyn & Bacon.

Rooke, J. (2013). *Transforming Writing: Final Evaluation Report*. London: National Literacy Trust.

Sims, D. (2001). *Improving Elementary School Students' Writing Using Reading and Writing Integration Strategies* (Thesis). Saint Xavier U. ERIC No. ED454502.

Taggart, A., and Laughlin, M. (2017). Affect matters: When writing feedback leads to negative feeling. *International Journal for the Scholarship of Teaching and Learning*, 11(2), 1–11.

Timperley, H., and Parr, J. (2009). What is this lesson about? Instructional processes and student understandings in writing classrooms. *The Curriculum Journal*, 20(1), 43–60.

Wiliam, D. (2011). *Embedded Formative Assessment*. Bloomington, IN: Solution Tree Press.

Wolfe, S., and Alexander, R. (2008). Argumentation and dialogic teaching: Alternative pedagogies for a changing world. www.beyondcurrenthorizons.org.uk.

Young, R. (2019). *What is it 'Writing For Pleasure' teachers do that makes the difference?* The University Of Sussex: The Goldsmiths' Company [Online]. Available: www.writing4pleasure.com.

Young, R., and Ferguson, F. (2020). *Real-World Writers: A Guide to Teaching Writing with 7–11 Year Olds*. London: Routledge.

Zumbrunn, S., Marrs, S., McBride, C., and Stringer, J.K. (2016). Exploring elementary student perceptions of writing feedback. *Journal on Educational Psychology*, 10(1), 16–28.

CHAPTER

23

Literacy for pleasure

Connect reading and writing

This chapter looks at the relationship between writers and their reading and, importantly, at the resulting implications for teaching writing.

An *integrated* approach, where reading and writing are taught alongside each other, has become something of the norm within the teaching of writing in recent years. However, Cremin et al. (2014) and Graham et al. (2018) caution that many so-called integrated programmes do not in fact provide a proper balance between reading and writing instruction, with a large number favouring reading instruction over writing. When this happens, writing attainment suffers (Graham et al. 2018). As we have seen throughout this book, specific and dedicated teaching of the craft of writing is essential if children are to learn to write most effectively (Fitzgerald and Shanahan 2000; Graham and Perin 2007; Glenn 2007; Graham and Sandmel 2011; McQuitty 2014; Graham et al. 2018).

According to Graham et al. (2018), there is still very little experimental research into how *exactly* reading and writing influence each other in the classroom. What we do know is that:

- Giving children ample time to read enhances the quality of their writing.
- Giving children the opportunity to write in response to the texts they have read significantly enhances their comprehension of those texts.
- The more children are given an opportunity to write, the more their reading comprehension improves.
- Instruction in writing supports reading; instruction in reading supports writing.

(Graham and Hebert 2011; Graham et al. 2018)

As Hansen (1987, p. 145) says: 'when writers write, they concentrate on their information; when they read they respond to another writer's knowledge. Thus, writing, reading, and content learning all move along, side by side'. Indeed, the idea that reading and writing have much to contribute to each other has a firm theoretical foundation (Tierney and Shanahan 1991; Heller 1999; Graham 2020). According to Fitzgerald and Shanahan (2000) and Kent and Wanzek (2016), the connection between reading and writing is apparent in three types of teacher orientation: rhetorical, procedural, and shared knowledge.

- **The rhetorical orientation** sees a connection between reading and writing on the basis that children gain an understanding of 'how communication works by being both a sender and receiver' of texts (Fitzgerald and Shanahan 2000, p. 39). Children create text from their understanding of being a reader and from considering what their audience may need from them as the writer (Holliway 2004).
- **The procedural orientation** sees both reading and writing as functional activities which can combine to help writers achieve their intentions, for example, note-taking from a text.
- **The shared knowledge orientation**, whose premise is that reading and writing share some of the same cognitive processes and so can influence one another. For example, the phonemic, orthographic, graphophonic, semantic, syntactic, and pragmatic knowledge children gain from reading is utilised when they write. Smith (1983) suggests that much of this type of learning happens implicitly as children become readers.

This chapter will consider the theoretical background and practices involved in teaching the interconnections between reading and writing, and how children can be helped to be better writers and readers. We will discuss how to teach what we currently know about the ways in which writers, both professional and recreational, use their reading to help them craft texts (Murray 1993; Prose 2006; Rosen 2018), including how:

- Writers read for pleasure.
- Writers are often inspired by their reading.
- Writers learn from their heroes and study their craft.

We will also discuss the potential for a *literacy for pleasure* classroom through a contemporary writing workshop model.

Reading for pleasure

Reading for pleasure, also known as voluntary, independent, leisure, ludic, hobbyist, or recreational reading, is defined by Clark and Rumbold (2006) as 'reading that we do of our own free will, anticipating the satisfaction that we will get from the act of reading. It also refers to reading that, having begun at someone else's request, we continue because we are interested in it'. Here we see parallels with our own definition of *Writing For Pleasure* given in Chapter 2.

Reading for pleasure has a significant and positive effect on reading attainment, children's general knowledge, their emotional health, the building of positive social classroom communities and, importantly, on writing ability (Anderson et al 1988; Clark and Rumbold 2006; Clark 2011; Clark and Douglas 2011; Graham and

Hebert 2011). Cremin et al. (2014) discuss the kinds of activities that promote a culture of reading for pleasure:

- Providing children with daily opportunities to hear their teacher read aloud stories and other material in an active and pleasurable way.
- Promoting interaction with stories, poetry, and other non-fiction texts through book talk, dialogic talk, and critical discussion.
- Building a community of readers.
- Choosing their own reading.
- Children sharing books with others.
- Bridging the gap between home and school reading.
- Participation in regular and ample reading time.

According to Clark and Rumbold (2006), children enjoy reading most of all because of the emotional response it elicits: children believe reading helps them understand different people and cultures, find information they need, and learn more about new subjects, hobbies, and topics of interest. All these are rich sources for writing – if children are taught how to tap into them. As will be discussed throughout this chapter, children having choice over what they read and making their own response to it through writing is fundamental to reading and writing development (Clark and Phythian-Sence 2008; Manak 2011; Parry and Taylor 2018; Attiyat 2019; Young and Ferguson 2020).

Reading for pleasure's impact on writing for pleasure

Francine Prose (2006, p. 4) explains how 'in the ongoing process of becoming a writer, I read and re-read the authors I most loved. I read for pleasure', adding that: 'what writers know is that, ultimately, we learn to write by practice, hard work, by repeated trial and error, success and failure, and from the books we admire'. When asked for advice on the best way of becoming a writer, published authors like Prose invariably recommend reading as much as possible because they know that, when writers read, ideas for writing occur (Cremin et al. 2017).

Ofsted's (2011) survey of 12 outstanding schools showed that pupils were motivated to read more and develop their own ideas for writing if they heard teachers read aloud regularly, were given opportunities to visit libraries, had ready access to a range of classic and high-quality up-to-date texts and participated in regular book talk. According to Griffith (2010) and Manak (2011), children learn a great deal about the *craft* of writing as they develop an 'inner ear' for language through listening to high-quality literature performed aloud, and having ample time in which to read for themselves (Hansen 1987; Heller 1999; Barrs and Cork 2001). In Manak's (2011) study, one teacher read aloud to the class at least three times a day. Children who read and listen to high-quality texts include more literary features and write better texts (Pantaleo 2010; Barrs and Cork 2011; Dombey 2013); children who read poetry include more imagery and other poetic devices in their own writing (Griffith 2010). Finally, children who read for pleasure write stories which are not only rich and coherent but also transcriptionally accurate (Sénéchal et al. 2018). We can therefore conclude, in agreement with Dombey (2013, p. 30), that 'children who read more write more and write better'.

Personal response

It is readers who breathe life into texts. According to Dyson (1997, 2013), Rosen (2018), and Young and Ferguson (2020), writers often develop strong affective bonds with the things they have read, experienced, watched or heard, and use aspects of some or all of these 'life texts' (experiences, film, pictures, music, games) in their own writing. It is imperative to tell young apprentice writers that this is an utterly natural thing writers do and encourage them to do it for themselves. 'Children don't only show their comprehension when they write in response to the books they're reading; they also give something of themselves to the text too. A fair exchange of ideas is made between the writer and what's read' (Young and Ferguson 2020, p. 91).

As writers read, they find their own identities. They link what they are reading to their own experiences, philosophies, cultures, knowledge and opinions – and so have a personal response to the text (Benton and Fox 1985; Rosenblatt 1995; Hansen 1987; Lewis 2000; Rief 2014). For example, one of the authors of this book connected strongly when a young reader with any texts that portrayed children escaping their circumstances or being subversive to authority. The personal response influences what writers decide to craft themselves, with children becoming highly invested and motivated to write accomplished texts as a result (Solsken et al. 2000; DeCristofaro 2001; Roswell and Pahl 2007; Harman 2008; Parry and Taylor 2018). Dyson (2013) calls this the 'textual process'.

Who possesses the text?

As long ago as 1921, George Sampson pointed to the absurdity of demanding 'that all boys in a class must be writing on the same subject at the same time ... a common feature of disliked writing tasks was that they were imposed' (cited by Creber 1990, p. 34). Some 50 years later, the poet Ted Hughes complained about much the same thing: 'out of her class of thirty, I recall that twenty-nine wrote on the same topic ... they had in the process become "false to themselves"' (ibid p. 36). These two observations support the view that writing in personal response to a text can often be impeded or even refused. Creber (1990, p. 62) writes that 'often the problem in literature teaching is also one of interposition, where the teacher gets between the students and the text'. Meek Spencer (2000, p. 207) warns that 'too much interpretive assistance and the reader flees, leaving the teacher ... in sole possession of the text', while Harold Rosen says uncompromisingly that under such circumstances 'the pleasure of the text is appropriated and turned to ashes. Like so many other things, children are not to be trusted with it' (Rosen 2017, p. 77).

Such occurrences are clearly in evidence when children are asked to respond in teacher-directed ways to a single teacher-chosen or scheme-chosen text (Knight 2009; Dutro 2010; Yandell 2016). Required to engage in set writing tasks linked to a single book, children are in effect being asked to write in a certain prescribed way, to comply with someone else's desires and even with someone else's response or interpretation. Creber (1990, p. 72) warns against it, fearing that literature may become 'debased into material for a certain kind of manipulative teaching; lest children start reading the stimuli instead of the poems'.

Barrs and Ellis (cited in Barrs and Cork 2001, p. 36) discuss aesthetic reading. They rightly say that certain texts 'lend themselves to discussion, reflective reading and creative interpretation'; these of course should be part of the class library and would be among Meek Spencer's (1988) texts that teach what readers learn. Writers learn from them too, studying the craft (in its deepest sense) which their authors have used to such engaging effect. However, we need to ask ourselves why there is the assumption that one of these texts, chosen by a teacher or scheme, will engage all the children in the class over a period of time and will offer all of them an aesthetic reading experience. Instead, we argue for children to be taught to use books as writers do, write in response to a self-chosen text and learn craft lessons from it. Barrs and Cork (2001, p. 43) describe what they see as the helpful part played in the development of children's responses by the teacher's interpretation, conveyed during reading aloud. However, Cushing (2018, p. 10) warns against the negative effect on reader-response when readers are led away from 'authentic and aesthetic' reading by having to consider strong 'teacher-led interpretations'. Teachers need to realise that their voice, whilst essential, is only one of many other important voices within the classroom.

More of the legwork, more of the rewards, more of the fun

It is reasonable to suppose that, when teachers plan for 'novel study' and mine a favourite text for potential ideas for writing, they do so with feelings of pleasure, anticipation, and excitement at the sense of creative possibility they feel they are offering their young writers (Barrs and Corks 2001; O'Sullivan and McGonigle 2010). In accordance with the view of the importance of affording children a degree of agency and responsibility during class writing projects (see Chapter 14), 'creative planning' should be taken out of the hands of the teacher or scheme and given over to the children as members of a community of writers. By explicitly and seriously teaching children the planning procedures typically used by their teachers, we enable them to experience the pleasure of planning their *own* creative possibilities inspired by a self-chosen text (Hansen 1987). As Shelley Harwayne (1992, p. 156) says: 'if our students are to take lessons from literature, they need to be doing more of the legwork, having more of the fun, reaping more of the rewards'.

Hansen (1987), Harwayne (1992), DeCristofaro (2001), Atwell (2014), and Young and Ferguson (2020) all show very practically how to encourage children to make connections between their reading and writing without asking them to spend their *writing* sessions memorizing a text by heart, analysing the content of a text, imitating an extract, or completing a set writing-task chained to that particular class novel. Children are instead immersed in a community of rich texts. Moved, inspired, and motivated by a personal response to a self-chosen text they have read for pleasure, they focus on what they want to write *and* how they can learn from and write like their hero authors. They are given explicit instruction in how writers read and use their reading.

Intertextuality

'Children are always in a high state of readiness to transform into story not only what [they] experience directly but also what they hear and read' (Rosen 1985, p. 12). Harold Rosen is talking here about intertextuality, also known as creative play(giarism) (Brownell 2018), cross-fertilization (Moffett and Wagner 1992), creative reconstruction (McGillis 1997), creating a mosaic of text (Keene and Zimmermann 1997), assemblage (Ranker 2007), sedimented identity (Rowsell and Pahl 2007), transactional transformation (Bearne and Watson 1999), remixing (Potter 2012), 'readingandwriting' (Oatley 2003), redesign (Kress 2010), appropriation (Bakhtin 1981), critical reading and reflective writing (Corden 2007), borrowing (Lancia 1997; Pantaleo 2010), volitional reading leading to volitional writing (Parry and Taylor 2018), and hybridisation (Young and Ferguson 2020).

Ray (cited in Griffith 2010) states that 'when we write we are not doing something that hasn't been done before. Everything we do as writers, we have known in some fashion as readers first'. Intertextuality is the way in which writers will draw on text, interpreting and critically reflecting on it and using it to influence their writing. The texts children create are like scrapbooks made from parts of their own reading history and developing identities (Compton-Lilly 2006; Parry and Taylor 2018). As children read they generate ideas, and as they write, these ideas become articulated (Tierney and Shanahan 1991; Frank 2001). Dyson's (1997, 2013) seminal work has repeatedly showcased even the youngest of children's abilities to take familiar plots, settings, and characters from their reading, experiences, and other popular culture, and reinterpret or convert them into other genres intelligently and critically. Brownell (2018) claims that inviting children to be intertextual is a good way to motivate and engage them in writing, while Rosen (2018) suggests that intertextuality is the foundation of writing for pleasure.

There are clear links between writing for pleasure and reading for pleasure. Teachers need to be knowledgeable about high-quality and engaging texts, know how to construct a successful classroom library, how to engage children in rich book talk (Grainger et al. 2005) and specifically how to teach children about intertextuality (Pantaleo 2006, 2007, 2010; Cremin et al. 2014; Rosen 2018; Young and Ferguson 2020). In their book *Real World Writers*, Young and Ferguson (2020, p. 95) use the work of Rosen (1998, 2018) to share some of the prompts that can engage children in thinking and talking about their relationship with books and how this can influence ideas for writing:

- Does this writing remind me of anything from my life?
- Does it remind me of anything else I've seen or read?
- What do I have in common with this writing?
- Why might the author have been moved to write? What's the one thing I want to write about this book?

Young and Ferguson suggest that, in response to these questions, children will begin to think:

- Mmm, I'm going to nick that for my writing …
- I would love to have a go at writing something like that …
- That reminded me of something … and I'm going to write about it …
- Why don't I draw, jot, and dabble with ideas that come in my mind as I'm reading or listening. Maybe it'll turn into some writing – maybe it won't …

It appears that when children draw on reading that has interested them, they feel naturally encouraged to rewrite it, critically reframe it, and so go about actively constructing a deeper meaning from the text. This opportunity not only improves children's writing but also their ability to deepen the understanding of the text for others who read their writing (Langer and Applebee 1987; Morrow et al. 1997; Graham 2020). However, for intertextuality to be at its most successful, teachers need to actively teach the strategies writers employ when wanting to reinterpret or write in response to the texts they have read (Ranker 2007; Harman 2013; Brownell 2018). According to Harman (2008), this rarely happens in school.

Thinking through writing: writing to learn

Teachers will often ask children to slavishly reproduce information learnt as a means of evaluating their understanding in the foundation subjects, a practice which usually has no effect on their learning of the content taught (Bangert-Drowns et al. 2004). More productive is giving children the opportunity to write in order to think and reflect on their learning, and invite them to learn about the typical genres associated with the subject disciplines, for example in history and science (The Talk Workshop Group 1982; Lipson et al. 1993; Bangert-Drowns et al. 2004; Graham and Hebert 2011; Olinghouse et al. 2015; Klein and Boscolo 2016; Graham et al. 2020).

We note that the novelist and essayist Flannery O'Connor once remarked that she wrote because she didn't know what she thought until she read what it was she had to say. Her insight is reflected in research which claims that giving children the opportunity to write in personal response to their learning and to integrate it with their other thoughts, feelings, knowledge, and experiences significantly increases retention of that learning (Bangert-Drown et al. 2004; Roelle et al. 2012). Graham and Hebert (2011) describe how in this way children create a kind of intertext connecting ideas with prior knowledge from and across other sources and experiences, which Carbone and Orellana (2010) beautifully call 'writing themselves into the text'. We would call it 'writing themselves into their learning' so that they can remain close to it. Research emphasises the need for teachers to explicitly teach, model, and even provide children with prompts for this type of instruction to be at its most profitable.

Non-fiction and voice

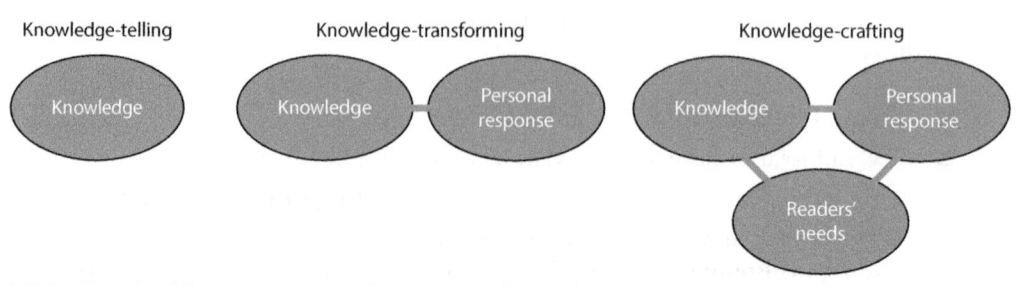

FIGURE 23.1 The different ways young writers can share knowledge through writing.

Both intertextuality and personal response have a powerful role to play in children's non-fiction writing, writing across the curriculum, and 'writing to learn'. If children are allowed to write in personal response to what they have read, watched, heard, experienced, or learnt, they can move from 'knowledge-telling' to 'knowledge-crafting' (see figure 23.1). In knowledge-telling, the writer is at the centre, stating and making a record of all they know or remember about a topic; this is typically what early writers do (Bereiter and Scardamalia 1987). However, the writer's presence is not overtly visible (a convention often overly encouraged in the production of non-fiction writing at school). In the transition from knowledge-telling to knowledge-transforming, the writer writes in their own voice and style, mixing knowledge with a personal response and transforming it into something new, valuable, and personally meaningful (Stein 1983; Chuy et al. 2011). In this way, not only are children more likely to retain the knowledge and use it in the future (Tierney and Shanahan 1991), but they will also produce a better text (Lipson et al. 1993; Olinghouse et al. 2015). Finally, when writers craft their knowledge with readers' needs in mind, they contribute to the building of their readers' knowledge and understanding too. This is what Scardamalia and Bereiter (2003) rightly call creating community knowledge.

Social collective responses and culturally sustaining texts

When a whole class (including the teacher) write in personal response and use intertextuality, they reveal to each other the different social and political conditions that can shape how texts are interpreted and rewritten. Harste and Leland (2000) claim that it opens up spaces for new, individual, and varied voices to be heard within a community of writers. Their observation is in welcome contrast to the situation where all the members of the class write a version of one person's (usually the teacher's or scheme's) interpretation of the text, a point made in our discussion of the *Literature-Based Approach* in Chapter 1 (Hansen 1987; Rief 2014; Rosen 2017; Young et al *in press*).

It is also possible for the community of writers to come together and write a social, collective response to their reading, or to produce what Harold Rosen calls a 'collaborative production of meaning' (Rosen 2017, p. 89). Some particularly good examples of this in action are to be found in the studies of Solsken et al. (2000), Hoewisch (2001), Lewison and Heffernan (2008), Lankshear and Knobel (2009), Laman (2014), and Ghiso (2015). In Lewison and Heffernan's study, for example, children wrote their own culturally sustaining 'social narratives' in response to the texts they were reading as part of reading workshop. Hoewisch's (2001) class reimagined gendered stereotypes in fairytales. In Ghiso's (2015) study, children were writing arguments based on issues within their local community that they felt were unfair. Young and Ferguson's (2019, 2020) and Young et al's (in press) work challenges children and teachers, through class writing projects, to consider how they can produce culturally sustaining texts, stressing the importance of children's freedom to reflect not only themselves and their local communities, but also others who may be under-represented in texts currently produced, for example, by some major children's publishers.

Writing about texts

Writing after reading can be a way of reiterating, revising, reimagining or even rejecting your comprehension. In their book *Real World Writers*, Young and Ferguson (2020, p. 94) use the work of Tennent et al. (2016) to share some of the ways children can write about the books they are reading. These could be adapted by practitioners and would suit a variety of reading abilities and textual genres.

What is it writers write when they are reading?

Connect with the book	Suggest	Question	Clarify
Write using what they know about the book so far. Write something that connects with the themes of the book. Relate parts of the book to their own lives and experiences and write about it.	They may write because they're inspired to make logical, plausible, or inventive suggestions as to what could happen next in the book, or about a character's personality and intentions.	Their writing may be a way for them to question the text. They may write in direct opposition to what the book is saying. They may write to share their opinion of the text.	They may rewrite the text in their own way to help them confirm or better understand what's going on.
Summarise	**Think aloud**	**Visualise**	**Reader in the writer**
They may write summaries for themselves or to share with others. They might write down things they've learnt.	Write a few sentences or a paragraph to talk about their thoughts so far.	Draw about what they have read.	Develop their own text inspired by or in personal response to what they have read.

Mentor texts: writers learn from their heroes

This section is about mentor authors, mentor texts, and how writers read. 'To learn how to write for newspapers you must read newspapers … For magazines, browse through magazines … To write poetry, read it' (Smith 1983, p. 560). In Smith's statement we see links between genre-study, setting product goals, writing-study mini-lessons, and the studying of mentor authors and texts.

According to Prose (2006), writers read differently from readers because they are aware that books are some of their best writing-teachers. The pebbles of knowledge children collect about writing from the book they read today become the diamonds on the shore of their writing compositions tomorrow. Children, like professional writers, have an innate desire to write something as great as the texts they are reading (Olthouse 2012; Young and Ferguson 2020). However, they also need specific mini-lessons showing how and when writers will borrow elements from their mentor authors and mentor texts to help them construct their own (Frank 2001; Corden 2007; Ranker 2009; Fletcher 2011; Rief 2014; Brownell 2018), and how leisure reading can profitably contribute to their 'writing toolkit' (Brodney et al. 1999; Parry and Taylor 2018). Gallagher (2014) also points out that children should continue to have access to mentor texts throughout a class writing project and not only at the start, with Griffith (2010, p. 51) stating that one goal of reading like a writer is to 'identify qualities of good writing and to further expand their current repertoire of crafting techniques' before, during, and after their writing process.

For example, Dix and Amoore (2010) were able to successfully teach children how focusing on authors' crafting techniques *whilst reading* could help them enrich and extend their own writing during writing time. They found that, once the writer-teacher had demonstrated the technique, children were perfectly capable of taking the best features of their own reading to use in their developing compositions. Being able to borrow from their favourite authors and mentor texts excited and motivated children when writing for themselves. Children understood that they were doing the things real writers do and so began to read with the understanding of a writer. We should walk into a classroom of writers and see a variety of book*s* across the tables, not multiple copies of a single book. It would appear that Calkins is right when she says: 'if our children see themselves as authors, they will read with admiration, marvelling at another author's efforts and learning vicariously from another author's successes and struggles' (1994, p. 228).

Literature-based mini-lessons

To teach about great craft, teachers need to know which books to go to (Griffith 2010). The knowledge they acquire as a writer who reads will not only directly help them showcase excellent examples of craft through mini-lessons but will also help them produce their own excellent writing. For example, the studies of Corden (2007), Hicks (2008), and Ranker (2009) showed how, in literature-based mini-lessons, teachers with good 'book knowledge' followed the routine of:

- **Noticing** examples of great craft from other authors.
- **Showcasing** how they themselves used it within their own writing.
- **Connecting** the lesson to the kinds of things children were currently trying to accomplish in their own writing.
- **Inviting** children to do it for themselves that day during writing time.

Young and Ferguson (2020, pp. 91–103) provide additional examples of the many strategies writers employ to read like writers, and how these processes can be taught to children. Once internalised, these strategies allow children to source, play with, and use language in the same way an artist might use a variety of materials to create their own unique collage. They include:

- Close reading and how to be 'squirrels' (keeping a writer's notebook for collecting inspirational vocabulary, sentences, paragraphs, narration, character, dialogue, sensory description, openings, endings, and writing ideas whilst reading).
- How to employ intertextuality and personal response to generate writing ideas.
- How to structure reading time to lead directly into writing time.
- How to teach 'dabbling' (drawing and 'painting with words' as you listen or read).

Finally, Graham (1998) warns against teachers using mentor texts as vehicles for devising a whole host of mechanical tasks. It is also claimed that any kind of rigidity towards the reading/writing connection may result in the shortening of valuable daily independent writing time (Hilton 2001 cited in Corden 2007).

Teachers as mentors: living the writerly life

Teachers as writers and readers need to show how they draw on their reading to create their own texts. Writer-teachers showcase how *they* take literary, linguistic, and grammatical features and vocabulary from their own reading when they are crafting (Schneider 2003; Rief 2014). Like their pupils, they come to know how certain texts are constructed, how to write them themselves, and what makes for great writing in a particular genre (Schneider 2003; Gallagher 2014). This idea is explored in more detail in Chapter 21.

Reading and talking about each other's writing

As discussed in Chapter 13, children rereading their own writing with regularity, reading and talking about each other's developing compositions through class sharing, and reading others' published writing are all vital elements in creating a rich community of writers and readers (Grainger et al. 2005; Graham 2020). Through such practices, the class can build a repertoire of metalanguage in which to discuss and evaluate their own texts with each other (Corden 2007). In addition, children begin to notice high-quality writing in their peers' compositions which they can then recreate in their own works (Griffith 2010). They start to think and talk as their future readership will think and talk (Holliway 2004). They become creators and consumers of texts concurrently.

Building a community of readers and writers: literacy for pleasure

'Engaging in literacy acts for the pursuit of personal interests and for daily living requirements is an educational goal that implies life-long learning and implies individuals controlling their literate lives' (Abbott 2000, p. 89). As we have said, access to a high-quality classroom and school library, full of a variety of books which are allowed to travel between home and school, will have a huge impact on young people's reading and writing attainment (Hansen 1987; Evans et al. 2010; Lindsay 2010; Clark and Poulton 2011). Building a classroom writing community in a rich reading environment provides the potential for a 'literacy for pleasure' classroom. For example, a study by Wharton-McDonald et al. (1998, p. 118) of exceptional writing teachers noted that in the highest-achieving classrooms, reading and writing were interwoven, with students 'frequently writing about what they were reading and using books to further develop topics they chose for writing.'

Reading For Pleasure	Writing For Pleasure
■ Providing children with daily opportunities to hear their teacher reading aloud stories and other material in an active and pleasurable way.	■ Providing children with opportunities to hear their teacher discuss their own writing and craft aloud in an active and pleasurable way.
■ Promoting interaction with stories, poetry and other non-fiction texts through book talk, dialogic talk, and critical discussion.	■ Promoting interaction about writing through dialogic talk, personal and social response, intertextuality, and critical discussion.
■ Building a community of readers.	■ Building a community of writers.
■ Choice over what they read.	■ Choice over what they write.
■ Children sharing books they've read with others.	■ Children sharing their writing with others.
■ Bridging the gap between home and school reading.	■ Bridging the gap between home and school writing.
■ Participation in regular and ample reading time.	■ Participation in regular and ample writing time.

Interweaving reading and writing: an example

In a contemporary writing workshop approach (Young and Ferguson 2020), children can be introduced to a whole-class project, such as writing a collection of short stories. Discussion is had about who these short stories should be written for and how they should be published or performed at the project's end. The class can then spend time hearing, reading, and discussing a variety of mentor texts (Lancia 1997; Hoewisch 2001; Corden 2007; Rief 2014). Next, the class can consider what they think their own short stories will have to include if they are to be successful and meaningful (Corden 2002; Laman 2014). Children can be taught strategies and techniques writers employ when generating writing ideas, and then generate their own (Hoewisch 2001; DeCristofaro 2001; Young and Ferguson 2020). As Harwayne (1992) and Frank (2001) suggest, literature is an important seedbed for children to discover their own topics, so children should continue to read high-quality texts, 'squirrelling', borrowing, and reimagining some of this reading as they craft their own writing throughout the project (Frank 2001; Grainger et al. 2005; Gallagher 2014). Every day children should receive a mini-lesson in vital craft knowledge, with examples taken from literature that will make a valuable contribution to their own developing manuscripts (Corden 2002; Ranker 2009; Griffith 2010; Manak 2011; Laman 2014). Within these mini-lessons, they can also look at examples from other experienced writers, including those within the school and their own writer-teacher (Hoewisch 2001; Schneider 2003; Corden 2007; Harman 2008). At the project's end, their writing feeds into the reading material in the classroom library and goes through the process of publication and performance beyond the classroom and school gates, thus completing the cycle of reader into writer.

In summary, this chapter has drawn together a range of educational research and literature and examples of what writers say they do when they read and write, to answer the following questions:

- What is it writers do *as* they read?
- How are writers *influenced* by their reading?
- How can we teach this knowledge successfully to young apprentice writers?

By connecting writing and reading authentically, humanely, and sincerely through a 'literacy for pleasure' paradigm, we give children access to the 'literacy club' (Smith 1988); a club which helps them to live a fully literate life and where they read and write with purpose, precision, pleasure, and power.

Examples of effective practice

In our research which observed exceptional teachers of writing (Young 2019), the most proficient clearly aimed to build a community of readers and writers concurrently. They had print-rich classrooms which included stories, non-fiction, poetry, newspapers, magazines, and the children's own published texts. However, only one teacher had in their class library a book *about writing* intended for a young audience. They read aloud every day to their classes with pleasure and enthusiasm from poetry, picture books, chapter books, non-fiction texts, and their own writing. They showed children how to read like writers and write like readers by encouraging them to make links between what they were reading, their own lives, and potential writing ideas. This included discussing themes, analysing the writer's craft, talking about aspects of intertextuality, and writing in personal response to texts read.

They understood that volitional reading can lead to volitional writing and ensured that during independent reading time children could also write in their personal writing project books if they felt the urge. Some children in these classes collected words, phrases, and other good examples of a writer's craft in the hope that they might come in useful later. For example:

- 'I like reading stories to myself and writing myself and stuff. Sometimes I write about books that have been made and copy some things about them and sometimes I just make my own.'
- 'She gives us personal writing project books. Right now everyone is doing 'cosy reading' but you don't just have to read – you can write. You can get blankets out and it's quite fun – it's not sitting at your desk reading a normal book – it's laying with your friends on cushions reading and writing together.'
- 'I just find it very enjoyable and I love reading – so I think it all comes together – I love to read my own books – and it's something I always try to do and I love writing in that sort of way.'
- When I've got a really good idea – I feel like a real writer writing it down. When I've read books, I've gotten ideas from them and it helps me to like write and feel like a writer because it's like what another writer has done.'

Practical things you can do

- Provide the children with a class library full of high-quality texts including poetry, fiction, classics, and non-fiction. Also ensure children have access to an ample number of texts relevant to the kind of writer they want to be at that time.
- Afford children the opportunity to bring books in from home to place into the class library.
- Regularly bring books in from the local library to supplement your classroom library.
- Ensure children's own writing can be published into the class, school, and local libraries.
- Consider setting up your own class publishing house. As part of this process, children could consider how culturally sustaining their classroom library is and who and what might be under-represented. This can then inform the type of writing they undertake throughout the year (Young and Ferguson 2020; Young et al. in press).
- Give children daily and ample time to read. As the year progresses, allow reading time to be followed by some personal writing time.
- Create a system that allows books from the class library and personal writing project books to go to and from home and school every day. This allows children to be in a constant state of reading and composition.
- Show children how they can write 'inspired by...' poems and create regular time for them to engage in this kind of intertextual writing.
- Show them how to dabble in their writer's notebook as they are reading.
- Show them how to appreciate certain character developments, setting descriptions, or beautifully crafted sentences in their reading, and how to make a note of it in their writers' notebook and then use those jottings to inform their own story, poetry, 'faction', or non-fiction writing.
- Use literature when you feel it can enhance the quality of your mini-lessons (see Chapter 20).
- Within class writing projects, allow children ownership and possession of the texts used to inform their writing.
- Show them how to 'hybrid' two or more of their favourite books to look for themes that they could exploit in their own writing.
- Show them examples from authors who 'hybridise' genres in new and unexpected ways using themes from their reading. For example, show some examples of strong personal voice within non-fiction texts, and allow children to think through writing by crafting their knowledge as opposed to simply 'telling' it.
- Share many mentor texts written by children and yourself in the past so children can see how others have approached certain class writing projects successfully. Make these available to read in the class library.
- Show them how to write 'fan-fiction' and allow children to be inspired and write in response to the texts they've chosen to read and enjoy.

> **QUESTIONS WORTH ASKING YOURSELF**
>
> - Does your classroom feel like a place where people come to talk, read, and write together?
> - Are you well informed about a *reading for pleasure* pedagogy (Open University 2020)?
> - Do you know what writers do as they read? Have you considered how you yourself use texts and your reading to inform your own writing? Does this reflect how you teach writing?
> - Do your children consider the writer, as a crafter, when they read? To what extent do you think your class realises that what they are reading has been crafted?
> - Do you and your class regularly ask why the author wrote this book?
> - Do children think about and discuss the future readership for their own texts? Do children collect information about their audience? (See Chapter 14).
> - How do your class currently use their reading and writing together?
> - Do you find yourself regularly saying after literature-based mini-lessons: 'you could give this a try in your own writing today …'?
> - Do you define 'texts' broadly to include, for example, films, music, pictures, multimedia, and lived experiences?
> - How can you involve families in talking about their 'life texts'? (Young & Kaufman 2020)

References

Abbott, J. (2000). 'Blinking out' and 'having the touch' two fifth-grade boys talk about flow experiences in writing. *Written Communication*, 17(1), 53–92.

Anderson, R.C., Wilson, P.T., and Fielding, L.G. (1988). Growth in reading and how children spend their time outside of school. *Reading Research Quarterly*, 23(3), 285–303.

Attiyat, N.M.A. (2019). The impact of pleasure reading on enhancing writing achievement and reading comprehension. *Arab World English Journal*, 10(1), 155–165.

Atwell, N. (2014). *In the Middle* (3rd Ed). Portsmouth, NH: Heinemann.

Bakhtin, M.M. (1981). Discourse in the novel (C. Emerson & M. Holquist, Trans.). In *The Dialogic Imagination*, Holquist, M. (Ed.) (pp. 259–422). Austin, TX: University of Texas Press.

Bangert-Drowns, R., Hurley, M., and Wilkinson, B. (2004). The effects of school-based writing-to-learn interventions on academic achievements: A meta-analysis. *Review of Educational Research*, 74, 29–58.

Barrs, M., and Cork, V. (2001). *The Reader in the Writer*. London: Centre for Language in Primary Education.

Bearne, E., and Watson, V. (1999). *Where Texts and Children Meet*. London: Routledge.

Benton, M., and Fox, G. (1985). *Teaching Literature*. Oxford: Oxford University Press.

Bereiter, C., and Scardamalia, M. (1987a). Knowledge telling and knowledge transforming in written composition. In *Advances in Applied Psycholinguistics: Vol. 2., Reading, Writing, and Language Learning*, Sternberg, R. (Eds.) (pp. 142–175). New York: Cambridge University Press.

Bereiter, C., and Scardamalia, M. (1987b). *The Psychology of Written Composition*. Mahwah, NJ: Lawrence Erlbaum Associates.

Brodney, B., Reeves, C., and Kazelskis, R. (1999). Selected prewriting treatments: Effects on expository compositions written by fifth-grade students. *The Journal of Experimental Education*, 68(1), 5–20.

Brownell, C. (2018). Creative language play(giarism). *Elementary English Language Arts Classroom,* 95(4), 218–228.

Calkins, L. (1994). *The Art of Teaching Writing*. Portsmouth, NH: Heinemann.

Carbone, P.W., and Orellana, M.F. (2010). Developing academic identities: Persuasive writing as a tool to strengthen emergent academic identities. *Research in the Teaching of English,* 44(3), 292–316.

Chuy, M., Scardamalia, M., and Bereiter, C. (2011). Development of ideational writing through knowledge building: Theoretical and empirical bases. In *Handbook of Writing: A Mosaic of New Perspectives,* Grigorenko, E., Mambrino, E., and Preiss, D. (Eds.) (pp. 175–190). New York: Psychology Press.

Clark, C. (2011). *Setting the Baseline: The National Literacy Trust's First Annual Survey into Reading – 2010*. London: National Literacy Trust.

Clark, C., and Douglas, J. (2011). *Young People's Reading and Writing An In-Depth Study Focusing on Enjoyment, Behaviour, Attitudes and Attainment*. London: National Literacy Trust.

Clark, C., and Phythian-Sence, C. (2008). *Interesting Choice: The (Relative) Importance of Choice and Interest in Reader Engagement*. London: The National Literacy Trust.

Clark, C., and Poulton, L. (2011). *Book Ownership and Its Relation to Reading Enjoyment, Attitudes, Behaviour and Attainment*. London: National Literacy Trust.

Clark, C., and Rumbold, K. (2006). *Reading for Pleasure a Research Overview*. London: The National Literacy Trust.

Compton-Lilly, C. (2006). Identity, childhood culture, and literacy learning: A case study. *Journal of Early Childhood Studies,* 6(1), 57–76.

Corden, R. (2002). Developing reflective writers in primary schools: Findings from partnership research. *Educational Review,* 54(3), 249–276.

Corden, R. (2007). Developing reading–writing connections: The impact of explicit instruction of literary devices on the quality of children's narrative writing. *Journal of Research in Childhood Education,* 21, 269–289.

Creber, P. (1990). *Thinking through English*. Maidenhead: Open University Press

Cremin, T., Mottram, M., Collins, F., Powell, S., and Safford, K. (2014). *Building Communities of Engaged Readers: Reading For Pleasure*. London: Routledge.

Cremin, T., Lillis, T., Myhill, D., and Eyres, I. (2017). Professional writers' identities. In *Writer Identity and the Teaching and Learning of Writing,* Cremin, T., and Locke, T. (Eds.) (pp. 19–36). London: Routledge.

Cushing, I. (2018). 'Suddenly, I am part of the poem': Texts as worlds, reader-response and grammar in teaching poetry. *English in Education,* 52(1), 7–19.

DeCristofaro, D. (2001). Author to author: How text influences young. Writers the Quarterly, 23(2), 8–12.

Dix, S., and Amoore, L. (2010). Becoming curious about cats: A collaborative writing project. *Australian Journal of Language & Literacy,* 33(2), 134–150.

Dombey, H. (2013). What we know about writing. *Preschool & Primary Education,* 1(1), 22–40.

Dutro, E. (2010). What 'hard times' means: Mandated curricula, class-privileged assumptions, and the lives of poor children. *Research in the Teaching of English,* 44(3), 255–291.

Dyson, A.H. (1997). *Writing Superheroes: Contemporary Childhood, Popular Culture, and Classroom Literacy*. New York: Teachers College Press.

Dyson, A.H. (2013). *Rewriting the Basics: Literacy Learning in Children's Cultures*. New York: Teachers College Press.

Evans, M.D.R., Kelley, J., Sikora, J., and Treiman, D.J. (2010). Family scholarly culture and educational success: Books and schooling in 27 nations. *Research in Social Stratification and Mobility,* 28, 171–197.

Fitzgerald, J., and Shanahan, T. (2000). Reading and writing relations and their development. *Educational Psychologist,* 35(1), 39–50.

Fletcher, R. (2011). *Mentor Author, Mentor Texts*. Portmsouth NH: Heinemann.

Frank, C. (2001). 'What new things these words can do for you': A focus on one writing-project teacher and writing instruction. *Journal of Literacy Research*, 33(3), 467–506.

Gallagher, K. (2014). Making the most of mentor texts. *Writing: A Core Skill*, 71(7), 28–33.

Ghiso, M. (2015). Arguing from experience: Young children's embodied knowledge and writing as inquiry. *Journal of Literacy Research*, 47(2), 186–215.

Glenn, W. (2007). Real writers as aware readers: Writing creatively as a means to develop reading skills. *Journal of Adolescent & Adult Literacy*, 51(1), 10–20.

Graham, J. (1998). Teaching, learning and the national literacy strategy. *Changing English*, 5(2), 115–121.

Graham, S. (2020). The Sciences of Reading and Writing Must Become More Fully Integrated. *Reading Research Quarterly*, 55(S1), S35–S44.

Graham, S., and Hebert, M. (2011). Writing to read: A meta-analysis of the impact of writing and writing instruction on reading. *Harvard Educational Review*, 81, 710–744.

Graham, S., and Perin, D. (2007). *Writing next: Effective Strategies to Improve Writing of Adolescents in Middle and High Schools*. Washington, DC: Alliance for Excellent Education.

Graham, S., and Sandmel, K. (2011). The process writing approach: A meta-analysis. *The Journal of Educational Research*, 104(6), 396–407.

Graham, S., Xinghua, L., Aitken, A., Ng, C., Bartlett, B., Harris, K., and Holzapfel, J. (2018). Effectiveness of literacy programs balancing reading and writing instruction: A meta-analysis. *Reading Research Quarterly*, 53(3), 279–304.

Graham, S., Kiuhara, S., and MacKay, M. (2020). The effects of writing on learning in science, social studies, and mathematics: A meta-analysis. *Review of Educational Research*, 90(2), 179–226.

Grainger, T., Goouch, K., and Lambirth, A. (2005). *Creativity and Writing: Developing Voice and Verve in the Classroom*. London: Routledge.

Griffith, R. (2010). Students learn to read like writers: a framework for teachers of writing. *Reading Horizons*, 50(1), 49–66.

Hansen, J. (1987). *When Writers Read*. Portsmouth, NH: Heinemann.

Harman, R. (2008). Systemic functional linguistics and the teaching of literature in urban school classrooms [Online]. Mick O' Donnell (Ed), International Systemic Functional Linguistics Association. www.isfla.org/Systemics/Print/index.html.

Harman, R. (2013). Literary intertextuality in genre-based pedagogies: Building lexical cohesion in fifth-grade L2 writing. *Journal of Second Language Writing*, 22(2), 125–140.

Harste, J., and Leland, C. (2000). Critical Literacy: Enlarging the Space of the Possible. *Primary Voices*, 9(2), 3–7.

Harwayne, S. (1992). *Lasting Impressions. Weaving Literature into the Writing Workshop*. Portsmouth, NH: Heinemann.

Heller, M. (1999). *Reading-Writing Connections: From Theory to Practice*. Mahwah, NJ: Lawrence Erlbaum Associates.

Hicks, J. (2008). *Writing identity and the writers' workshop: Looking back at my second grade classroom* [USFSP Honors Program Theses (Undergraduate)], 83.

Hoewisch, A. (2001). 'Do I have to have a princess in my story?': Supporting children's writing of fairytales. *Reading and Writing Quarterly*, 17, 249–277.

Holliway, D. (2004). Through the eyes of my reader: A strategy for improving audience perspective in children's descriptive language. *Journal of Research in Childhood Education*, 18(4), 334–349.

Keene, E., and Zimmermann, S. (1997). *Mosaic of Thought: Teaching Comprehension in a Reader's Workshop*. Portsmouth, NH: Heinemann.

Kent, S.C., and Wanzek, J. (2016). The relationship between component skills and writing quality and production across developmental levels: A meta-analysis of the last 25 years. *Review of Educational Research*, 86(2), 570–601.

Klein, P., and Boscolo, P. (2016). Trends in research on writing as a learning activity. *Journal of Writing Research*, 7, 311–350.

Knight, A. (2009). Re-engaging students disengaged with English: A unit of work on Othering. *English Teaching: Practice & Critique,* 8(1), 112–124.

Kress, G. (2010). *Multimodality: A Social Semiotic Approach to Contemporary Communication.* London: Routledge.

Laman, T. (2014). Transforming literate identities: Writing and multilingual children at work. *Learning English as a New Language,* 26(1), 2–10L.

Lancia, P. (1997). Literary borrowing: The effects of literature on children's writing. *The Reading Teacher,* 50(6), 470–475.

Langer, J., and Applebee, A. (1987). *How Writing Shapes Thinking: A Study of Teaching and Learning* (Research Rep No.22). Champaign, IL: National Council of Teachers of English.

Lankshear, C., and Knobel, M. (2009). More than words: Chris Searle's approach to critical literacy as cultural action. *Race & Class,* 51(2), 59–78.

Lewis, C. (2000). Critical issues: Limits of identification: The personal, pleasurable, and critical in reader response. *Journal of Literacy Research,* 32(2), 253–266.

Lewison, M., and Heffernan, L. (2008). Rewriting writers workshop: Creating safe spaces for disruptive stories. *Research in the Teaching of English,* 42(4), 435–465.

Lindsay, J. (2010). *Children's Access to Print Material and Education-Related Outcomes: Findings from a Meta-Analytic Review.* Washington, DC: Learning Point Associates.

Lipson, M., Valencia S., Wixson, K., and Peters, C. (1993). Integration and thematic teaching: Integration to improve teaching and learning. *Language Arts,* 70, 252–264.

Manak, J. (2011). The social construction of intertextuality and literary understanding: The impact of interactive read-alouds on the writing of third graders during writing workshop. *Reading Research Quarterly,* 46(4), 309–311.

McGillis, R. (1997). Self, other, and other self: Recognizing the other in children's literature. *The Lion and the Unicorn,* 21(2), 215-229.

McQuitty, V. (2014). Process-oriented writing instruction in elementary classrooms: Evidence of effective practices from the research literature. *Writing & Pedagogy,* 6(3), 467–495.

Meek Spencer, M. (1988). *How Texts Teach What Readers Learn.* Stroud: Thimble Press.

Meek Spencer, M. (2000). Afterword: Transitional transformation. In *Where Texts and Children Meet* (pp. 198–213). London: Routledge

Moffett, J., and Wagner, B. (1992). *Student-Centered Language Arts K-12* (4th Ed). Dover, NH: Boynton/Cook.

Morrow, L., Pressley, M., Smith, J., and Smith, M. (1997). The effect of a literature-based program integrated into literacy and science instruction with children from diverse backgrounds. *Reading Research Quarterly,* 32(1), 54–76.

Murray, D. (1993). *Read to Write* (3rd Ed.). San Diego, CA: Harcourt.

Oatley, K. (2003). Writingandreading. In *Cognitive Poetics in Practice,* Gavins, J.A., and Gerard, S. (Eds.) (pp. 161–175). London: Routledge.

Office for Standards in Education. (2011). *Excellence in English: What we can learn from 12 outstanding schools.* Available at: http://www.ofsted.gov.uk/resources/excellence-english.

Olinghouse, N., Graham, S., and Gillespie, A. (2015). The relationship of discourse and topic knowledge to fifth graders' writing performance. *Journal of Educational Psychology,* 107(2), 391–406.

Olthouse, J. (2012). Why I write: What talented creative writers need their teachers to know. *Gifted Child Today,* 35(2), 117–121.

Open University. (2020). *Reading for pleasure.* Available: https://researchrichpedagogies.org/research/reading-for-pleasure.

O'Sullivan, O., and McGonigle, S. (2010). Transforming readers: Teachers and children in the centre for literacy in primary education power of reading project. *Literacy,* 44(2), 51–59.

Pantaleo, S. (2006). Readers and writers as intertexts: Exploring the intertextualities in student writing. *Australian Journal of Language and Literacy,* 29(2), 163–181.

Pantaleo, S. (2007). The reader in the writer: Exploring elementary students' metafictive texts. *The Journal of Reading, Writing and Literacy*, 2(3), 42–74.

Pantaleo, S. (2010). Developing narrative competence through reading and writing metafictive texts. *Literacy Research and Instruction*, 49(3), 264–281.

Parry, B., and Taylor, L. (2018). Readers in the round: Children's holistic engagements with texts. *Literacy*, 52(2), 103–110.

Potter, J. (2012). *Digital Media and Learner Identity: The New Curatorship*. Basingstoke: Macmillan.

Prose, F. (2006). *Reading Like a Writer*. New York: HarperCollins.

Ranker, J. (2007). Designing meaning with multiple media sources: A case study of an eight-year-old student's writing processes. *Research in the Teaching of English*, 41, 402–434.

Ranker, J. (2009). Student appropriation of writing lessons through hybrid composing practices: Direct diffuse, and indirect use of teacher-offered writing tools in an ESL classroom. *Journal of Literacy Research*, 41, 393–431.

Rief, L. (2014). *Read Write Teaching: Choice and Challenge in the Reading-Writing Workshop*. Portsmouth, NH: Heinemann.

Roelle, J., Krüger, S., Jansen, C., and Bertford, K. (2012). The use of solved example problems for fostering strategies of self-regulated learning in journal writing. *Educational Research International*, 2012, 1–14.

Rosen, H. (1985). *Stories and Meanings*. Sheffield UK: National Association of Teachers of English.

Rosen, H. (2017). Neither bleak house nor liberty hall: English in the curriculum. In *Harold Rosen Writings on Life, Language and Learning 1958–2008*, Richmond, J., (Ed.) (pp. 73–90). London: UCL IOE Press.

Rosen, M. (1998). *Did I Hear You Write?* (2nd Ed.). London: Five Leaves Publications.

Rosen, M. (2018). *Writing for Pleasure*. London: Michael Rosen.

Rosenblatt, L. (1995). *Literature as Exploration* (5th Ed.). New York: Modern Language Association.

Rowsell, J., and Pahl, K. (2007). Sedimented identities in texts: Instances of practice. *Reading Research Quarterly*, 42(3), 388–404.

Scardamalia, M., and Bereiter, C. (2003). Knowledge building. In *Encyclopedia of Education* (2nd Ed.) (pp. 1370–1373). New York: Macmillan Reference.

Schneider, J. (2003). Contexts, genres, and imagination: An examination of the idiosyncratic writing performances of three elementary children within multiple contexts of writing instruction. *Research in the Teaching of English*, 37, 329–379.

Sénéchal, M., Hall, S., and Malette, M. (2018). Individual differences in grade 4 children's written compositions: The role of online planning and revising, oral storytelling, and reading for pleasure. *Cognitive Development*, 45, 92–104.

Smith, F. (1983). Reading like a writer. *Language Arts*, 60(5), 558–567.

Smith, F. (1988). *Joining the Literacy Club*. Portsmouth, USA: Heinemann.

Solsken, J., Willett, J., and Wilson-Keenan, J. (2000). Cultivating hybrid texts in multicultural classrooms: "Promise and challenge". *National Council of Teachers of English*, 35(2), 179–212.

Stein, N. (1983). On the goals, functions, and knowledge of reading and writing. *Contemporary Educational Psychology*, 8, 261–292.

Tennent, W., Reedy, D., Hobsbaum, A., and Gamble, N. (2016). *Guiding Readers – Layers of Meaning*. London: UCL Press.

The Talk Workshop Group. (1982). *Becoming Our Own Experts*. London: Redwood Burn.

Tierney, R., and Shanahan, T. (1991). Research on the reading-writing relationship: Interactions, transactions, and outcomes. In *Handbook of Reading Research Volume II*, Barr, R., Kamil, M.L., Mosenthal, P., and Pearson, P.D. (Eds.) (pp. 246–280). New York: Longman.

Wharton-McDonald R., Pressley, M., and Mistretta-Hampston, J. (1998). Literacy instruction in nine first-grade classrooms: Teacher characteristics and student achievement. *The Elementary School Journal*, 99(2), 101–128.

Yandell, J. (2016). Growth and the Category of Experience. *English in Australia*, 51(3), 19–26.

Young, R., and Ferguson, F. (2019). *Power English Writing: Teacher's Guide Year 6*. Oxford: Pearson.

Young, R., and Ferguson, F. (2020). *Real-World Writers: A Handbook for Teaching Writing with 7–11 Year Olds*. London: Routledge.

Young, R., and Kaufman, D. (2020). *Supporting children writing at home* [Available: https://writing4pleasure.com/supporting-children-writing-at-home/]

Young, R., Govender, N., and Kaufman, D. (in press). *Writing Realities*. Leicester: UKLA.

CHAPTER

24

Conclusion

An action plan for world-class writing teaching

While it is amazing to think that we all begin our journey towards being writers when we are toddlers at home, the parts played by parents, schools, and society all have a fundamental impact on whether we are able to build on this early learning and on the possibility of becoming empowered, successful, and life-long writers, writers who make meaning and communicate effectively, writers who write *as* and *for* pleasure, and writers who write with enjoyment and for personal and professional satisfaction.

However, for too long, too many children across the world have not learnt to write successfully (Cremin and Locke 2017; UNESCO 2017). For example, in 2015, '758 million adults 15 years and older still cannot read or write a simple sentence' (UNESCO 2016). In the United States, around two-thirds of 8th and 12th grade pupils write at or below the basic level (National Center for Educational Statistics 2012). Prior to curriculum reform in England, one in five primary pupils did not attain the expected standard in English, with a far greater proportion failing to achieve the standard in writing (Ofsted 2009, 2012). Sadly, we see this again in 2017, where 'attainment at the expected standard, as measured by teacher assessment … is lowest in writing. This is similar to the pattern in 2016' (DfE 2017). In 2019, only one in five children in England were writing above the basic 'met' standard (DfE 2019b). Finally, the DfE (2012, p. 3) remarks that 'writing is the subject with the worst performance compared with reading, maths and science at Key Stages 1 and 2'. For too long, writing has been disregarded and its importance underestimated, and children have been underperforming. It is imperative that we find an approach to teaching writing and developing writers which satisfies both teachers and policymakers. The dominant approaches have simply not worked.

However, there is the possibility for a radical change in how writing is taught. This book has shared:

- What educational researchers across differing contexts and for the past four decades have consistently identified as the most effective teaching practices.
- What we know the most exceptional writing teachers do to achieve high levels of attainment and elicit pleasure from their pupil-writers.
- What we know about how professional writers work.

We have been able to communicate this knowledge in the form of 14 enduring principles of world-class writing teaching (see Chapter 10), and each principle has been investigated and examined in detail in its own dedicated chapter. However, despite all that we presently know, children are failing to receive this world-class writing teaching. Why? And how can we change this situation? In this chapter we outline a very clear action plan detailing exactly what can be done.

Firstly, we would do well to establish a National Commission on Writing, basing it on the great US initiative of 2002 set up in response to a growing concern about the level and quality of writing across all sectors of American society. The commission's vision is to press for a national writing and writing-teaching revolution by creating a comprehensive writing policy and a national agenda, and to support teachers' professional development. The first task of a UK equivalent would be to unite and then urge all policymakers, teacher educators, literacy associations, school leaders, teachers, educational publishers and consultants to consider the evidence embodied in the 14 principles with the very greatest seriousness. This is an endeavour which we should be currently and determinedly pursuing. Stakeholders must then focus their attention on:

- Raising the profile of writing.
- Teachers' beliefs.
- Teachers writing.
- Teachers' knowledge.
- Initial teacher education.
- Research-informed continued professional development.

Raising the profile of writing

The reasons children are moved to write, as outlined in Chapter 2, are the reasons we can all be moved to write. We write to find out what we think, to entertain, reflect, teach, give opinions, paint with words, and to make a record. However, many adults dismiss these writing goals as irrelevant, or perhaps feel they are unattainable (Cremin et al. 2017). Interestingly, we have been unable to find any mention of recreational writing in surveys seeking to ascertain how UK adults spend their free time, while reading is regularly listed. With this said, we acknowledge the fact that in some ways people are writing more than ever before. The majority of people now have to write as part of their work (CollegeBoard 2004; Schanzenbach et al. 2016; WEF 2016; OECD 2017) and many now text, write email, and create and use 'memes' and other technology and modalities via social and online multimedia. However, does this fact make us a nation of writers?

Getting the nation writing

According to The US National Commission on Writing (2003, p. 9), one of the prerequisites for the creation of a generation of confident and extraordinary writers is 'a commitment to writing, not simply among educators but also among policymakers and the general public'. Therefore, writing is everybody's business. It is heartening to know that there are organisations in the UK promoting adult writing education and hobbyist and community writing, although they could be better supported and established across the country. There are already good models to work with, including The Federation of Worker Writers and Community Publishers (now The FED), Transforming Lives, The Workers' Educational Association, QueenSpark, and The Scotland Road Writers' Workshop to name but a few. Organisations such as these give inclusive entry to a great variety of writing communities and audiences, and access to print not controlled by the whims and commercial priorities of major publishers. Gregory (1984, p. 224), for example, talks about how such organisations can transform public perceptions of writing from a 'hated and daunting chore (as so often at school) to a preferred and … intoxicating way of life'. And with the rise of the internet, free social media, blogging, multimedia platforms, self-publishing and cheap printing costs, there has never been a better time for accessing audiences, publication, and performance (Woodin 2018).

Making the nation knowledgeable about writing

According to Graham (1999) and Frank (2003) the general public, parents, and teachers may know little about why writers write and how they craft their writing. Charitable organisations have much expertise and knowledge to share. Charities such as First Story, Ministry Of Stories, The Poetry Society, Society of Authors, Story Planet, The Writers' Guild, The Poetry Trust, National Centre For Writing, Arvon, The National Literacy Trust, The Children's Literacy Charity, The Centre for Literacy in Primary Education, National Writing Day, National Poetry Day, World Book Day, The Book Trust and The Reading Agency should all work together and be given more publicity, column inches and airtime to support their promotion of writing for pleasure.

The United Kingdom Literacy Association, The English Association, National Association of Teachers of English, The London Association of Teachers of English, The National Writing Project UK, and The National Association of Writers in Education all have a potential key role in campaigning and advocating for more public exposure to the benefits of writing and world-class writing teaching, and for the sharing of knowledge and expertise with the press, media, the government, and other policymakers. Establishing an organised special interest group (SIG) with the specific role of raising the profile and teaching of writing (as The National Commission on Writing in the United States has done) would help these organisations work together in a more coordinated way.

Raising the profile of children's writing

We call on children's book publishers to seek out ways to make publicly available writing by children in all genres. Good models include initiatives such as the Amazon Young Storytellers, Story Makers Company, Young City Poets, the Fabled Kids podcast, the Writing Web blogging platform, and publications like *England: Poems from a School* by Kate Clanchy or *Stepney Words* by Chris Searle. Adults gain much from reading children's writing, and children are very drawn to reading what their contemporaries have written, often using it intertextually in their own writing.

Policymakers understanding writing and writers

We need to discover the extent to which policymakers understand how writers craft their texts. We should be asking whether our education secretary, members of governmental education committees, or subject leads for Ofsted have ever attended a writers' workshop or a writing retreat alongside teachers. For example, do government-designed curricula really reflect all that is presently known about how young apprentice writers develop, and are they ambitious enough? We would argue that they are not, and that as a result many misconceptions are perpetuated within education policy.

Teachers' beliefs

In Chapter 1, we stated our view that a teacher's experience of learning to write at school will in one way or another colour their present perceptions of writing and of themselves as writers. Many will enter the profession with negative views (Graham et al. 2001; Street 2003; Gardner 2014; Cremin et al. 2019; Gusevik 2020). How teachers were trained, their private writing practices, and successive government policies will also exert a powerful influence. We have put forward evidence that writing teaching has long been inadequate across many parts of the world and that this cycle is difficult to break in the face of teachers' entrenched beliefs and misconceptions about what it means to write (Parker 1988; McKinney and Giorgis 2009; Hall and Grisham-Brown 2011). It appears that teachers often go about teaching writing in the possibly detrimental ways they themselves were taught (Parker 1988; Frank 2003; McCarthey et al. 2014; Dobson 2016; Yoo 2018). It is also likely that they are either not aware of research-informed practices or that they lack the confidence to enact them (Theriot and Tice 2008; Hall 2016; Helfrich and Clark 2016; Gusevik 2020). Clearly, we need to work hard to change beliefs and improve teachers' writing self-efficacy. We suggest a three-pronged approach: nurture writer-identities, develop subject knowledge, and improve pedagogical knowledge.

Teachers writing

In summary so far, we think it necessary for teachers to reflect on their attitudes towards writing and on their own experience of learning to write and being a writer, and to understand how these factors inevitably affect their teaching. We then propose that teachers try to gain an understanding of how writers live and work in a community of writers. By participating in writing groups, teachers can begin to identify themselves as writer-teachers who will be well-placed to teach effectively since they can share with children their own knowledge and experience of writing (Morgan 2017; Whitney 2017).

The National Writing Project UK

One effective way of developing teachers as writers is through the National Writing Project (Whyte et al. 2007; Andrews 2008; Kaplan 2008; Locke et al.

2011). In keeping with the views of its US counterpart, the aim of the NWPUK is to give teachers professional development opportunities in writing. In the United States, this has been particularly successful, with the NWP establishing over 200 sites and with universities entering into partnership with local schools, giving teachers an opportunity to write and talk as a community of writers, and gain professional accreditation. Similar initiatives could be adopted in the UK, with teachers, lecturers, and consultants invited to take part in summer institutes and holiday writing retreats, reading, writing, sharing, and then reflecting on their teaching practices, as illustrated in the process below (see also Woodard 2017; Cremin et al. 2019). In this way teachers would gain greater expertise and feel reprofessionalised (Smyth 1998).

School-based writer-teacher groups

Schools should be encouraged to set up internal writer-teacher groups, much in keeping with the highly successful OU/UKLA teachers' reading groups (Open University 2020). Through school-based writer-teacher groups (Smith and Wrigley 2012; Young and Ferguson 2020b), or by participating in online writing groups like #WritersByNight (Young and Ferguson 2020d), practitioners can access a network of committed teachers who write and writers who teach. In such a space they can reflect on their developing writer-identities, extend their subject and pedagogical knowledge, and share examples of practice from action research projects (see Figure 24.1).

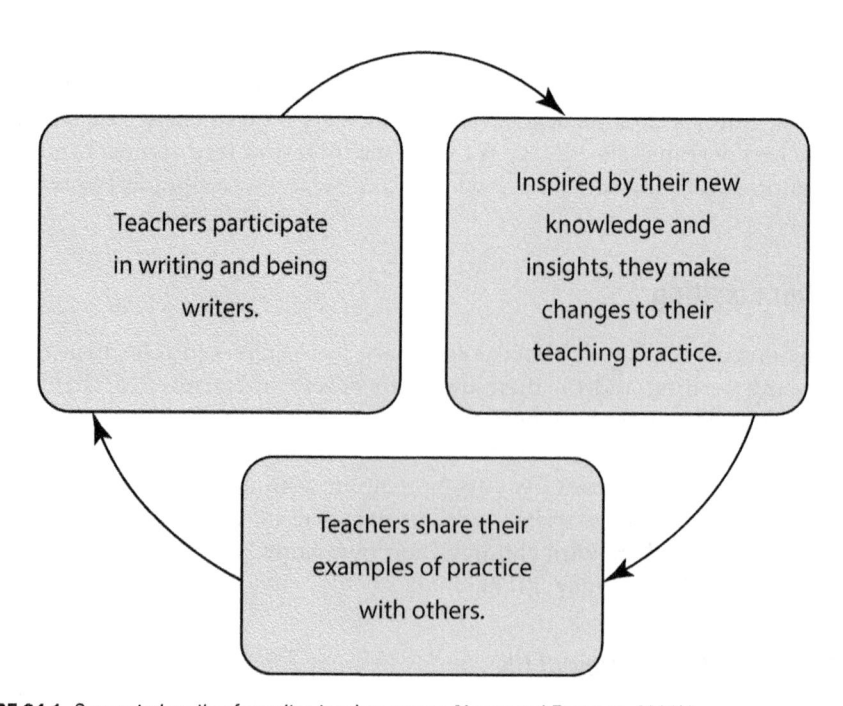

FIGURE 24.1 Suggested routine for writer-teacher groups (Young and Ferguson 2020b).

Teachers' subject knowledge

Teachers' knowledge

We need to increase teachers' writing subject knowledge through an understanding of the knowledge writers acquire and use, including the following:

- **Craft knowledge** involved in creating texts, including:
  - **Process knowledge,** knowledge about the processes, procedures, strategies, and techniques writers employ as they go through their writing process, generating ideas, planning, drafting, revising, editing, publishing, and performing.
  - **Genre knowledge**, the typical textual, linguistic, literary, and grammatical features genres employ to be at their most meaningful and successful.
  - **Goal knowledge**, how writers set themselves goals and manage their writing deadlines.
  - **Knowledge about their reader**, how writers will meditate on the purpose for their writing, gather information about and consider their future readership.
  - **Knowledge about a writerly environment**, how writers live and work with others, and the conditions which are conducive to writing productively and happily.
- **Transcriptional knowledge,** including spelling and punctuation conventions and keyboard and handwriting skills .
- **Knowledge of how writers use their reading**, including how they read to enhance their craft knowledge and search for content material.
- **Knowledge of technology** and other modalities.
- **Knowledge of the affective domains** used by writers as they craft and publish texts. This includes giving attention to their confidence, motivation, desire, competence and their personal and collective responsibilities.

Teachers' pedagogical knowledge

Teachers' pedagogical decisions need to be guided by sound conceptual principles. For children to become great writers they require: a positive and writerly classroom environment; quality daily writing instruction; opportunities to be moved to write; meaningful practice; ample time to craft and refine their writing; regular opportunities to prepare, publish, and perform their writing products, and committed writer-teachers who prioritise responsive teaching. A *Writing For Pleasure* pedagogy has made the principles of world-class writing teaching entirely explicit so as to provide schools with a consistent vision and a shared understanding and vocabulary and give teachers increased and research-based pedagogical knowledge.

It is our view that children deserve more than to encounter just one exceptional teacher of writing. Instead they must experience many – one after the other (Block and Mangieri 2009; Rubie-Davies et al. 2014). In the UK, this would require the regular conducting and dissemination of research into what teaching practices are used by typical teachers of writing compared with those of exceptional teachers of writing, with Dockrell et al. (2015b) and Young's (2019) studies being good templates to work from. We can then continually promote what it is exceptional teachers do that makes the difference. While significant progress has been made in understanding writing in and out of school over the past four decades (MacArthur et al. 2016; Graham et al. 2019), it is essential to bear in mind that these principles can always be further explored and refined.

The 14 principles of world-class writing teaching

- Create a community of writers.
- Treat every child as a writer.
- Read, share, think, and talk about writing.
- Pursue authentic and purposeful class writing projects.
- Pursue personal writing projects.
- Teach the writing processes.
- Set writing goals.
- Teach mini-lessons.
- Pupil conference: meet children where they are.
- Balance composition and transcription.
- Be a writer-teacher.
- Be reassuringly consistent.
- Literacy for pleasure: connect reading and writing.
- Interconnect the principles.

These principles are broad and open-ended enough to give teachers the liberty and the room to teach sensitively and creatively in accordance with their knowledge of their own school context and the particular needs of their children.

Growing whole schools of extraordinary writers

We know from research that having an evidence-based and consistent approach to the teaching of writing across school is vital to children's pleasure and academic progress (Ings 2009; Locke 2017). It is necessary for every school to develop a shared understanding of the reasons we are moved to write, what good writing is, and what effective writing teaching encompasses. The full long-term commitment and engagement of the senior leadership team must be secured if teachers are to be properly supported in their endeavours. Young and Ferguson (2020b) give writing coordinators and senior leaders much practical advice on how to create a whole school of extraordinary writing through a *Writing For Pleasure* pedagogy.

The role of literacy associations

It seems imperative to establish a central body similar to the US National Commission on Writing to help draw together the work of different literacy associations, enabling them to have a collective impact and to achieve the following outcomes:

- Through the dissemination, discussion, and critique of what is known about world-class writing teaching, government departments for education would be in a position to monitor the quality of commercial writing materials (McKinney and Giorgis 2009). Writing programmes could then be responsibly and systematically reviewed (Dockrell et al. 2015a). It comes as no surprise to note that, while reviews of materials promoting early reading and maths mastery (DfE 2014, 2018) have been carried out, no such review of commercial writing programmes has taken place.
- Literacy associations would work together to make educational research findings meaningful and useful to the practice of classroom teachers (Wyse 2020). For example, researchers could more regularly produce teacher-facing articles to accompany their more academic work.
- Associations working together could support the organisation of writing institutes offering teachers research-based and high-quality professional development, an opportunity to immerse themselves in the literary life, and the chance of full interchange and dialogue, much as the acclaimed US Teachers' College Reading and Writing Project does.
- Finally, a National Commission could assist in expanding initiatives like the DfE's sponsored 'English Hubs' to include as much about writing teaching as about phonics and early reading.

Initial Teacher Education

As discussed in Chapter 1, despite the importance of learning about writing instruction it is the case that, in most ITE programmes, little emphasis is placed on how to teach writing (and writers) effectively (Graham 1999; Norman and Spencer 2005; Kaufman 2009; Myers et al. 2016; Cushing 2019). In England, the Department for Education's (DfE 2019a) Initial Teacher Training (ITT) Core Content Framework puts forward only one objective on the subject of teaching writing. It should also be noted that the framework fails to use the word 'writers' or the phrase 'writing for pleasure' at all. In contrast, 'readers' and 'reading for pleasure' are frequently used. Only one statement is related to writing: 'discussing and analysing with expert colleagues how to teach different forms of writing by modelling planning, drafting and editing'. This is, at best, ill-informed about the processes involved in crafting writing and, at worst, fails to articulate how we develop exceptional writers. In addition, The Office for Standards in Education, Children's Services and Skills, which inspects the quality of ITE within England, fails to use the word 'writing' or 'writers' in their draft inspection framework at all (Ofsted 2020). In contrast, the word 'reading' is used on nine occasions and the document goes on to cite eight papers on the teaching of phonics and early reading. Again, no papers related specifically to the teaching of writing are cited.

It is clear, therefore, that more emphasis is given to instructing preservice teachers in the teaching of reading than in the teaching of writing (Domaille and Edwards

2006; Andrews 2008), with a resulting low degree of confidence in writing teaching among teachers (Gannon and Davies 2007; Andrews 2008; Morgan 2010; Morgan and Pytash 2014). This lack of balance seems even more unwise in view of the fact that, as is noted by Cremin and Myhill (2012), Cremin et al. (2019), and Cushing (2019), a great many teachers come to teaching with a love of reading and not writing. Worth noting too, are the observations made by Cremin (2006), Bifuh-Ambe (2013), Dobson (2016), and Yoo (2018) that those knowledgeable teachers who do wish to employ the kinds of effective practices described in this book are often prevented from doing so by poorly designed governmental curricula and subsequent ill-informed school policy.

The inadequate attention given on ITE courses to the teaching of writing, coupled with the promotion of misconceptions about the writing processes and the craft of writing, is gravely concerning. If we have any ambition to promote world-class writing teaching and so develop generations of extraordinary writers, then current ITE courses need to be carefully reviewed and redesigned to include some of the following initiatives: teacher trainers being asked to reflect on their own writer identities and to model their writerly life (Kaufman 2002, 2009; Gaitas and Martins 2015; Locke et al. 2020); modules devoted to the teaching of writing; an annual national survey of the writing teaching taking place on ITE programmes (Morgan and Pytash 2014; Myers et al. 2016), and the establishment of more initiatives like The Centre For Research In Writing (Exeter University) or The Center for the Study and Teaching of Writing (Ohio State University).

Finally, another common complaint from preservice teachers transitioning from the lecture theatre to their own school classroom is the disparity between what is learnt about writing teaching while at university and what is learnt once they enter schools. To combat this, longitudinal studies observing teachers' journeys from university to classrooms would be welcomed (Morgan and Pytash 2014).

Time for another Dartmouth seminar?

In 1966, a three-week long seminar took place in Dartmouth (USA) with some 50 leading educators from the United States and the UK attending. There were two aims: to work towards defining English as a school subject, and to consider how it could be taught most effectively. The seminar and its impact were very impressively recorded in the UK's John Dixon's *Growth through English* (1969) and the United States's Herbert Muller's *The Uses of English* (1967). However, although there has been a significant increase in educational research since then, such a seminar has not to our knowledge been adequately repeated (Harris 1991; Smith 2019). We would suggest that the time is now right for a new expanded Dartmouth, with the proviso that more serving teachers and countries be involved now than was the case in 1966.

Research-informed continued professional development

There is certainly a need for the principles of research-informed CPD to be better understood by providers. For example, research has shown that traditional CPD fails to change or embed new practices within schools (CUREE 2011;

Bifuh-Ambe 2013; Johnson 2013; McCarthey and Geoghegan 2016; Fletcher-Wood and Zuccollo 2020). What needs to change is explained below.

Establishing and participating in a professional learning community

Evidence shows that professional development projects should last *at least* a year and provide teachers with opportunities for follow-up, consolidation, and additional support. Affordable initiatives such as *The Writing For Pleasure Centre's* school residency and affiliate programme (Young and Ferguson 2020c) ensures that a training project continues in this way. CPD providers must act as coaches, co-researchers, and mentors to teacher participants. Teachers must feel part of the process and be treated as peers and co-learners alongside providers. Schools must set explicit and high expectations for providers and have a clear plan for how they are to evaluate the CPD project. For example, how do they know it has been effective? What impact has it had on pupils? What change has the school seen in outcomes?

Promoting internal specialists and school dialogue

A training project should be a collective enterprise. It is crucial for providers of CPD to identify in advance of the project what subject knowledge is needed by teachers, what are the areas of strength, and what areas need to be developed. This can be done through an audit of individual practice, the results of which are shared amongst the whole staff and then with the trainers.

The aim during training should be for all staff members to develop an understanding of the 14 principles and the rationale behind each one; an understanding of the writing processes and the language to talk about them, and to construct a shared vision of the future of writing teaching in the school. The staff must then work to create or at least refine their own policy and practice in collaboration with colleagues, supported by an 'internal specialist', a staff member who has been equipped to carry on the training role after the providers have physically left the school.

Teachers and schools as action researchers

The idea of teachers engaging in action research must be taken up so that practitioners can contribute towards educational policy and practice (Woodard 2017). Again, in keeping with *The Writing For Pleasure Centre's* school residency and affiliate programme (Young and Ferguson 2020c), schools can contribute to and learn from other teachers and school affiliates within a growing professional and international network. Schools can become professional learning communities by participating in and eventually organising teacher writing institutes. Taking *The Writing For Pleasure Centre's* school residency and affiliate programme as the example, providers should ensure that as part of their training they create knowledge-sharing teachers through the promotion of writer-teacher groups, internal lesson study, the publication and dissemination of action research, and examples of practice (Young and Ferguson 2020a). This requires schools, after initial input from a provider, to engage in subsequent in-class experimentation and collaboration with colleagues. Providers should also ensure there are opportunities for teachers to collaborate with others in person and online; for example, through Twitter chats like @WritingRocks_17 and through The Writing For Pleasure Centre's website.

A nationally recognised site

Finally, there is an urgent need for a nationally recognised site specifically dedicated to the establishment of a strong nationwide professional learning community; to be a meeting place for educational publishers, relevant charities, providers of CPD, researchers, local education authorities, academy trusts, school leaders, and a centre where teachers can gather. Ideally, the site would be attached to a teacher-education university with the scope to provide a school residency training programme, multi-day teacher institutes or festivals, and even a physical home for The National Writing Project and a National Commission On Writing.

Lastly

This book has been written with the conviction that there can be a bright future for writing teaching in our schools and for what writing can mean for generations of young people. To achieve this, fundamental changes need to be made to a culture of education which does not officially assert the status and significance of children being and becoming writers. Happily, if we all work together, it will be possible to address this failure and bring about significant change through collective agreement and practice. We should no longer deny children the means of exploring and expressing through writing their diversity of knowledge, histories, and identities, and instead teach them to write for themselves and others with power, precision, purpose and pleasure – for life.

References

Andrews, R. (2008). *The Case for a National Writing Project for Teachers*. Reading: CfBT Educational Trust.
Bifuh-Ambe, E. (2013). Developing successful writing teachers: Outcomes of professional development exploring teachers' perceptions of themselves as writers and writing teachers and their students' attitudes and abilities to write across the curriculum. *English Teaching*, 12, 137–156.
Block, C., and Mangieri, J. (2009). *Exemplary Literacy Teachers* (2nd Ed.). New York: Guilford Press.
Centre for the use of research evidence in education (CUREE) (2011). *Understanding What Enables High Quality Professional Learning: A Report on the Research Evidence*. London: Pearson.
CollegeBoard. (2004). *Writing: A ticket into work or a ticket out*. Available: https://archive.nwp.org/cs/public/download/nwp_file/21479/writing-a-ticket-to-work-or-a-ticket-out.pdf?x-r=pcfile_d.
Cremin, T. (2006). Creativity, uncertainty and discomfort: Teachers as writers. *Cambridge Journal of Education*, 36(3), 415–433.
Cremin, T., and Locke, T. (2017). *Writer Identity and the Teaching and Learning of Writing*. London: Routledge.
Cremin, T., and Myhill, D. (2012). *Creating Communities of Writers*. London: Routledge.

Cremin, T., Lillis, T., Myhill, D., and Eyres, I. (2017). Professional writers' identities. In *Writer Identity and the Teaching and Learning of Writing*, Cremin, T., and Locke, T. (Eds.) (pp. 19–36). London: Routledge.

Cremin, T., Myhill, D., Eyres, I., Nash, T., Wilson, A., and Oliver, L. (2019). Teachers as writers: Learning together with others. *Literacy*, 54(2), 49–59. doi.org/10.1111/lit.12201.

Cushing, I. (2019). Grammar policy and pedagogy from primary to secondary school. *Literacy*, 53(3), 170–179.

DfE. (2012). *What is the Research Evidence on Writing? Education Standards Research Team*. London: Department for Education.

DfE. (2014). *Phonics: Choosing a Programme*. London: Department for Education. [Available: https://www.gov.uk/government/collections/phonics-choosing-a-programme].

DfE. (2017). *National Curriculum Assessments at Key Stage 2 in England, 2017 (revised)*. London: Department for Education.

DfE. (2018). *Join the Maths Teaching for Mastery Programme*. London: Department for Education. [Available: https://www.gov.uk/guidance/join-the-maths-teaching-for-mastery-programme].

DfE. (2019a). *ITT Core Content Framework*. London: Department for Education.

DfE. (2019b). *National Curriculum Assessments at Key Stage 2 in England, 2019 (revised)*. London: Department for Education.

Dixon, J. (1969). *Growth through English* (2nd Ed). Oxford: Oxford University Press.

Dobson, T. (2016). 'Just because I'm not a published author does not mean that I'm not a writer': Primary trainee teachers' identities as creative writers. *Writing in Practice: The Journal of Creative Writing Research*, 2.

Dockrell, J., Marshall, C., and Wyse, D. (2015a). *'Talk For Writing': Evaluation Report*. London: Education Endowment Fund.

Dockrell, J., Marshall, C., and Wyse, D. (2015b). Teachers' reported practices for teaching writing in England. *Reading & Writing: An Interdisciplinary Journal*, 29, 409–434.

Domaille, K., and Edwards, J. (2006). Partnerships for learning: Extending knowledge and understanding of creative writing processes in the ITT year. *English in Education*, 40(2), 71–84.

Fletcher-Wood, H., and Zuccollo, J. (2020). *The effects of high-quality professional development on teachers and students: A rapid review and meta-analysis*. London: Wellcome Trust.

Frank, C. (2003). Mapping our stories: Teachers' reflections on themselves as writers. *Language Arts*, 80(3), 185–195.

Gaitas, S., and Martins, M. (2015). Relationships between primary teachers' beliefs and their practices in relation to writing instruction. *Research Papers in Education*. 30(4), 492–505.

Gannon, S., and Davies, C. (2007). For love of the word: English teaching, affect and writing. *Changing English*, 14(1), 87–98.

Gardner, P. (2014). Becoming a teacher of writing: Primary student teachers reviewing their relationship with writing. *English in Education*, 48(2), 128–148.

Graham, R. (1999). The self as writer: Assumptions and identities in the writing workshop. *Journal of Adolescent & Adult Literacy*, 43(4), 358–364.

Graham, S., Harris, K.R., Fink, B., and MacArthur, C.A. (2001). Teacher efficacy in writing: A construct validation with primary grade teachers. *Scientific Studies of Reading*, 56, 177–202.

Graham, S., MacArthur, C., and Hebert, M. (2019). *Best Practices in Writing Instruction* (3rd Ed.). New York: Guildford Press.

Gregory, G. (1984). Community-published working-class writing in context. In *Changing English: Essays for Harold Rosen*, Meek, M., and Miller, J. (Ed.) (pp. 220–235). London: Heinemann.

Gusevik, R. (2020). *Writing for pleasure and the teaching of writing at the primary level: A teacher cognition case study*. Unpublished Dissertation, University of Stavanger [Available: https://writing4pleasuredotcom.files.wordpress.com/2020/08/gusevik_rebeccamarie.pdf]

Hall, A. (2016). Examining shifts in preservice teachers' beliefs and attitudes toward writing instruction. *Journal of Early Childhood Teacher Education*, 37(2), 142–156.

Hall, A., and Grisham-Brown, J. (2011). Writing development over time: Examining preservice teachers' attitudes and beliefs about writing. *Journal of Early Childhood Teacher Education*, 32, 148–158.

Harris, J. (1991). After dartmouth: Growth and conflict in English. *College English*, 53(6), 631–646.

Helfrich, S., and Clark, S. (2016). A comparative examination of pre-service teacher self-efficacy related to literacy instruction. *Reading Psychology*, 37, 943–961.

Ings, R. (2009). *Writing Is Primary: Final Research Report*. London: Esmee Fairbairn Foundation.

Johnson, R. (2013). The impact of professional development in writing instruction on the implementation of writing strategies in the classroom. In *Association of Literacy Educators and Researchers Yearbook: Literacy is Transformative*, Szabo, S., Martin, L., Morrison, T., Haas, L., and Garza-Garcia, L. (Eds.) (Vol. 35, pp. 157–172) Michigan: Association of Literacy Educators and Researchers.

Kaplan, J. (2008). The national writing project: Creating a professional learning community that supports the teaching of writing. *Theory Into Practice*, 47, 336–344.

Kaufman, D. (2002). Living a literate life: Revisited. *English Journal*, 91(6), 51–57.

Kaufman, D. (2009). A teacher educator writes and shares: Student perceptions of a publicly literate life. *Journal of Teacher Education*, 60, 338.

Locke, A., Smith, C., Walsh, C., Baldwin, L., and Rooke, J. (2020). *Student-teachers becoming writer-teachers* [Available: https://writing4pleasure.com/student-teachers-becoming-writer-teachers/]

Locke, T. (2017). Developing a whole-school culture of writing. In *Writer Identity and the Teaching and Learning of Writing*, Cremin, T., and Locke, T. (Eds.) (pp. 132–148). London: Routledge.

Locke, T., Whitehead, D., Dix, S., and Cawkwell, G. (2011). New Zealand teachers respond to the 'national writing project' experience. *Teacher Development*, 15(3), 273–291.

MacArthur, C., Graham, S., and Fitzgerald, J. (2016). *Handbook of Research on Writing* (2nd Ed.). New York: Guilford Press.

McCarthey, S., and Geoghegan, C. (2016). The role of professional development for enhancing writing instruction. In *Handbook of Writing Research*, MacArthur, C., Graham, S., Fitzgerald, J. (Eds.) (2nd Eds) (pp. 330–345). New York: Guildford Press..

McCarthey, S., Woodard, R., and Kang, G. (2014). Elementary teachers negotiating discourses in writing instruction. *Written Communication*, 31(1), 58–90.

McKinney, M., and Giorgis, C. (2009). Narrating and performing identity: Literacy specialists' writing identities. *Journal of Literacy Research*, 41, 104–149.

Morgan, D. (2010). Preservice teachers as writers. *Literacy Research and Instruction*, 49, 352–365.

Morgan, D. (2017). I'm not a good writer. In *Writer Identity and the Teaching and Learning of Writing*, Cremin, T., and Locke, T. (Eds.) (pp. 39–52). London: Routledge.

Morgan, D., and Pytash, K. (2014). Preparing preservice teachers to become teachers of writing: A 20-year review of the research literature. *National Council of Teachers of English*, 47(1), 6–37.

Muller, H. (1967). *The Uses of English: Guidelines for the Teaching of English from the Anglo-American Conference at Dartmouth College*. New York: Holt, Rinehart and Winston.

Myers, J., Scales, R. Q., Grisham, D. L., Wolsey, T. D., Dismuke, S., Smetana, L., Kreider, K., Ikpeze, Y., Ganske, K., and Martin, S. (2016). What about writing?: A national exploratory study of writing instruction in teacher preparation programs. *Literacy Research & Instruction*, 55, 309–330.

National Center for Educational Statistics. (2012). *The Nation's Report Card: Writing 2011* (NCES 2012–470). Washington, DC: U.S. Department of Education: Institute of Educational Sciences.

National Commission On Writing. (2003). *The neglected 'R': The need for a writing revolution* Available: http://www.collegeboard.com/prod_downloads/writingcom/neglectedr.pdf.

Norman, K., and Spencer, B. (2005). Our lives as writers: Examining preservice teachers' experiences and beliefs about the nature of writing and writing instruction. *Teacher Education Quarterly*, 32(1), 25–40.

OECD. (2017). *PISA 2015 Results (Volume V): Collaborative Problem Solving*. Paris: PISA OECD.

Ofsted. (2009). *English at the Crossroads*. London: Ofsted.

Ofsted. (2012). *Moving English Forward*. London: Ofsted.

Ofsted. (2020). *Initial Teacher Education Inspection Framework and Handbook*. London: Ofsted.

Open University. (2020). OU/UKLA Teachers' Reading Groups [Available: https://researchrich pedagogies.org/research/teachers-reading-groups].

Parker, R. (1988). Theories of writing instruction: Having them, use them, change them. *English Education*, 20(1), 18–40.

Rubie-Davies, C., Weinstein, R., Huang, F., Gregory, A., Cowan, P., and Cowan, C. (2014). Successive teacher expectation effects across the early school years. *Journal of Applied Developmental Psychology*, 35, 181–191.

Schanzenbach, D., Nunn, R., Bauer, L., Mumford, M., and Breitwiesser, A. (2016). *Seven Facts of Noncognitive Skills from Education to the Labor Market*. Washington, CD: The Hamilton Project.

Smith, J., and Wrigley, S. (2012). What has writing ever done for us? The power of teachers' writing groups. *English in Education*, 46(1), 69–84.

Smith, L. (2019). 'We're not building worker bees.' What has happened to creative practice in england since the dartmouth conference of 1966? *Changing English*, 26(1), 48–62.

Smyth, J. (1998). Reprofessionalising teaching: A university research institute engages teachers in creating dialogic space in schools. *Teacher Development*, 2(3), 339–350.

Street, C. (2003). Pre-service teachers' attitudes about writing and learning to teach writing: Implications for teacher educators. *Teacher Education Quarterly* Summer, 30(3), 33–50.

Theriot, S., and Tice, K. (2008). Teachers' knowledge development and change: Untangling beliefs and practices. *Literacy Research and Instruction*, 48(1), 65–75.

UNESCO (United Nations Educational, Scientific and Cultural Organisation). (2016). *International Literacy Day*. Retrieved from https://www.worldcoo.com/blog/en/international-literacy-day/.

UNESCO. (2017). *Reading the Past, Writing the Future* [Available: https://unesdoc.unesco.org/ark:/48223/pf0000247563].

WEF (World Economic Forum). (2016). *The future of Jobs*. Cologny/Geneva: World Economic Forum.

Whitney, A. (2017). Developing the teacher-writer in professional development. In *Writer Identity and the Teaching and Learning of Writing*, Cremin, T., and Locke, T. (Eds.) (pp. 67–79). London: Routledge.

Whyte, A., Lazerte, A., Thomson, I., Ellis, N., Muse, A., and Talbot, R. (2007). The national writing project, teachers' writing lives, and student achievement in writing. *Action in Teacher Education*, 29(2), 5–16.

Woodard, R. (2017). Working towards 'I'm a writer and a pretty good writer'. In *Writer Identity and the Teaching and Learning of Writing*, Cremin, T., and Locke, T. (pp. 115–131). London: Routledge.

Woodin, T. (2018). *Working-Class Writing and Publishing in the Late Twentieth Century: Literature, Culture and Community*. Manchester: Manchester University Press.

Wyse, D. (2020). Presidential address: The academic discipline of education reciprocal relationships between practical knowledge and academic knowledge. *British Educational Research Journal*, 46, 6–25.

Yoo, J. (2018). Teachers as creative writers: Needs, desires and opportunities for growth. *New Writing*, 15(3), 300–310.

Young, R. (2019). *What is it 'writing for pleasure' teachers do that makes the difference?* The University Of Sussex: The Goldsmiths' Company [Online]. Available: www.writing4pleasure.com.

Young, R., and Ferguson, F. (2020a). *Explore the principles and read examples of classroom practice.* Available: www.writing4pleasure.com/explore-the-principles-read-examples-of-practice.

Young, R., and Ferguson, F. (2020b). *Real-World Writers: A Handbook for Teaching Writing with 7–11 Year Olds.* London: Routledge.

Young, R., and Ferguson, F. (2020c). *Teacher and pupil writing retreats.* Available: www.writing4pleasure.com/training.

Young, R., and Ferguson, F. (2020d). *#WritersByNight.* Available: www.writing4pleasure.com/writersbynight.

Index

Page numbers in **bold** denote tables, in *italic* denote figures

Abbott, J. 52, 58–59, 168, 230
adventurer 39, **179**
agency 3, 21, 23, 26, 29–30, 35, 39, 42–47, *46*, 51, 55, 62, 71, 96, 114, 117–119, 127–129, 144, 154, 167–172, *204*, 224
Alber, S. 96
Alber-Morgan, S. 32, 35, 36, 38, 52, 135, 187–188, 193
Alexander, R. 21, 102, 212
Alford, K. 203
Allal, L. 3, 38, 132, 211
Alves, R. 29–32, 129, 177, 181–182, 189
Ames, C. 144, 151–153
Amoore, L. 229
Amtmann, D. 177–179
Anderson, C. 214–215
Anderson, J. 134
Applebee, A. N. 160, 226
Archer, J. 144, 151–153
Atwell, N. 37, 51, 68–70, 103, 107, 159, 166, 180, 187, 200, 224
Au, W. 21, 65, 68
Author's Chair 31, 103, 107, 109, 162, 192, 217
Axelrod, Y. 26, 49

Baker, S. 199, 204, *204*
Bakhtin, M. M. 102, 225
Barrs, M. 65, 72, 200, 222, 224
Bazerman, C. 6, 12, 44, 160
Beach, S. 65, 86, 89
Beard, R. 2, 12, 21, 117
Becker, A. 131, 132
Behizadeh, N. 42–43, 112–113, 120
Bereiter, C. 1, 12, 116, 131–132, 166, 179, 227
Berkeley, S. 39, 191, 201–202
Berninger, V. W. 125, 177–179, 181, 190
Bernstein, B. 4

Bifuh-Ambe, E. 205, 248–249
bilingual 88, 96
Bloodgood, J. 125, 136, 146, 180
Boscolo, P. 30, 49, 51–53, 64–65, 67–68, 113, 226
Breetvelt, I. 115, 145, 179
Britton, J. 13, 101, 105
Brown, M. 65, 67, 86
Brownell, C. 225–226, 228
Bruner, J. 20, 102
Bruning, R. 21, 29, 35, 43, 49–54, 58, 61, 88, 112, 190
Burchinal, M. 88, 94, 96

Calkins, L. M. 31, 68, 70, 114, 127, 145, 159, 166–167, 180, 187, 200, 212, 215, 229
Carbone, P. W. 169, 226
Casey, M. 86, 178
Cawkwell, G. 106, 132, 134, 199
Cazden, C. 11, 37
Chamberlain, L. 61, 65, 70, 166
Chambers, A. 75
Chanquoy, L. 132, 134, 181
characters 8, 39, 66, 134, 191, 225, 228–229, 233
Chelsea, S. 65, 68–70
Clanchy, K. 242
Clark, C. 14, 20–21, 88, 112, 221–222, 230
Clark, N. 212
Cleary, T. J. 211
Collier, D. R. 14, 37, 42, 64–65, 67, 94, 127, 166, 168, 170
Colognesi, S. 27, 58–59
Colwell, R. P. 96
community of writers 11, 13–14, 30, 36–38, 43, 51, 55, 59, 62, 66, **76**, 77, 83, 86, 88, 90, 94, 96, 101, 118, 120, 129, 144, 147, 172, 193, 199–200, 205, 215, 224, 227, 230, **231**, 243–244, 246
Cooper, H. M. 99

Corden, R. 31, 107, 146, 149, 167, 177, 180, 189, 225, 229–231
Cork, V. 200, 222, 224
Cornelius-White, J. 95
creative writing 4, 129
Creber, P. 223
Cremin, T. 1, 6, 8–9, 13, 21, 70, 82–83, 86, 101–102, 105, 107, 168, 171, 180, 187, 189, 191, 199–201, 203–205, 217, 220, 222, 225, 240–241, 243–244, 248
Cummins, J. 68
Cushing, I. 205, 224, 247–248

Damasio, A. 26
Davis, D. 213
Davis, T. 70
Day, J. 66, 70
De La Paz, S. 132
DeCristofaro, D. 223–224, 232
Deegan, J. 205
Department for Education (DfE) 14, 20–21, 168, 240, 247
DeSmedt, F. 21, 49–51, 53, 54, 58–59, 75, 77–79, 83
dialogue 11, 38, 102, 104, 202, 213, 229, 247, 249
Dignath, C. 21, 35
Dix, S. 101, 103, 106, 132, 134, 199, 229
Dixon, J. 1, 6, 9, 116, 248
Dobson, T. 1, 205, 243, 248
Dockrell, J. 246–247
Dombey, H. 76–82, 95, 114, 120, 182, 222
Drummond, L. 36–38, 101, 193
Durran, J. 153
Dutro, E. 6, 66, 70, 116, 127, 168–169, 223
Dyson, A. H. 21, 43, 68, 89, 101, 113, 116, 118, 124, 167, 169, 223, 225

Early, J. 203
Eccles, J. 49–50, 53–54, 58–59
Edelsky, C. 68, 116–117
educational research 21, 26, 75, 80, 83, 231, 240, 247–248
Elbow, P. 5, 59, 128, 130, 137
Eliot, T. S. 22, 125
Elliott, V. 211–212
Ellis, N. 224
Eltringham, K. 146–147, 149
Englert, C. S. 35–36, 39, 126, 145–146, 150, 188, 190, 192, 202
English as a second language 66, 96
entertain 12, 22, 61, 114, 241

Faust, M. 203–204
feedback 5, 32, 37–39, **76**, 77, 81, 83, 87, 89, 107–108, 151, 159, **160**, 162, 183, 203, 211–216; oral/verbal 81, 205, 212, 214, 216; written 81, 212–213, 216
Ferguson, F. 13–14, 22, 37, 39, 44–45, 47, 51, 55, 61, *61*, 65, 69–70, 79, 82, 86, 89, 91, 96, 103, 106–108, 114, *115*, 117–120, *124*, 126, 128–133, *131*, *134*, 135–137, 146, 148–150, 152–154, 159, 161, 163, 166, 169, 171, 173–174, 178–180, **179**, 182, 187, 189–192, 200–202, 205, 212–214, 222–225, 228–229, 231, 233, 244, *244*, 246, 249
Fisher, T. 42, 44, 68, 86
Fitzgerald, J. 220–221
Fletcher, A. 30, 42–45
Fletcher, R. 192, 228
Flint, A. S. 10, 42, 44, 86, 118
Flower, L. 115, 124, 132, 190
Fowler, G. 22
Fox Tree, J. 212
Frank, C. R. 1, 64, 86, 89, 113, 126–127, 129, 135–136, 167, 181, 199–201, 205, 225, 228, 231, 242–243
free writing 4–5, 37, 128, 130, 137, 170
Freire, P. 2, 10, 104

Gadd, M. 32, 43, 52, 76, 78, 80, 82–83, 88, 95, 113–114, 118, 120, 144, 150, 161
Gallagher, K. 148, 228, 230–231
Gambrell, L. B. 57, 113
Gardner, P. 1, 12, 64, 200, 203–204, 243
Garrett, L. 49, 58–62, 87, 89, 114, 150
Gee, J. 66
Gelati, C. 52, 67, 113
genre 3, 5–8, 10–14, 20, 37, 42, 44–45, 47, 53, 61, 65, 67, **76**, 80, 87, 108, 112–113, 119, 128, 144–148, *146*, 150, 155, 159, 166–167, 170–171, 180, 188, 225–226, 228, 230, 233, 242, 245; *see also* orientation
Ghiso, M. 227
Gibson, S. 103–104
Giorgis, C. 205, 243, 247
Glasswell, K. 95, 213, 215
goals: distant 31, 54, 79, 118, 137, 144–145, *146*, 148, 152–154; process 31, 38, 46, 79, 138, 144, *146*, 151–154; product 31, 33, 38, 44, 54, 79–80, 97, 105, 109, 132–133, 138, 144, 146, *146*, 148–151, 153–155, 183, 192, 212, 228; *see also* writing
Goodman, E. 22
Goouch, K. 42, 45, 65, 69, 167–168, 170
Gourd, K. 21, 65, 68
Graham, J. 1, 230
Graham, L. 20, 170
Graham, R. 204, 242, 247
Graham, S. 1, 3, 6, 9, 29, 32, 35–39, 49, 71, 75–83, 94, 96–97, 120, 126, 129–130, 159–161, 177–178, 182, 187–191, 204, 215, 220, 222, 226, 243, 246
Grainger, T. 8, 42, 45, 65, 69, 89, 114, 116–117, 167–168, 180, 199–200, 202–203, 225, 230–231
grammar 2, 7, **76**, 81, 98, 125, 147, 183, 189–190; functional **76**, 81, 103, 189–191, 193–195
Graves, D. 43, 58, 67, 69, 88, 114, 116–117, 129, 159, 166–168, 171, 181, 199–200
Green, J. 101
Gregory, G. 242

Griffith, R. 222, 225, 229–231
Grossman, P. L. 76, 78, 80–81, 83, 187
Gutiérrez, K. 10–11, 64, 116

Hadwin, A. 37
Hall, A. 1, 27, 49, 204, 243
Halliday, M. 6–7, 101, 115, 130, 132, 147, 149
handwriting 2, 36, 177–180, 182–183, 188, 245
Hansen, J. 200, 214, 220, 222–224, 227, 230
Harman, R. 223, 226, 231
Harmey, S. 43, 49, 130, 177
Harris, K. R. 9, 35, 75–78, 81, 94, 96, 127, 129, 159–161, 178, 188, 190–191
Harste, J. 227
Harwayne, S. 10, 71, 200, 224, 231
Hattie, J. 75, 211
Hayes, J. R. 53, *53*, 115, 124, 130–133, 135, 182, 190
Hayler, M. 205
Heffernan, L. 86, 227
Heller, M. 129, 220, 222
Hemenway, S. 86, 178
Hemingway, E. 22, 131
Henderson, J. 17, 70
Hicks, J. 65–71, 88–89, 95–96, 101, 114, 161, 168, 187, 229
Hidi, S. 49, 51, 64–65, 113, 118, 167
Hillock, G. 1, 6, 14, 21, 75–76, 78–82, 148, 151, 159, 192, 212
Hmelo-Silver, C. 6, 32, 126, 151–152, 161, 187–188, 192
Hoewisch, A. 68, 86, 94, 116, 129, 227, 231
Holliway, D. 132, 221, 230
Hoogeveen, M. 52, 105, 126, 148
Horn, C. 21, 43, 49–54, 58, 61, 88, 112
Hughes, T. 223
Hyland, K. 1, 4–5, 8, 146

Immordino-Yang, M. 26
influence 1, 22, 27, 29, 54, 65–66, 69, 83, 88, 94, 102, 106, 130, 149, 177, 204–205, 211, 217, 220–221, 223, 225, 232, 243
Ivanič, R. 1, 4
Izibili, N. 172

Jasmine, J. 126
Jay, T. 102
Jeffrey, B. 168
Johnson, A. 20, 170
Johnston, P. 64, 66, 70, 86
Jones, S. 133, 135

Kaufman, D. 12, 30, 67, 99, 199–201, 203, 205, 214, 234, 247–248
Kellogg, R. T. 1, 125–126, 129–130, 160, 178–179, 188–189, 193
Kent, S. C. 177, 221
Kinneavy, J. 1, 60
Knapp, M. S. 177, 182

Knobel, M. 11, 227
Konrad, M. 33, 35, 160–161, 214
Koster, M. 75, 79–81, 126, 144, 148, 187
Kucirkova, N. 172

Laman, T. T. 10, 43, 65, 68, 70, 96, 118, 227, 231
Lamb, M. 51
Lambirth, A. 42, 45, 65, 69, 167–168, 170, 180
Langer, J. A. 76, 78, 80–81, 83, 116, 126, 151, 160–161, 226
language 4, 6, 8, 10–11, 66, 87–88, 95–96, 101, 104–105, 130, 145, 147, 190, 215, 222, 229, 249; body 134; meta- 104–105, 108–109, 215, 230
Lankshear, C. 11, 227
Laughlin, M. 211
Lave, J. 21, 193
Leland, C. 227
Lensmire, T. 5–6, 11–12, 14, 26, 29, 37, 64, 67, 168, 172
Leung, C. 65–71, 88–89, 95–96, 101, 114
Levitt, R. 126
Lewison, M. 227
Limbrick, L. 76–77, 79–83, 95
Limpo, T. 29–32, 129, 177, 182, 189
linguistics 4, 6–7, 11, 66, 79, 81–83, 89, 94, 104, 116, 132, 149–150, 155, 178, 183, 187–189, 192–193, 195, 230, 245
Lipson, M. 125–127, 130, 135, 152, 160, 213–214, 226, 227
literacy: club 13, 43, 65, 86, 232; critical 5, 10–12, 43, 60; for pleasure 62, 70, **76**, 82, 200, 221, 230–232, 246
Littleton, K. 102
Locke, T. 1, 3, 8, 12, 70, 113, 203, 205, 240, 244, 246, 248

MacArthur, C. 3, 32, 36, 132, 134, 136, 246
McCarthey, S. 68
McCutchen, D. 113, 131–132, 134, 177, 179, 182, 187
McGee, P. 211, 214
MacKenzie, N. 100, 129–130, 178, 182
McKinney, M. 205, 243, 247
McQuitty, V. 35, 105, 126–127, 180, 189–191, 215, 220
Magnifico, A. 51–52
make a record 22, 114, 241
Maloch, B. 52, 113, 118
Manak, J. 222, 231
Marchisan, M. 96
Martin, J. R. 6, 145–148, 150
Maybin, J. 1, 6–7, 10
Medwell, J. 76–78, 80–83, 178, 182, 189
Meece, J. 31, 49, 51–54
Meek Spencer, M. 223–224
Mercer, N. 101–102, 106, 202
Miller, S. 31, 49, 51–53
mini-lesson 31–32, 37–38, 54, 69, 76, 77, 80–82, 95, 97–98, 103–104, 133, 138, 151, 154–155,

159–160, **160**, 162–163, 171, 173, 183, 187, 189–195, *191*, 199, 206–207, 213, 216–217, 228–229, 231, 233–234, 246; daily 31, 38, 54, 69, 97, 159, 199
Mkhize, D. 1, 68
Moffett, J. 128, 166–167, 225
Moje, E. 64
Moll, L. 73, 168
Moltzen, R. 49, 58–62, 87, 89, 114, 150
Morizawa, G. 77–83, 120, 124, 127
Morrell, J. 67
motivation 3, 20–21, 23, 26, 29–30, 35, 38–39, 42, 45, *46*, 49–53, *53*, 54–55, 58, 61, 65, 71, 95, 114, 117–118, 136, 144, 151, 153–154, 167–168, 170, 188, 191–192, 201, 211–212, 245
Muller, H. 248
multilingual 66, 88, 96
Murray, D. 5, 130, 136, 166, 200, 202, 214, 221
Myhill, D. 6, 13, 81, 86, 102–103, 105–107, 133, 135, 149, 168, 171, 180, 187, 189, 205, 248

National Literacy Trust 20–21, 55, 242
Nauman, A. 58–62
Neitzel, C. 43, 213
Niemiec, C. 42, 46, 58
Niwese, M. 27, 58–59
Nolen, S. 51, 54, 89, 167–168

Oates, J. C. 22
O'Connor, F. 226
Ofsted 14, 20–21, 222, 240, 243, 247
Oldfather, P. 50–52
Olinghouse, N. G. 96, 113, 145, 182, 226, 227
Oliver, L. 21, 82, 200–201, 217
Olthouse, J. 59, 89, 95, 228
Orellana, M. F. 169, 226
orientation: community 10, 12, 14, 51, 82; environmental 10, 12, 14; genre 6, 9; literacy 10, 43, 60; literature-based 8; presentational 1, 4, 8, 14; teacher 15, 221
Oshige, M. 37

Pahl, K. 11, 66, 86, 88, 223, 225
paint with words 22, 61, 114, 190, 241
Pajares, F. 29–30, 32, 49, 167, 182
paragraph 2, 102, 108, *133*, 137–138, **179**, **228**, 229; piler 39, 108, 138, **179**
Paris, S. G. 35–38, 42, 44, 49–51, 145, 161, 187–189, 191–193
Parr, J. M. 52, 76–83, 95, 101, 104, 113–114, 120, 144–145, 148, 151–152, 213, 215
Parry, B. 129, 170, 222–223, 225, 228
Pekrun, R. 167
Perin, D. 6, 36, 75, 77–83, 120, 126, 187, 189–190, 220
Perl, S. 94
Perry, N. E. 36–39, 191, 193
personal writing projects 8, 14, 44–45, 47, 54, 60–62, 69, 78, 90, 98, 118, 153–155, 166–174, *169*, 183, 200, 217, 232, 246

persuade 22, 114, 150, 180
Peterson, R. 87
Piazza, C. 26–27, 67
planner 39, 137, **179**
policymakers 240–243
Pollard, A. 88, 117, 150
Pressley, M. 49, 52, 76–80, 82, 125, 130, 151, 160–161, 187, 189, 191, 193
Prose, F. 221–222, 228
punctuation 2, 36, 81, 83, 127, 135, 137, 177–181, 183, 188, 195, 245
pupil conference 32, 39, 45, 54, 67, 70, **76**, 77, 81, 95, 97, 104, 161, 183, 200–201, 206–207, 216–217, 246
Purcell-Gates, V. 21, 42, 44, 112, 145, 147, 169

Ranker, J. 169, 172, 193, 225–226, 228–229, 231
Raphael, L. 30–31, 51–52, 54
Raphael, T. E. 145–146, 150
Rathmann, K. 86
Ray, K. 65, 225
reading: instruction 9, 220; material 10, 231; for pleasure 21, 82, 221–222, 225, **231**, 234, 247; programme 9; proof- 39, 79, 81, 124–125, 130, 134–135, 137–138, 173, 181, 193, 202; and writing 9, 62, 70, **76**, 82, 104, 200, 220–222, 224, 230–234, 246–247
reflection 9, 11–12, 22, 30, 37, 39, 43, 60–61, 67, 83, 90–91, 104, 109, 114, 116–120, 125, 126, 128, 133, 147, 192–193, 199, 202, 204–205, 207, 213, 215–216, 224–227, 234, 241, 243–244, 248
Regan, K. 39, 191, 201–202
Reutzel, D. R. 95, 150, 161
Rief, L. 42, 167, 223, 227–228, 230–231
Risemberg, R. 35, 37–38
Robson, D. 35
Rogers, L. 75, 80–81
Rojas-Drummond, S. M. 102–103, 105–106
Rose, D. 4, 6, 18, 145, 147–148
Rosemberg, C. R. 88
Rosen, H. 4, 6–7, 9, 13, 68, 129, 181, 223–224, 227
Rosen, M. 168, 221, 223, 225
Rosenthal, R. 94, 96
Rothery, J. 146
Rowlands, K. 67
Rowsell, J. 11, 66, 86, 88, 225
Rubie-Davies, C. M. 94–96, 150, 245
Rumbold, K. 221–222
Ruttle, K. 88, 106
Ryan, R. 42, 46, 58

Saddler, B. 187, 190
Sampson, G. 223
Sandmel, K. 36, 75, 77–79, 82, 190, 220
Satchwell, C. 94, 96
Scardamalia, M. 1, 12, 42, 116, 131–132, 166, 179, 227
Schneider, J. 7, 37, 106, 124, 126–127, 130, 134, 146, 230–231

schools: effective 160; elementary 108; library 119–120, 137, 230; primary 20, 87; writing 68, 230; Searle, C. 10–11, 242
Seban, D. 44, 64–68, 70
self-efficacy 23, 26, 29–32, 35, 38–39, 42–43, 45–47, *46*, 49, 51, 53, 58, 62, 71, 88, 94–95, 97–98, 103–104, 119, 144–145, 148–149, 152, 161–162, 167, 169, 171, 181, 193, 211, 213, 216, 243
self-expression 4–6, 13–14, 51, 150, 159, 166–167
self-regulated strategy development (SRSD) 97–98, 190–191
self-regulation 23, 26, 29–30, 35–39, 42–43, 45–47, *46*, 51, 53, 55, 58, **76**, 77, 79–80, 87, 95, 97–98, 104–105, 116–117, 126–127, 144–145, 148, 161–162, 169, 171, 178, *179*, 181, 190–195, 202–203, 211–213, 216
sentence 2, 81, 102, 105–106, 108, 127, 130, *133, 134*, 137–138, 177–178, **179**, 182, 190, 194, **228**, 229, 233, 240; combine 81, 189–190; stacker 39, 108, 138, **179**
Shanahan, T. 8–10, 130, 132, 145, 220–221, 225, 227
Sharples, M. 128–130, 133
Sibert, C. 26–27, 67
Smith, F. 2, 13, 43, 86, 89, 124, 147–148, 178, 180, 182, 201, 221, 228, 232
Smith, K. 116–117
Smith, M. 10, 124
Snyders, B. 65, 68–70
Solsken, J. 113, 169, 223, 227
special educational needs 30, 96
spelling 2, 36, 81–82, 125, 127, 130, 135, 137, 177–183, 188, 245
Splitter, L. J. 112
Stein, N. 129, 227
Street, B. 1, 4, 10
Street, C. 1, 201, 204, 243
Subero, D. 9–10, 13, 66, 88–89, 118, 168

Taggart, A. 211
Tarrés, E. 66
Tavsanli, Ö. 44, 64–68, 70
Taylor, L. 129, 170, 222–223, 225, 228
Taylor, M. 12, 201
teacher/pupil relationship 2, 4, 6, 8, 11, 13, 88, 202
teaching strategies 2, 5, 7–8, 11, 13, 97, 119, 151, 182
Tennent, W. 228
Teravainen, A. 14, 20–21, 113
Thompson, N. 95
Timperley, H. 52, 144–145, 148, 151–152, 211, 213
Tolchinsky, L. 193
Tom, D.Y. H. 95
Tompkins, G. E. 86–88, 180
Troia, G. A. 49–50, 53–54, 58, 79–80, 82, 96–97, 160, 181
Tway, E. 86–88

Van Keer, H. 75, 77–79, 83
Vanderburg, R. 151

Vanknin-Nusbaum, V. 52
Vass, E. 105
vocabulary 2, 104–105, 132, 135, 138, 150, 178, 181–182, 194, 229–230, 245
volition 20–21, 23, 26, 29, 35–36, 38, 45, *46*, 49, 51, 58–62, 65, 71, 89, 95, 114, 129, 204, 225, 232
vomiter 39, 108, 137, **179**
Vygotsky, L. S. 66, 102, 167

Wagner, B. 128, 167, 225
Walker, B. J. 167
Wanzek, J. 177, 221
Ward, A. 65, 86, 89
Warrington, M. 178
Wedell, M. 51
Weiner, W. 126
Wenger, E. 21, 193
Wharton-McDonald, R. 230
White, C. 88, 108, 118
Whitney, A. E. 112–113, 117, 152, 154, 199–200, 204, 243
Whyte, A. 200, 205, 243
Wigfield, A. 49–50, 53–54, 58–59
Wiggins, G. 112, 144
Wiliam, D. 211–212
Willinsky, J. 116
Wilson, N. 94
Winograd, P. 35–38, 145, 161, 187–189, 191–193
Wolfe, S. 212
Woodside-Jiron, H. 66, 70
Wray, D. 2, 117, 182
writer-identity 23, 26, 31, 39, 42, *46*, 49, 58, 64–71, 79, 95, 107, 127, 168, 207
writing: curriculum 2, 5, 7–8, 11, 13, 67–68, *113*, 118, 166, 168, 170–172, 188; goals 9, 29, 31, 36, 38, 44, 54, 75, **76**, 79–80, 97, 104, 115, 144, 150, 152–153, 162, 189, 192, 194, 200, 216, 241, 246; as pleasure 22, 58; for pleasure 14, 20–24, 26, 30, 35, 39, 42, 49, 58, 64, 82, 86, 90, 116–117, 146, 167, 171, 199, 203, 222, 225, 230–231, 242, 247; process 3–4, 13, 31, 36–37, 39, 42–44, 46, 50, 54, *53*, 55, 62, 64, 67–68, 70, **76**, 79, 82, 96, 102–105, 107–108, 116–117, 120, 124–125, *124*, 126–127, 135, 137–138, 144, 151–155, 159, 161, 167, 170–172, 180–183, 188–190, 192–193, 199, 203, 206–207, 214–216, 229, 245–245, 248–249; study 80–81, 133, 187–189, 191, 193–195, 199, 206–207, 228; time 31–32, 38–39, 67, 69, 79–82, 98, 106–109, 138, 153, 159–163, **160**, 171, 173, 187, 189, 191, 193–195, 202, 217, 229–230, **231**, 233; workshops 12–13, 35, 37, 51, 65, 67–69, **76**, 77, 79, 82, 90–91, 96, 103, 107, 126, 135, 146, 159–160, **160**, 162, 166, 178, 190, 202, 205, 213, 221, 231; *see also* reading, school
Writing for Pleasure: classrooms 37, 103–104, 161, 171, 215; defining 21; pedagogy 23, 77, 83, 101, 103, 153, 168, 177, 213, 245–246; practice 103–104; teachers 19, 23–24, 32, 45, 55, 62, 71, 90, 95–97, 102, 108, 114–115, 117, 126, 137,

145–148, 150–153, 160–162, 171–172, 177, 180–183, 188, 190–191, 193, 199–200, 203, 214, 216

Yandell, J. 169, 172, 223
Yoo, J. 205, 243, 248
Young, R. 10, 13–14, 21–23, 26–27, *26*, 29–30, 33, 36–37, 39, 42–45, *46*, 47, 51, 55, 61–62, *61*, 65, 68–71, 76, 79–83, 86, 88–91, 96–97, 99, 103, 106–108, 113–114, *115*, 116–120, *124*, 126, 128–130, 132–133, *131*, *134*, 135–137, 144, 146–150, 152–154, 159, 161–163, 166, 168–169, 171–174, 178–180, **179**, 182, 187, 189–193, 200–202, 205–206, 212–214, 222–225, 227–229, 231–234, 244, *244*, 246, 249

Zimmerman, B. J. 30–32, 35–38, 211
Zoellner, R. 3
Zumbrunn, S. 21, 35, 42, 51–52, 62, 64–65, 67, 70, 160, 190, 192–193, 200–201, 211